G.C.S.E. PHYSICS

C. Boyle
B.Sc.(Hons.), M.Sc., P.G.C.E., C.Phys., M.Inst.P., A.F.I.M.A.

CHECKMATE GOLD

© C. BOYLE 1987

First published in Great Britain 1987 by Checkmate Gold Publications,
4 Ainsdale Close, Bromborough, Wirral L63 0EU.

British Library Cataloguing in Publication Data
Boyle, C.
GCSE Physics
1. Physics
I. Title
530   QC23

ISBN 1 85313 001 X

All rights reserved. No part of this publication may be reproduced, stored in a retrieval system, or transmitted in any form or by any means, electronic, photocopying, recording, or otherwise, without prior permission of Checkmate Gold at 4 Ainsdale Close, Bromborough, Wirral L63 0EU.

Text set in 10/12 pt Times
by Merseyside Graphics Ltd., 130 The Parade, Meols, Wirral L47 5AZ
Printed by Billing & Sons Limited, Hylton Road, Worcester WR2 5JU.

Cover design by Merseyside Graphics Ltd.

PREFACE

The introduction of the G.C.S.E. to replace the G.C.E. and C.S.E. presents a challenge to both students and teachers. Needless to say, this challenge also extends to authors!

Not only has the subject material been reviewed but also the underlying philosophy has changed with the major shift being towards the reward of positive achievement and the development of experimental skills and investigations.

The purpose of this book is to provide a coherent framework of study which fully covers the material included in the syllabuses of the four English examining groups together with that of the International G.C.S.E. examination offered by the University of Cambridge Local Examinations Syndicate.

In order to achieve the discrimination necessary to stretch the more able student, the text of each chapter is organised into core and supplementary material. The core material is designed for all students with the supplementary material also being required for those students aiming for grades A to B.

Physics is, by its nature, experimental. It is accordingly important that an assessment of students' knowledge and understanding of physics should contain a component relating to practical work and experimental skills. Success in this domain cannot be achieved by reading a textbook. Accordingly, any experimental work described in this text has been minimised and describes only how the fundamental concepts may be practically demonstrated and investigated. More sophisticated experiments, such as the determination of the density of an insoluble powder, are now more appropriate for investigation and development of the more able student in a laboratory situation.

Bearing in mind that physics does not operate in a vacuum, wherever appropriate its scientific and technological applications with their social, economic and environmental implications are described.

In order to both re-inforce the presented material and prepare the student for the examination, questions appropriate to the core and supplementary material are included at the end of each chapter.

C.B.

DEDICATED TO MY PARENTS.

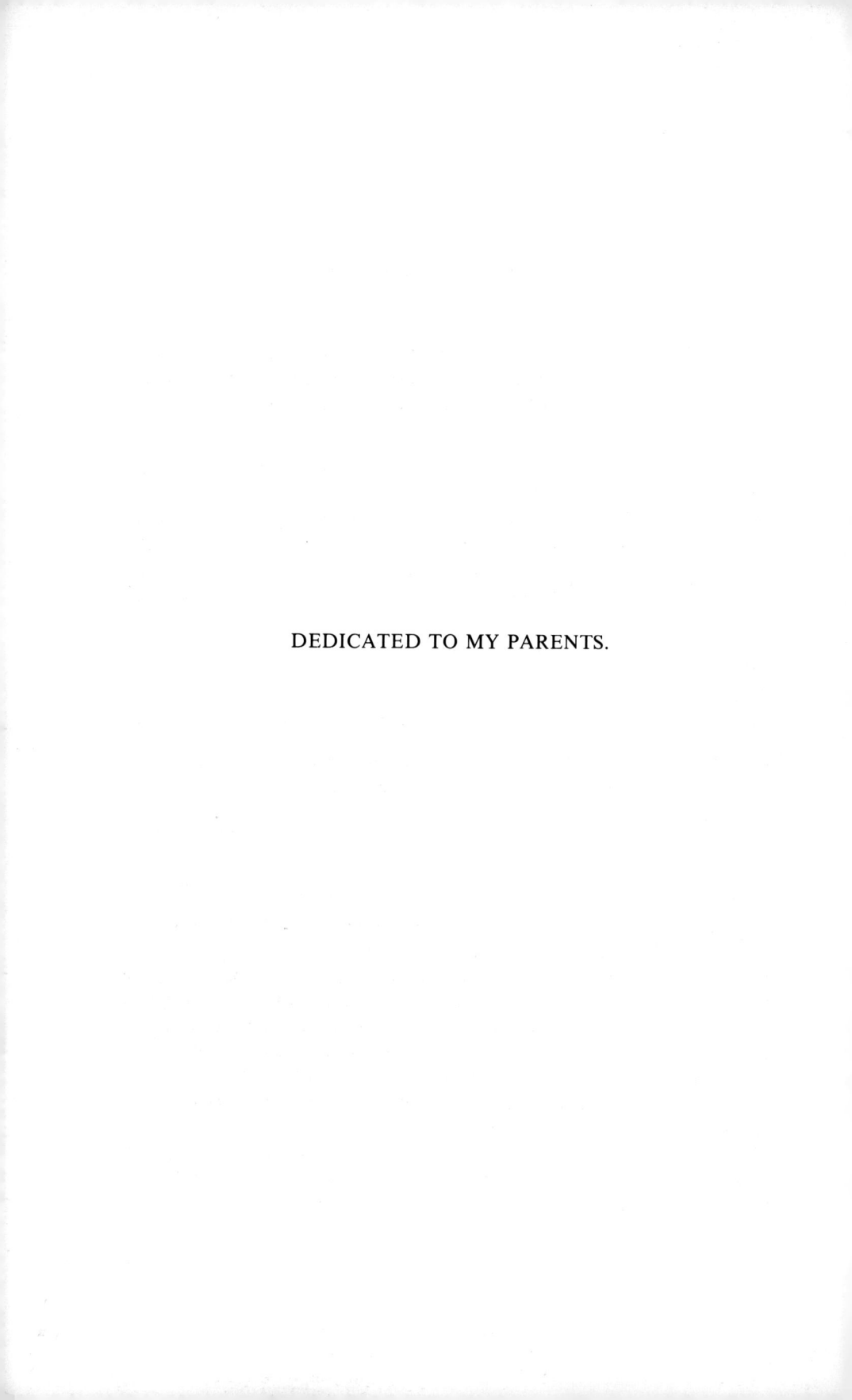

ACKNOWLEDGEMENTS

I am indebted to the staff of Merseyside Graphics Ltd. for so skilfully transcribing my initial manuscript and illustrations to their final form and also to P.S. Dennison, H.N.C., B.A.(HONS.), T.CERT. of North Cheshire College for reading the proofs.

I tnank the following examination boards for allowing me to reproduce specimen G.C.S.E. examination questions:

N.E.A. — The Northern Examining Association (comprising Associated Lancashire Schools Examining Board, Joint Matriculation Board, North Regional Examination Board, North West Regional Examination Board and Yorkshire & Humberside Regional Examination Board).
L.E.A.G. — London and East Anglian Group.
M.E.G. — Midlands Examining Group.
S.E.G. — Southern Examining Group.

The answers are provided by the author and are not the only answers possible.

My thanks are due to Ian Tasker and Michael Kellett of the Cheshire School of Art & Design for providing Fig. 2.2 and Fig. 2.3.

Finally, I am grateful to the following sources for supplying and allowing me to use photographs:
British Airways — PHOTOGRAPH 3; Central Electricity Generating Board — PHOTOGRAPHS 9, 10, 25 and 26; Philip Harris Ltd — PHOTOGRAPHS 14, 15, 23, 24, 27 and 28; Hoverspeed — PHOTOGRAPH 2; J.E.T. Joint Undertaking — PHOTOGRAPHS 30 and 31; Department of Engineering, University of Lancaster — PHOTOGRAPH 5; Department of Physics and Astronomy, University College, London — PHOTOGRAPHS 16 and 17; University of Manchester — PHOTOGRAPH 18; Oertling — PHOTOGRAPH 1; Plessey Radar Ltd. — PHOTOGRAPHS 19, 20 and 21; Riso National Laboratory, Denmark — PHOTOGRAPHS 6, 7 and 8; Department of Applied Acoustics, University of Salford — PHOTOGRAPH 22; Department of Orthopaedic Mechanics; University of Salford — PHOTOGRAPH 4; S.E.R.C. Daresbury Laboratory — PHOTOGRAPH 29 (COVER); Swan Housewares Ltd — PHOTOGRAPHS 12 and 13 and Department of Physics, University of York — PHOTOGRAPH 11.

TABLE OF CONTENTS

PREFACE I
ACKNOWLEDGEMENTS II
CHAPTER
1. BASIC QUANTITIES IN PHYSICS 1
2. MOTION 19
3. SCALARS AND VECTORS 44
4. FORCES 51
5. TURNING 77
6. PRESSURE 87
7. WORK, POWER AND ENERGY 102
8. MATTER 116
9. THERMAL EXPANSION OF SOLIDS, LIQUIDS AND GASES 129
10. TEMPERATURE 137
11. THERMAL CAPACITY 145
12. MELTING AND BOILING 150
13. THE TRANSFER OF HEAT 159
14. WAVES 171
15. REFLECTION OF LIGHT 188
16. REFRACTION OF LIGHT 203
17. THIN CONVERGING LENSES 215
18. ELECTROMAGNETIC WAVES 223
19. SOUND 230
20. MAGNETISM 241
21. ELECTROSTATICS 258
22. ELECTRIC CURRENTS 271
23. ELECTRIC CIRCUITS 290
24. PRACTICAL ELECTRIC CIRCUITRY 303
25. ELECTROMAGNETIC INDUCTION 313
26. THE MAGNETIC EFFECT OF AN ELECTRIC CURRENT 327
27. FORCE ON A CURRENT CARRYING CONDUCTOR 335
28. THERMIONIC EMISSION, THE CATHODE RAY OSCILLOSCOPE AND RECTIFICATION 344
29. ELECTRONIC DEVICES 357
30. THE ATOM 374
31. RADIOACTIVITY 379
ANSWERS 394–404
INDEX 405–413

Chapter 1
BASIC QUANTITIES IN PHYSICS

At the end of this chapter you will know:
CORE: what is meant by length, area, volume, mass, time and density and how they are measured.
SUPPLEMENTARY: how to measure small lengths and time intervals; what is meant by inertia and how to find the density of irregular objects.

CORE
1.1 LENGTH

Length is a one dimensional measurement of size.

It is measured in metres, symbol m.

The actual length of one metre is defined in terms of the light given out by krypton gas.

1.2 AREA

Area is a two dimensional measurement of size.

It is measured in square metres, symbol m^2.

As shown in Fig. 1.1

FIG. 1.1

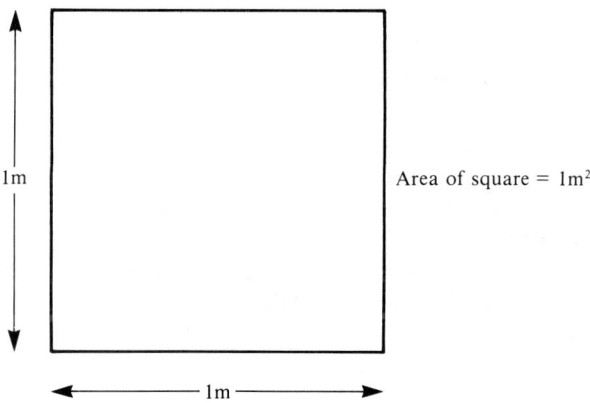

A square of side 1 metre has an area of 1 square metre.

1.3 VOLUME

Volume is a three dimensional measurement of size.

2 Basic Quantities in Physics

It is measured in cubic metres, symbol m³.

As shown in Fig. 1.2

FIG. 1.2

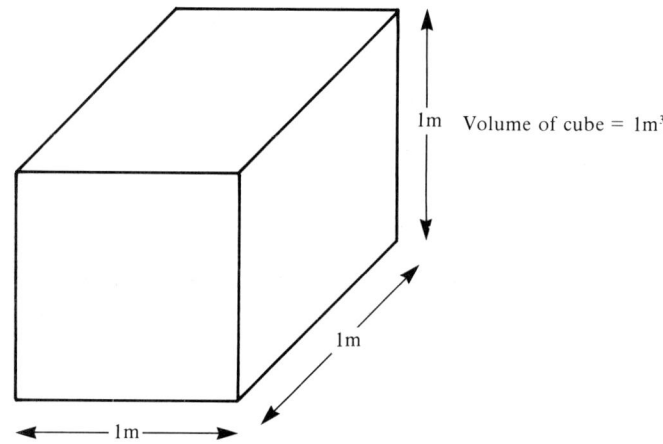

A cube of side 1m has a volume of 1 cubic metre.

1.4 MASS

Mass is a measure of how much substance an object contains.

It is measured in kilograms, symbol kg.

The actual mass of one kilogram is defined in terms of the mass of a block of platinum-iridium alloy kept near Paris.

1.5 TIME

Time is a measure of the passage of events.

It is measured in seconds, symbol s.

The actual time of one second is defined in terms of a particular number of vibrations in a caesium atom.

1.6 THE S.I. SYSTEM AND LARGER AND SMALLER MEASUREMENTS

(i) When we measure mass, length or time, our answer will be a certain number of kilograms, metres or seconds. Kilograms, metres and seconds are the first three basic units of the International System of Units known as the S.I. system. Other units of measurement, known as derived units, may be obtained from them.

Basic Quantities in Physics 3

(ii) Often, measurements may be very large or very small. We need bigger and smaller units.

In order to arrive at a big unit we use the prefix kilo, symbol k, which has the effect of multiplying a unit by 1000.

As an example   1 kilometre = 1000 metres
       or   1km = 1000m.

PROBLEM
CONVERT 25km to metres.

Now   1km = 1000m
so   25km = 25 × 1000 = 25,000m.

ANSWER: 25km = 25,000m.

In order to arrive at a small unit we use the prefixes centi, symbol c, and milli, symbol m, which have the effect of dividing a unit by 100 and 1000.
As examples

$$1 \text{ centimetre} = \frac{1}{100} \text{ metre}$$

So   100 centimetres = 1 metre
or   100cm = 1m.

$$1 \text{ millimetre} = \frac{1}{1000} \text{ metre}$$

So   1000 millimetres = 1 metre
or   1000mm = 1m.

From the above we can see that
         1 centimetre = 10 millimetres
or   1cm = 10mm.

PROBLEM
CONVERT 3.5m to MILLIMETRES
Now   1m = 1000mm
so   3.5m = 3.5 × 1000 = 3,500mm.

ANSWER: 3.5m = 3,500mm.

For extremely small units, we use the prefix micro, symbol μ, which has the effect of dividing the unit by 1,000,000.
As an example

$$1 \text{ micrometre} = \frac{1}{1,000,000} \text{ metre}$$

So   1,000,000 micrometres = 1 metre
or   1,000,000 μm = 1m.

1.7 CONVERSION OF AREA UNITS

In the same way that we can split the unit of length, the metre, into smaller units, we can do the same with the unit of area.

Now $1m = 100cm$
so $1m^2 = 1m \times 1m = 100cm \times 100cm = 10,000cm^2$
and so 1 square metre $= 10,000$ square centimetres
or $1m^2 = 10,000cm^2$

Also $1m = 1000mm$
so
$1m^2 = 1m \times 1m = 1000mm \times 1000mm = 1,000,000mm^2$
and so 1 square metre $= 1,000,000$ square millimetres
or $1m^2 = 1,000,000mm^2$

PROBLEM
CONVERT $0.5m^2$ to SQUARE CENTIMETRES

Now $1m^2 = 10,000cm^2$
so $0.5m^2 = 0.5 \times 10,000 = 5000cm^2$

ANSWER: $0.5m^2 = 5000cm^2$.

1.8 CONVERSION OF VOLUME UNITS

In a similar way, volume units may be changed from cubic metres to cubic centimetres or cubic millimetres.

Now $1m = 100cm$
so
$1m^3 = 1m \times 1m \times 1m = 100cm \times 100cm \times 100cm = 1,000,000cm^3$
and so 1 cubic metre $= 1,000,000$ cubic centimetres
or $1m^3 = 1,000,000cm^3$.

We may write cm^3 as c.c.

Also $1m = 1000mm$
so
$1m^3 = 1m \times 1m \times 1m = 1000mm \times 1000mm \times 1000mm = 1,000,000,000mm^3$
and so 1 cubic metre $= 1,000,000,000$ cubic millimetres
or $1m^3 = 1,000,000,000mm^3$

PROBLEM
CONVERT $0.002m^3$ to CUBIC MILLIMETRES.

Now $1m^3 = 1,000,000,000mm^3$
so $0.002m^3 = 0.002 \times 1,000,000,000 = 2,000,000mm^3$

ANSWER: $0.002m^3 = 2,000,000mm^3$

1.9 THE VOLUME OF LIQUIDS

For historical reasons, the volume of liquids is measured in litres, symbol ℓ.

$$1 \text{ litre} = 1000 \text{ cubic centimetres}$$
or
$$1\ell = 1000 \text{cm}^3$$

The litre is split into a small unit, the millilitre, symbol $m\ell$.

$$1 \text{ litre} = 1000 \text{ millilitres}$$
or
$$1\ell = 1000 m\ell.$$

and so giving
$$1000 m\ell = 1000 \text{cm}^3$$
$$1 m\ell = 1 \text{cm}^3$$

1.10 DENSITY

The density of a substance is an important quantity. It is equal to the mass of a particular quantity of substance divided by its volume.

$$\text{DENSITY} = \frac{\text{MASS}}{\text{VOLUME}}$$

or
$$D = \frac{m}{V}$$

where
D = density
m = mass
V = volume.

Mass is measured in kg and volume in m^3 and so density is measured in kg/m^3.

A knowledge of the density of a material is important in many situations. To the chemist it may be used to find if a substance is pure and to the engineer it is a measure of the strength of a material.

Some typical values of density are given in the Table.

SUBSTANCE	DENSITY in kg/m^3
WATER	1000
AIR	1.26
ICE AT 0°C	920
METHYLATED SPIRIT	800
STEEL	7800
SAND	2600
MERCURY	13600
GOLD	19300

Sometimes density is quoted in units of g/cm³. Using the relationship between kg and g and m³ and cm³ we find that

$$1000 \text{ kg/m}^3 = 1 \text{ g/cm}^3$$

It follows from the definition of density that if we were to consider a number of identical sized cubes of different substances, those made of denser material would have the greater mass.

PROBLEM
THE GLASS CUBE SHOWN IN FIG. 1.3 HAS A SIDE OF LENGTH 0.25m.

FIG. 1.3

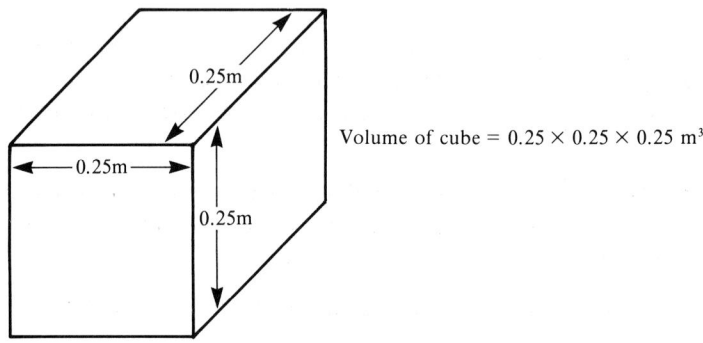

Volume of cube = 0.25 × 0.25 × 0.25 m³

IF THE DENSITY OF GLASS IS 2592 kg/m³, CALCULATE THE MASS OF THE CUBE.

THE VOLUME OF THE CUBE IS
$$0.25 \times 0.25 \times 0.25 \text{ m}^3$$
USING THE SAME SYMBOLS AS EARLIER
$$D = \frac{m}{V}$$
AND SUBSTITUTING THE VALUES
$$2592 = \frac{m}{0.25 \times 0.25 \times 0.25}$$
so
$$m = 2592 \times 0.25 \times 0.25 \times 0.25$$
$$= 40.5 \text{kg}$$

ANSWER: MASS OF CUBE IS 40.5kg.

In the above example, the volume has been found using the formula from mathematics. Obviously for other shapes, different formulae would have to be used.

Basic Quantities in Physics 7

In the case of unevenly shaped — or irregular — objects their volume must be found in other ways and this is studied in section 1.13(iii).

1.11 READING SCALES

(i) Suppose we are using a scale to measure the length of some object as in Fig. 1.4. We are trying to measure the length of the shaded object using the scale marked in whole units.

FIG. 1.4

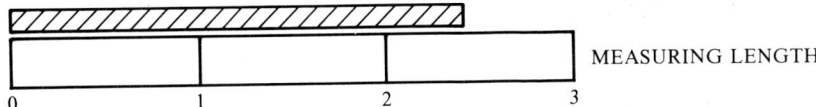

MEASURING LENGTH

We can use this scale to measure with certainty to the nearest whole number on the scale. Here, this reading would be 2 units. Usually though we can measure to the nearest half division giving a reading here of 2.5 units.

In general we can say that whenever we read a scale, we can read with certainty to the nearest division on the scale and with reasonable accuracy to the nearest half division.

(ii) Whenever a scale is being read, it should be viewed from directly above as shown in Fig. 1.5.

FIG. 1.5

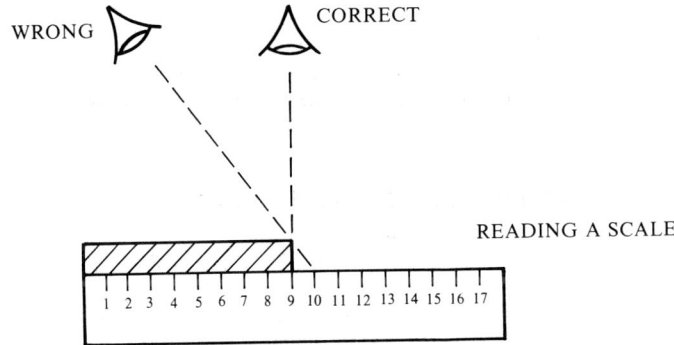

READING A SCALE

This would give a correct reading of 9 units. If this is not done an incorrect reading — 10 units in this diagram would result because the eye looks in a straight line. A correct reading is said to have "no parallax".

8 Basic Quantities in Physics

(iii) A large number of modern measuring instruments do not have scales. Instead the values are displayed as numbers in what is known as a digital format. They are convenient because you do not have to interpret a scale and the problem of parallax is avoided.

Such displays are now common on clocks, particularly those in video recorders. They use a seven segment display in which from one to seven segments is activated. As a result the figure shown often looks angular. A seven segment display is shown in Fig. 1.6 and will be discussed again in Chapter 29.

FIG. 1.6

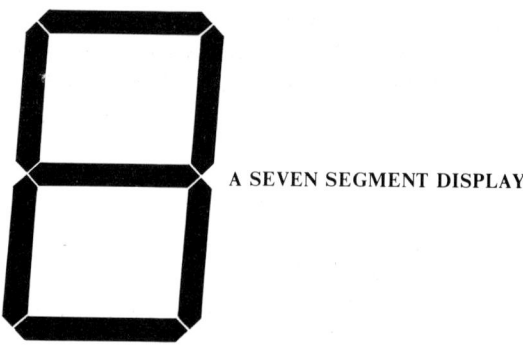

A SEVEN SEGMENT DISPLAY

1.12 MEASURING LENGTH AND AREA

In order to measure length we use a metre rule. As its name implies, this is a rule which is one metre long with a scale calibrated — or graduated — in mm marked upon it. The maximum measurement, one metre, is called the range.

When measuring the length of an object it is better to not place the end of the object on the zero just in case the zero is damaged or worn. Thus in Fig. 1.7 the length of the object is

FIG. 1.7

READING A METRE RULE
(Not to scale)

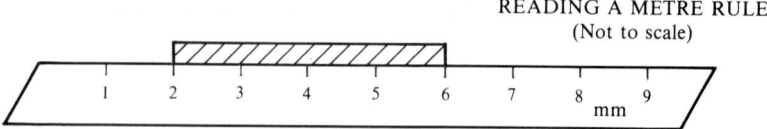

Length of object = Higher reading — Lower reading
= 6 — 2
= 4 mm.

In order to measure area, we substitute appropriate length measurements into mathematical expressions.

1.13 MEASURING VOLUME

(i) In order to measure the volume of a regular solid, we use a metre rule to measure its length in each dimension and substitute these values into the appropriate mathematical expression.

(ii) In order to measure the volume of a liquid, we use a measuring cylinder. The cylinder is usually made from glass or, if it is used in an environment where it is likely to receive rough treatment, plastic. The device measures in cm^3 or ml but the actual scale calibration depends upon the range being used.

The surface of a liquid in a container is never flat. At the edges it bends upwards in most liquids. However in some liquids it bends downwards. This downward bending occurs noticeably with mercury. (Mercury should never be measured in an open measuring cylinder because it is a hazard to health). In all cases we measure the height of the flat liquid surface as shown in Fig. 1.8

FIG. 1.8

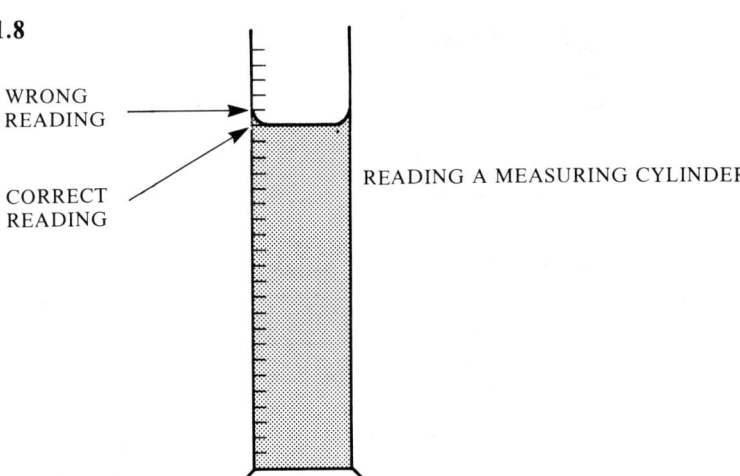

READING A MEASURING CYLINDER

The scale is only accurate at one particular temperature and the value of this will be marked on the cylinder by the manufacturer.

Other devices such as beakers, pipettes and burettes are used by chemists.

(iii) In order to measure the volume of uneven — or irregularly shaped — solids we use a displacement technique with a measuring cylinder.

We fill a measuring cylinder to a suitable level with water and note the volume. The object whose volume is wanted is then lowered on a fine thread so that it is completely under the water. The water level rises

10 Basic Quantities in Physics

because the object pushes out of the way a volume of water equal to its own volume. The new volume reading represents the volume of the water and the volume of the object. By subtracting from this reading the original water volume we find the volume of the object.

In Fig. 1.9 we have

FIG. 1.9

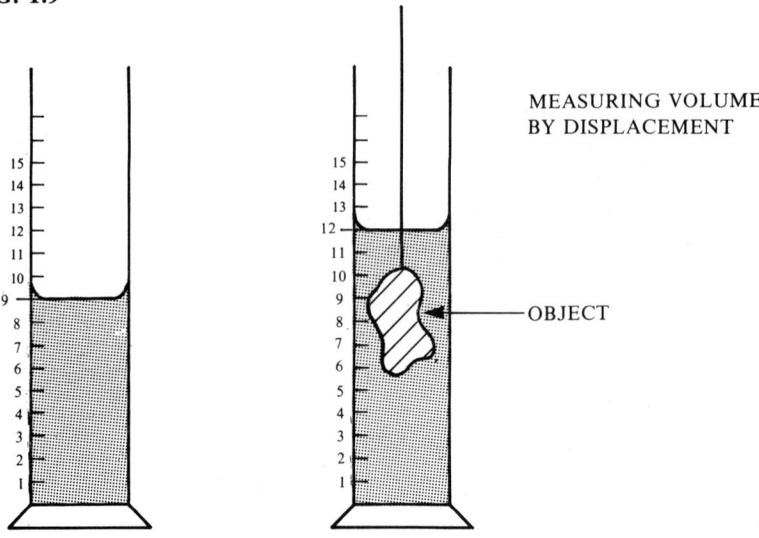

MEASURING VOLUME BY DISPLACEMENT

OBJECT

Original volume of water = 9 ml
Volume of water and object = 12 ml

So

Volume of object = 12 - 9 = 3 ml

1.14 MEASURING MASS

In order to measure mass we use a balance.

Originally beam balances and lever balances were used. Your school may have examples of these. However for modern determination of mass we use a top pan balance as shown in Photograph 1.

Basic Quantities in Physics 11

PHOTOGRAPH 1

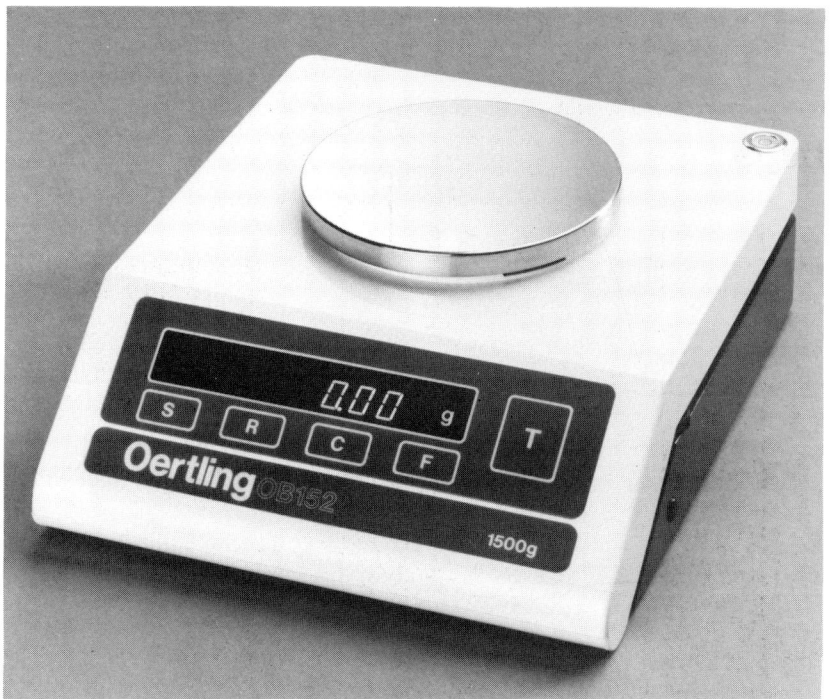

The object whose mass is required is placed on the pan gently and the balance switched on. The scale is read or as in the case of this balance, the digital display is read.

We have said that the unit of mass is the kilogram. However this is quite large and as we would imagine from the prefix, it may be split into 1000 parts known as grams, symbol g. The balance shown in Photograph 1 has a range of 1500 g and is calibrated in $\frac{1}{100}$ g.

Incidentally, because the kg is the unit of mass we need a new unit for larger quantities. We use the tonne.
$$1 \text{ tonne} = 1000 \text{ kilograms}$$

1.15 MEASURING TIME

In order to measure time we use a stopwatch or clock. We must always ensure that it is set to zero before we begin timing and that it is sufficiently well wound.

Because time is not measured metrically — in large units of 10s, 100s — we use different larger units.

12 Basic Quantities in Physics

	1 minute = 60 seconds
or	1 min = 60 s
and	1 hour = 60 minutes
or	1 h = 60 min
And so	1 h = 60 × 60 = 3600 s.

The second is split into smaller units, as we would expect, of centiseconds, milliseconds and microseconds.

1.16 MEASURING DENSITY

(i) In order to measure the density of a solid of regular shape, we measure its mass using a balance. We measure its dimensions using a metre rule and obtain its volume from the appropriate formula. The mass is then divided by the volume.

(ii) In order to measure the density of a liquid, we find the mass of an empty measuring cylinder using a balance. A known volume of the liquid is then poured into the measuring cylinder. The measuring cylinder is again placed on the balance and the mass of the cylinder and liquid is found. By subtracting from this the mass of the empty cylinder we find the mass of the liquid. The mass is then divided by the volume.

(iii) In general, the density of solids is greater than liquids and this is greater than that of gases. An important exception is mercury. This is the only metal which is a liquid at room temperature and it has a very high density compared with that of other liquids. Because the density of gases is so low, very sophisticated balances need to be used to measure the mass of a given volume in order that their densities may be found.

SUPPLEMENTARY

1.17 MEASURING SMALL LENGTHS

(i) If we are measuring small lengths then the metre rule is an unsatisfactory device because its scale is only calibrated in mm. This leads to inaccuracy. In order to improve the accuracy, greater precision is needed, i.e. a scale with divisions representing smaller lengths.

Two devices are available. One is a vernier caliper and the other is a micrometer screw gauge.

(ii) A vernier caliper is shown in Fig. 1.10

FIG. 1.10

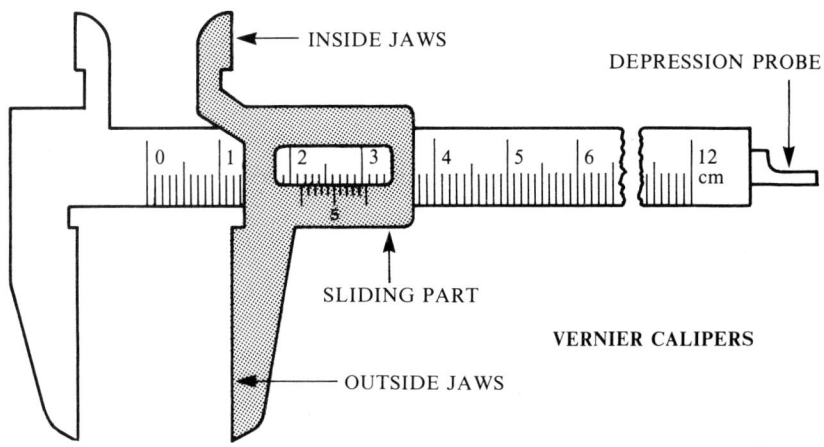

VERNIER CALIPERS

It has a range of 0 to 12 cm and enables measurements to be made to the nearest 0.1 mm by incorporating a vernier scale. It consists of a sliding part, shown shaded in the figure, attached to a large static part.

In order to measure a straightforward length we place the object between the outside jaws, move the sliding part until the outside jaws touch the object, then read the scale. To measure an inside length, such as the diameter of a pipe, we move the sliding part until the inside jaws touch, place the inside jaws into the pipe and then move the sliding part to the right until both are in contact with the object being measured. The scale is then read.

As the sliding part is moved to the right, a depression probe emerges as shown. This may be used to measure the depth of a depression such as a groove. It should be noted that this probe is sharp and dangerous. It should never be pointed at the body.

To read the scale on the instrument we must be able to read a vernier scale. To see how to do this, consider Fig. 1.11.

To obtain a reading to the nearest whole mm we look at the zero mark.

It is lying between 2.3 and 2.4 cm.

To increase the precision of the reading we need the next figure which will give the reading to the nearest 0.1 mm. We look at the marks on the static scale and the vernier scale and decide which two are most in line. Here the fourth vernier mark coincides with a static mark and so the next figure is a 4.

14 Basic Quantities in Physics

FIG. 1.11

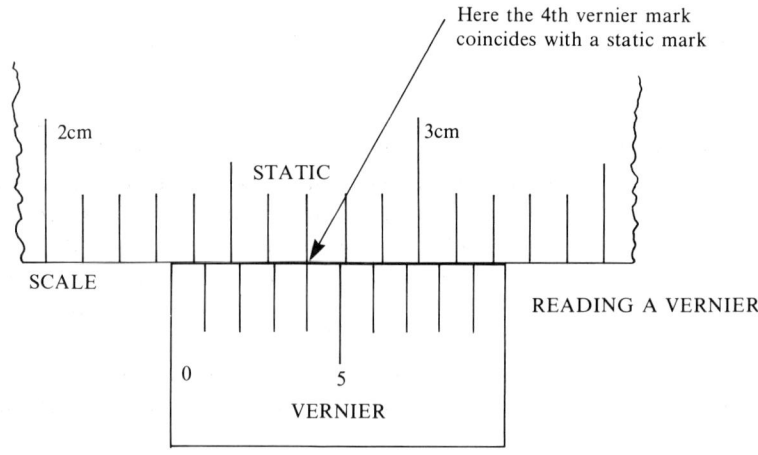

The complete reading is 2.34 cm.

Returning to a consideration of Fig. 1.10, it will be seen that the reading is 2.17 cm.

An exact reading of 2.1 cm, because of the precision available, should be recorded as 2.10 cm.

(iii) A micrometer screw gauge is shown in Fig. 1.12.

FIG. 1.12

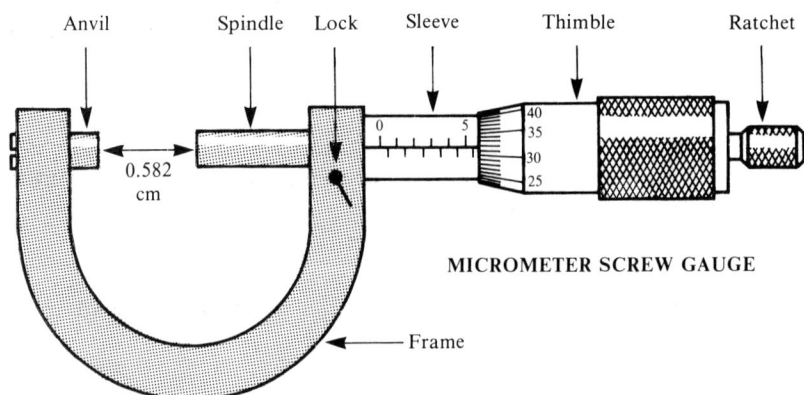

It has a range of 0 to 25 mm and enables measurements to be made to the nearest 0.01 mm.

In order to take a measurement we turn the thimble to move the spindle to the right. The object is then placed between the anvil and

Basic Quantities in Physics 15

the spindle and the spindle closed onto the object by turning the ratchet until the ratchet slips, indicated by a clicking noise. This prevents compression of the object. The lock is engaged, the object removed and the reading taken.

The thimble scale goes from 0 to 50 and 2 complete revolutions corresponds to 1 mm so each scale division on the thimble corresponds to 0.01 mm. But we need to know whether the thimble has turned through less or more than one revolution — that is, does a reading of 40 represent 40 or 1 revolution plus 40, i.e. 50 + 40 = 90. In order to decide this we look at the sleeve scale. The divisions on it are 1 mm apart. However on the lower scale the divisions are also 1 mm apart but each lies exactly half way between the top divisions. If one of these lower divisions is also visible before the thimble then we know that the thimble has already made 1 of its 2 revolutions needed for each 1 mm.

Returning to a consideration of Fig. 1.12. We have gone past the 5 mm mark on the sleeve scale and the next $\frac{1}{2}$ mm mark. The thimble reading is found by looking which horizontal line is next to the horizontal line of the sleeve scale. Here it is 32.

The complete reading is
$$5 + \tfrac{1}{2} + \tfrac{32}{100} = 5+0.5+0.32 = 5.82 \text{ mm} = 0.582 \text{ cm}$$
(sleeve) (sleeve) (thimble)

An exact reading of $\frac{1}{2}$ cm should be quoted, because of the precision available as 0.500 cm.

(iv) If we are measuring the thickness of small objects of which we have a few, it is better to obtain an average value and gain increased precision.

Suppose we are trying to measure the thickness of a paper towel. We may measure one, using a micrometer screw gauge, as 0.31 mm. However, it would be better practice to measure 10. If this reading is 2.49 mm it gives an average of
$$\frac{2.49}{10} = 0.249 \text{ mm}$$
Note that we have also increased the precision of our reading to 0.001 mm.

1.18 MEASURING SMALL TIME INTERVALS
(i) In order to measure small time intervals there are two methods available in order to obtain greater accuracy by increasing the precision. One is an electrically operated timing device and the other is to time a large number of events.

16 Basic Quantities in Physics

(ii) Electrically operated timing devices are ideal in situations where a clock can be started and stopped electrically by breaking and making an electrical circuit. A centisecond timer, measuring to 0.01 s is often used in a free fall experiment to time the journey of a falling object.

(iii) The scale on a stopwatch reads to the nearest 0.1 s. This lack of precision matters if we are measuring the period of a pendulum, i.e. the time for one complete swing. Suppose we time one swing and find it to be 2.0 s. However, it would be better practice to time 10 swings. If this reading is 19.6 s, it gives an average of

$$\frac{19.6}{10} = 1.96 \text{ s}$$

Note that we have increased the precision of our reading to 0.01 s.

1.19 INERTIA

An object with a large mass resists motion and if it is moving it resists being stopped. This unwillingness is known as inertia. The larger the mass of a body, the greater is its inertia and we may regard the mass of a body as a measure of its inertia.

1.20 MEASURING THE DENSITY OF AN IRREGULAR SOLID

In order to measure the density of an irregular solid, we measure its mass using a balance. We measure its volume using a displacement technique. The mass is then divided by the volume.

PROBLEM

THE MASS OF A LUMP OF GLASS IS FOUND TO BE 55 g. IT IS TIED TO A PIECE OF THREAD AND IMMERSED IN SOME LIQUID CONTAINED IN A MEASURING CYLINDER CAUSING THE LEVEL OF THE LIQUID TO RISE FROM 34 TO 56 mℓ. CALCULATE THE DENSITY OF THE GLASS, IN kg/m^3.

MASS OF GLASS = 55 g
$$= \frac{55}{1000} = 55 \times 10^{-3} \text{ kg}$$

VOLUME OF GLASS = CHANGE IN READING
$$= 56 - 34 = 22 \text{ m}\ell$$
$$= 22 \text{ cm}^3$$

TO CONVERT FROM cm^3 TO m^3, DIVIDE BY 1,000,000

So $\quad 22 \text{ cm}^3 = \dfrac{22}{1,000,000} = 22 \times 10^{-6} \text{ m}^3$

Now $\quad$ DENSITY $= \dfrac{\text{MASS}}{\text{VOLUME}} = \dfrac{55 \times 10^{-3}}{22 \times 10^{-6}}$
$$= 2500 \text{ kg/m}^3$$

ANSWER: DENSITY OF GLASS = 2500 kg/m³.

NOTE TO STUDENT: ALTERNATIVELY THIS PROBLEM COULD HAVE BEEN WORKED THROUGH IN g and cm³ AND CONVERTED FROM g/cm³ TO kg/m³ USING THE CONVERSION FACTOR OF 1000.

QUESTIONS

CORE
1. State the units of a) length, b) area, c) volume.
2. Convert 2.5 m to cm.
3. Convert 2.5m² to cm²
4. Convert 250000 mℓ to m³.
5. A piece of steel of mass 120 g has a volume of 15 cm³. Calculate its density in a) g/cm³, b) kg/m³.
6. The density of air is 1.26 kg/m³. Calculate the mass of air in a room of dimensions 10 m by 5 m by 3 m.
7. What is the length of the object shown in Fig. 1.13?

FIG. 1.13

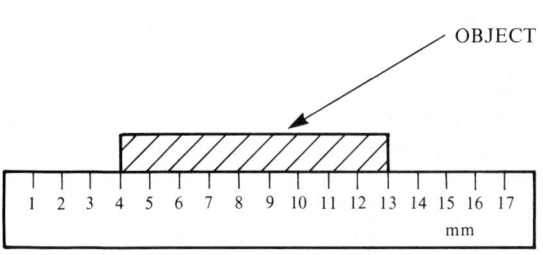

MEASURING A LENGTH

8. What is the volume of the stone shown in Fig. 1.14?

FIG. 1.14

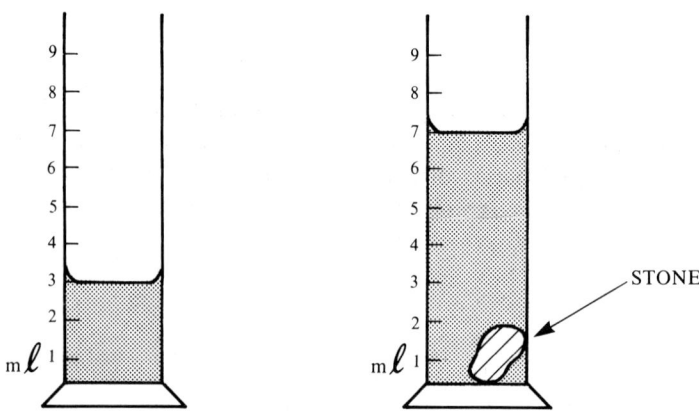

MEASURING A VOLUME BY DISPLACEMENT

SUPPLEMENTARY

9. A piece of glass of approximate size 10 cm by 8 cm by 1 cm is to be measured. Name the instrument used for each measurement.
10. What is meant by inertia?
11. A stone of mass 60 g is lowered into a measuring cylinder causing the liquid level to rise from 15 to 35 ml. Calculate the density of the stone in g/cm^3.
12. A steel block of sides 100 cm by 10 cm by 10 cm is joined to an aluminium block of sides 54 cm by 50 cm by 10 cm. If the density of steel is 7800 kg/m^3 and the density of aluminium is 2700 kg/m^3, calculate the average density of the shape formed when the blocks have been joined together.

Chapter 2
MOTION

At the end of this chapter you will know:

CORE: what is meant by speed, displacement, velocity and acceleration; how to make measurements using a ticker-tape timer and trolley; how changes in distance, displacement, speed and velocity with time may be shown using graphs and what is represented by the area under speed-time and velocity-time graphs.

SUPPLEMENTARY: how non-uniform motion may be shown by graphs; how speed may be found from a distance-time graph, velocity from a displacement-time graph and acceleration from a velocity-time graph; what is meant by terminal velocity and how the Equations of Motion may be used to solve problems on motion.

CORE

2.1 SPEED

A moving object has speed.

$$\text{Speed} = \frac{\text{Distance moved}}{\text{Time taken}}$$

If the distance is measured in km and the time in h then speed is measured in km/h.

If the distance is measured in m and the time in s then speed is measured in m/s.

PROBLEM

A CAR TRAVELS 45 m IN 3 s. CALCULATE ITS SPEED.

$$\text{SPEED} = \frac{\text{DISTANCE MOVED}}{\text{TIME TAKEN}}$$
$$= \frac{45}{3}$$
$$= 15 \text{ m/s}$$

ANSWER: SPEED = 15 m/s.

In this problem the speed of the car is steady or uniform over the 3 s period.

Over a longer period of time, unless the car was on a motorway, it would have to keep changing the speed because of varying traffic conditions. In such a case we would measure an average speed.

$$\text{Average speed} = \frac{\text{Total distance moved}}{\text{Total time taken.}}$$

PROBLEM

A TRAIN TRAVELS 320 km FROM MANCHESTER TO LONDON IN 2½ h. CALCULATE ITS AVERAGE SPEED.

$$\text{AVERAGE SPEED} = \frac{\text{TOTAL DISTANCE MOVED}}{\text{TOTAL TIME TAKEN}}$$
$$= \frac{320}{2\tfrac{1}{2}}$$
$$= 128 \text{ km/h}$$

ANSWER: AVERAGE SPEED = 128 km/h.

2.2 DISPLACEMENT

Displacement is distance moved in a given direction.

It is measured in distance units with the direction added.

Suppose a person walks 5 km along a road from south to north. The distance moved is 5 km but the displacement is 5 km due north.

2.3 VELOCITY

(i) A moving object not only has speed but it has velocity.

$$\text{Velocity} = \frac{\text{Distance moved in a particular direction}}{\text{Time taken}}$$

and remembering what is meant by displacement we may write

$$\text{Velocity} = \frac{\text{Displacement}}{\text{Time taken}}$$

But, also remembering what is meant by speed we may write

Velocity = Speed in a particular direction.

So, velocity is measured in km/h or m/s in the direction of travel.

Now because velocity is really speed in a particular direction this means that the velocity of an object may change if either its speed or its direction of motion changes. We shall only consider motion in a straight line and so any velocity changes we look at will be caused only by a change in speed.

PROBLEM

A CAR TRAVELS ALONG A STRAIGHT ROAD. IF IT MOVES 125 m in 5 s, CALCULATE ITS VELOCITY.

$$\text{VELOCITY} = \frac{\text{DISTANCE MOVED IN A PARTICULAR DIRECTION}}{\text{TIME TAKEN}}$$

$$= \frac{125}{5}$$

$$= 25 \text{ m/s}$$

ANSWER: VELOCITY = 25 m/s IN DIRECTION OF TRAVEL.

The velocity of the car is steady over the period of time considered.

When an object is moving at a steady velocity in a constant direction we say that it is travelling at a uniform velocity.

We could measure average velocity as

$$\text{Average Velocity} = \frac{\text{Total displacement}}{\text{Total time taken}}$$

But it is not very practical to do this unless we are able to travel in the same direction over the time period considered. Even motorways and railway tracks go round bends!

PROBLEM
A CAR TRAVELS AT A UNIFORM VELOCITY OF 15 m/s. CALCULATE ITS DISPLACEMENT AFTER 20 s.

$$\text{UNIFORM VELOCITY} = \frac{\text{DISPLACEMENT}}{\text{TIME TAKEN}}$$

So

$$\text{DISPLACEMENT} = \text{UNIFORM VELOCITY} \times \text{TIME TAKEN}$$
$$= 15 \times 20$$
$$= 300 \text{ m}$$

ANSWER: DISPLACEMENT = 300 m IN DIRECTION OF TRAVEL.

(ii) As an example of the difference between speed and velocity, consider Fig. 2.1.

THE DIFFERENCE BETWEEN SPEED AND VELOCITY

FIG. 2.1

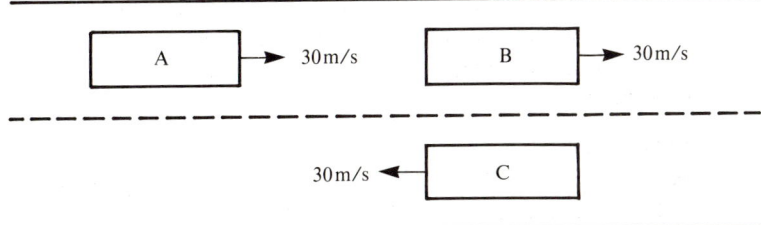

22 Motion

Two lorries A and B are travelling in the same direction at a uniform speed of 30 m/s along a straight piece of road. Lorry C is travelling at a uniform speed of 30 m/s in the opposite direction.

All the lorries have the same speed. Lorries A and B also have the same velocity because they are travelling in the same direction. However, the velocity of C is different to that of A and B because it is travelling in the opposite direction.

The speedometer in a car does not show the direction of motion and so it would be wrong to call it a velocity meter.

2.4 ACCELERATION

(i) Suppose an object is travelling in a straight line at a constant velocity and its velocity is steadily increased to a larger constant velocity. We say that an acceleration is taking place.

$$\text{Acceleration} = \frac{\text{Change of velocity}}{\text{Time taken}}$$

Change of velocity is measured in m/s and time in s and so acceleration is measured in m/s^2, or metres per second squared, in the direction of motion.

When an object is moving with a steadily increasing velocity in a constant direction, we say that it is moving with a uniform acceleration.

If the velocity is decreasing, we say that the object is decelerating or undergoing a retardation.

PROBLEM

THE UNIFORM VELOCITY OF A CAR INCREASES FROM 20 TO 30 m/s IN 5 s. CALCULATE ITS UNIFORM ACCELERATION.

$$\text{ACCELERATION} = \frac{\text{CHANGE OF VELOCITY}}{\text{TIME TAKEN}}$$
$$= \frac{30 - 20}{5} = \frac{10}{5}$$
$$= 2 \text{ m/s}^2$$

ANSWER: ACCELERATION = 2 m/s^2 IN DIRECTION OF MOTION.

NOTE TO STUDENT: IN PROBLEMS, WE USUALLY ASSUME VELOCITIES AND ACCELERATIONS ARE UNIFORM WITHOUT ACTUALLY STATING IT.

PROBLEM
THE VELOCITY OF A TRAIN IS REDUCED FROM 150 TO 60 m/s BY APPLYING THE BRAKES FOR 30 s. CALCULATE THE DECELERATION OF THE TRAIN.

$$\text{ACCELERATION} = \frac{\text{CHANGE OF VELOCITY}}{\text{TIME TAKEN}}$$

IN CALCULATING THE CHANGE OF VELOCITY, WE SUBTRACT THE SMALLER VELOCITY FROM THE LARGER. BECAUSE THE LARGER VELOCITY IS THE INITIAL VELOCITY, WE ARE DEALING WITH A DECELERATION.

$$\text{DECELERATION} = \frac{150 - 60}{30} = \frac{90}{30}$$
$$= 3 \text{ m/s}^2$$

ANSWER: DECELERATION = 3 m/s²

(ii) A very important example of a uniform acceleration can be seen all around us. If we hold an object such as an apple and release it, it falls to the ground. Gravity causes this motion and accelerates the apple towards the ground at a rate of 9.8 m/s². This acceleration is known as the acceleration due to gravity or acceleration of free fall. Although it is uniform in any particular place, its value does change slightly depending upon whether we are at the pole or the equator or whether we are above or below sea level.

2.5 THE TICKER-TAPE TIMER
(i) The ticker-tape timer is shown in Fig. 2.2.

FIG. 2.2

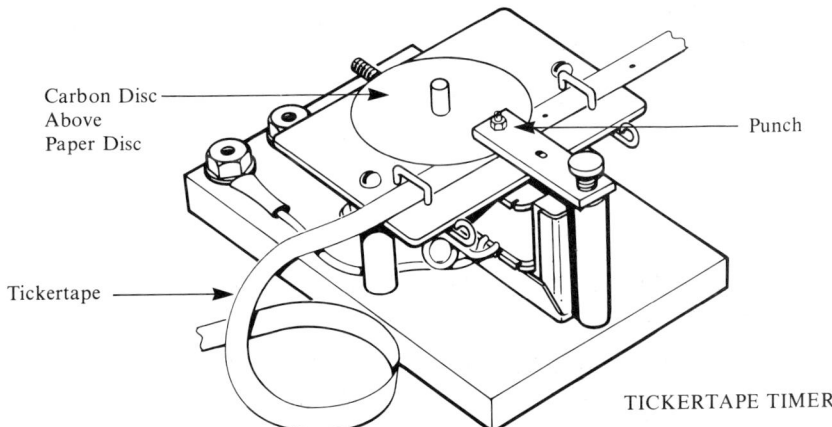

TICKERTAPE TIMER

It consists of a vibrating metal bar which hits a piece of carbon paper above a piece of ticker-tape 50 times every second.

The ticker-tape moves along underneath the carbon paper because it is attached to a moving trolley as shown in Fig. 2.3.

FIG. 2.3 TROLLEY AND TICKERTAPE TIMER

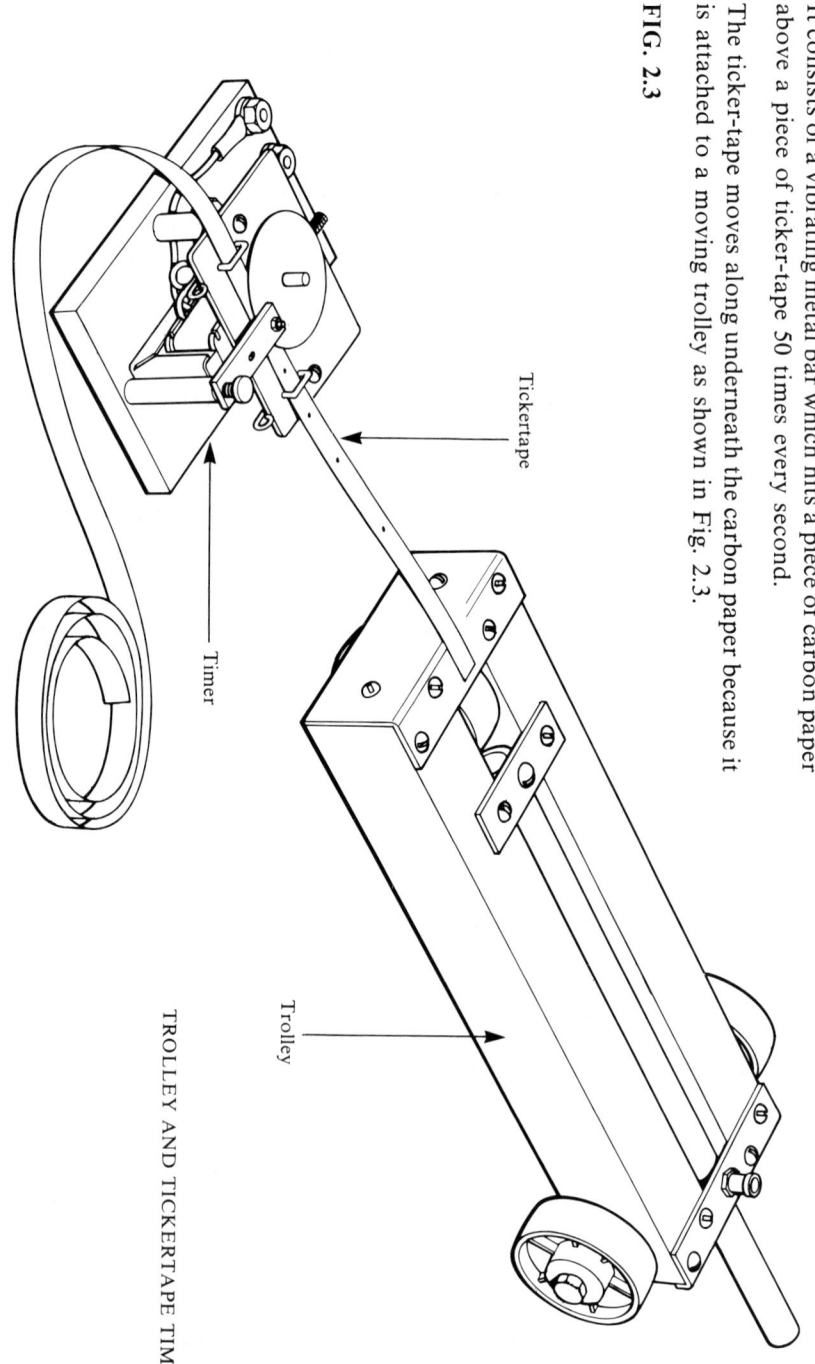

As the trolley moves it pulls the ticker-tape along and the timer prints a dot on the ticker-tape every $\frac{1}{50}$ s. The way in which the trolley is made to move will be seen in Chapter 4.

We can use this arrangement to measure:
either how far the trolley moves in a particular time by measuring the distance between a certain number of dots;
or how long the trolley takes to move a given distance by counting how many dots there are on a particular length of tape.

(ii) In order to see if the trolley is accelerating, the ticker-tape timer is switched on while the trolley is moving away from it. After a suitable length of ticker-tape has passed through the timer, we cut the ticker-tape into pieces with each piece having the same number of dots.

Now a dot is printed every $\frac{1}{50}$ s so the distance between two dots is the distance moved in $\frac{1}{50}$ s. Similarly, the distance between eleven dots is the distance moved in ten time intervals, that is,
$$10 \times \tfrac{1}{50} = \tfrac{1}{5} \text{ s}$$

If the trolley is moving with a uniform velocity then all the dots will be the same distance apart and so all the pieces are of equal length, as shown in Fig. 2.4.

FIG. 2.4

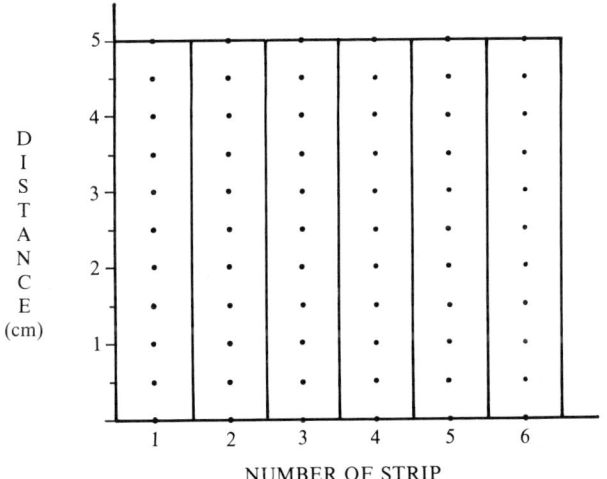

TROLLEY MOVING WITH UNIFORM VELOCITY
OR ZERO ACCELERATION

26 Motion

If the trolley is uniformly accelerating then the dots become further apart and the strips become longer. The line joining the top dots on each strip is straight and slopes upwards. This is shown in Fig. 2.5.

FIG. 2.5

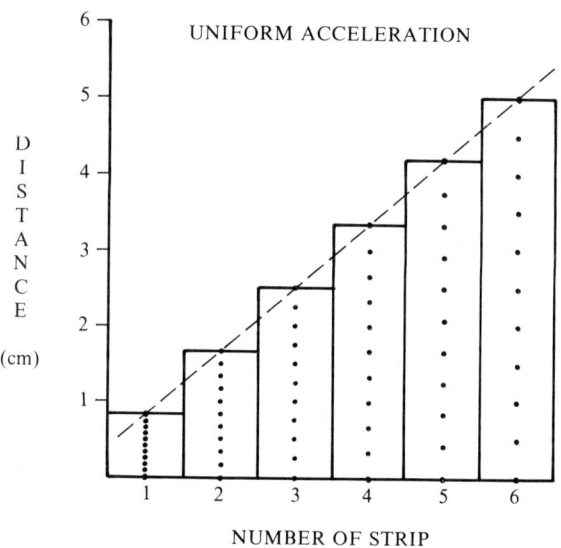

2.6 DISTANCE-TIME GRAPHS

We can represent information about the distance which an object travels in any particular time by drawing a distance-time graph.

FIG. 2.6

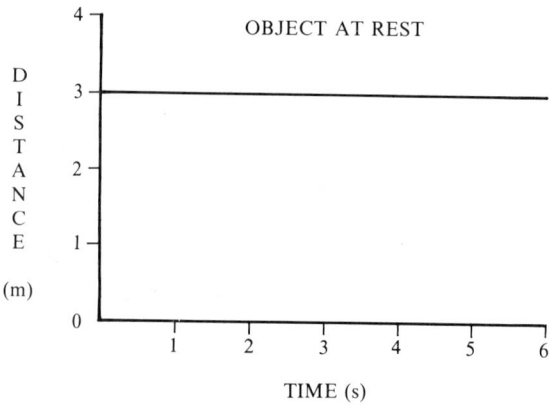

Fig. 2.6 shows a graph of distance against time for an object which is at rest. It is a straight line parallel to the time axis.

Fig. 2.7 shows a graph of distance against time for an object moving at a uniform speed. It is a straight line which slopes upwards.

FIG. 2.7

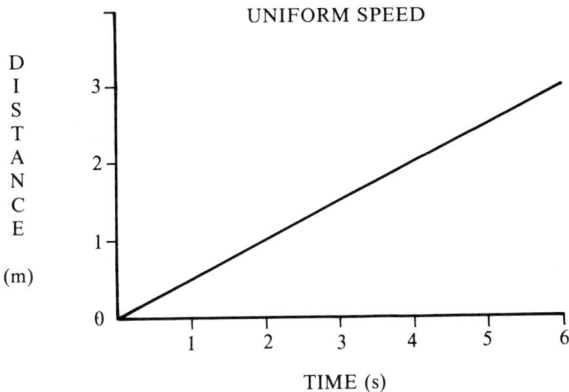

2.7 DISPLACEMENT-TIME GRAPHS

A displacement-time graph shows how the displacement of an object changes with time.

FIG. 2.8

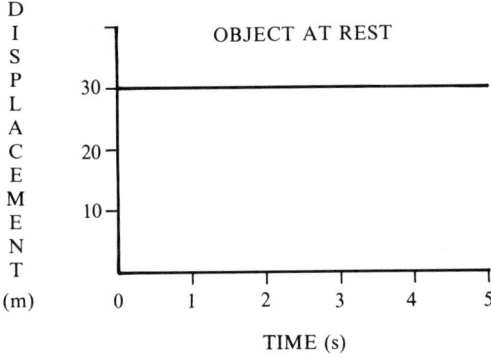

Fig. 2.8 shows a graph of displacement against time for an object which is at rest. It is a straight line parallel to the time axis.

Fig. 2.9 shows a graph of displacement against time for a moving object.

FIG. 2.9

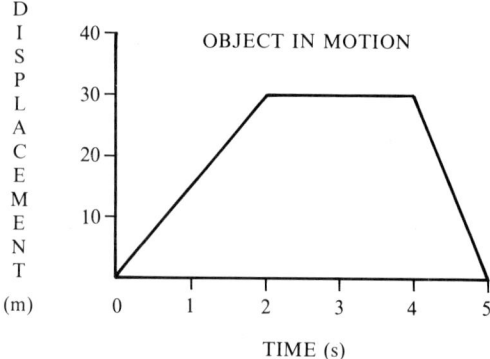

In the first 2 s it moves at a uniform velocity, shown by the straight line sloping upwards. It then remains at rest for a further 2 s as shown by the line parallel to the time axis. Finally, in the remaining 1 s, it returns to its starting point again at a uniform velocity. Because it has reversed its direction its displacement decreases, causing the line to slope downwards. A reversal of direction always causes the slope to change direction.

2.8 SPEED-TIME GRAPHS

A speed-time graph shows how the speed of an object changes with time.

FIG. 2.10

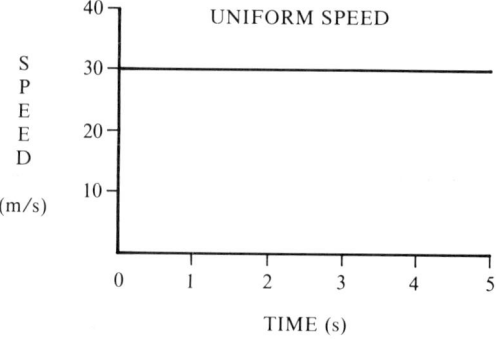

Fig. 2.10 shows a graph of speed against time for an object moving with a uniform speed. It is a straight line parallel to the time axis.

FIG. 2.11

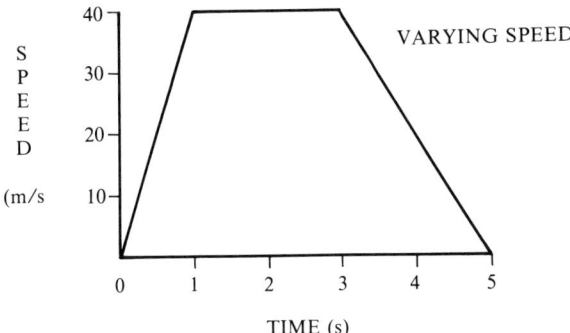

In Fig. 2.11 for the first 1 s it moves at a uniformly increasing speed, shown by the straight line sloping upwards. For the next 2 s it moves at a uniform speed shown by the straight line parallel to the time axis. Finally, in the remaining 2s, its speed decreases uniformly to zero, shown by the straight line sloping downwards.

The area underneath a speed-time graph is equal to the distance travelled.

PROBLEM

FIG. 2.12

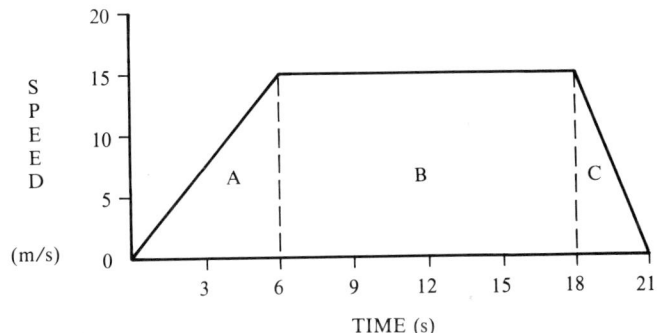

FIG. 2.12 SHOWS THE MOTION OF A CAR OVER A 21s PERIOD. CALCULATE THE TOTAL DISTANCE TRAVELLED BY THE CAR.

TOTAL DISTANCE = AREA UNDER GRAPH
= AREA OF TRIANGLE A + AREA OF RECTANGLE B + AREA OF TRIANGLE C.
= ½ × 6 × 15 + 12 × 15 + ½ × 3 × 15
= 45 + 180 + 22.5
= 247.5 m

ANSWER: DISTANCE TRAVELLED = 247.5 m.

2.9 VELOCITY-TIME GRAPHS

A velocity-time graph for an object moving in a particular direction shows how its velocity changes with time.

FIG. 2.13

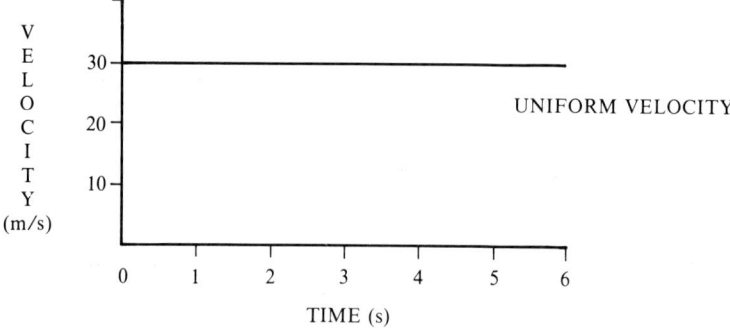

Fig. 2.13 shows a velocity-time graph for an object moving at a uniform velocity. It is a straight line parallel to the time axis.

FIG. 2.14

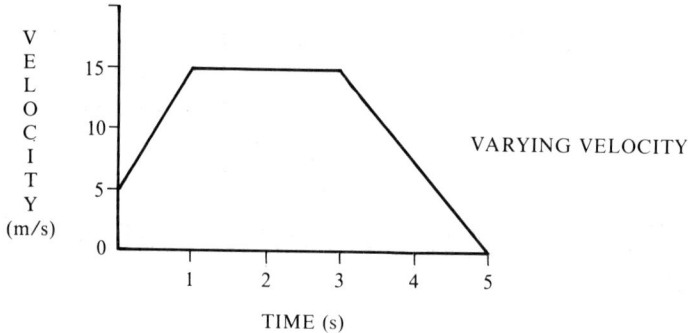

In Fig. 2.14 the object starts with a velocity of 5 m/s and its velocity increases uniformly for 1s, shown by the straight line sloping upwards. For the next 2s it moves at a uniform velocity, shown by the straight line parallel to the time axis. Finally in the remaining 2s its velocity decreases uniformly to zero, shown by the straight line sloping downwards.

We can see that an acceleration is represented by an upward sloping line and a deceleration is represented by a downward sloping line.

The area underneath a velocity-time graph is equal to the total displacement.

PROBLEM

FIG. 2.15

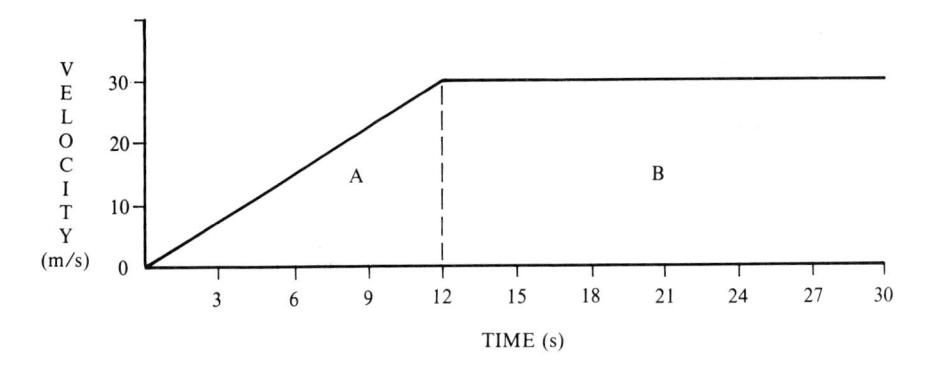

A CAR STARTS FROM REST AND ACCELERATES UNIFORMLY FOR 12s UNTIL IT ACHIEVES A VELOCITY OF 30 m/s. IT THEN TRAVELS AT THIS VELOCITY FOR ANOTHER 18s. CALCULATE ITS DISPLACEMENT.

TOTAL DISPLACEMENT = AREA UNDER GRAPH
= AREA OF TRIANGLE A + AREA OF RECTANGLE B
= ½ × 12 × 30 + 18 × 30
= 180 + 540
= 720 m

ANSWER: DISPLACEMENT = 720 m IN DIRECTION OF TRAVEL.

SUPPLEMENTARY

2.10 NON-UNIFORM MOTION

In all the graphs so far considered, the changes in distance, displacement, speed and velocity have been uniform. If the changes are non-uniform the straight lines become curves.

FIG. 2.16

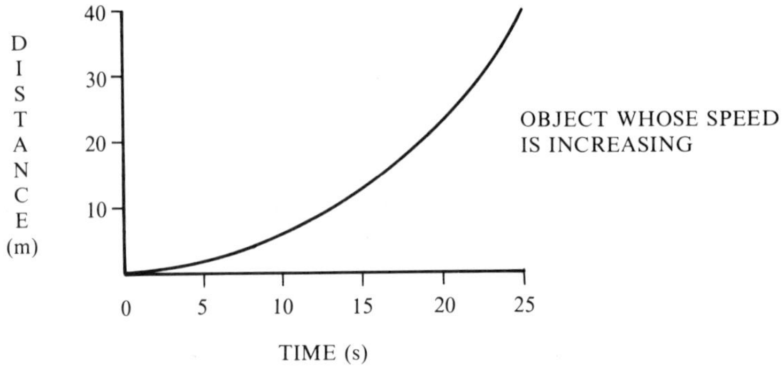

Fig. 2.16 shows a distance-time graph for an object whose speed is increasing.

FIG. 2.17

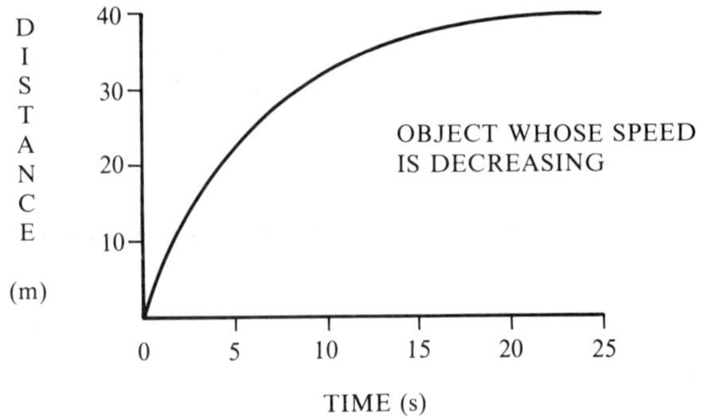

Fig. 2.17 shows a distance-time graph for an object whose speed is decreasing.

Displacement-time graphs for objects whose velocity is increasing or decreasing have similar shapes.

FIG. 2.18

```
40
SPEED 30
(m/s) 20
       10              OBJECT WHOSE SPEED
                       INCREASES MORE RAPIDLY
        0  5  10  15  20  25
               TIME (s)
```

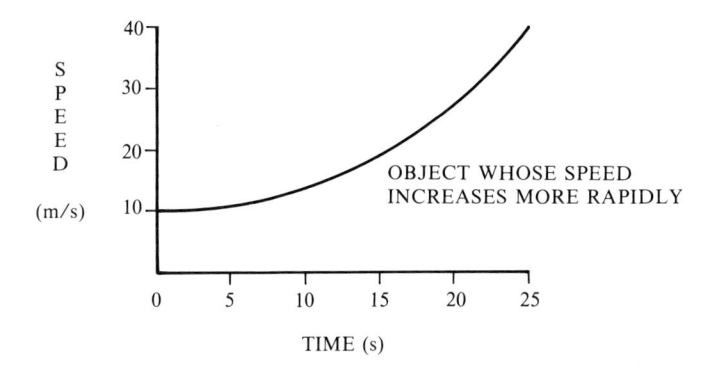

Fig. 2.18 shows a speed-time graph for an object whose speed increases more rapidly as time goes by.

FIG. 2.19

```
40
SPEED 30
(m/s) 20        OBJECT WHOSE SPEED
                INCREASES LESS RAPIDLY
       10
        0  5  10  15  20  25
               TIME (s)
```

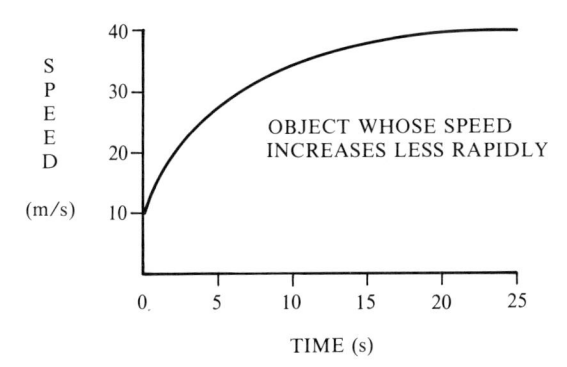

Fig. 2.19 shows a speed-time graph for an object whose speed increases less rapidly as time goes by.

Velocity-time graphs for objects whose velocity is increasing more or less rapidly have similar shapes.

2.11 THE GRADIENT OF A DISTANCE-TIME GRAPH

The gradient of a distance-time graph is speed. For an object moving with a uniform speed, this is simply the gradient of the straight line. If the gradient is zero, the object is at rest.

In Fig. 2.7

$$\text{Speed} = \text{Gradient of line} = \frac{3-0}{6-0} = \frac{3}{6} = 0.5 \text{ m/s}$$

34 Motion

If the speed is not uniform, we can find its value at any particular time by measuring the gradient of the tangent drawn to the curve at the required time.

In Fig. 2.20, the speed at time t is given by the gradient of the tangent.

FIG. 2.20

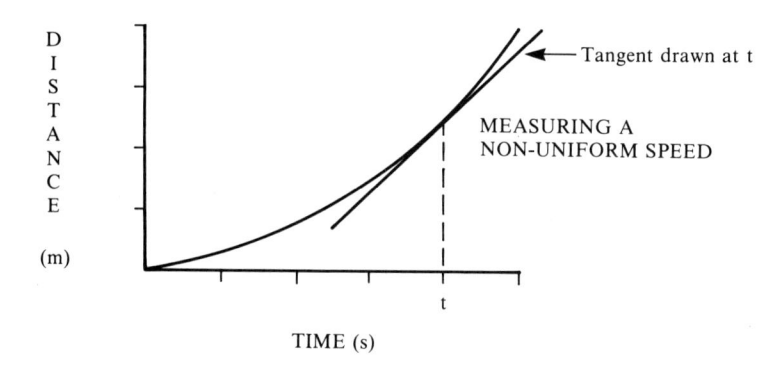

MEASURING A NON-UNIFORM SPEED

Tangent drawn at t

PROBLEM
FIG. 2.21 SHOWS THE DISTANCE MOVED BY AN OBJECT.

FIG. 2.21

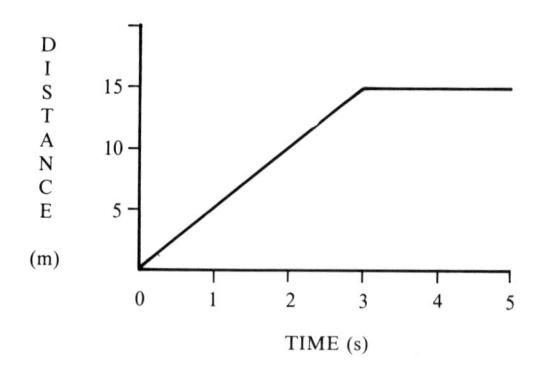

CALCULATE ITS SPEED IN THE FIRST 3 s.

$$\text{SPEED} = \text{GRADIENT OF LINE} = \frac{15-0}{3-0} = \frac{15}{3} = 5 \text{ m/s}.$$

ANSWER: SPEED = 5 m/s.

2.12 GRADIENT OF A DISPLACEMENT-TIME GRAPH

The gradient of a displacement-time graph is velocity. For an object moving with a uniform velocity, this is simply the gradient of the straight line. If the gradient is zero, the object is at rest.

In Fig. 2.9

$$\text{Velocity in first 2s} = \text{Gradient of line} = \frac{30-0}{2-0} = \frac{30}{2} = 15 \text{ m/s}$$

$$\text{Velocity in final 1s} = \text{Gradient of line} = \frac{30-0}{4-5} = \frac{30}{-1} = -30 \text{ m/s}$$

This final negative velocity means that the object has reversed its direction of travel.

If the velocity is not uniform, we can find its value at any particular time by measuring the gradient of the tangent drawn to the curve at the required time.

In Fig. 2.22, the velocity at time t is given by the gradient of the tangent.

FIG. 2.22

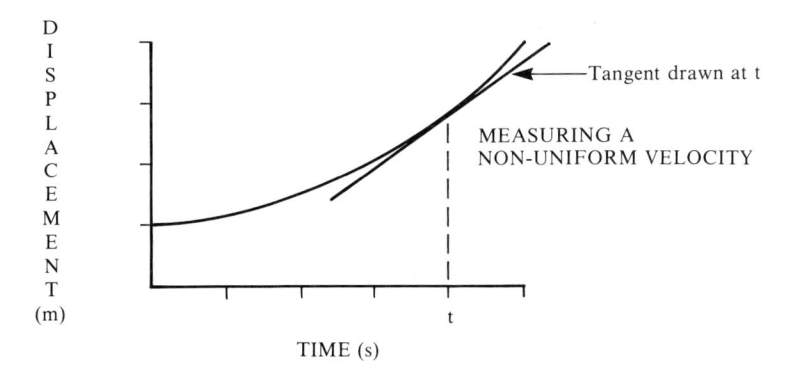

MEASURING A NON-UNIFORM VELOCITY

Tangent drawn at t

DISPLACEMENT (m)

TIME (s)

PROBLEM

FIG. 2.23 SHOWS THE DISPLACEMENT OF AN OBJECT WITH TIME.

36 Motion

FIG. 2.23

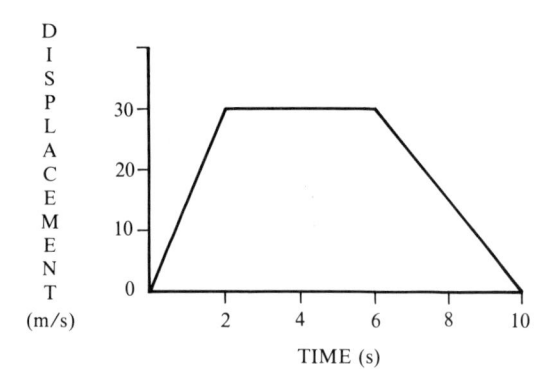

DISPLACEMENT (m/s) vs TIME (s) graph showing a trapezoid: rising from (0,0) to (2,30), flat from (2,30) to (6,30), falling from (6,30) to (10,0).

FIND THE VELOCITY DURING EACH PART OF ITS MOTION.

IN THE FIRST 2s
 VELOCITY = GRADIENT OF LINE = $\frac{30-0}{2-0} = \frac{30}{2} = 15$ m/s

IN THE NEXT 4s
VELOCITY = GRADIENT OF LINE = 0 m/s

IN THE FINAL 4s
VELOCITY = GRADIENT OF LINE = $\frac{30-0}{6-10} = \frac{30}{-4} = -7.5$ m/s

ANSWER: VELOCITY IS 15 m/s, 0 m/s and −7.5 m/s.

2.13 GRADIENT OF A VELOCITY-TIME GRAPH

The gradient of a velocity-time graph is acceleration. For an object moving with a uniform acceleration, this is simply the gradient of a straight line. If the gradient is zero, the object is moving with a uniform velocity.

In Fig. 2.14

Acceleration in first 1s = Gradient of line = $\frac{15-5}{1-0} = \frac{10}{1} = 10$ m/s²

Acceleration in next 2s = Gradient of line = 0 m/s²

Acceleration in final 2s = Gradient of line = $\frac{15-0}{3-5} = \frac{15}{-2} = -7.5$ m/s²

The minus sign shows a deceleration.

If the acceleration is not uniform we can find its value at any particular time by measuring the gradient of the tangent drawn to the curve at the required time.

Motion 37

In Fig. 2.24, the acceleration at time t is given by the gradient of the tangent.

FIG. 2.24

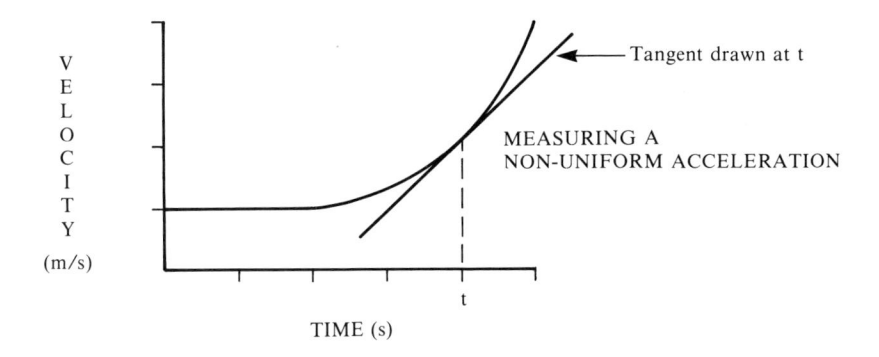

VELOCITY (m/s) vs *TIME (s)*

Tangent drawn at t

MEASURING A NON-UNIFORM ACCELERATION

PROBLEM
FIG. 2.25 SHOWS THE VELOCITY OF A CAR WITH TIME. CALCULATE THE ACCELERATION IN THE FIRST 2s AND THE FINAL 3s.

FIG. 2.25

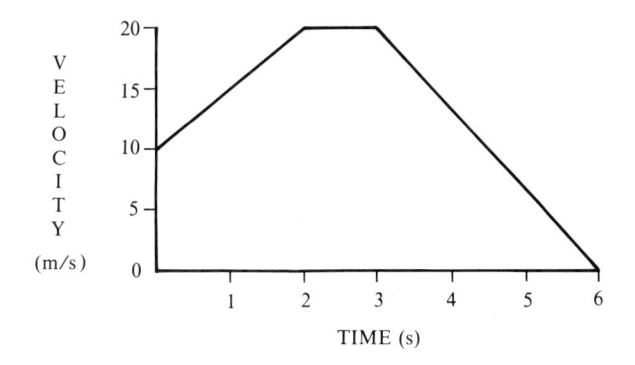

VELOCITY (m/s) vs *TIME (s)*

In the first 2s, Acceleration = gradient of line = $\frac{20-10}{2-0} = \frac{10}{2} = 5$ m/s^2

In the final 3s, Acceleration = gradient of line = $\frac{20-0}{3-6} = \frac{20}{-3} = -6.7$ m/s^2

ANSWER: ACCELERATION = 5 m/s^2, −6.7 m/s^2.

2.14 ACCELERATION USING A TICKER-TAPE TIMER

The acceleration of a trolley may be found using a ticker-tape timer.

38 Motion

In Fig. 2.5,

$$\text{Average velocity for first strip} = \frac{\text{Total displacement}}{\text{Total time}} = \frac{0.8}{1/5} = 4 \text{ cm/s}$$
$$= 0.04 \text{ m/s}$$

$$\text{Average velocity for sixth strip} = \frac{\text{Total displacement}}{\text{Total time}} = \frac{5}{1/5} = 25 \text{ cm/s}$$
$$= 0.25 \text{ m/s}$$

NOTE TO STUDENT: Although we do not usually use the term average velocity, here we do so because during the motion the direction of travel is constant.

Now these average values of velocity represent the values at the middle of each strip, that is at the middle of the first strip and the sixth strip.

The time from the middle of one strip to the middle of the next is $1/5$ s so the time from the middle of the first to the middle of the sixth is

$$5 \times 1/5 = 1 \text{ s}$$

$$\text{Acceleration} = \frac{\text{Change of Velocity}}{\text{Time taken}} = \frac{0.25 - 0.04}{1} = 0.21 \text{ m/s}^2$$

2.15 TERMINAL VELOCITY

Galileo released balls of different mass and material from the top of the leaning tower of Pisa. He found that they all reached the ground together, because they fall under the influence of gravity.

However, if we were to repeat the experiment with a parachute tied to one of the balls, we would find that it would take a greater time to reach the ground. The acceleration of the ball would no longer be equal to the acceleration due to gravity. The air resistance will immediately begin to reduce the acceleration of the ball. Eventually the acceleration will be reduced to zero and the ball will move with a uniform velocity known as terminal velocity.

A graph of velocity-against time will be as in Fig. 2.26.

A real parachute relies on this principle for its effectiveness. The large volume of raindrops, compared with their mass, also means that they reach a terminal velocity. If they did not and accelerated as they fell to earth they could cause damage to whatever they hit.

FIG. 2.26

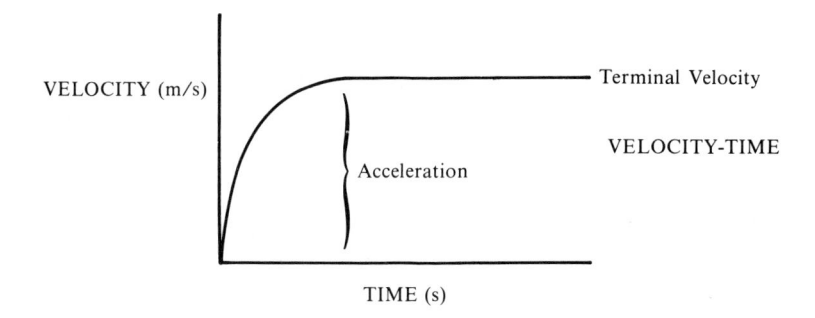

```
VELOCITY (m/s)                    ── Terminal Velocity

                                     VELOCITY-TIME
                    Acceleration

                    TIME (s)
```

2.16 THE EQUATIONS OF MOTION

Information concerning the motion of objects travelling in straight lines and uniformly accelerating from one uniform velocity to another may be obtained using the equations of motion.

Using
- u = initial velocity
- v = final velocity
- a = acceleration
- t = time of motion
- s = distance travelled or displacement

then

$$v = u + at$$
$$v^2 = u^2 + 2as$$
$$s = ut + \tfrac{1}{2}at^2$$

For objects starting from rest, u = 0
For objects falling under gravity, a = g
For objects thrown up against gravity, a = −g — because gravity is acting to slow down the object.

PROBLEM

A TRAIN STARTS FROM REST AT A STATION AND TRAVELS WITH A UNIFORM ACCELERATION OF 0.5m/s^2. WHAT IS THE VELOCITY OF THE TRAIN AFTER 30s AND HOW FAR HAS IT TRAVELLED?

$$u = 0 \text{ m/s}$$
$$a = 0.5 \text{ m/s}^2$$
$$t = 30 \text{ s}$$

Using
$$v = u + at$$
$$= 0 + 0.5 \times 30$$
$$= 15 \text{ m/s}$$

40 Motion

Using $s = ut + \frac{1}{2}at^2$
$= 0 + \frac{1}{2} \times 0.5 \times 30^2$
$= 225\,m$

ANSWER: VELOCITY AND DISTANCE = 15 m/s, 225 m.

PROBLEM
A STONE IS THROWN VERTICALLY UPWARDS WITH A VELOCITY OF 20 m/s. FIND HOW HIGH IT WILL GO AND THE TIME TAKEN TO REACH THIS HEIGHT. ASSUME $g = 10\,m/s^2$.

$u = 20\,m/s$
$v = 0\,m/s$ at maximum height
$a = -10\,m/s^2$

Using $v = u + at$
$0 = 20 - 10t$
$t = {}^{20}\!/_{10} = 2\,s$

Using $s = ut + \frac{1}{2}at^2$
$= 20 \times 2 - \frac{1}{2} \times 10 \times 2^2$
$= 40 - 20$
$= 20\,m$

ANSWER: TIME AND HEIGHT = 2s and 20 m.

2.17 MEASUREMENT OF THE ACCELERATION DUE TO GRAVITY
In order to measure the acceleration due to gravity we use the apparatus shown in Fig. 2.27.

FIG. 2.27

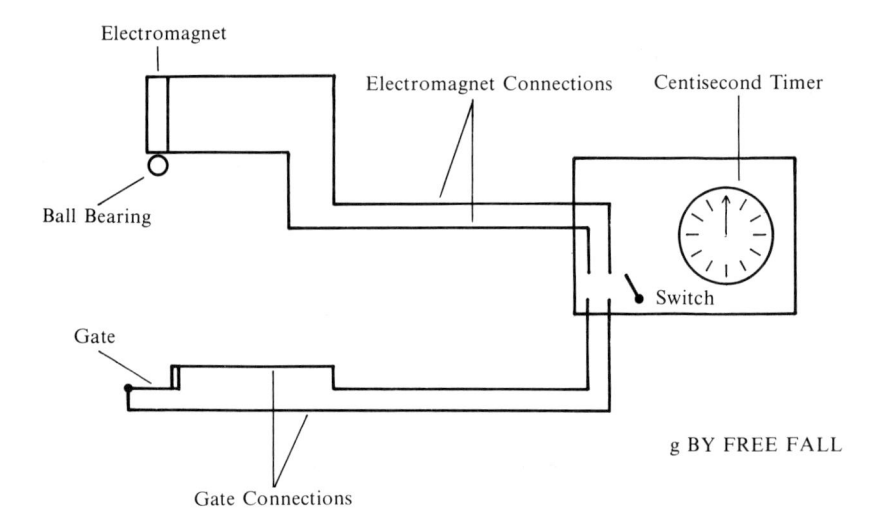

g BY FREE FALL

The fall of a ball bearing over a known distance is timed. The centi-second timer, measuring to $\frac{1}{100}$ s, is switched on and the ball bearing is released. When the ball bearing hits the gate, it stops the timer. The experiment is repeated for five different distances. A graph is then plotted of distance against time².

Using $s = ut + \frac{1}{2}at^2$
here $s = \frac{1}{2}gt^2$

If a graph is plotted of distance against time² it will be a straight line of gradient $\frac{1}{2}g$. So we find g by doubling the gradient of the graph we have plotted.

QUESTIONS

CORE

1. Calculate the speed of a runner who travels 200 m in 25 s.
2. Calculate the average speed of a train which travels 48 km in $\frac{3}{4}$ h.
3. Explain why two cars travelling at the same speed along roads which cross have different velocities.
4. A car travels at a uniform velocity of 15 m/s. Calculate its displacement in 1 min.
5. A car accelerates at 3 m/s² for 10 s. If it started with a velocity of 20 m/s, calculate its final velocity.
6. A piece of ticker-tape attached to a trolley passes through a ticker-tape timer. The trolley moves at a uniform speed for $\frac{3}{10}$ s then a higher uniform speed for another $\frac{2}{10}$ s. If the ticker-tape were cut into pieces as in Fig. 2.5, describe their appearance.
7. A man runs a race against a dog. Fig. 2.28 is a graph showing how they moved during the race

FIG. 2.28

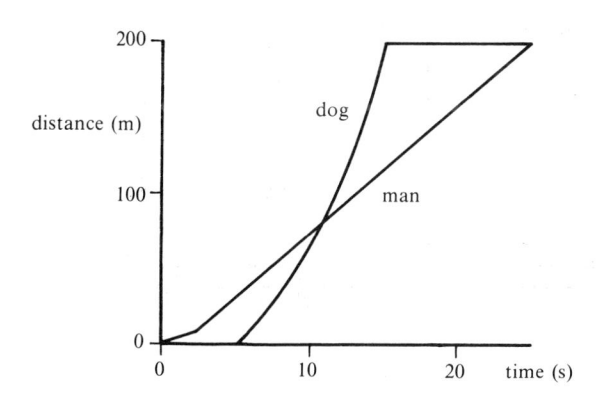

(a) What was the distance for the race?
(b) After how many seconds did the dog overtake the man?
(c) How far from the start did the dog overtake the man?
(d) What was the dog's time for the race?
(e) Use the equation v = s/t to calculate the average speed of the man.
(f) After 8 seconds is the speed of the man increasing, decreasing or staying the same?
(g) What is the speed of the dog after 18 s? *(N.E.A.)*

8. What can be said about the speed of the object shown in Fig. 2.29?

FIG. 2.29

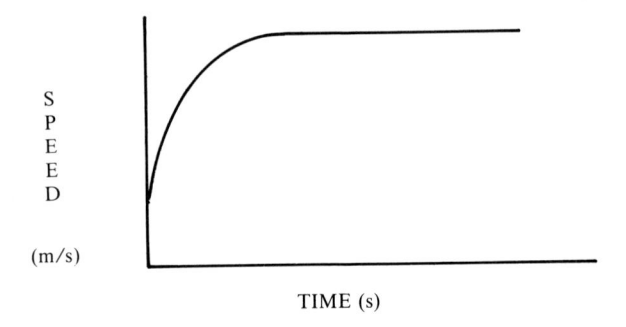

SPEED (m/s) vs TIME (s)

9. In Fig. 2.30, calculate the acceleration during the first 5 s and the total displacement.

FIG. 2.30

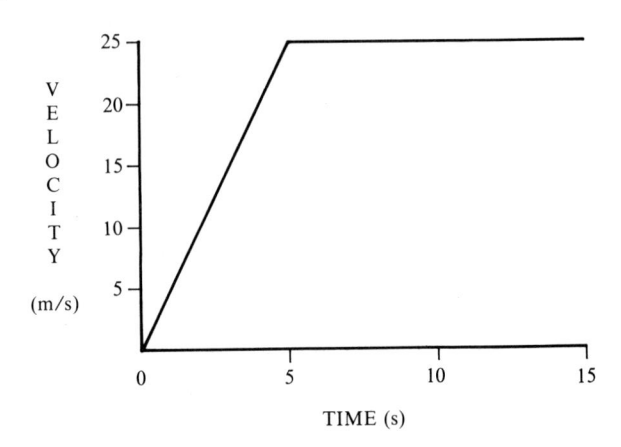

VELOCITY (m/s) vs TIME (s)

10. A ball bearing is gently dropped into a cylinder of oil which resists its motion. Describe what will happen to the ball bearing.
11. In a free fall experiment, the ball bearing falls 78.4cm in 0.4s. Use this information to calculate a value for the acceleration due to gravity.
12. The sketch graph in Fig. 2.31 represents a journey in a lift in a department store.

FIG. 2.31

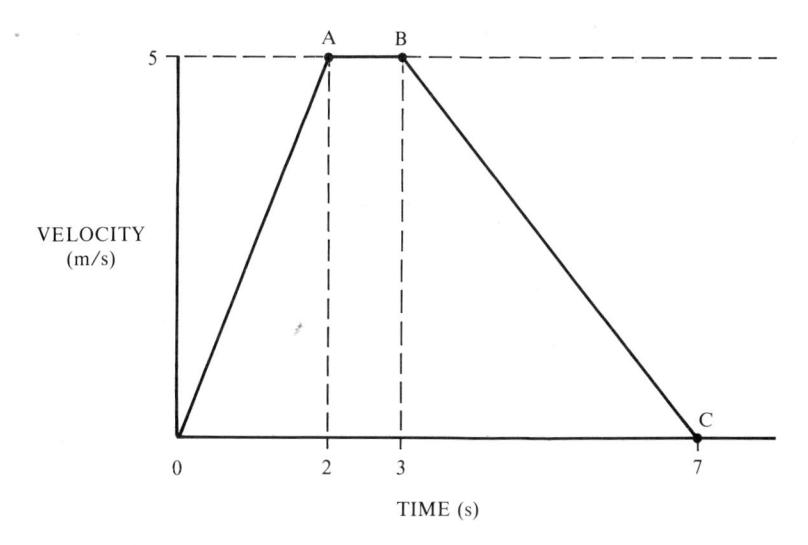

(a) Briefly describe the motion represented by (i) OA, (ii) AB, (iii) BC.
(b) Use the graph to calculate
(i) the initial acceleration of the lift.
(ii) the total distance travelled by the lift.
(iii) the average speed of the lift for the whole journey.

(N.E.A.)

Chapter 3
SCALARS AND VECTORS

At the end of this chapter you will know:
CORE: what is meant by scalars and vectors and examples of each; how scalars may be added; how vectors may be added and how vectors may be resolved.
SUPPLEMENTARY: how vectors may be added to give a resultant using the polygon of vectors.

CORE

3.1 SCALAR QUANTITIES
Scalar quantities have size but no direction.

We have already met two examples — distance and speed.

Other important examples, which will be met later, include energy, work, power and temperature.

3.2 VECTOR QUANTITIES
Vector quantities have size and direction.

We have already met three examples — displacement, velocity and acceleration.

Other important examples, which will be met later, include force, magnetic fields and electric fields.

3.3 THE ADDITION OF SCALAR QUANTITIES
Scalar quantities are added together by adding together their sizes.

We shall consider a problem in which the scalars are distances.

PROBLEM
A CAR TRAVELS 160km IN A DAY. THE NEXT DAY IT TRAVELS 230km. CALCULATE THE TOTAL DISTANCE TRAVELLED.

TOTAL DISTANCE TRAVELLED = 160 + 230 = 390km

ANSWER: TOTAL DISTANCE TRAVELLED = 390km.

3.4 THE ADDITION OF VECTOR QUANTITIES
(i) We can represent a vector with a straight line, drawn to scale, in the correct direction.

Scalars and Vectors 45

Suppose we wish to represent a displacement of 5 km in an easterly direction. If we choose a scale of 1 cm to represent 1 km then 5 cm represents 5 km. The line is drawn horizontally with an arrow at its end making it point to the east. This is shown in Fig. 3.1.

FIG. 3.1

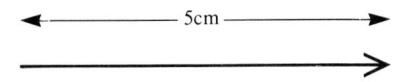

◄──────── 5cm ────────►

─────────────────────►

The addition of two or more vectors gives us a resultant vector.

The resultant of two vectors is greatest when they are in the same direction. We perform the addition by representing each vector by a line, drawn to scale, in the correct direction. The lines are placed end to end and their resultant is that given by the total line formed which acts in the same direction as each vector.

Suppose we wish to add a displacement of 5 km to one of 4 km with both acting in an easterly direction. Using a scale of 1 cm to represent 1 km, we can represent the addition in Fig. 3.2.

FIG. 3.2

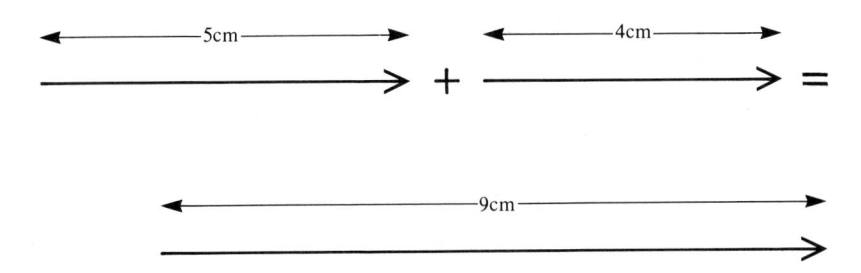

◄──── 5cm ────►   ◄──── 4cm ────►

──────────────► + ──────────────► =

◄──────────── 9cm ────────────►

──────────────────────────────►

The resultant is 9 cm long, representing a total displacement of 9 km east.

(ii) The resultant of two vectors is smallest when they are in opposite directions. As an addition, we represent the vectors by lines, drawn to scale, in the correct direction. This time, the lines are placed so that the start of one lies over the end of the other. The resultant is represented by the line needed to go from the starting point to the end of the other line in that direction.

Suppose we wish to add a displacement of 5 km east to a displacement of 4 km west. Using a scale of 1 cm to represent 1 km we can represent the addition in Fig. 3.3.

FIG. 3.3

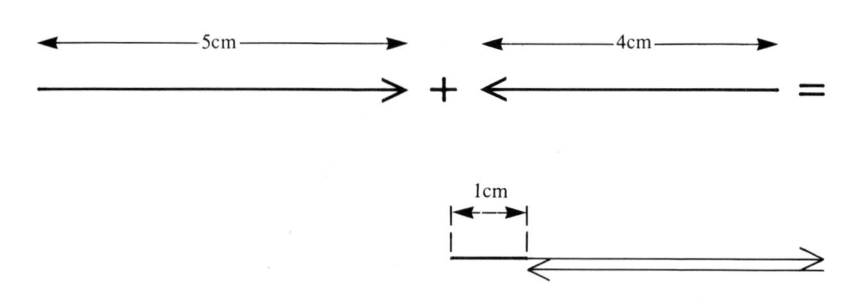

In order to return us to the starting point, we need to move 1 cm. This represents a displacement of 1 km. The direction is the same as the 5 km displacement, that is easterly.

(iii) The addition of vectors which are not in the same or opposite directions is more difficult.

Suppose we wish to add together two vectors as shown in Fig. 3.4.

FIG. 3.4

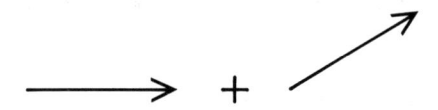

We arrange the lines so that they both start out from the same point and point in their correct directions. These two lines act as two sides of a parallelogram. We complete the parallelogram and draw the diagonal from the vectors' starting point. This diagonal represents their resultant in both size and direction, as shown in Fig. 3.5.

FIG. 3.5

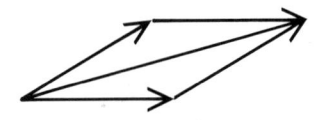

PROBLEM
FIND THE RESULTANT OF A DISPLACEMENT OF 4 km EAST AND 6 km SOUTH-EAST.

WE SHALL CHOOSE A SCALE OF 1 cm TO REPRESENT 1 km. THE LINES ARE THEN DRAWN FROM THE SAME STARTING POINT, AS IN FIG. 3.6.

FIG. 3.6

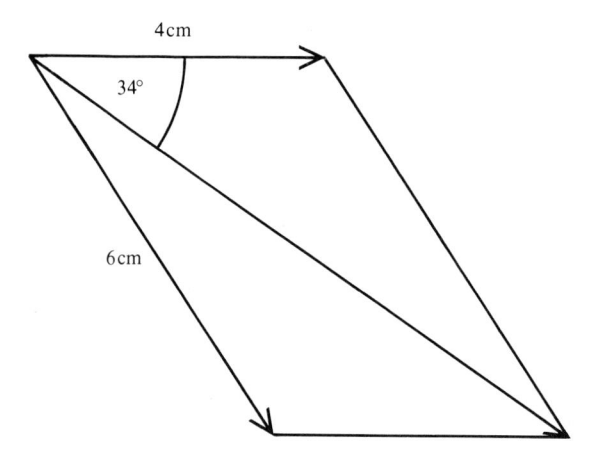

```
        4cm
   ┌─────────→
  /34°      /
 /  \      /
/    \    /
6cm   \  /
       \/
       /\
      /  \
     ↓    ↘
```

THESE TWO LINES ARE MADE TO REPRESENT THE TWO SIDES OF A PARALLELOGRAM. THE RESULTANT IS THE DIAGONAL. IT IS 8.8 cm AT AN ANGLE OF 34°. USING THE SCALE WE GET:

ANSWER: RESULTANT IS 8.8 km IN DIRECTION 34° SOUTH OF EAST.

3.5 THE RESOLUTION OF A VECTOR

We can add together two vectors to obtain a resultant. We can also work backwards and split a vector into two others. When we split a vector into the two vectors which make it up we say that we are resolving a vector into its two components. We choose these components to be at right angles with one being horizontal and the other vertical.

Suppose we wish to split a displacement of 5 km into a horizontal component and a vertical component, as in Fig. 3.7.

FIG. 3.7

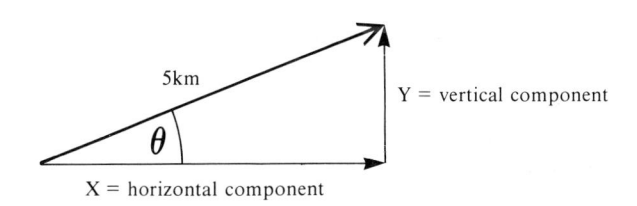

```
              ↗
         5km /|
            / | Y = vertical component
           /θ |
          ─────→
    X = horizontal component
```

The displacement is at an angle of θ to the horizontal.

48 Scalars and Vectors

X is the horizontal component of the displacement and Y is the vertical component of the displacement.

From trigonometric definitions we can see that
$$X = 5 \cos \theta$$
$$Y = 5 \sin \theta$$

PROBLEM

FIG. 3.8

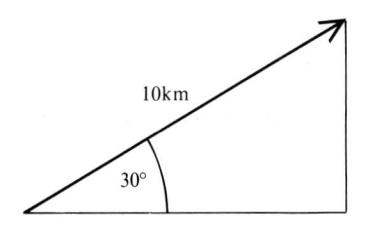

RESOLVE THE DISPLACEMENT OF 10 km AT 30° TO THE HORIZONTAL INTO HORIZONTAL AND VERTICAL COMPONENTS.

HORIZONTAL COMPONENT = 10 cos 30 = 10 × 0.866 = 8.66 km.
VERTICAL COMPONENT   = 10 sin 30 = 10 × 0.500 = 5.00 km.

ANSWER: HORIZONTAL AND VERTICAL COMPONENTS = 8.66 km AND 5.00 km.

SUPPLEMENTARY

3.6 THE POLYGON OF VECTORS

Suppose we wish to add a large number of vectors in various directions, as shown by the vectors drawn to scale in Fig. 3.9.

FIG. 3.9

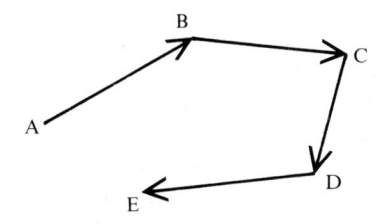

In order to add vectors, AB, BC, CD and DE we find their resultant by closing the polygon — that is by joining E to A. This line represents the resultant in the direction of starting point to finishing point — that is from A to E.

PROBLEM
FIND THE RESULTANT OF THE DISPLACEMENTS SHOWN IN FIG. 3.10.

FIG. 3.10

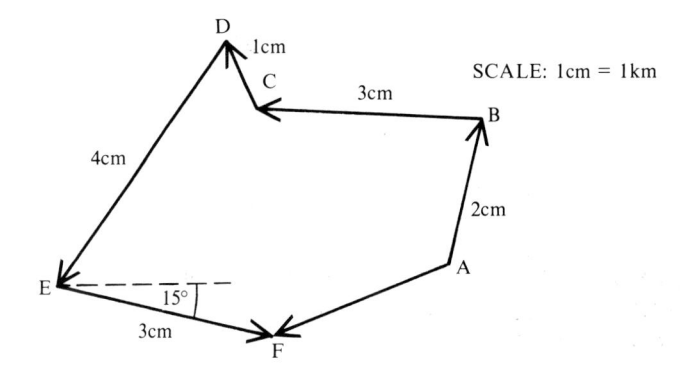

WE JOIN A TO F. THIS LINE IS 2.5cm LONG. USING THE SCALE GIVEN IT CORRESPONDS TO 2.5km.

ANSWER: RESULTANT DISPLACEMENT = 2.5km IN DIRECTION AF.

QUESTIONS

CORE
1. Define a scalar quantity.
2. Define a vector quantity.
3. Which of the following is a scalar quantity — electric field, magnetic field, speed?
4. Which of the following is a vector quantity — energy, acceleration, work?
5. (a) (i) State a difference between a vector quantity and a scalar quantity.
    (ii) Name two vector quantities.
    (iii) Name two scalar quantities.
   (b) Explain in simple language the difference between adding two vector quantities and adding two scalar quantities.
   (S.E.G.)

50 Scalars and Vectors

6. A man walks 1.73 km due east than 1 km due north. What is his total displacement?
7. A displacement of 5 km is to be combined with a displacement of 3 km. Over what range of values could the resultant be?

SUPPLEMENTARY
8.

FIG. 3.11

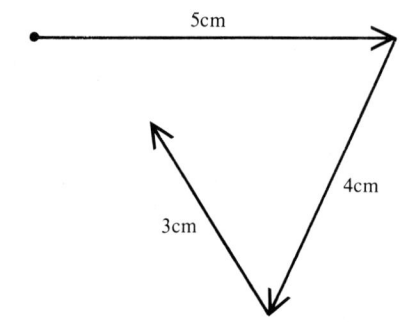

Calculate the resultant displacement in Fig. 3.11.

Chapter 4
FORCES

At the end of this chapter you will know:
CORE: what is meant by force and how it is measured; what is meant by a free body, resultant force and equilibrium and what happens to a free body when a resultant force acts on it; what is meant by friction; Newton's Laws of Motion; how we define the newton; what is meant by weight and how it is measured; what is meant by centre of of gravity; what is meant by shearing and bending; the effect of forces on wires and springs and what is meant by a field of force.
SUPPLEMENTARY: what is meant by limit of proportionality, centripetal force and how mass is a measure of inertia; how the position of a centre of gravity may be found; how $F = ma$ may be verified and what is meant by gravitational and electrical field strength.

CORE

4.1 WHAT IS FORCE?
A force is a push or a pull or a twist.

FIG. 4.1

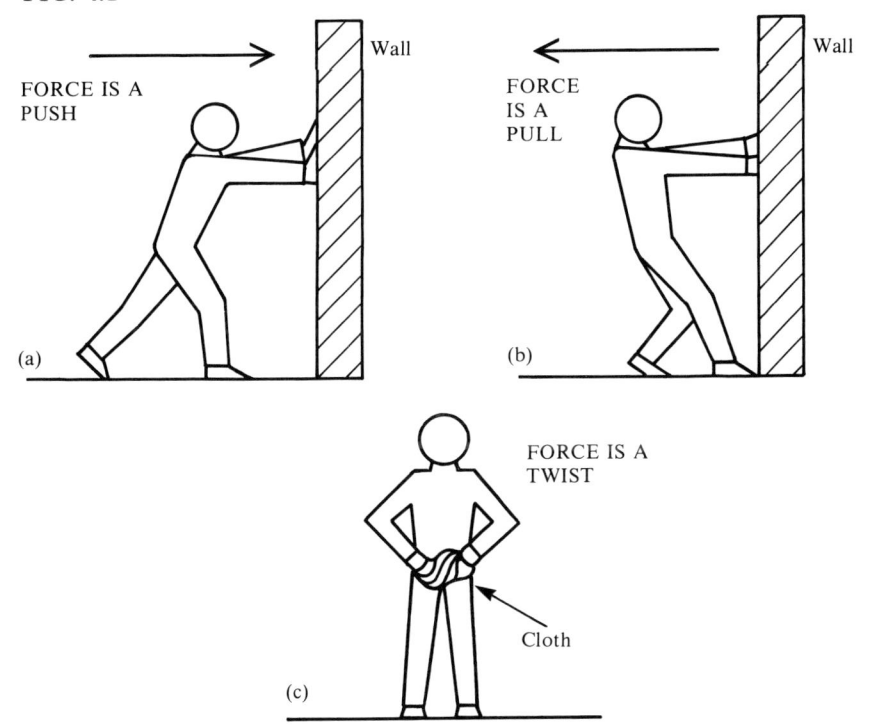

52 Forces

Whenever it acts upon a fixed object it may damage it, depending upon how hard the object is. For example, if we push on a house wall we will just tire ourselves out, but if we push on a garden fence we may push it over. If the object is fixed to the ground but is not very hard we may damage it by changing its shape. This is called deformation.

Force is measured in newtons, symbol N.

We have seen that a force is a push or pull and so it is obviously a vector quantity.

4.2 FREE BODIES, RESULTANT FORCE AND EQUILIBRIUM

(i) If an object is not firmly fixed down but is free to move we say that it is a free body.

(ii) A number of forces may act on a free body. Because forces are vectors we can always calculate the resultant force acting on a body.

Suppose forces of 5N and 4N act on a free body to the right, as shown in Fig. 4.2. The resultant force will be $5 + 4 = 9N$ to the right.

FIG. 4.2

RESULTANT = 9N

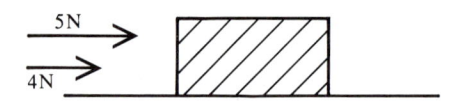

If now the 4N force acts to the left, as in Fig. 4.3 then the resultant

FIG. 4.3

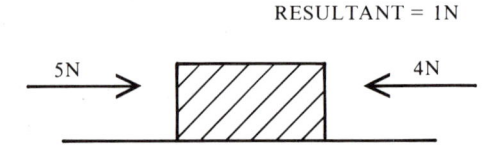

RESULTANT = 1N

force will be $5 - 4 = 1N$ to the right.

(iii) If now two identical forces of 5N act, but both in opposite directions, then the resultant force will be $5 - 5 = 0N$. When the forces are exactly equal but in opposite directions, the resultant force is zero, as in Fig. 4.4.

FIG. 4.4

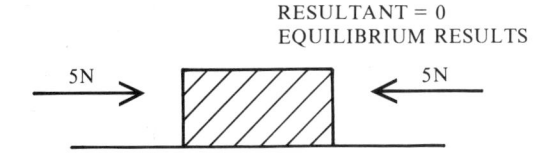

```
                    RESULTANT = 0
                    EQUILIBRIUM RESULTS
   5N  →  [////]  ←  5N
```

We say that the body is in equilibrium, i.e. it is balanced. We shall say more about equilibrium in the next chapter.

(iv) Usually unless we are dealing with forces applied to walls, fixed rods, wires or springs we are always talking about free bodies and so we usually leave out the word "free". Also, when considering forces acting on such a body we sometimes use the word force instead of resultant force.

PROBLEM

A MAN AND A WOMAN ON EACH SIDE OF A GARDEN FENCE PUSH IT, AS SHOWN IN FIG. 4.5. WHAT WILL HAPPEN TO THE FENCE?

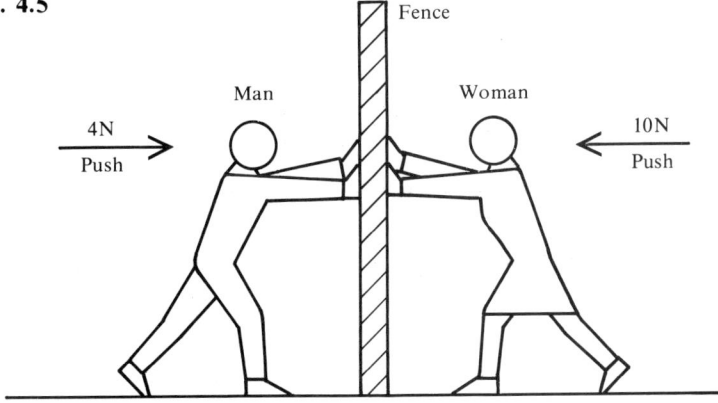

FIG. 4.5

ANSWER: THERE IS A RESULTANT FORCE OF 10 – 4 = 6N TO THE LEFT. SO THE FENCE WILL FALL OVER TO THE LEFT.

4.3   RESULTANT FORCE ON A FREE BODY

Whenever a resultant force acts upon a free body it can cause the following three things to happen:

(i)   If the body is at rest, it will move in the direction of the force.

(ii) If the body is already moving and the direction of the force is in the same direction of the motion, then the velocity of the body will increase due to a change in speed.

54 Forces

(iii) If the body is already moving and the direction of the force is not in the same direction as the motion, then the velocity of the body will change because the direction of motion will change.

We are usually interested in cases (i) and (ii) when a force causes a change of speed although an example of case (iii) will be discussed in the supplementary section of this chapter.

4.4 FRICTION

Friction is a very important force.

It arises whenever one surface moves or tries to move over another surface and it is due to the fact that surfaces are never really smooth but consist of a series of hills and hollows. These hinder motion.

Friction always acts in a direction to oppose the motion.

Sometimes friction is a useful force. It enables us to walk around. The friction between our shoes and the ground prevents our feet from sliding backwards and enables us to push ourselves forwards, as shown in Fig. 4.6.

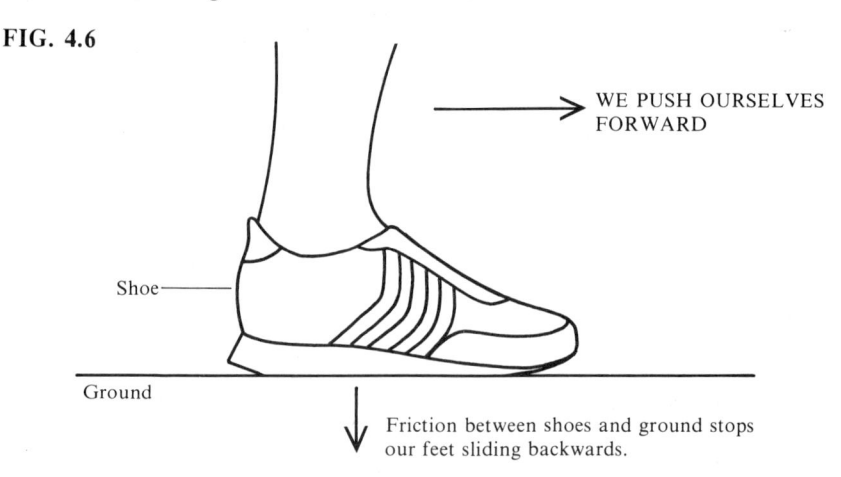

FIG. 4.6

WE PUSH OURSELVES FORWARD

Shoe

Ground

Friction between shoes and ground stops our feet sliding backwards.

We can observe what happens in the absence of friction when we walk over icy ground. The ice reduces the friction and our feet slide backwards.

Similarly there is friction between a motor car tyre and the road surface. If water fills the tyre tread it reduces the friction and the car may aquaplane or skate on water. Cars, just like human beings, slip on ice!

However, friction can also be a nuisance. If it arises in a machine, a great deal of damage can be done. In these situations, it is reduced by

PHOTOGRAPH 2

lubrication. A film of oil between the moving and the fixed surface is used to provide lubrication.

Friction between the bottom of a hovercraft and the water over which it moves is eliminated by blowing air from the hovercraft, as shown in Photograph 2.

As a result the hovercraft floats on a cushion of air.

4.5 NEWTON'S LAWS OF MOTION
There are three of these laws.

(i) The first law really is a statement of what a force causes a free body to do.

Newton's First Law says that every object remains at rest or if it is moving it continues in a straight line at a uniform speed unless a resultant force acts upon it.

(ii) The second law tells us the relationship between a resultant force and the acceleration which it causes.

Suppose a resultant force acts upon a body causing it to accelerate in the direction of the force.

Newton's Second Law says that
$$\text{Force} = \text{Mass} \times \text{Acceleration}$$
where the force and the acceleration are in the same direction.

We sometimes write this as
$$F = ma$$
where
- F = force
- m = mass
- a = acceleration.

(iii) The third law tells us that forces never occur singly but in pairs.

Newton's Third Law says that if body 1 exerts a force on body 2 then body 2 exerts an equal force in the opposite direction on body 1.

It is important to realise that this does not mean that there is no resultant force because the forces are acting on different bodies.

So in Fig. 4.7, the man pushes on the wall with a force F newtons, but the wall pushes back on the man with an equal force of F newtons. One force is acting on the wall and the other on the man.

If we consider Fig. 4.5 again. The man pushes on the fence with a force 4 N. The fence will push on the man with an equal force of 4 N.

FIG. 4.7

Man pushes on wall with force F Newtons →

← Wall pushes back on man with force F Newtons

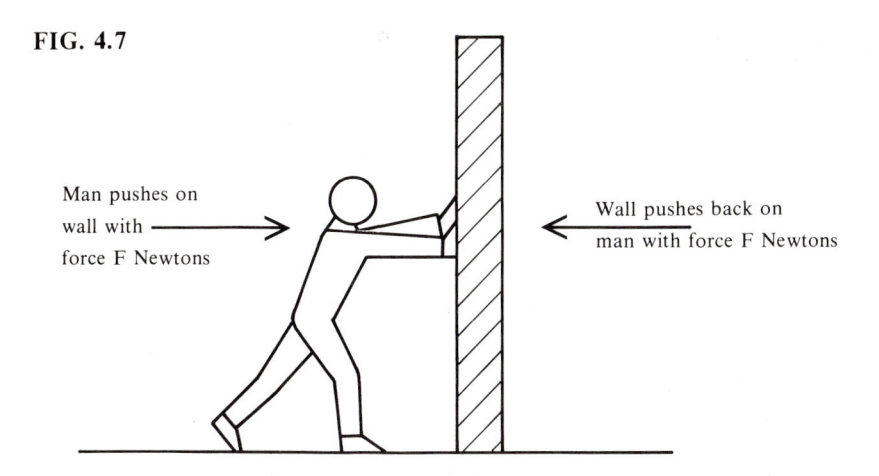

The woman pushes on the fence with a force of 10N and the fence will push on the woman with an equal force of 10N. There will still be a resultant force of 6N acting on the fence causing it to fall over. However, when this happens, the fence will no longer be pushing back on the man and woman and so they will shoot forwards under the action of their pushing forces.

In the hovercraft the air pushes down on the water which pushes up on the air.

Because of Newton's Third Law, we can consider friction again in a little more detail. When we walk forwards, equal and opposite forces are involved. When we step forwards our foot pushes backwards on the ground. The ground pushes our foot forwards with an equal force. Friction prevents our foot sliding backwards as we push backwards.

(iv) Newton's Laws of Motion are very important whenever we think about the motion of bodies.

Suppose a car is travelling at a constant velocity. It still needs the driving force of the engine to maintain its steady motion. This is because forces are acting to oppose its motion including friction in its moving parts and friction caused by its motion through the air — air resistance. When the driving force of the engine equals the opposing forces then the car will move at a steady velocity.

Concorde has a special "streamlined" shape in order that air resistance is reduced as it cruises at 2,150 km/h.

58 Forces

PHOTOGRAPH 3

PROBLEM
CALCULATE THE RESULTANT FORCE NEEDED TO PRODUCE AN ACCELERATION OF 8m/s^2 ON A VAN OF MASS $1,600 \text{kg}$.

Using $\quad\quad\quad$ F = ma
here $\quad\quad\quad$ m = 1600 kg
$\quad\quad\quad\quad\quad$ a = 8m/s^2

so
$\quad\quad\quad\quad\quad$ F = 1600 × 8
$\quad\quad\quad\quad\quad\quad$ = 12,800N

ANSWER: RESULTANT FORCE = 12.8 kN.

PROBLEM
A CAR OF MASS 1000 kg ACCELERATES UNIFORMLY FROM REST. AFTER 30s IT HAS REACHED A SPEED OF 60 m/s. CALCULATE ITS ACCELERATION AND THE RESULTANT FORCE NEEDED. EXPLAIN WHY THE DRIVING FORCE OF THE ENGINE WILL BE GREATER THAN THIS.

Now $\quad\quad\quad$ ACCELERATION = $\dfrac{\text{CHANGE OF VELOCITY}}{\text{TIME TAKEN}}$

so
$\quad\quad\quad\quad\quad$ ACCELERATION = $\dfrac{60 - 0}{30}$ = 2m/s^2

Using $\quad\quad\quad$ F = ma
here $\quad\quad\quad$ m = 1000 kg
$\quad\quad\quad\quad\quad$ a = 2m/s^2

so
$\quad\quad\quad\quad\quad$ F = 1000 × 2
$\quad\quad\quad\quad\quad\quad$ = 2000 N.

THE RESULTANT FORCE IS 2000N BUT THIS IS EQUAL TO THE DRIVING FORCE OF THE ENGINE MINUS THE OPPOSING FORCES. SO THE DRIVING FORCE IS GREATER THAN 2000N.

ANSWER: 2m/s^2, 2000N, GREATER BECAUSE OF THE OPPOSING FORCES.

4.6 THE NEWTON

We have

$$\text{Force} = \text{Mass} \times \text{Acceleration}$$

If $\quad$ Mass $= 1\,\text{kg}$
and $\quad$ Acceleration $= 1\,\text{m/s}^2$
then $\quad$ Force $= 1 \times 1$
$\quad\quad\quad\quad = 1\,\text{N}.$

From Newton's Second Law we can define the force of 1N as the force needed to give a mass of 1kg, an acceleration of $1\,\text{m/s}^2$ in the direction of the force.

4.7 WEIGHT

(i) The weight of a body is the force of gravity on the body.

Like all forces, weight is a vector with its direction being towards the ground.

From Newton's Second Law we know that

$$\text{Force} = \text{Mass} \times \text{Acceleration}.$$

When we are talking about gravity the force is the weight and the acceleration acting is the acceleration due to gravity.
So

$$\text{Weight} = \text{Mass} \times \text{Acceleration due to gravity}$$

We usually represent weight by W so

$$W = mg$$

A mass of 1kg has a weight of gN and taking our value of g as $9.8\,\text{m/s}^2$ this means that a mass of 1kg has a weight of 9.8N.

(ii) We must also remember that g varies on the earth and so the weight of a body varies.

Two important differences between weight and mass are that weight is a vector, mass is a scalar and weight varies but mass is always the same.

On other planets, gravity is not the same as on the earth and so the acceleration which it causes it not the same. g on the moon is about $\frac{1}{6}$ of g on the earth and so on the moon bodies weigh only about $\frac{1}{6}$ of what they do on the earth.

(iii) The weight of a body may be found by hanging it on a spring balance or dynamometer with newtons marked on its scale, as in Fig. 4.8

FIG. 4.8

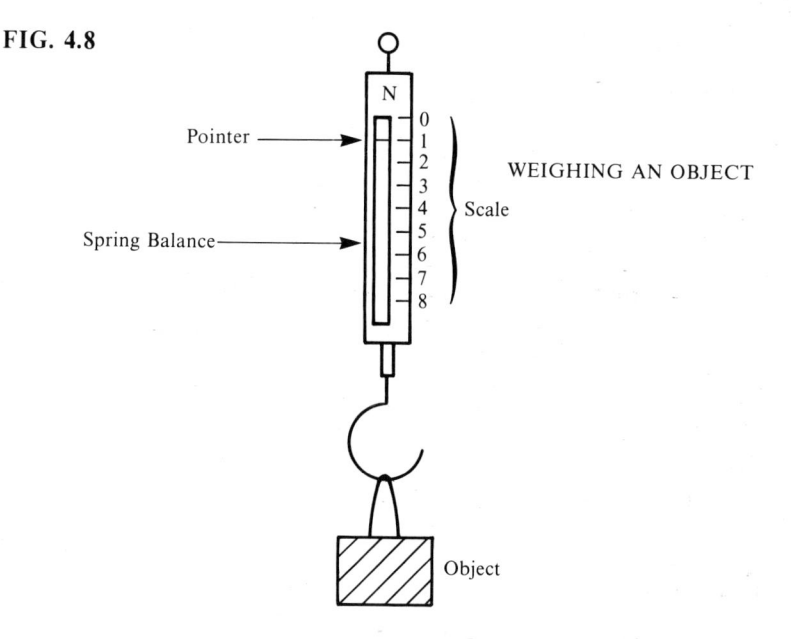

WEIGHING AN OBJECT

The force of gravity on the object stretches the spring and a pointer moves over the scale.

(iv) Weight is a very important force. If it were not present we would float around above the ground rather like astronauts in a space ship.

However, it also has its disadvantages which we easily feel if we fall off a ladder and fall to earth with an increasing velocity.

The bones in our bodies constantly have to support our weight as we stand and move around over the surface of the earth.

If our body isn't working properly, then mechanical help is needed to enable our weight to move around. Photograph 4 shows such a device, the Salford Swivel Walker pioneered for spina bifida children by the Department of Orthopaedic Mechanics at the University of Salford.

4.8 CENTRE OF GRAVITY

(i) A body behaves just as if all its weight were concentrated at a point known as its centre of gravity.

The centre of gravity of symmetrical objects is always located at their centre and so the centre of gravity of a metre rule lies 50 cm along it.

If an object is supported at its centre of gravity it will balance. The metre rule shown in Fig. 4.9 will balance perfectly because it is supported at its 50 cm mark.

62 Forces

PHOTOGRAPH 4

FIG. 4.9

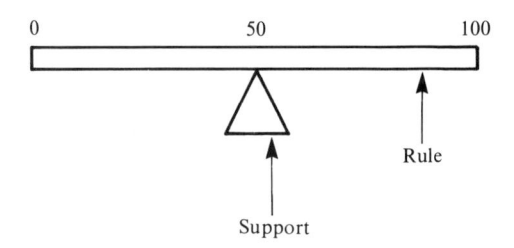

(ii) The position of the centre of gravity of a body influences whether or not it topples over. A body topples over when the vertical line drawn through its centre of gravity does not pass through its base.

We shall talk about this again in Chapter 5.

4.9 SHEARING AND BENDING

(i) Suppose we have a cube of material and we clamp its lower surface so that it is unable to move. If we now apply a force along the top surface, as shown in Fig. 4.10, we might find that the layers of the

FIG. 4.10

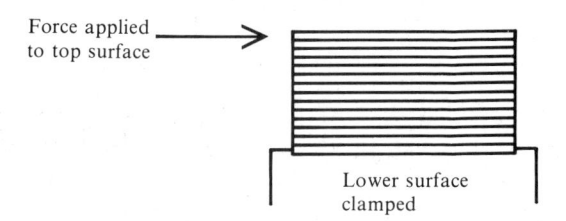

Force applied to top surface →

Lower surface clamped

material slide over each other, as shown in Fig. 4.11.

FIG. 4.11

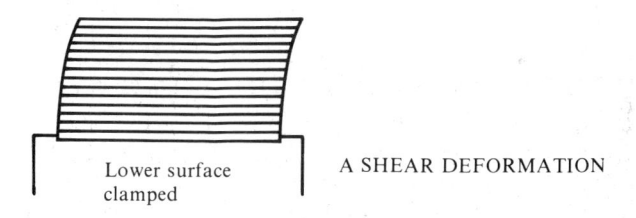

Lower surface clamped

A SHEAR DEFORMATION

This sort of deformation is known as a shear.

Usually only small shears are seen with most hard solids. The effect can be seen most noticeably with a soft solid such as a liquorice allsort made of layers of sweet and liquorice!

Liquids very easily shear and we can see this very easily if we have a thin layer of water between two glass microscope slides and we slide the top slide over the bottom one.

(ii) If a rod of material is clamped at one end and a downwards force is applied to the other end, the rod will bend, as shown in Fig. 4.12.

FIG. 4.12

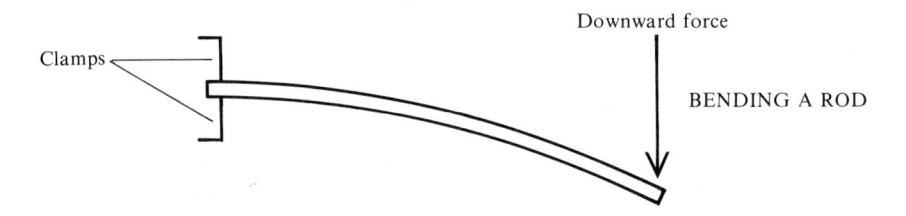

Clamps

Downward force

BENDING A ROD

This bending would occur if the force were applied anywhere along the bar but most bending takes place when the force is applied at the other end of the bar, as shown in Fig. 4.12.

In this diagram the top surface is stretched and the bottom surface is compressed. Half way between these one surace called the neutral filament remains the same. This is shown in Fig. 4.13.

FIG. 4.13

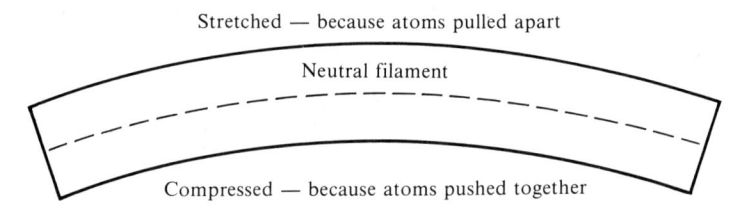

Stretched — because atoms pulled apart

Neutral filament

Compressed — because atoms pushed together

STRETCHING AND COMPRESSING
WHEN BENDING A ROD

This happens when a beam is bent also. I shaped steel girders are used in large structures, as shown in Fig. 4.14.

FIG. 4.14

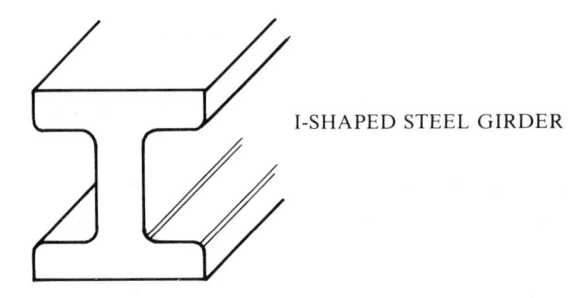

I-SHAPED STEEL GIRDER

They are made to weigh less by removing material from around the neutral filament.

In order to make the bending of the beams in a bridge as small as possible, supporting columns are added, as shown in Fig. 4.15.

FIG. 4.15

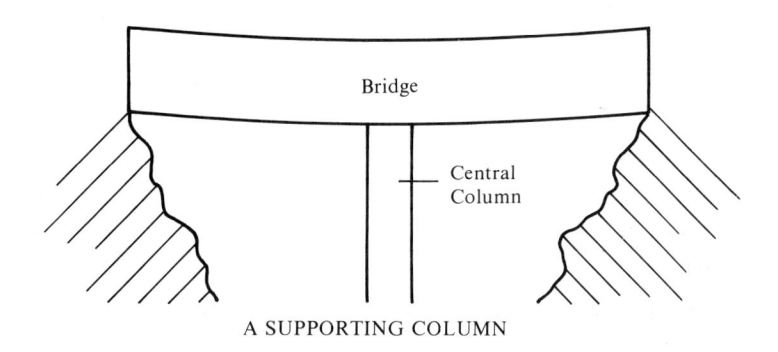

A SUPPORTING COLUMN

4.10 THE EFFECT OF FORCES ON WIRES AND SPRINGS

(i) If we squeeze together the ends of a rod, as shown in Fig. 4.16, we make the rod shorter because we are applying a compressive force.

FIG. 4.16

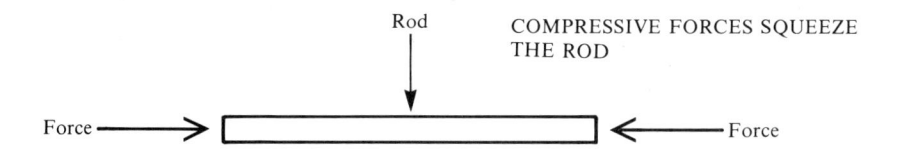

COMPRESSIVE FORCES SQUEEZE THE ROD

(ii) If we stretch the ends of a rod, as shown in Fig. 4.17, we make the rod longer because we are applying a tensile force.

FIG. 4.17

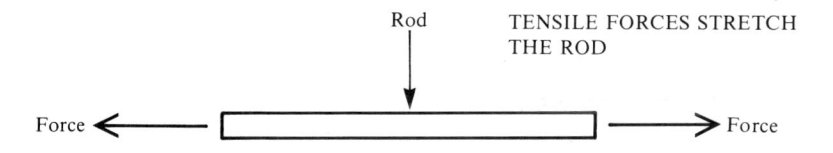

TENSILE FORCES STRETCH THE ROD

(iii) Elastic materials always return to their original shape after an applied force has been removed. Rubber is an example of an elastic substance.

Plastic materials do not return to their original shape after an applied force has been removed. Plasticine is an example of a plastic substance.

66 Forces

Most elastic materials only behave elastically up to a maximum force beyond which they behave plastically. This changeover point from elastic to plastic behaviour is known as the elastic limit of the material.

(iv) Hooke's Law says that providing the elastic limit is not exceeded then we can write

$$\text{Force} = \text{Constant} \times \text{Extension}$$

or $F = kx$

where
$F = \text{force}$
$k = \text{Hooke's Constant}$
$x = \text{extension}$

In other words, to produce twice the extension we need to apply twice the force.

PROBLEM
A WIRE IS STRETCHED 1 mm BY A FORCE OF 100N. WHAT LOAD WOULD BE NEEDED TO STRETCH THE WIRE BY 4 mm, ASSUMING THE WIRE IS STILL ELASTIC.

NOW A FORCE OF 100N CAUSES AN EXTENSION OF 1 mm. IF THE EXTENSION IS MULTIPLIED BY 4 TO OBTAIN 4 mm THEN THE FORCE MUST ALSO BE MULTIPLIED BY 4 TO GIVE

$$4 \times 100 = 400\text{N}$$

ANSWER: FORCE NEEDED = 400N.

(v) We can plot a graph of force against extension, as in Fig. 4.18.

FIG. 4.18

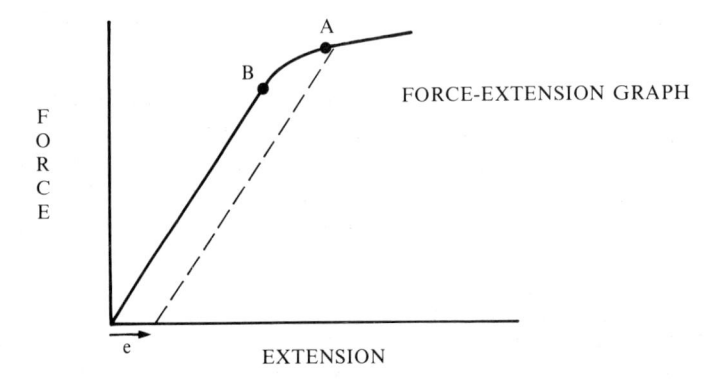

FORCE-EXTENSION GRAPH

Along the straight line to B Hooke's Law applies. Point A is the elastic limit. If we stretch the material just beyond this point and then remove the force it will not return to its original length but will have gained a permanent extension, e, as shown in the graph.

We can investigate the behaviour of force and extension for materials in the shape of wires or cylinders in the laboratory. We hang a wire, as shown in Fig. 4.19 and measure its extension for various loads.

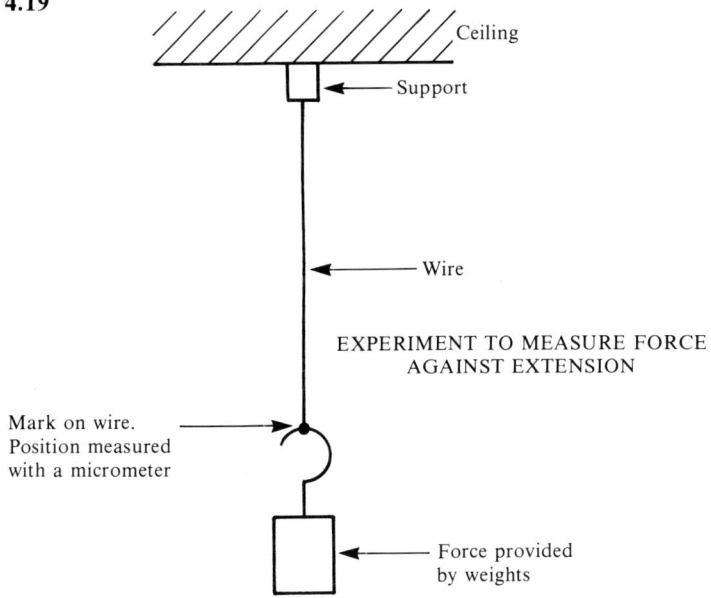

FIG. 4.19

EXPERIMENT TO MEASURE FORCE AGAINST EXTENSION

Ceiling — Support — Wire — Mark on wire. Position measured with a micrometer — Force provided by weights

Usually the extension observed will be small and will need to be measured with a micrometer.

Whenever this experiment is performed you must wear safety glasses to avoid the wire injuring your eyes if it breaks.

(vi) If we do this experiment for rubber, nylon and copper we find that the rubber extends quite easily, the nylon less and the copper least of all. In fact the extension of the rubber will be about 100 times that of the nylon which will be about 100 times that of the copper for any particular force when we use identically shaped wires. This is too difficult to represent on a graph accurately but the comparison is shown in Fig. 4.20.

If our material is in the form of a spring then we will observe large extensions all the way to the elastic limit. The spring balance, used to measure weight makes use of Hooke's Law in its operation. We only use it to point B of the graph in Fig. 4.18.

FIG. 4.20

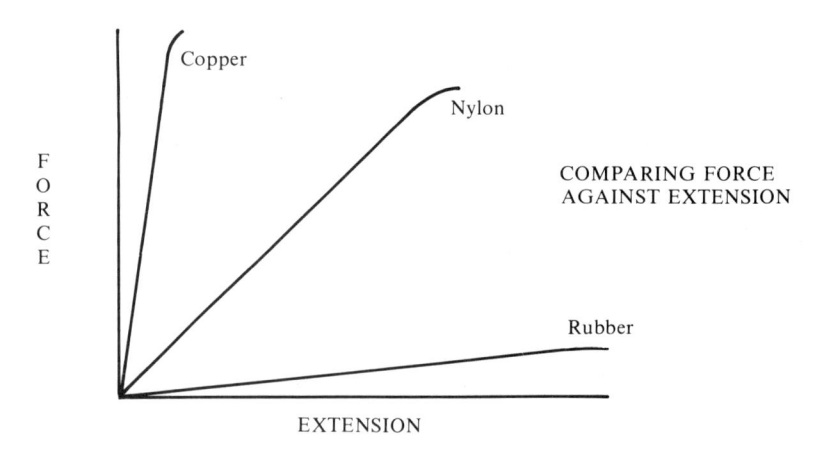

```
F
O
R
C
E
```

Copper
Nylon
Rubber

COMPARING FORCE
AGAINST EXTENSION

EXTENSION

PROBLEM

A SPRING IS 30 cm LONG. WHEN IT IS PULLED BY AN UNKNOWN FORCE IT IS 45 cm LONG. WHEN IT IS PULLED BY A FORCE OF 2.5N IT IS 55 cm LONG. WHAT IS THE VALUE OF THE UNKNOWN FORCE?

NOW FORCE = CONSTANT × EXTENSION

A FORCE OF 2.5N CAUSES AN EXTENSION OF 55 − 30 = 25 cm. THE UNKNOWN FORCE CAUSES AN EXTENSION OF 45 − 30 = 15 cm.

THIS IS $\frac{15}{25}$ OF THE EXTENSION CAUSED BY 2.5N

SO THE UNKNOWN FORCE MUST BE $\frac{15}{25} \times 2.5 = 1.5$N.

ANSWER: UNKNOWN FORCE = 1.5N.

4.11 A FIELD OF FORCE

We have already met the force of gravity. This force acts through space and causes a body which is not in contact with the earth to fall to the ground. We say that the earth has a gravitational field of force which exerts a force on any other body in the field.

Because it can act upon a body not in contact with the earth we speak of it as an action at a distance force. Action at a distance forces always become smaller as the distance increases. So when an object is further from ground the force, i.e. its weight, will decrease.

We have already seen that g is less when we are above sea level.

Since $\qquad$ W = mg

a smaller value of g will result in a smaller value of W, the weight. This agrees with our reasoning in terms of an action at a distance force.

The force is always attractive in a gravitational field of force, as shown in Fig. 4.21.

FIG. 4.21

GRAVITATIONAL FIELD OF THE EARTH
ATTRACTING AN OBJECT ON ITS SURFACE

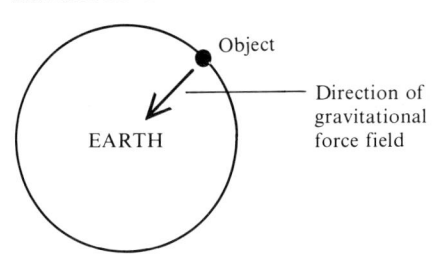

In the same way that a gravitational field is associated with the earth and all planets there are other fields of force.

The space around an electric charge is surrounded by an electric field of force. Any other charges moving into the field will feel the electric field. If the charges are the same the force will be repulsive; if they are different it will be attractive.

FIG. 4.22

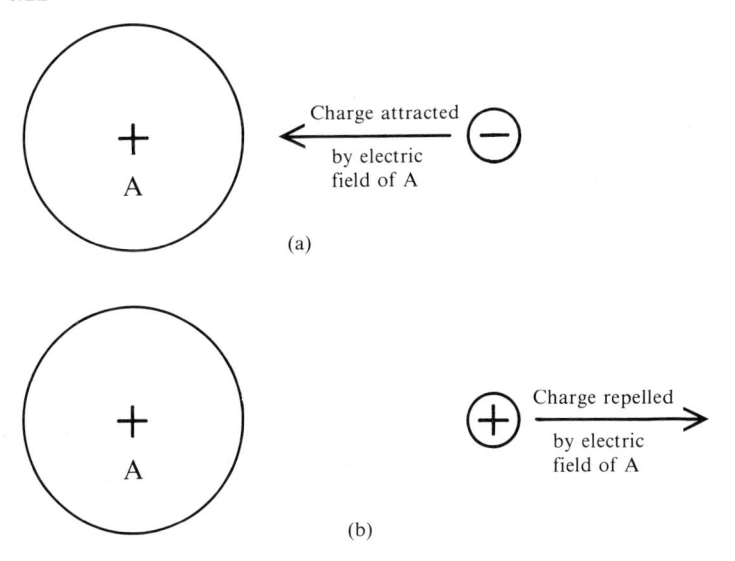

The space around the end of a magnet is surrounded by a magnetic field of force. Any other end of a magnet moving into the field will feel the magnetic field. If the ends of the magnet are the same — both north or south the force will be repulsive, but if one is north and the other is south, it will be attractive.

FIG. 4.23

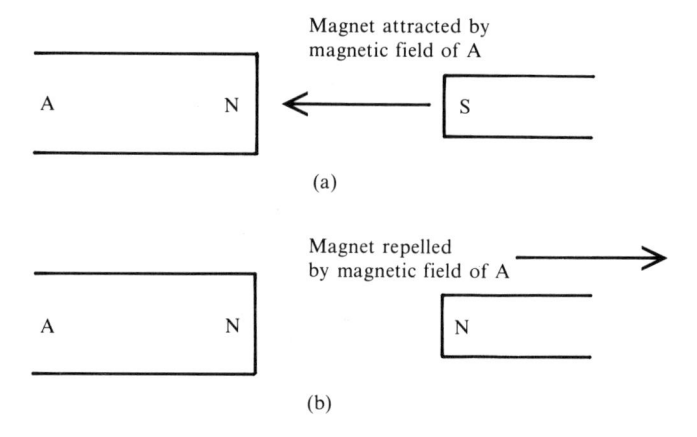

```
┌─────────────┐
│             
│  A        N │   ←——————  ┌─────────────┐
│             │   Magnet attracted by   │
└─────────────┘   magnetic field of A S │
                            └─────────────┘
                    (a)

┌─────────────┐
│             │            ┌─────────────┐  ——————→
│  A        N │            │             
│             │   Magnet repelled      N │
└─────────────┘   by magnetic field of A │
                            └─────────────┘
                    (b)
```

SUPPLEMENTARY

4.12 THE LIMIT OF PROPORTIONALITY

In Fig. 4.18 the point B is called the limit of proportionality. Up to this point Hooke's Law is obeyed and the extension produced is directly proportional to the applied force. From B to A the material is still behaving elastically but the extension is no longer directly proportional to the force. With some materials there is a large separation on the graph between B or A but with others B and A occur together.

Obviously we could not use a spring balance if it had been stretched beyond the limit of proportionality.

The gradient of the straight line to B gives us the constant in Hooke's Law.

4.13 CENTRIPETAL FORCE

In all our problems on forces we have dealt with motion in a straight line with a resultant force producing a change in velocity, i.e. an acceleration by a change in speed.

Of course we can also produce a change in velocity by causing a change in direction with the speed staying constant.

An important type of acceleration caused by a change of direction is centripetal acceleration.

Whenever a body is travelling in a circle at constant speed there is an acceleration acting known as centripetal acceleration. It acts towards the centre of the circle, as in Fig. 4.24.

FIG. 4.24

CENTRIPETAL ACCELERATION

Instantaneous direction of travel

Centripetal Acceleration

Body travelling in a circle at constant speed

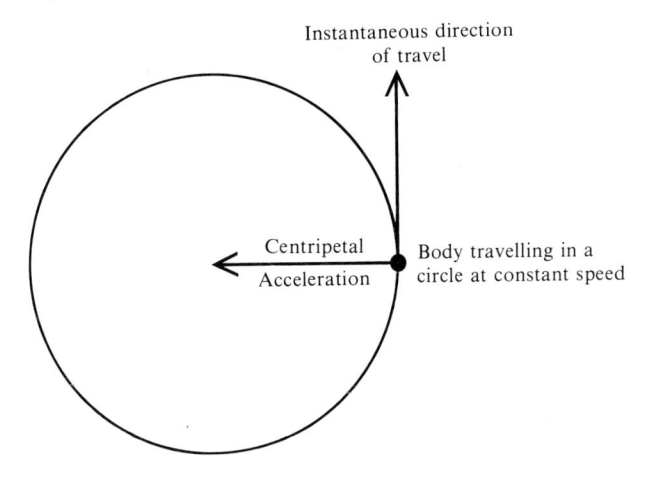

By Newton's Second Law there will be a force acting. This is known as centripetal force. It acts towards the centre of the circle and is equal to the mass of the body multiplied by its centripetal acceleration. There must of course be a force acting on the body in order to change the direction.

Whenever we whirl an object round on a piece of string, we provide the centripetal force by pulling on the string.

4.14 MASS AND INERTIA

We have already seen in Chapter 1, section 19, that the larger a mass, the greater its inertia.

This follows from Newton's Second Law. Suppose a force F acts upon a mass m causing an acceleration a
Then $F = ma$.
For a given force, the greater the mass, the smaller will be the acceleration and so the greater will be the resistance of the mass to motion or the greater its inertia.

So, the greater the mass, the greater its inertia.

72 Forces

A similar argument applies in the case of a moving object being slowed down.

4.15 FINDING THE POSITION OF A CENTRE OF GRAVITY

(i) If we have a rod or bar of non-uniform shape or material, we arrange it on a support, as in Fig. 4.9. We continue to move it until it balances perfectly on the support. When this happens, the centre of gravity will lie above the support.

(ii) In the case of an irregular flat-shaped object, known as a lamina we have to use a more complex procedure.

We drill three holes around its edge. Then using a piece of thread through one hole we suspend it from a stand. We also suspend from the stand a lead sphere on a piece of string so that the sphere lies below the lamina with the string touching the lamina. Very carefully we draw the position of the string as it passes over the lamina, as shown in Fig. 4.25.

FIG. 4.25

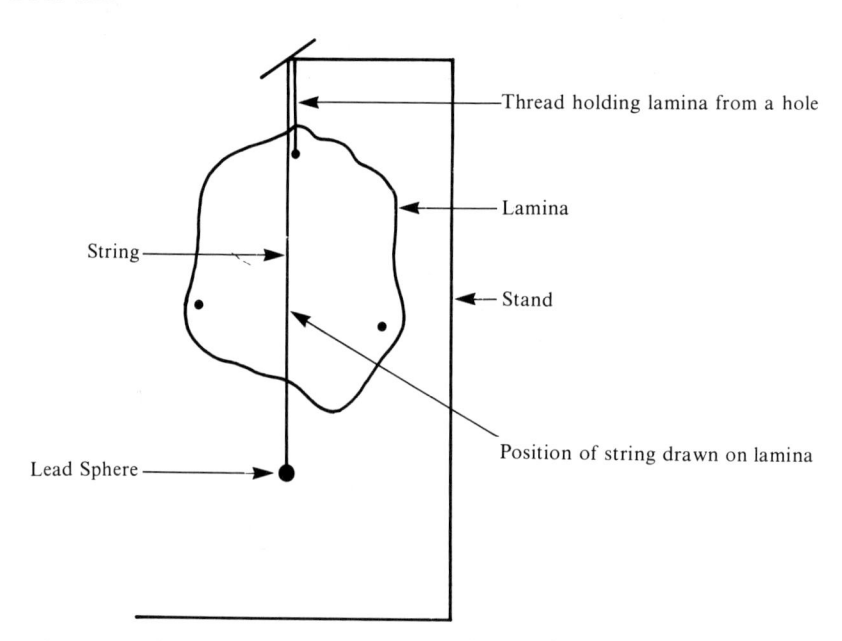

FINDING THE CENTRE OF GRAVITY
OF A LAMINA EXPERIMENT

We then repeat the process twice by suspending the lamina in turn from each of the other two holes. The centre of gravity will then lie at the point where all the string positions cross, as in Fig. 4.26.

FIG. 4.26

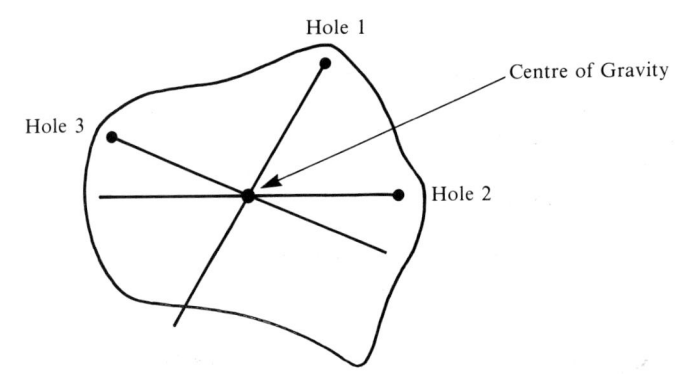

LOCATING THE CENTRE OF GRAVITY

4.16 VERIFICATION OF FORCE = MASS × ACCELERATION

We use a trolley attached to a ticker-tape timer, as shown in Fig. 2.3.

The trolley is situated on a smooth long piece of wood known as a runway and forces are applied to the trolley by hanging weights on the trolley via a pulley, as shown in Fig. 4.27.

FIG. 4.27

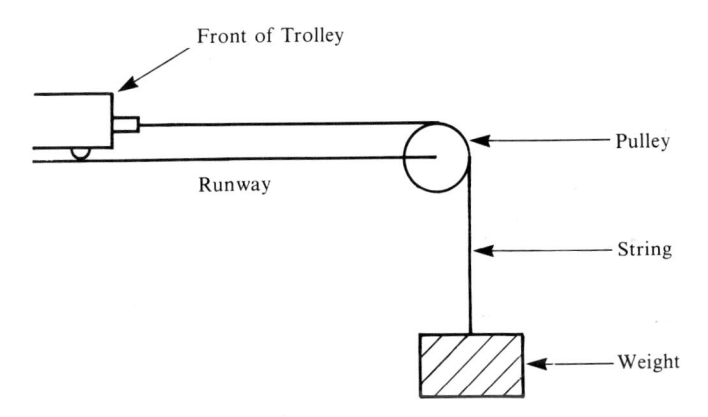

PROVIDING FORCE ON TROLLEY

Initially with no force applied to the trolley, the runway is tilted until the trolley just begins to move. At this point the tilt of the runway just compensates for any frictional forces acting to prevent the motion of the trolley. Known weights are now applied to the trolley and the accelerations they produce are measured as described in Section 14, Chapter 2.

A graph is then drawn of force against acceleration. This will be found to be a straight line through the origin, the gradient of the line being equal to the mass of the trolley.

4.17 FIELD STRENGTH

The strength of a gravitational field is defined as the force acting on unit mass in the field.

Now the force acting on a mass in a gravitational field is its weight and we know that
$$W = mg$$
For a unit mass of 1 kg
$$W = g$$
g is therefore the gravitational field strength. In terms of a field strength definition it is measured in newtons per kilogram from the equation $W = mg$.

Accordingly, g may be either measured in m/s^2 or N/kg.

The strength of an electric field is defined as the force acting on unit charge in the field.

We represent field strength by the symbol E.

Then the force F acting on a charge q in the field is given by
$$F = Eq$$
E is therefore measured in force units divided by charge units and because charge is measured in Coulombs, symbol C, then the units of E are newtons per Coulomb, N/C.

QUESTIONS

CORE
1. State two ways in which a force can change a fixed object.
2. State three ways in which a force can change a rod fixed at one end.
3. What name is given to the effect when layers of a material slide over one another?
4.

FIG. 4.28

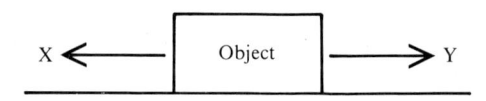

X ← [Object] → Y

In Fig. 4.28 if Y is a force of 10N and the object moves with a constant velocity, what is the value of the force X?

5.

FIG. 4.29

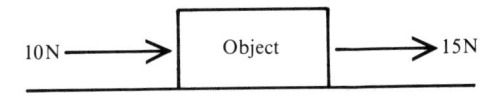

10N ⟶ Object ⟶ 15N

In Fig. 4.29 what is the resultant force acting on the object?
6. State three effects of a resultant force on a free body.
7. Calculate the resultant force needed to produce an acceleration of 4 m/s² in a car of mass 1500 kg.
8. Calculate the weight of an astronaut of mass 100 kg (a) on the earth where $g = 9.8$ m/s² and (b) on the moon where $g = 1.6$ m/s².
9. A front wheel drive car is travelling at a constant velocity. The forces acting on the car are shown in Fig. 4.30.

FIG. 4.30

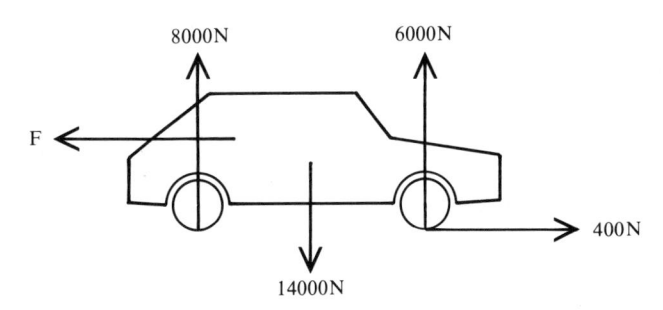

8000N ↑   6000N ↑
F ←
↓ 14000N   → 400N

F is the push of the air on the car.
(i) Name the 400N force to the right.
(ii) What is the value of F, the force to the left?
(iii) Taking the weight of 1 kg to be 10N, calculate the mass of the car.
(iv) The force to the right is now increased. Describe and explain what effect this has on the speed of the car.

(L.E.A.G.)

SUPPLEMENTARY
10. Explain why a spring balance cannot be used beyond its limit of proportionality.
11. A stone is whirled round in a horizontal circle. In what direction is the stone being accelerated?

76 Forces

12. Fig. 4.31 shows a plywood lamina suspended by a thin thread at point A. If it were then suspended at points B and C where would the centre of gravity be found?

FIG. 4.31

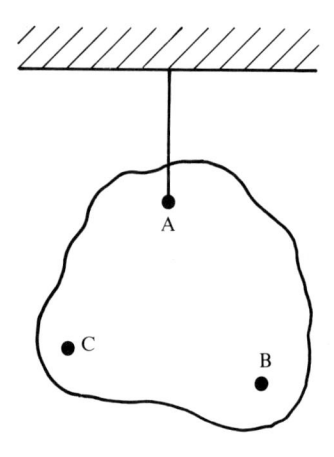

Chapter 5
TURNING

At the end of this chapter you will know:
CORE: what is meant by a moment; the Principle of Moments; why objects are stable and how to deal with problems on moments.
SUPPLEMENTARY: how the Principle of Moments is verified and how to deal with more complicated problems where rods are not balanced at their centre of gravity.

CORE

5.1 THE MOMENT OF A FORCE

If a rod is hinged at one end and a force is applied at the other end, as shown in Fig. 5.1, the rod turns on the hinge.

FIG. 5.1

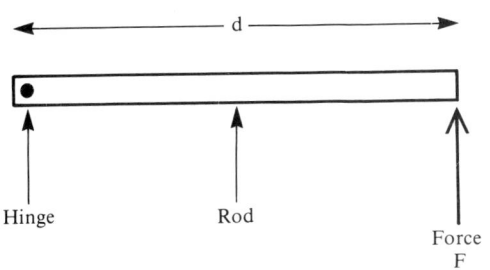

A FORCE EXERTING A MOMENT

Because the force is upwards, the rod will turn anti-clockwise. If the force were downwards, the rod would turn clockwise.

The hinge is known as a fulcrum and whenever an object turns about a fulcrum, as in Fig. 5.1, we say that the force has a moment. The moment is clockwise or anti-clockwise depending upon the direction of the rotation it produces.

The moment is given by
$$\text{force} \times \text{perpendicular distance from the fulcrum}$$
So in Fig. 5.1
$$M = F \times d \qquad \text{where } M = \text{moment.}$$

Force is measured in newtons and distance in metres so moments are measured in newton metres, symbol Nm.

In Fig. 5.2

FIG. 5.2

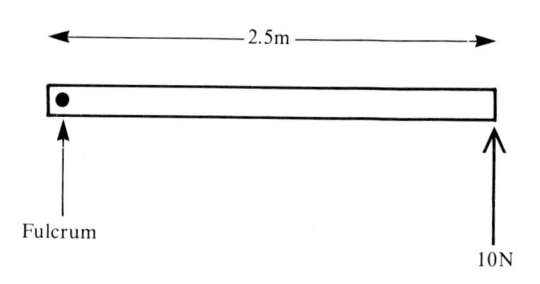

```
|←——— 2.5m ———→|
┌─────────────────────┐
│ •                   │
└─────────────────────┘
  ↑                 ↑
Fulcrum            10N
```

$$\text{Moment} = 10 \times 2.5$$
$$= 25\,\text{Nm}$$

We can increase the value of a moment by increasing either the force or its perpendicular distance from the fulcrum.

Whenever an object turns about a fulcrum the moment of the force must overcome the friction at the fulcrum. A smaller moment is always needed to open a door on a well oiled hinge than one on a dry, rusty hinge.

The handle on a door is always at the edge opposite the hinge so that the smallest force necessary can be used. For the same reason it is always easier to use a spanner which is as long as possible whenever we loosen a nut.

PROBLEM
FIND THE RESULTANT MOMENT ACTING ON THE SEE-SAW IN FIG. 5.3.

FIG. 5.3

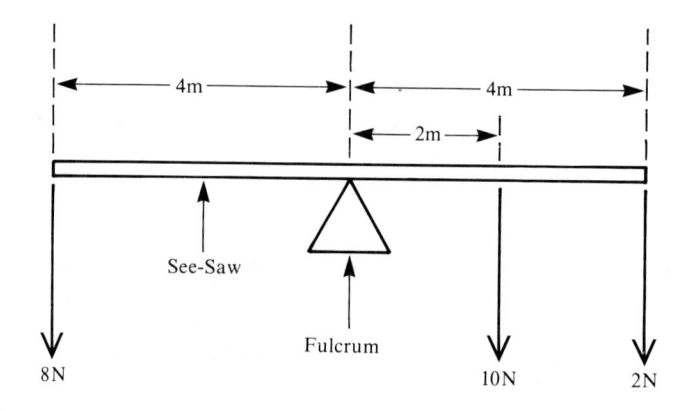

Turning 79

CLOCKWISE MOMENT DUE TO 2N FORCE = 2 × 4 = 8Nm
CLOCKWISE MOMENT DUE TO 10N FORCE = 10 × 2 = 20Nm
TOTAL CLOCKWISE MOMENT = 28Nm
ANTI-CLOCKWISE MOMENT DUE TO 8N FORCE = 8 × 4 = 32Nm
RESULTANT MOMENT = 32Nm ANTI-CLOCKWISE
  − 28Nm CLOCKWISE
  = 4Nm ANTI-CLOCKWISE

ANSWER: RESULTANT MOMENT = 4Nm ANTI-CLOCKWISE.

5.2 THE PRINCIPLE OF MOMENTS

The Principle of Moments says that whenever a body is in equilibrium
  Total clockwise moment = Total anti-clockwise moment.

So whenever an object is balanced on a fulcrum, there is no resultant moment acting.

PROBLEM
THE SEE-SAW IN FIG. 5.4 IS BALANCED.

FIG. 5.4

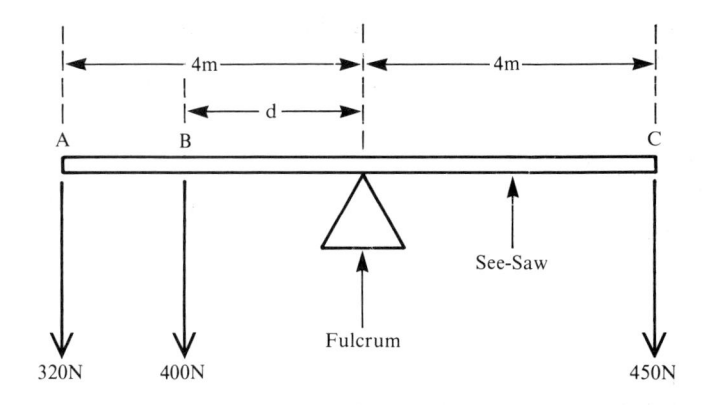

JANE WEIGHS 320N AND IS AT A, JOHN WEIGHS 400N AND IS AT B AND BILL WEIGHS 450N AND IS AT C. HOW FAR IS JOHN FROM THE FULCRUM?

SUPPOSE d REPRESENTS THE DISTANCE OF JOHN FROM THE FULCRUM.

CLOCKWISE MOMENT = 450 × 4 = 1800Nm
ANTI-CLOCKWISE MOMENT = 320×4+400×d = 1280+400d Nm.
AT EQUILIBRIUM

80 Turning

CLOCKWISE MOMENT = ANTI-CLOCKWISE MOMENT
$1800 = 1280 + 400d$
$520 = 400d$
$d = \frac{520}{400} = 1.3m$

ANSWER: JOHN IS 1.3m FROM THE FULCRUM.

We may add the Principle of Moments to what we already know about bodies in equilibrium.

So, whenever a body is in equilibrium:
The total force acting on it is zero.
The total moment acting on it is zero.

5.3 WHY OBJECTS TOPPLE

We have already seen in Chapter 4, Section 8 that a body topples over when the vertical line drawn through its centre of gravity does not pass through its base.

This can be explained in terms of moments and their action.

In Fig. 5.5, the weight acts downwards through the centre of gravity, G. The cone remains at rest in a state of stable equilibrium.

FIG. 5.5

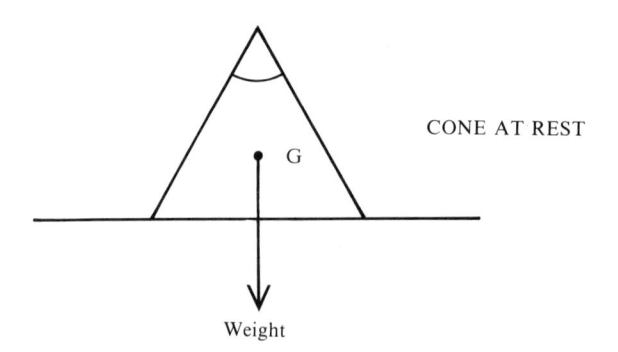

CONE AT REST

Weight

In Fig. 5.6, the weight still acts downwards through the centre of gravity, G. However, the cone is balanced on one edge which acts as a fulcrum. The weight has an anti-clockwise moment about this fulcrum and so the cone turns anti-clockwise and returns to position as in Fig. 5.5 — it will return to stable equilibrium when released.

FIG. 5.6

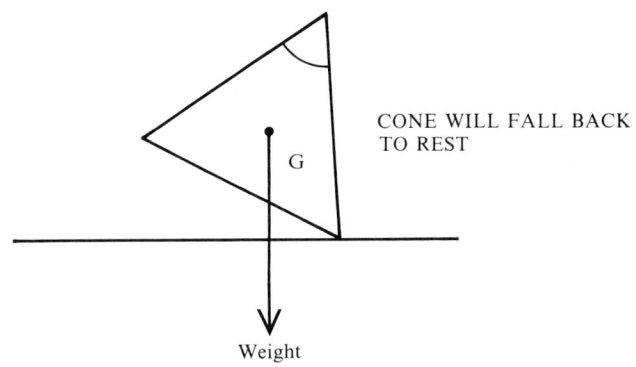

CONE WILL FALL BACK TO REST

Weight

In Fig. 5.7, the weight is still acting downwards through the centre of gravity, G. The weight now has a clockwise moment about the fulcrum and causes the cone to topple over. When it is balanced on its point it is in a state of unstable equilibrium.

FIG. 5.7

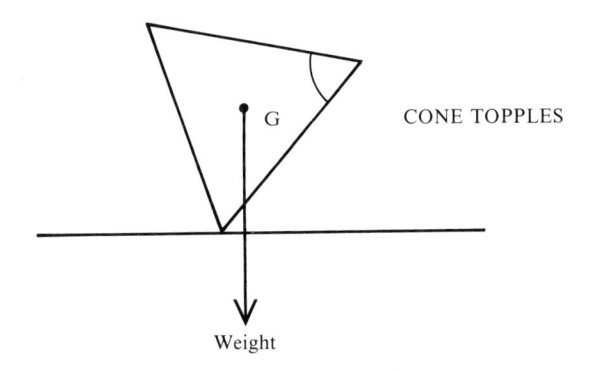

CONE TOPPLES

Weight

If the cone is lying on its side, as in Fig. 5.8, then it is in a meta-stable state. It will rotate if pushed and then stop but it will also stay exactly where it is if it is not pushed.

FIG. 5.8

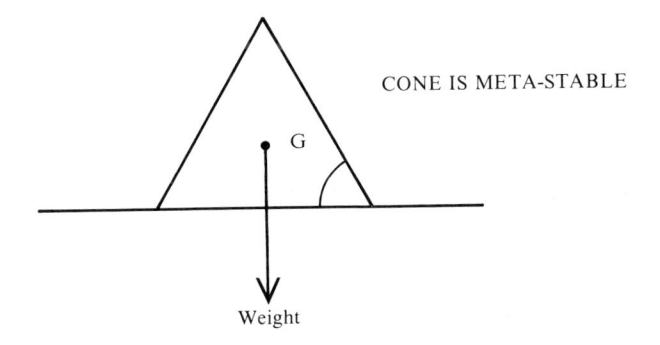

CONE IS META-STABLE

Weight

82 Turning

In order to increase stability and reduce toppling in a bus, we need to make the centre of gravity as low as possible. This is why extra passengers are always made to go downstairs instead of upstairs.

SUPPLEMENTARY

5.4 VERIFICATION OF THE PRINCIPLE OF MOMENTS

In order to verify the Principle of Moments we use the arrangement shown in Fig. 5.9.

FIG. 5.9

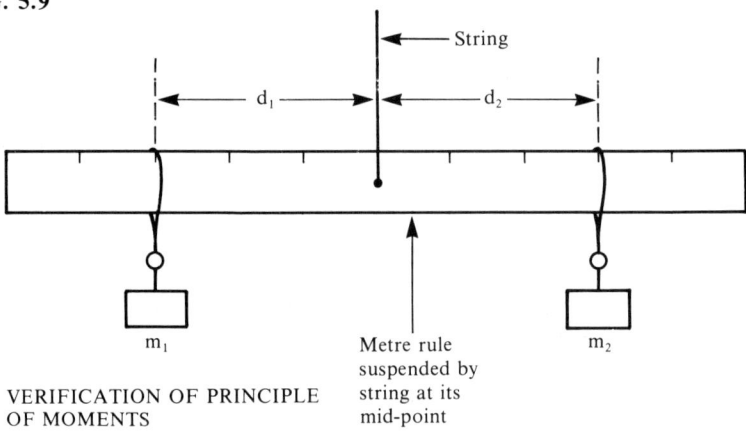

VERIFICATION OF PRINCIPLE OF MOMENTS

A metre rule is suspended by a string which passes through a hole at its mid-point, the 50 cm mark. If the rule is not horizontal, plasticine is added to one side or the other until it is. Masses m_1 and m_2 are then attached by loops of string onto the rule, one a distance d_1 from the string and the other d_2 from the string on its other side. Then d_1 and d_2 are adjusted until the rule is horizontal again and their values recorded. The experiment is repeated a further four times and all values of d_1 and d_2 noted. The values of m_1 and m_2 are also noted and then the following table constructed, with F_1 and F_2 being the weights of m_1 and m_2.

m_1 (kg)	$F_1=m_1g$ (N)	d_1 (m)	Anti-Clockwise Moment F_1d_1 (Nm)	m_2 (kg)	$F_2=m_2g$ (N)	d_2 (m)	Clockwise Moment F_2d_2 (Nm)

From this table we will see that the clockwise moment is equal to the anti-clockwise moment in each case.

5.5 RODS NOT BALANCED AT THEIR CENTRE OF GRAVITY

In the problems we have met so far, we have been concerned with rods balanced at their centre of gravity. In such cases the weight of the body does not exert a moment because the weight acts through the fulcrum.

If however the fulcrum is not under the centre of gravity, then the weight of the rod itself exerts a moment.

PROBLEM
A UNIFORM ROD OF WEIGHT 2N IS PIVOTED ON A FULCRUM, AS SHOWN IN FIG. 5.10. FORCES OF 1N AND 4N ACT AS SHOWN. CALCULATE THE RESULTANT MOMENT.

FIG. 5.10

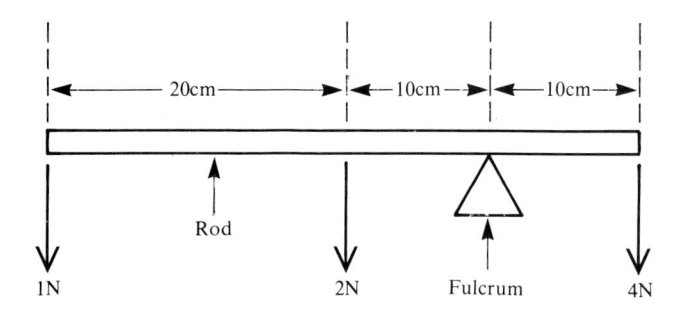

THE WEIGHT OF THE ROD WILL ACT AT ITS MID-POINT, AS SHOWN.

CLOCKWISE MOMENT = 4 × 0.1 = 0.4Nm
ANTI-CLOCKWISE MOMENT = 2 × 0.1 + 1 × 0.3 = 0.5Nm
RESULTANT MOMENT = 0.5Nm ANTI-CLOCKWISE
           − 0.4Nm CLOCKWISE
         = 0.1Nm ANTI-CLOCKWISE

ANSWER: RESULTANT MOMENT = 0.1Nm ANTI-CLOCKWISE.

Unless the weight of a rod is negligible, it will always exert a moment when the fulcrum does not lie beneath its centre of gravity.

QUESTIONS

CORE

1. Explain what is meant by the moment of a force.
2. A force F is needed to open a door when it is pushed at the far side from the hinge. What will be the value of the force needed to open the door by pushing it halfway between the hinge and the far side?
3. The metre rule shown is balanced and is supported at its centre. Calculate x.

FIG. 5.11

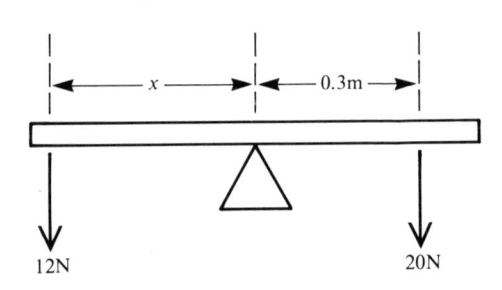

4. In Fig. 5.12 the distance XY = YZ. Calculate the value of the force F which will keep the system at rest.

FIG. 5.12

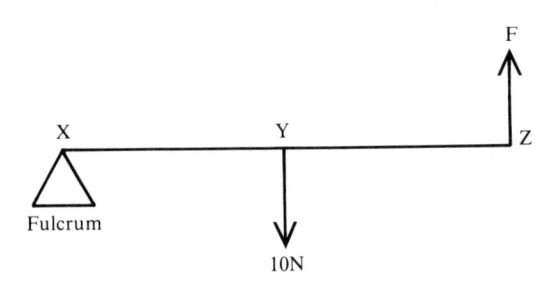

5. The diagram shows a uniform metre rule pivoted at its centre.

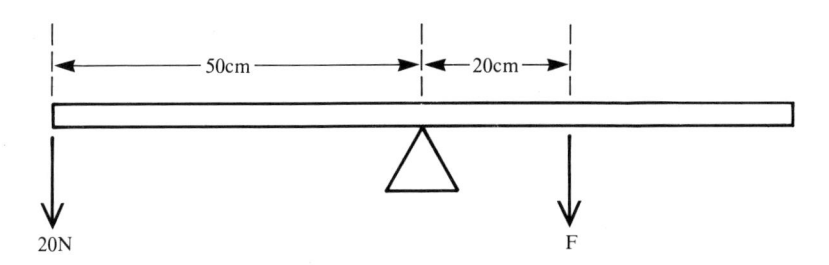

If the rule is balanced, the force F is

    A   8N
    B   25N
    C   40N
    D   50N   *(S.E.G.)*

6. The diagram shows a lever being used to lift a lid from a paint tin.

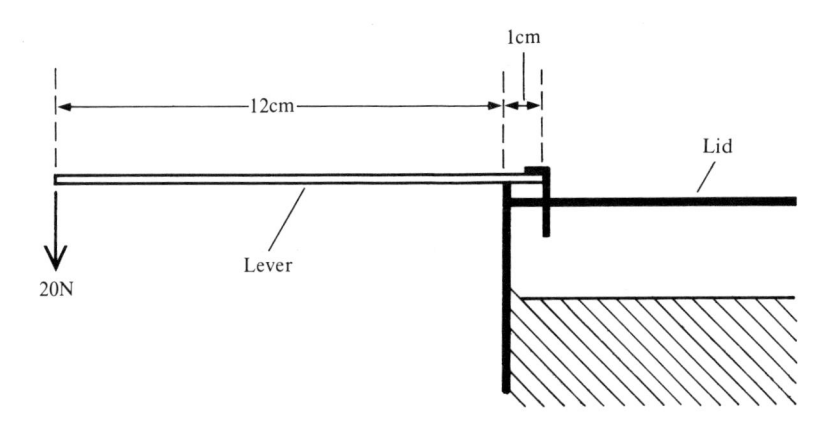

(a) State the principle of moments. *(3 marks)*
(b) Use the principle of moments to help you calculate the force F exerted by the lever on the lid. Show your working clearly. *(4 marks)*
(c) What are the size and direction of the force exerted by the lever on the pivot? *(2 marks)*
(d) State TWO changes which could be made to increase the size of the force F if it proved to be too small to lift the lid. *(2 marks)*
(S.E.G.)

86 Turning

SUPPLEMENTARY

7. Suggest why a tight rope walker carries a pole.
8.

FIG. 5.13

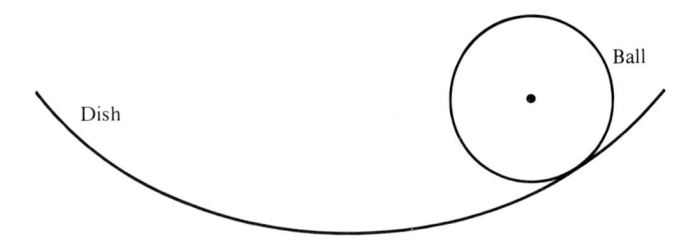

Explain why the ball rolls down the dish when it is released.

9. The weight of the uniform bar shown in Fig. 5.14 is 5N.

FIG. 5.14

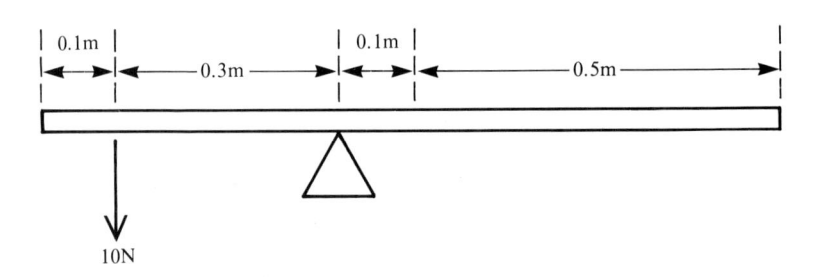

What will happen to the bar?

10. Calculate the weight of the uniform metre rule shown in Fig. 5.15.

FIG. 5.15

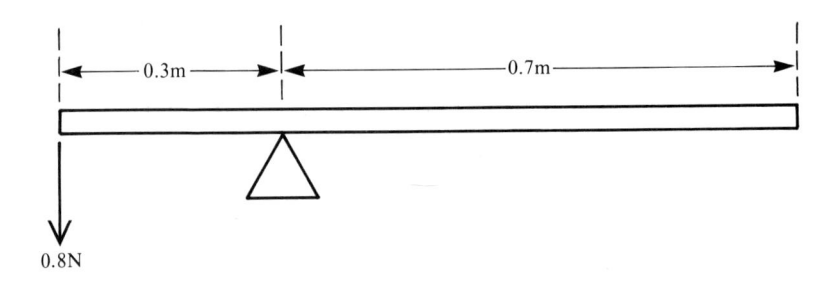

Chapter 6
PRESSURE

At the end of this chapter you will know:
CORE: what is meant by pressure, how it is measured and how devices depend upon it for their operation; why liquids exert a pressure, what it depends upon and how syringes work; how pressure is transmitted in a braking system; why gases exert a pressure; that the atmosphere exerts a pressure, how this varies with height and applications of it and how atmospheric pressure and gas pressure may be measured.
SUPPLEMENTARY: how the pressure at a depth in a liquid may be calculated and how atmospheric pressure governs the weather.

CORE

6.1 THE MEANING OF PRESSURE
Fig. 6.1 shows a block resting on a table.

FIG. 6.1

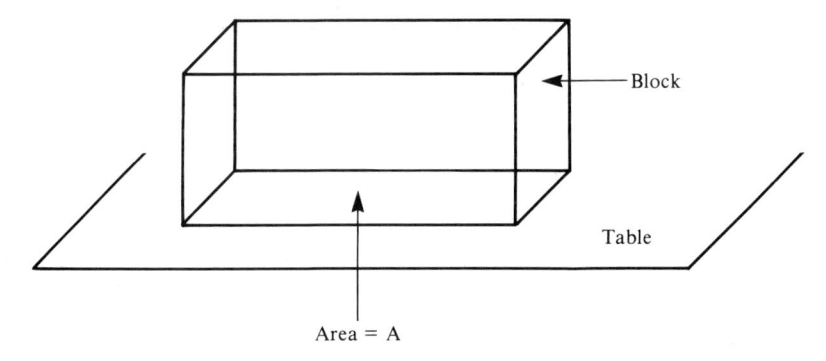

The force, F, acting on the table is the weight of the block, and the area of the base of the block is A.

We say that the block is exerting a pressure on the table.

The pressure, p, is given by

$$\text{PRESSURE} = \frac{\text{FORCE}}{\text{AREA}}$$

or $\quad p = \dfrac{F}{A}$

As in this diagram we always measure the area perpendicular to the force.

Force is measured in newtons and area in square metres and so pressure is measured in newtons per square metre, N/m², or pascals, symbol Pa.

For any particular object, the greatest pressure will result when it rests on its smallest face area and the least pressure when it rests on its largest face area.

PROBLEM
IN FIG. 6.1 THE WEIGHT OF THE BLOCK IS 36N AND THE BASE MEASURES 3m BY 4m. FIND THE PRESSURE.

$$FORCE = 36N$$
$$AREA = 3m \times 4m = 12m^2$$

So $$PRESSURE = \frac{36}{12} = 3\,Pa$$

ANSWER: PRESSURE = 3 Pa

In order to calculate the pressure which you exert on the ground you need to find your mass using a set of scales marked in kg. Multiply this reading by 9.8 to get your weight. Then measure the area of your shoe soles. This is best done by drawing around the shape of your soles when they are resting on 1cm graph paper. By counting the number of squares you will know the area in cm² and can convert to m². Now divide your weight by this area, remembering to measure the area of both shoes.

Stiletto heels damage floors so easily because they have a very small area and so exert a large force. A knife is able to cut as it moves over a surface because it has a very small area and exerts great pressure. A needle punctures the skin for the same reason. Things such as snow shoes and skis have a large surface area and exert only a small pressure so that you don't sink into the snow.

6.2 PRESSURE IN A LIQUID
(i) At all points in a liquid there is a pressure because of the weight of the liquid above.

The pressure increases with depth. This can be seen with the spouting can shown in Fig. 6.2.

The pressure causes the water to escape through the spouts. The water coming from the bottom spout travels furthest showing that it is under the greatest pressure.

FIG. 6.2

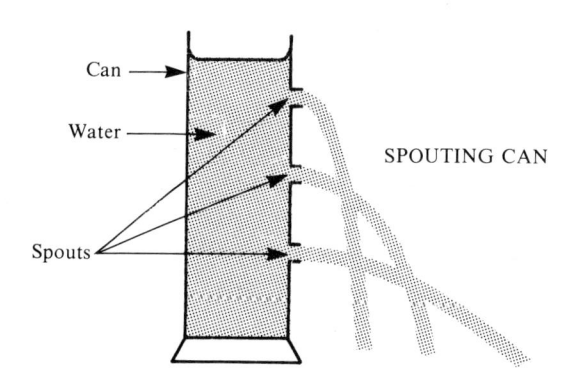

```
                    SPOUTING CAN
```
(Can, Water, Spouts labeled on diagram)

(ii) The pressure also increases with density. We can see this if we repeat the spouting can experiment using a liquid of different density. If we use methylated spirit which has a lower density than water, we observe that the liquid escaping from the lowest spout will not travel as far. In fact it travels less from each spout than it did before.

(iii) The pressure at any point in a liquid acts equally in all directions. This can be seen using the apparatus shown in Fig. 6.3.

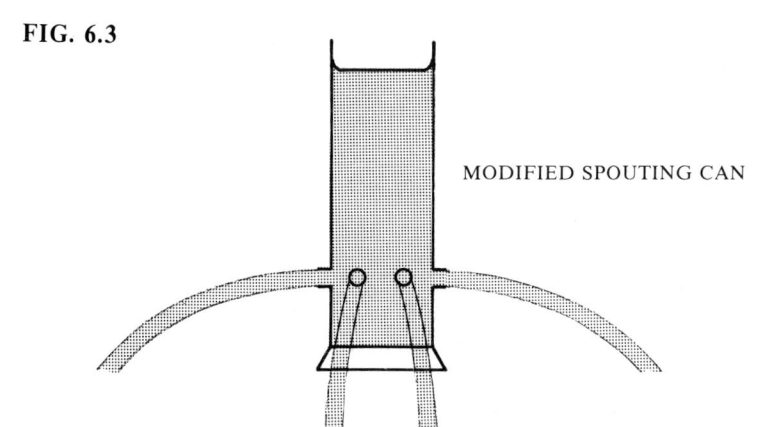

FIG. 6.3

```
                    MODIFIED SPOUTING CAN
```

A modified spouting can is used with a series of spouts all at the same depth.

We find that the water travels the same distance from all the spouts.

(iv) The fact that pressure increases with depth is very important. Because of it, reservoirs must be carefully built. The dam holding back the water must be thicker at the bottom to be able to withstand the increased water pressure at the greater depth. Divers' ears are

FIG. 6.4

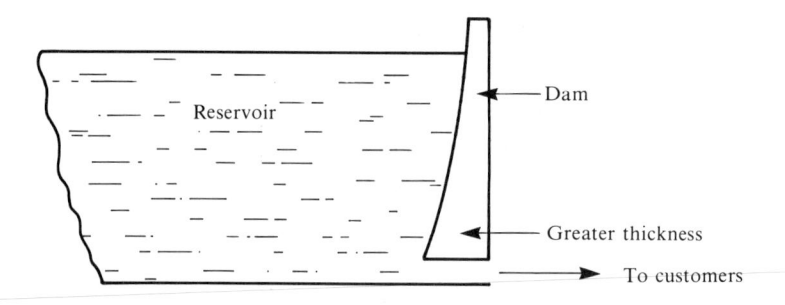

[Diagram: Reservoir with Dam showing Greater thickness at bottom, water flowing To customers]

subjected to increased pressure because of the water. This increased pressure causes extra gas to be dissolved in the blood supply. If a diver does not surface slowly, the dissolved gas leaves the blood because of the reduction in pressure. A painful, even fatal, condition known as the bends results.

6.3 THE SYRINGE

Syringes are used by doctors, dentists and nurses to give injections. As shown in Fig. 6.5 it consists of a piston which fits tightly into a barrel. Pushing down on the piston causes the liquid to be forced out of the needle.

FIG. 6.5

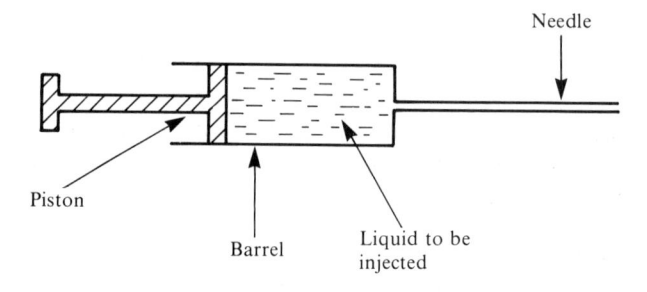

[Diagram of a syringe labeled: Piston, Barrel, Liquid to be injected, Needle]

6.4 TRANSMISSION OF PRESSURE IN A LIQUID

Liquids cannot be compressed much, that is, their volume cannot be decreased by pressure. Instead they transmit or pass on any pressure which is applied to them. We make use of this fact in hydraulic machines.

A hydraulic car jack is a very good example. It is shown in Fig. 6.6.

FIG. 6.6

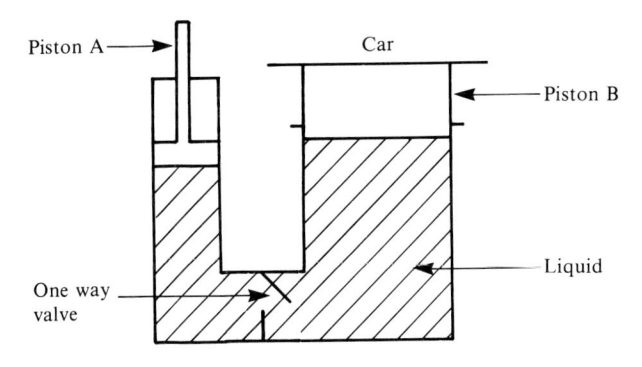

```
Piston A          Car
                                  Piston B


                                  Liquid
One way
valve
```

HYDRAULIC CAR JACK

Pressure is applied to the liquid by piston A. This piston has a small area and so the force applied to piston A generates a large pressure. This pressure is transmitted through the liquid and presses on piston B. Piston B has a very large area and so the pressure acting upon it applies a very large force, large enough to lift a car placed on the piston. A one-way valve is fitted so that when piston A has been pushed down, the liquid which it displaces moves upwards following piston B and does not return when the force has been removed from piston A. In real jacks, a release switch is added so that the valve may be released and there is also a liquid reservoir to top up the liquid to compensate for any liquid escape.

Car brakes also work hydraulically. When the brake pedal is pressed down, a piston in the master cylinder exerts a force on the brake fluid (an oil) and this pressure is transmitted equally to two pistons at each wheel. These pistons press the brake shoes or discs against the wheels and cause braking.

6.5 PRESSURE IN A GAS

A gas is made up of molecules moving very quickly. They are constantly hitting the walls of their container, as shown in Fig. 6.7.

When they hit the wall they bounce off and travel in the opposite direction. The wall changes their direction of motion. To do this the wall must exert a force on the molecules. (From Newton's First Law of Motion).

From Newton's Third Law of Motion this means that the molecules exert a force on the container walls. They must then also exert a pressure on the container walls.

FIG. 6.7

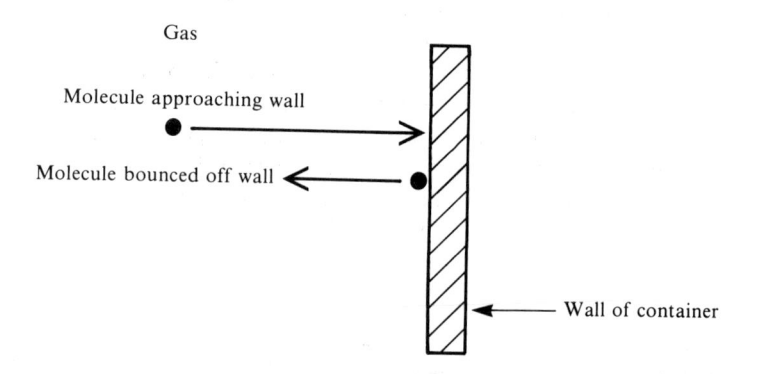

```
                            Gas
        Molecule approaching wall
                    ●  ──────────→ │▓│
                                   │▓│
        Molecule bounced off wall  │▓│
                    ←──────── ●    │▓│
                                   │▓│
                                   │▓│ ←── Wall of container
```

We can see that a gas exerts a pressure due to molecular bombardment.

6.6 ATMOSPHERIC PRESSURE

(i) On earth we are surrounded by air. This is a gas and so it exerts a pressure, known as atmospheric pressure.

On a normal day atmospheric pressure is equal to 101,325 Pa which is known as 1 atmosphere pressure.

Atmospheric pressure acts on us from all directions, as shown in Fig. 6.8.

FIG. 6.8

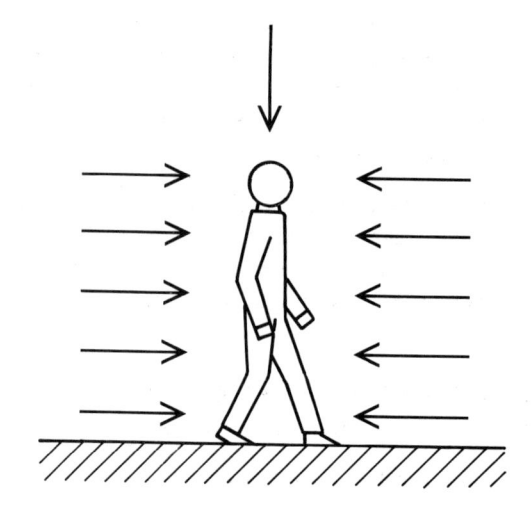

Our blood pressure prevents us from being compressed.

(ii) A good demonstration of the presence of atmospheric pressure is shown in the crushing can experiment. When it is empty it contains air! This will exert a pressure outwards on the walls. The air outside will exert a pressure inwards on the walls. They will cancel each other out. If we boil a little water inside the can, remove the heater, seal the can and cool the can under cold water then the steam which has pushed the air out will condense. There will be no air inside the can and so the atmospheric pressure which is now acting only outside the can collapses it, as shown in Fig. 6.9.

FIG. 6.9

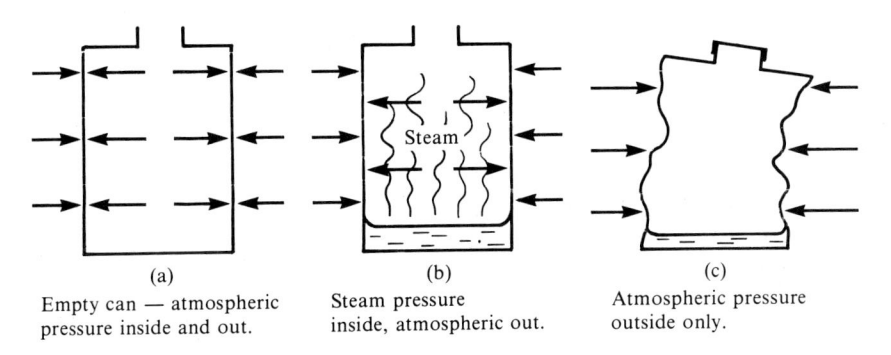

(a) Empty can — atmospheric pressure inside and out.

(b) Steam pressure inside, atmospheric out.

(c) Atmospheric pressure outside only.

(iii) Atmospheric pressure is less the higher we go. This is because the air becomes less dense at higher altitudes and so there are less molecules to cause bombardment.

In order that this loss of pressure does not affect our breathing, aircraft cabins have to be pressurised. Air is pumped around the inside of an aircraft, not usually at exactly atmospheric pressure but typically equal to atmospheric pressure at 1500 m. This is why aircraft travel can be rather tiring.

Now since the pressure inside the aircraft is greater than it is outside the windows and doors must fit tightly in order to prevent air rushing outwards causing decompression. If a window were to break, the resulting decompression would cause bodies to be sucked out of the aircraft.

6.7 MEASUREMENT OF ATMOSPHERIC PRESSURE

Atmospheric pressure is measured with devices known as barometers.

A mercury barometer is shown in Fig. 6.10.

It consists of a long glass tube held upside down in a bowl of mercury. The air above the mercury in the tube has been removed leaving a

94 Pressure

FIG. 6.10

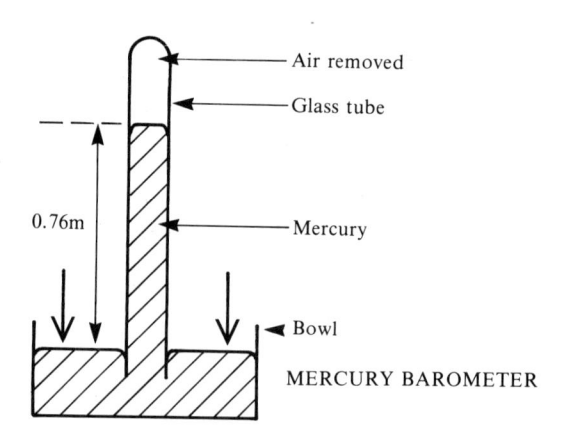

[Diagram of mercury barometer: glass tube with air removed at top, mercury column of 0.76m, bowl at base, with arrows showing atmospheric pressure on mercury surface]

MERCURY BAROMETER

Torricellian vacuum. The atmospheric pressure acting on the mercury surface in the bowl, shown by arrows, has pushed the mercury up the tube as shown. If the atmospheric pressure is 1 atmosphere then the height of the mercury column above the mercury surface will be 0.76m, usually expressed as 760 mm. So, on a normal day we may express atmospheric pressure as 760 mm Hg because Hg is the chemical symbol for mercury.

An aneroid barometer is shown in Fig. 6.11.

FIG. 6.11

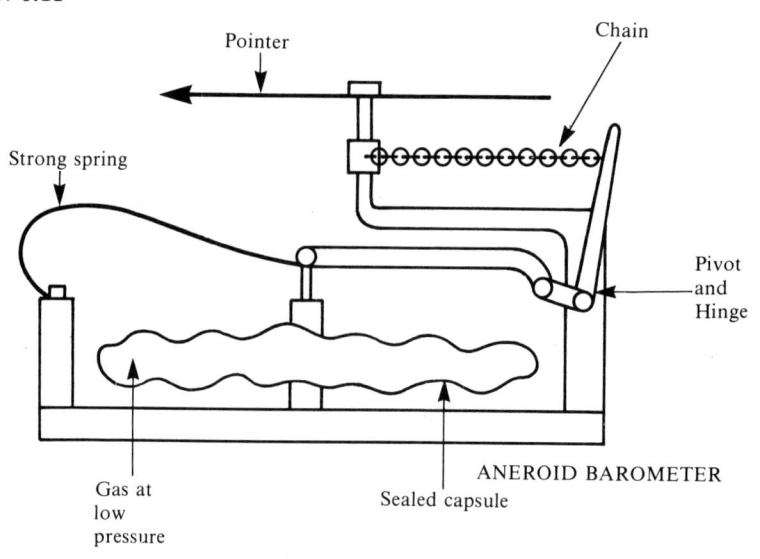

[Diagram of aneroid barometer showing: Pointer, Chain, Strong spring, Pivot and Hinge, Sealed capsule, Gas at low pressure]

ANEROID BAROMETER

It consists of a sealed capsule containing a gas at low pressure. A strong spring prevents the capsule from collapsing. When the atmospheric pressure increases, the capsule is squeezed in slightly. The movement is magnified using a series of rods and hinges and then moves a chain causing a pointer to move over a scale. Initially this barometer always has to be calibrated.

Aneroid barometers are used as altimeters to measure the height of an aircraft since the atmospheric pressure decreases as we go higher.

6.8 SOME USES OF ATMOSPHERIC PRESSURE

Fig. 6.12 shows the rubber sucker.

FIG. 6.12

RUBBER SUCKER

Smooth Surface

Atmospheric Pressure

Vacuum

Rubber Sucker

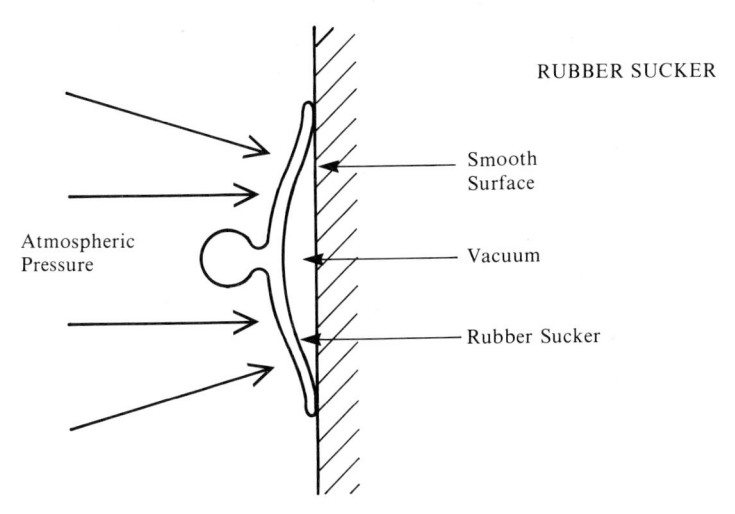

FIG. 6.13

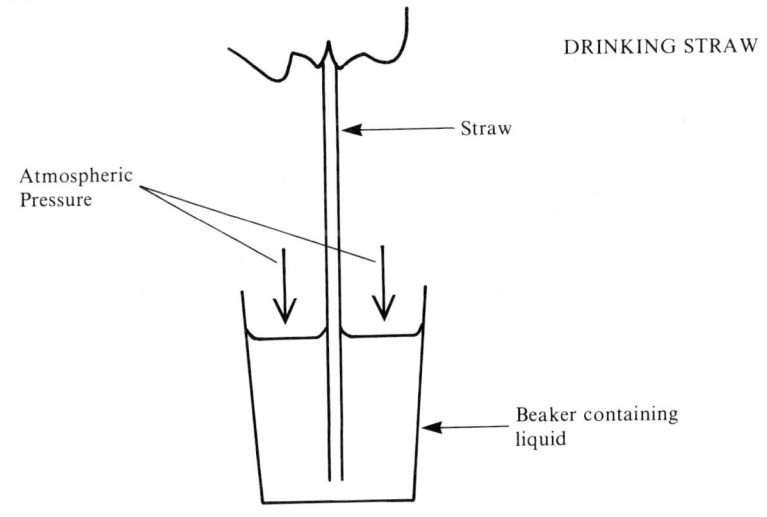

DRINKING STRAW

Straw

Atmospheric Pressure

Beaker containing liquid

When the sucker is wetted and pressed onto a flat smooth surface, the air inside is pushed out, leaving a vacuum. The atmospheric pressure on the outside then holds the sucker firmly against the surface. Suckers are not only used on toy arrows but are used to attach car licences to windscreens and in industry for lifting large sheets of metal and glass.

Fig. 6.13 shows the drinking straw.

When you suck on a straw you suck the air from inside it. The atmospheric pressure acting on the surface of the liquid then pushes the liquid up the straw and into your mouth.

6.9 PRESSURE GAUGES

These measure the pressure exerted by a gas or liquid.

Fig. 6.14 shows the U tube manometer, used for measuring gas pressure.

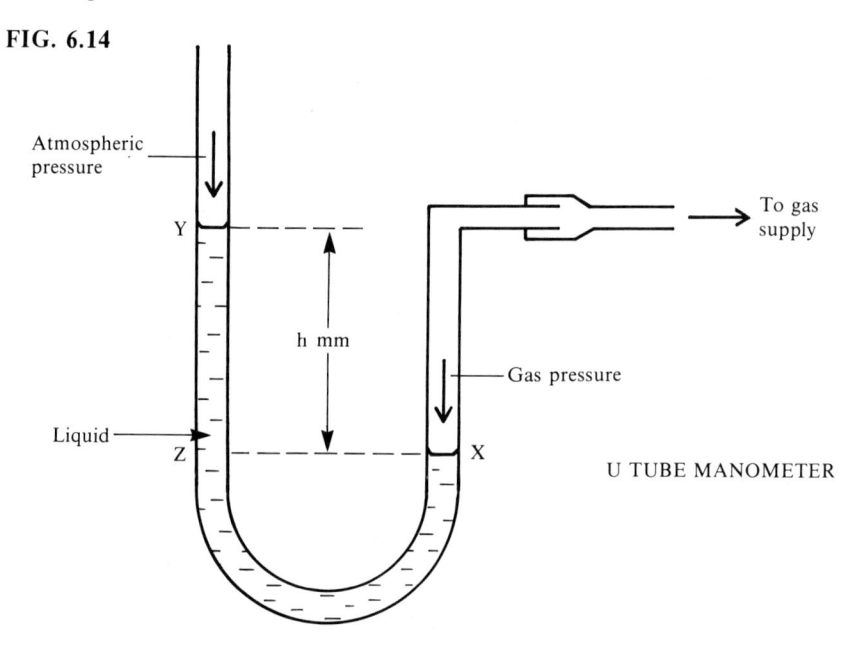

FIG. 6.14

U TUBE MANOMETER

It consists of a glass tube full of liquid with one side open to the atmosphere and the other connected to the gas supply to be measured. When the gas is switched on it exerts a pressure on surface X and causes level Y to rise. When it has stopped rising

Gas Pressure = Atmospheric Pressure + Pressure due to liquid column YZ

or

Gas Pressure − Atmospheric Pressure = Pressure due to liquid column YZ

Now Gas Pressure − Atmospheric Pressure = Excess pressure (of gas above atmosphere)

So Excess Pressure = Pressure due to liquid column YZ
= h mm of liquid.

If we are measuring low excess pressures the liquid used would be a light oil and for large excess pressures we would use mercury.

Fig. 6.15 shows the Bourdon gauge used for measuring either gas or liquid pressure, i.e. fluids.

FIG. 6.15

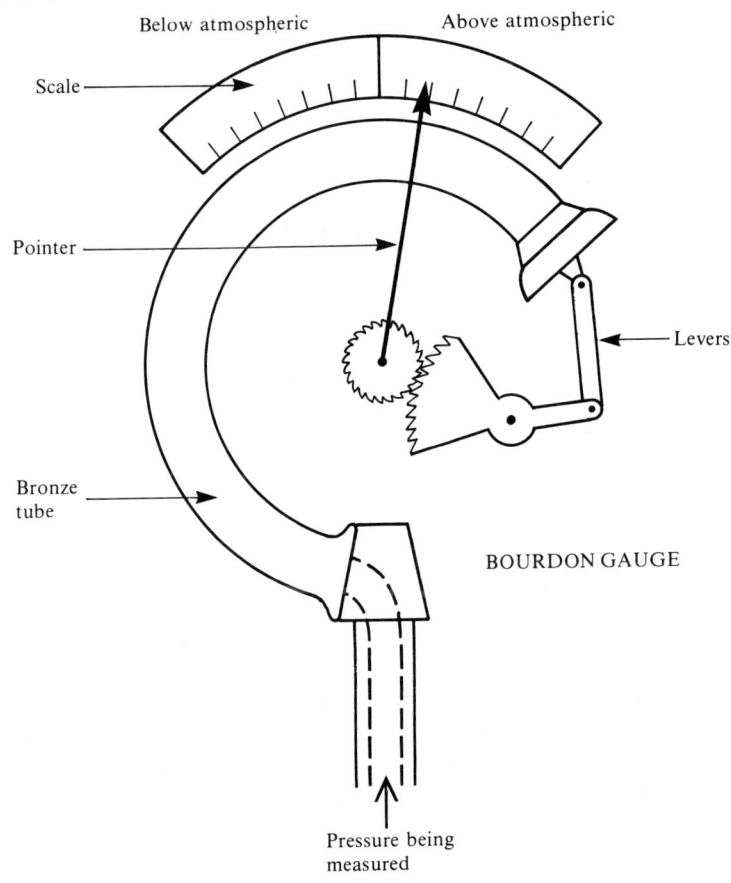

BOURDON GAUGE

It consists of a curved bronze tube connected via a system of levers to a pointer.

When the fluid pressure is being measured it causes the bronze tube to curl up more or less. If the pressure increases it will uncurl and cause the pointer to move to the right. If the pressure is reduced it will curl up more and cause the pointer to move to the left.

These gauges are used to measure the pressure in gas cylinders and to measure the oil pressure in a car.

SUPPLEMENTARY

6.9 CALCULATION OF A PRESSURE IN A LIQUID

We have seen that the pressure in a liquid depends upon depth and the density of the liquid.

The pressure p is given by

$$p = Dgh$$

where D = liquid density
g = acceleration due to gravity
h = depth in the liquid.

Not only does this equation enable us to calculate pressure but it enables us to convert a pressure from a height of mercury to Pascals. We can change a normal atmospheric pressure of 0.76 mm Hg into Pa by multiplying by g and the density of mercury.

PROBLEM

CALCULATE THE PRESSURE DUE TO 100 m OF SEA WATER IF THE DENSITY OF SEA WATER IS 1150 kg/m³ AND THE ACCELERATION DUE TO GRAVITY IS 9.8 m/s².

Using $p = Dgh$
$p = 1150 \times 9.8 \times 100$
$= 1.127 \times 10^6 \, Pa$

ANSWER: PRESSURE DUE TO SEA = 1.127×10^6 Pa.

We need to remember that this is the pressure due to the liquid alone. Atmospheric pressure also acts on the surface of the liquid and is transmitted by it.
So
Total pressure = Dgh + Atmospheric Pressure.

6.10 CALCULATIONS INVOLVING PRESSURE TRANSMISSION IN A LIQUID

We have already seen how a hydraulic car jack works and shall now consider a calculation.

PROBLEM

IN A HYDRAULIC CAR JACK A FORCE OF 20N IS APPLIED TO THE SMALL PISTON OF AREA $0.20\,m^2$. IF THE AREA OF THE LARGE PISTON IS $2\,m^2$, CALCULATE THE PRESSURE TRANSMITTED THROUGH THE LIQUID AND THE FORCE APPLIED TO THE LARGE PISTON.

Now $\quad p = \dfrac{F}{A}$

$\qquad\qquad F = 20\,N \qquad A = 0.20\,m^2$

So $\qquad p = \dfrac{20}{0.20} = 100\,Pa$

THIS IS THE PRESSURE TRANSMITTED THROUGH THE LIQUID. IT IS APPLIED TO THE LARGE PISTON. THE FORCE ACTING ON THIS IS

$\qquad\qquad F = pA$

with $\qquad p = 100\,Pa, \qquad A = 2\,m^2$

$\qquad\qquad F = 100 \times 2$

$\qquad\qquad\quad = 200\,N.$

ANSWER: PRESSURE = 100 Pa, FORCE = 200 N.

6.11 THE WEATHER

The atmospheric pressure at ground level can vary and weather conditions are related to these variations. Meteorologists refer to regions of high or low pressure and these are areas of air which move over the earth's surface in which the atmospheric pressure is higher or lower than normal. Regions of high pressure called anticyclones usually bring fine, settled weather. Regions of low pressure, called cyclones or depressions usually bring rain and storms. This is because winds tend to blow into low pressure areas so the lower the pressure, the stronger the winds.

High and low pressure areas can be seen on a weather map. Lines on the map called isobars join places where the atmospheric pressure is the same. When the isobars are close together the winds will be strong, blowing to where the isobars are less close together.

Atmospheric pressure on a weather chart is usually given in bars. A pressure of one atmosphere is equal to one bar.

QUESTIONS

CORE

1. Explain why a woman wearing stiletto heels is more likely to damage a wooden floor than an elephant.
2. Calculate the pressure exerted on a table by a block of weight 50N and base area 5 m².
3.

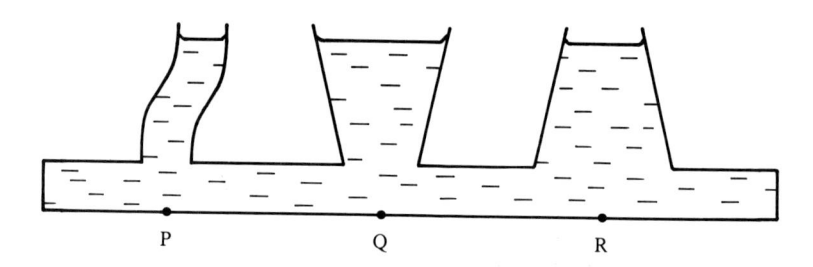

The apparatus in the diagram contains water.
Which of the following statements, about the pressure at P, Q and R is correct?

      A   P is the lowest
      B   Q is the highest
      C   R is the lowest
      D   P, Q and R are equal.   (L.E.A.G.)

4. What property of a liquid is important so that it can be used in a hydraulic jack?
5. A rectangular block measures 8 cm by 4 cm by 5 cm and has a mass of 1.25 kg.
    (a) (i) If the gravitational field strength is 10N/kg, what is the weight of the block?
    (ii) What is the area of the smallest face of the block?
    (iii) What pressure (in N/cm²) will the block exert when it is resting on a table on its smallest face?
    (iv) What is the least pressure the block could exert on the table?
    (b) (i) What is the volume of the block?
    (ii) Calculate the density of the material from which the block is made.   (N.E.A.)
6. Why is a person with high blood pressure likely to have a nosebleed at a high altitude?
7. The instrument shown in the diagram measures gas pressure.

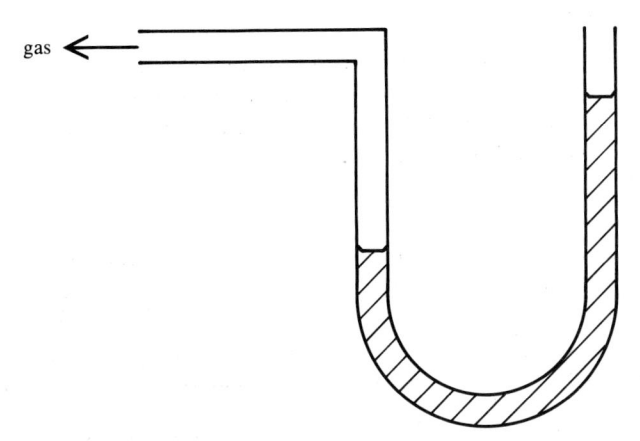

It is called a
A   barometer
B   Bourdon gauge
C   manometer
D   thermometer.   (S.E.G.)

SUPPLEMENTARY
8. Why is water not used in a barometer?
9. Calculate the total pressure 20 mm below the surface of some mercury in a dish assuming it is a normal day.
10. What is an isobar?

Chapter 7
WORK, POWER AND ENERGY

At the end of this chapter you will know:
CORE: what is meant by work; what a machine is; what is meant by power; what is meant by energy, the various forms of energy and the types of energy reserves; types of energy conversion; what is meant by the Principle of Conservation of Energy and how we define efficiency.
SUPPLEMENTARY: how work can be done by and against a force; how certain energy sources are exhaustible and equations for kinetic energy, change in potential energy and energy-mass equivalence.

CORE

7.1 WORK

Work is done whenever a force moves.

Work done = Force × Distance moved by force

We always measure the distance moved in the same direction as the force.

The work done, W, when a force, F, moves a distance, s, is then
$W = F \times s$

Force is measured in newtons and distance in metres and so work is measured in newton metres, Nm. We call a newton metre a joule, symbol J.

PROBLEM
CALCULATE THE WORK DONE WHEN A FORCE OF 20N MOVES THROUGH A DISTANCE OF 5m.

Using $\qquad W = F \times s$
$\qquad\qquad F = 20N, \qquad s = 5m$
So $\qquad\qquad W = 20 \times 5 = 100 J$

ANSWER: WORK DONE = 100 J.

Whenever work is done, energy is transferred. We shall say more about this later in the chapter.

Any device which can do work is known as a machine. The human body is a machine because it can do work — we are all used to lifting objects!

We have already met in Chapter 5 another type of machine, the lever. A lever is simply a rod positioned on a fulcrum. We apply a small force known as the effort to move a large force known as the load. The effort is small but moves through a large distance and the load is big but moves through a small distance. Consider Fig. 7.1.

FIG. 7.1

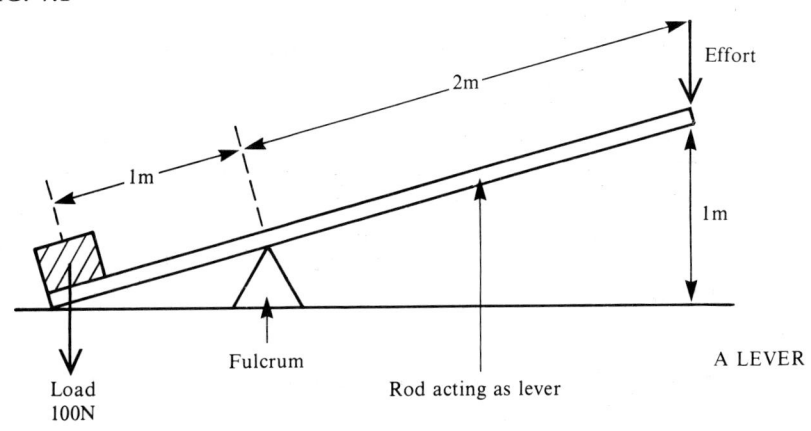

A LEVER

Load 100N
Fulcrum
Rod acting as lever
Effort

If the effort pushes its end of the lever to the ground it will move 1 m. By geometry, the load will rise by 0.5 m.

Applying work in = work out
    load × distance moved by load = effort × distance moved by effort
If E = effort then
$$100 \times 0.5 = E \times 1$$
$$E = 50.$$
We only need to apply an effort of 50N.

FIG. 7.2

A single pulley, as shown in Fig. 7.2, does not reduce the force we need to apply — the effort — although we may have to do work against friction.

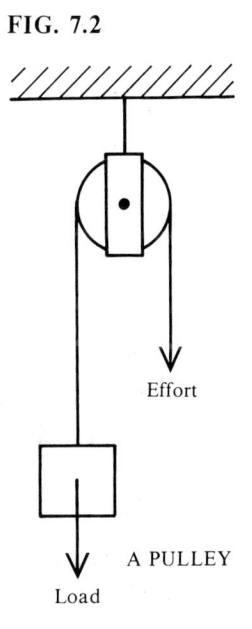

A PULLEY

Its main advantage is that it enables us to pull down in order to lift a load.

Block and tackle systems comprise a large number of moving and fixed pulleys, as shown in Fig. 7.3.

FIG. 7.3

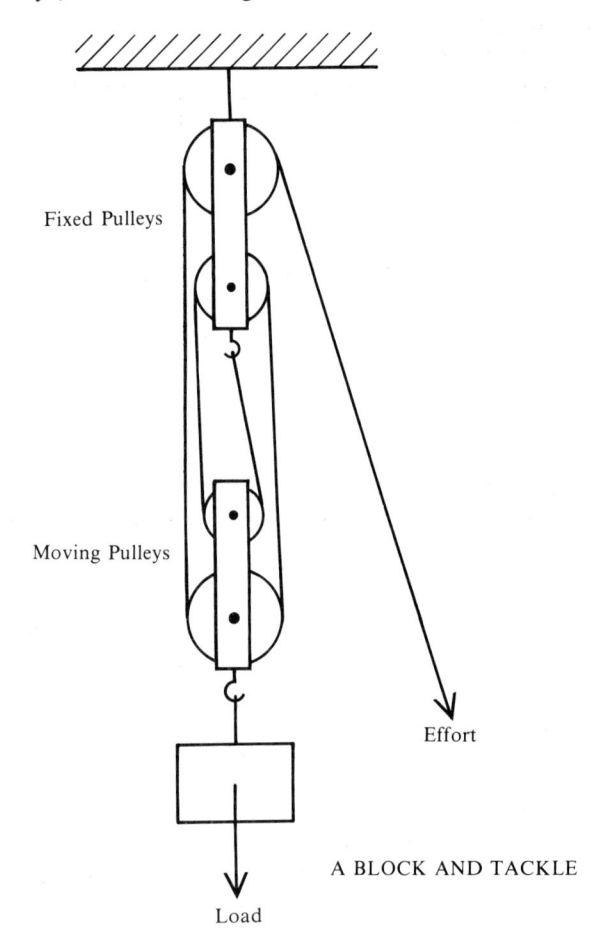

Fixed Pulleys

Moving Pulleys

Effort

A BLOCK AND TACKLE

Load

Extremely large loads may be lifted by the application of only small efforts.

7.2 POWER

Power is

$$\frac{\text{Work done}}{\text{Time taken}} \quad \text{or} \quad \frac{\text{Energy transfer}}{\text{Time taken}}$$

Work is measured in joules and time in seconds so work is measured in joules per second, J/s. We call a joule per second a watt, symbol W.

If W joules of work are done in t seconds this represents a power of P where
$$P = \frac{W}{t}$$

PROBLEM
A BOY WEIGHING 400N CAN RUN UP A FLIGHT OF STAIRS IN 5s. IF THE HEIGHT OF THE STAIRS IS 7m, CALCULATE THE POWER DEVELOPED BY THE BOY.

Using $\quad P = \dfrac{W}{t}$

Now $\quad W = F \times s$
$\qquad F = 400N, \quad s = 7m$
and $\quad t = 5s$
So $\quad P = \dfrac{400 \times 7}{5} = 560 W$

ANSWER: POWER DEVELOPED = 560 W.

7.3 ENERGY

In order that work can be done, a machine needs energy. Energy is always needed to do work and since energy is converted into work it is measured in joules.

Energy is found in many different forms — chemical, nuclear, thermal (or heat), wind, wave, sound, electromagnetic radiation, kinetic, electrical and four types of potential energy — magnetic, electric, elastic and gravitational.

Some of these types of energy come from reserves:
(1) fossil fuels — coal, oil and natural gas.
(2) vegetable fuels — wood, charcoal and peat.
Both fossil and vegetable fuels contain chemical energy.
(3) nuclear fuel such as uranium which contains nuclear energy.

7.4 ENERGY CONVERSIONS

Energy can be changed from one form into another by suitable devices known as transducers.

Although energy can be changed from one form to another, it can never be made or destroyed. The Principle of Conservation of Energy states that energy can never be made or destroyed and can only change into a different form.

Some types of energy conversions are given below:

106 Work, Power and Energy

fossil and vegetable fuels are burned to convert chemical into thermal energy;
nuclear fuels convert some of their mass into thermal energy;
wind energy can turn a generator to give electrical energy — this is used by a windmill generator, shown in Photograph 5.

PHOTOGRAPH 5

the vanes and generator are shown in Photographs 6 and 7;

PHOTOGRAPH 6

PHOTOGRAPH 7

wave energy can move a vane connected to a generator to generate electricity — this is used in a wave machine, shown in Photograph 8, which is a $\frac{1}{40}$th model of the Lancaster Flexible Bay;

the sun converts mass into electromagnetic energy in the form of thermal and light and is the origin of wind and wave energy;
in a piezoelectric lighter, a quartz crystal converts elastic potential energy into electrical energy;
in the earth, radioactive decay generates thermal energy known as geothermal energy;
in plants, electromagnetic energy in the form of light is converted by chloroplasts into chemical energy.

7.5 KINETIC AND POTENTIAL ENERGY

All moving bodies have kinetic energy. It is the energy of motion.

Potential energy is energy which a body has because of its position or condition. For a mass in a gravitational field it is gravitational and increases with height, for a charge in an electric field it is electric and for a magnet in a magnetic field it is magnetic. If a fixed object is pulled, pushed or twisted it has elastic potential energy.

7.6 MORE COMPLICATED ENERGY CONVERSIONS

(i) The human body is a transducer. It converts chemical energy in food into thermal energy (keeping us warm), kinetic energy (allowing

108 Work, Power and Energy

PHOTOGRAPH 8

us to move around) and new chemical energy (rebuilding our tissues).

Some foods supply large amounts of energy — chocolate contains 2300 kJ per 100 g but some such as rhubarb only contain 20 kJ per 100 g.

In order to lose weight you need to take in less energy than you use. The body then converts some of its weight into energy. If you eat more food than you need, your body will store the excess energy as fat. A person working in an office uses about 10,000 kJ per day but a heavy manual worker uses about 21,000 kJ per day.

(ii) In the wind and wave machines we really need to include kinetic energy. The wind is changed into the kinetic energy of the vanes which drive the generator to make electricity. Similarly, in a wave machine the energy of the wave is changed into kinetic energy of the vane which then drives a generator to make electricity.

More complicated conversions occur in power stations. A coal fired station is shown in Photograph 9. This is at Eggborough near Selby. Here coal is burned to boil water. The steam given is used to drive a turbine attached to a generator which generates electricity. During this process the energy changes from chemical to thermal to potential to kinetic to electrical. We can represent this on a block diagram shown in Fig. 7.4.

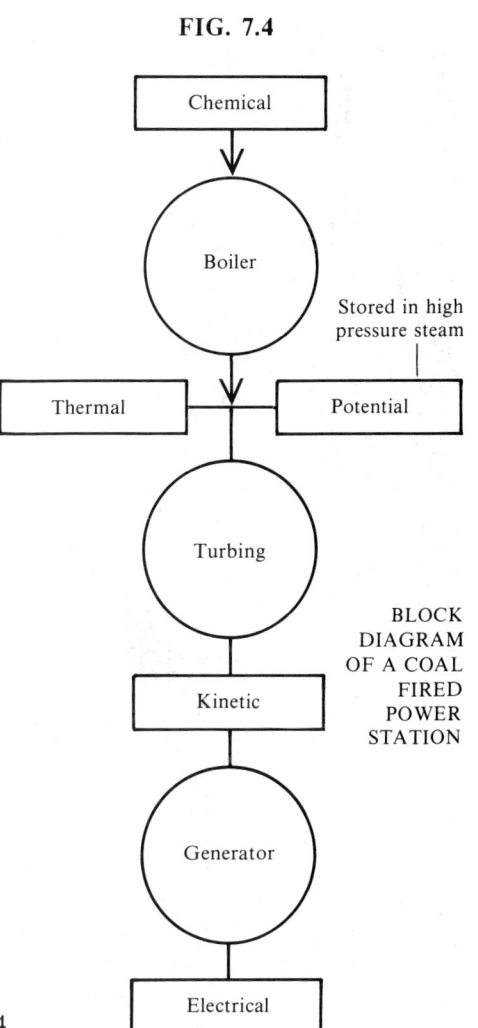

FIG. 7.4

Chemical → Boiler → Thermal / Potential (Stored in high pressure steam) → Turbing → Kinetic → Generator → Electrical

BLOCK DIAGRAM OF A COAL FIRED POWER STATION

PHOTOGRAPH 9

PHOTOGRAPH 10

The circles represent transducers and the rectangles represent energy forms.

In a nuclear power station, nuclear energy replaces chemical energy, the reactor replacing the boiler. Photograph 10 shows the Oldbury Power Station in Gloucestershire.

7.7 ENERGY LOSSES

In machines and transducers there is usually some energy loss with the work output being less than the work input. We talk of efficiency where

$$\text{Efficiency} = \frac{\text{Work output}}{\text{Work input}} \times 100 = \frac{\text{Energy output}}{\text{Energy input}} \times 100$$

The answer is given as a percentage.

112 Work, Power and Energy

SUPPLEMENTARY

7.8 WORK DONE BY AND AGAINST A FORCE

When a force is due to a field then work may be done by or against the force.

In Fig. 7.5 a negative charge B is in the field due to a positive charge A.

FIG. 7.5

B will be attracted towards A. The field does work in attracting charge B and the electric potential energy of B falls.

In Fig. 7.6 a positive charge C is in the field due to a positive charge A.

FIG. 7.6

C will be repelled from A. If C is pushed towards A work will be done against the field and the electric potential energy of C increases.

In a similar way objects are always attracted to the ground by the earth's gravitational field and as they fall to the ground their gravitational potential energy falls.

7.9 EXHAUSTIBLE ENERGY RESERVES

Certain energy sources are exhaustible — that is, they can be used up. All fossil fuels and nuclear fuel are of this type. Although new fuel is always being formed, it takes so long to form that if we use up our current supplies it will have gone completely.

7.10 ENERGY EQUATIONS

The kinetic energy, K.E., of a body is given by

$$K.E. = \frac{1}{2}mv^2$$

where its mass is m and its speed is v.

PROBLEM
CALCULATE THE KINETIC ENERGY OF A CAR OF MASS 500 kg TRAVELLING AT A SPEED OF 40 m/s.

Use
$$K.E. = \tfrac{1}{2} mv^2$$
$$m = 500 \text{ kg} \quad v = 40 \text{ m/s}$$
$$K.E. = \tfrac{1}{2} \times 500 \times 40 \times 40 = 4 \times 10^5 \text{ J}.$$

ANSWER: KINETIC ENERGY = 4×10^5 J.

(ii) The change in potential energy or P.E. of a body is given by
$$\text{Change in P.E.} = \text{Weight} \times \text{change in height}$$
$$= Wh$$
where W = weight and h = change in height.

We normally take ground level as the zero level of potential energy and so if an object is moved up from ground level the actual potential energy is given by weight × height above ground.

PROBLEM
CALCULATE THE CHANGE IN POTENTIAL ENERGY OF A BOY OF WEIGHT 600N WHO CLIMBS UPWARDS BY 10m.

Use
$$\text{CHANGE IN P.E.} = Wh$$
$$W = 600 \text{ N}, \quad h = 10 \text{ m}$$
$$\text{CHANGE IN P.E.} = 600 \times 10 = 6 \times 10^3 \text{ J}$$

ANSWER: CHANGE IN P.E. = 6×10^3 J.

When an object falls its potential energy changes into kinetic energy.

(iii) In a nuclear reactor the mass of the nuclear substance changes into thermal energy.

Mass itself is a form of energy. The relationship between mass and its energy equivalence is given by
$$E = mc^2$$
when
E = energy equivalence
m = mass
c = speed of electromagnetic radiation in vacuum.

QUESTIONS

CORE
1. Calculate the work done when a weight of 10N is raised by 2 m.
2. A lift of weight 2000N is raised by an electric motor through a height of 15 m in 20 s. Calculate the power output of the motor.
3. Explain what is meant by kinetic energy.
4. Explain what is meant by potential energy.

5. State the Principle of Conservation of Energy.
6. Which of the following is DESIGNED to convert electrical energy into sound energy?
   A. Transformer, B. Loudspeaker, C. Microphone, D. Recording Tape. *(L.E.A.G.)*
7. A steam engine drives a generator which lights a lamp. Which of the following lines best describes the energy changes which occur?

A	Heat	— Electrical	— Heat and Light
B	Electrical	— Heat	— Kinetic
C	Heat and Light	— Kinetic	— Electrical
D	Heat	— Heat and Light	— Electrical

   (L.E.A.G.)
8. A worker on a building site raises a bucket full of cement at a slow steady speed, using a pulley like that shown in the diagram.

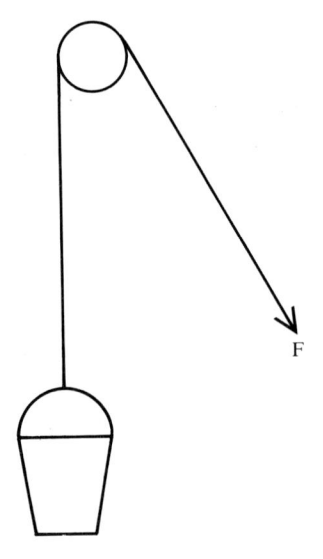

   The weight of the bucket and cement is 200 newtons. The force F exerted by the worker is 210 newtons.
   (a) Why is F bigger than the weight of the bucket and cement? *(1 mark)*
   (b) The bucket is raised through a height of 4 metres.
      (i) Through what distance does the worker pull the rope?
      (ii) How much work is done on the bucket and cement?
      (iii) What kind of energy is gained by the bucket?
      (iv) How much work is done by the worker?
      (v) Where does the energy used by the worker come from? *(6 marks)*
   (S.E.G.)

9. In a hydro-electric generating station, water falls through pipes from a high reservoir to a turbine. The turbine drives an alternator.
   (a) Label the block diagram below, with the three parts of the system. On the diagram show clearly the main energy changes in the system. *(4 marks)*

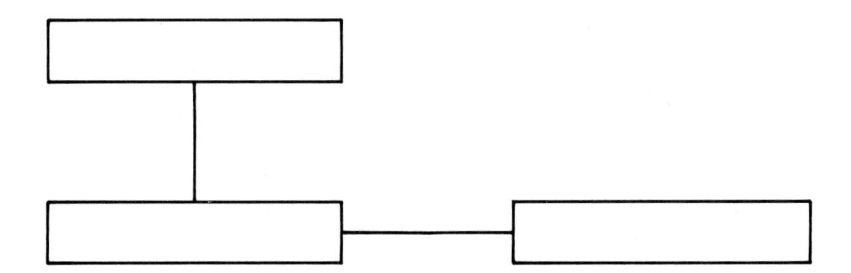

   (b) Write down the names of THREE different sources of energy which are used for driving an electrical generating system. *(3 marks)*
   (S.E.G.)

SUPPLEMENTARY
10. A girl walks up a flight of steps. Does she do work against gravity or does gravity do work on her?
11. A cricket ball of mass 0.2 kg has a kinetic energy of 40 J. Calculate its speed.
12. Calculate the gain in potential energy of a weight of 50 N which rises by 5 m.

116 Matter

Chapter 8
MATTER

At the end of this chapter you will know:
CORE: the states of matter and their characteristic properties; what is meant by Brownian motion, diffusion and evaporation; the effect of thermal energy on solids, liquids and gases; why there is a large change in volume when a liquid changes into a gas; why the pressure of a gas increases as its temperature increases and what is meant by the absolute zero of temperature.
SUPPLEMENTARY: why large particles can be moved by small particles when observing Brownian motion; how temperature, surface area and draught effect evaporation; the variation in pressure and volume of a gas; the variation in pressure and temperature of a gas and the ideal gas equation.

CORE

8.1 SOLIDS, LIQUIDS AND GASES

(i) All substances are made up of tiny particles called atoms. The atoms group themselves together in three ways so that the substance is either a solid, a liquid or a gas. Solids, liquids and gases are called the three states of matter.

(ii) In solids, the atoms are arranged in a pattern which continually repeats itself. The atoms do not wander around but stay in their own positions. The particular pattern in which the atoms are arranged varies from substance to substance. We say that each substance has its own particular crystal lattice on which the atoms are arranged. Of course, we cannot see the lattice because it is just a mathematical way of representing the pattern. A typical lattice arrangement is shown in Fig. 8.1.

FIG. 8.1

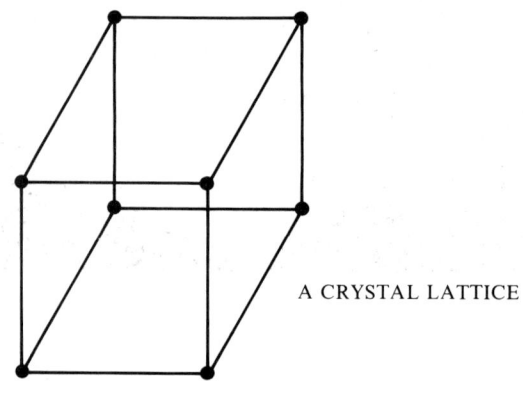

A CRYSTAL LATTICE

The black dots show the atoms and the lines represent the lattice structure. This is a simple cubic lattice and we can think of the atoms as being fixed at the corners of a cube.

The atoms are very close together. In most solids the distance from one atom to the next is about $\frac{1}{10,000,000,000}$ m and so obviously they cannot be seen with the eye or even a microscope. Instead we have to use X rays to observe them. A much more complicated lattice structure obtained using X rays is shown in Photograph 11.

PHOTOGRAPH 11

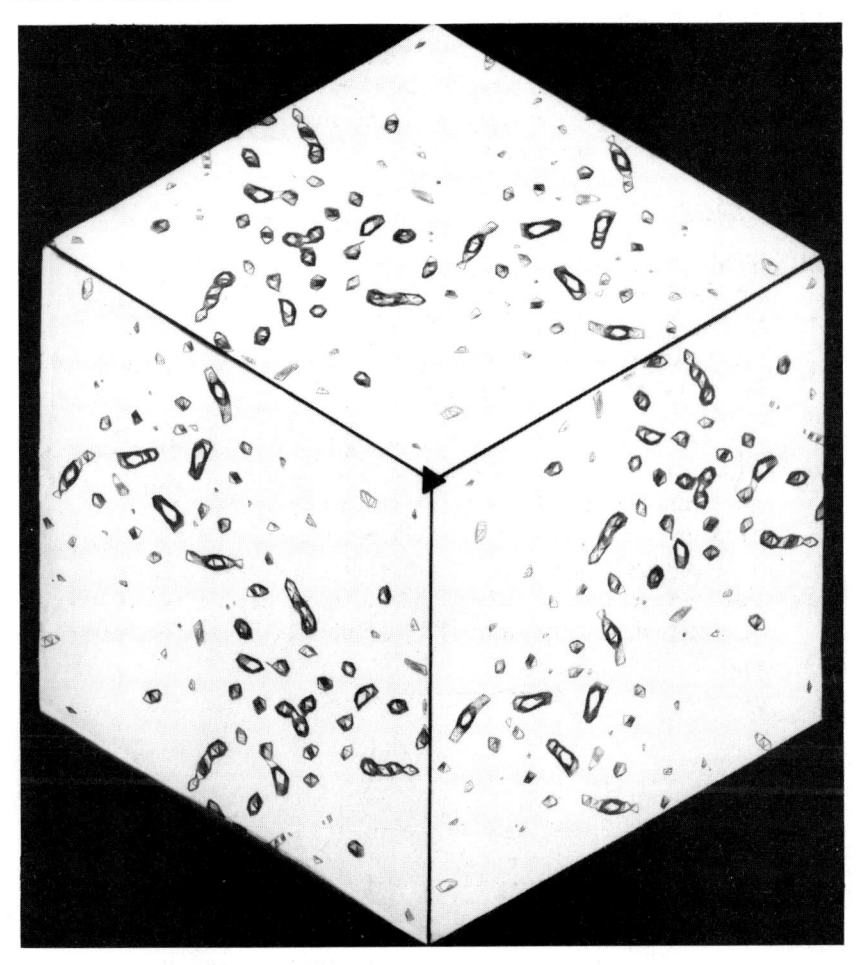

118 Matter

The atoms are not at rest on the lattice. They vibrate to and fro about their rest position. As two neighbouring atoms approach each other they repel each other. This stops them and makes them begin to move away from each other. As they pass through their rest position they then begin to attract each other. This again stops them and makes them begin to move towards each other and their motion is repeated. This is shown in Fig. 8.2.

FIG. 8.2

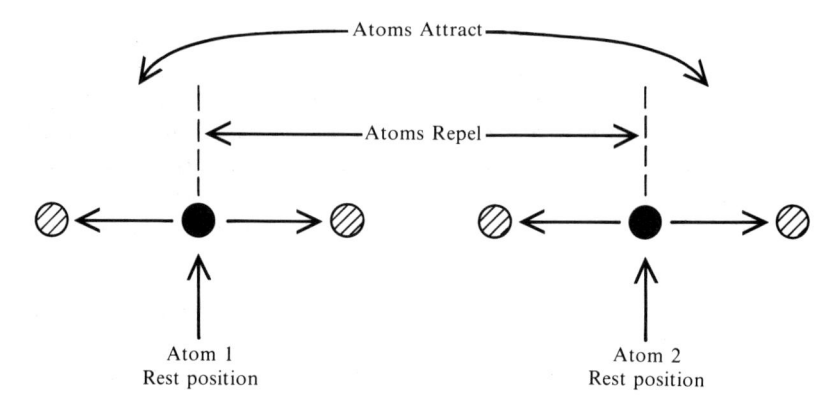

This vibration is going on through the whole lattice.

(ii) In liquids the atoms are not arranged in a pattern. We say that a liquid is not as ordered as a solid. Instead of being arranged in a pattern, the atoms wander around at random, still vibrating slightly. The average distance between the atoms is only slightly greater than in a solid but this means that there is a slight attractive force between the atoms.

(iii) In gases the atoms are moving around very rapidly. The average distance between atoms is about ten times greater than in a solid or a liquid and is $\frac{1}{1,000,000,000}$ m.

The atoms move randomly in all directions. They move in straight lines until their direction is changed when they hit other atoms or the walls of their container. Because they move so rapidly, they move completely independently of each other and attractive forces only act between them for the short times when they are close enough together. This theory of gases is called the kinetic theory.

8.2 THE PROPERTIES OF SOLIDS, LIQUIDS AND GASES

(i) Because the atoms in a solid are arranged on a lattice, a solid is rigid and is not able to flow.

If we try to squeeze the atoms together we have to apply a force to overcome the repulsion between them. Equally, if we try to pull the atoms apart we have to apply a force to overcome the attraction between them. This is the origin of compressive and tensile forces which we discussed in Chapter 4, Section 10 and it explains why solids are effectively incompressible.

(ii) There is less order in a liquid and so liquids flow. It is because a liquid has no crystal lattice that it does not have a shape of its own and must be kept in a container. Liquids are slightly more compressible than solids. This is because there is a slight attractive force between their atoms and we can therefore push them closer together. Very soon, though, the repulsive forces take over and prevent us squeezing the atoms any closer together.

(iii) There is no order at all in a gas. Gases flow very easily and require a container. Because the atoms are widely separated, they may easily be compressed until their atoms are much closer together and they will feel the repulsive forces.

Because the atoms move independently of each other, a gas always expands to completely fill its container. The atoms are frequently hitting the walls of the container and because of this, a gas always exerts a pressure on the walls of its container as discussed in Chapter 6, Section 5.

(iv) Because of the nearness of their atoms, the density of solids and liquids is greater than the density of gases, as can be seen in the table of densities shown earlier.

However, most liquids are less dense than most solids. This is due to differences in the masses of their atoms. Mercury has a very high density and is the only metal which is a liquid at room temperature.

8.3 BROWNIAN MOTION

Atoms can exist by themselves or group together with similar or different atoms to form molecules.

The first experiment in which the motion of molecules of a liquid was observed was performed by Robert Brown, a botanist, in 1827. We call it Brownian motion.

He was using a microscope to look at some pollen particles in water and he saw that they were continually moving around in all directions and often changed direction without warning. At the time Brown could not explain what was happening. In fact what was happening was that the water molecules were continually moving around, invisible to the naked eye. They frequently collided with the pollen particles and the force which they exerted on the particles during the collisions made the particles move around in all directions.

So although the actual motion of the water molecules could not be seen, the effect of the collisions between the water molecules and the pollen particles could be seen quite easily through the microscope.

A Brownian motion experiment is shown in Fig. 8.3.

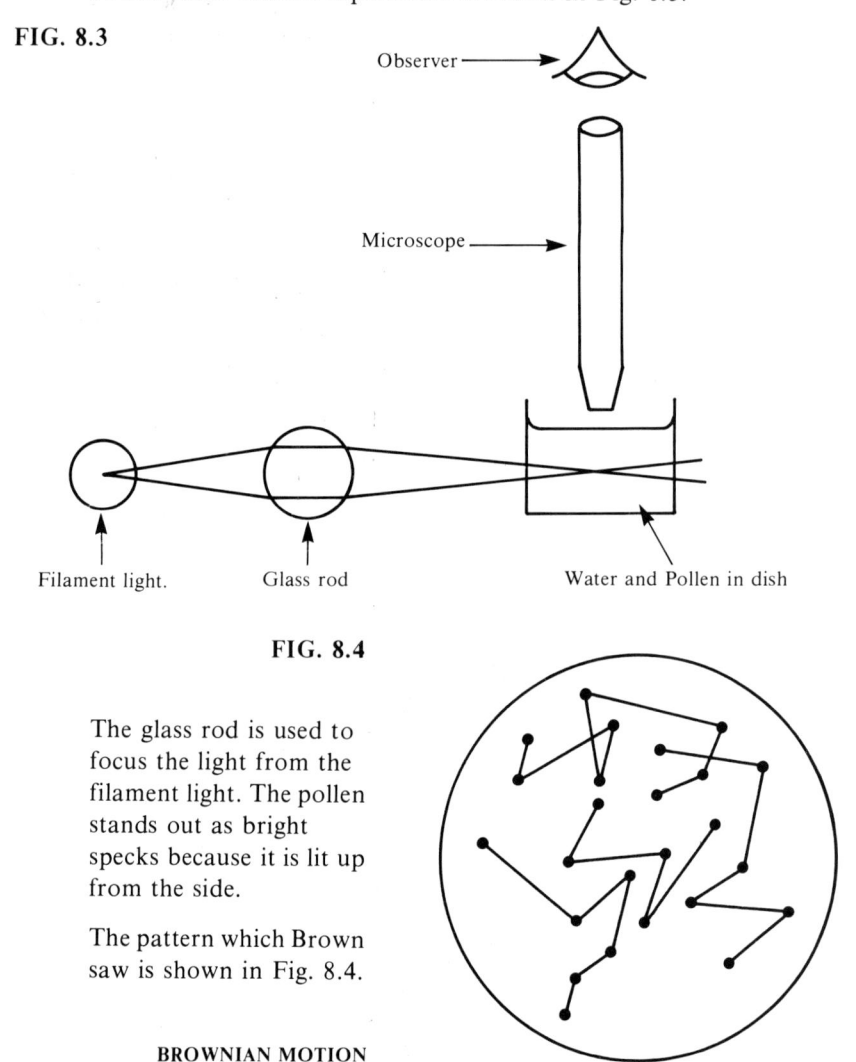

FIG. 8.3

Observer

Microscope

Filament light.   Glass rod   Water and Pollen in dish

FIG. 8.4

The glass rod is used to focus the light from the filament light. The pollen stands out as bright specks because it is lit up from the side.

The pattern which Brown saw is shown in Fig. 8.4.

BROWNIAN MOTION

If the experiment is repeated using warmer water we find that the distance between collisions is less and so the directions change more often. The time between collisions is also very much less.

Brownian motion may also be seen with smoke in air and is very clear when a smoker sits beneath the projection beam in a cinema. We can observe the behaviour of smoke in the laboratory. The apparatus shown in Fig. 8.3 is used but the water and pollen are replaced by a smoke cell. This is a small glass cylinder with a base and a removable lid. It is about 3 cm in diameter and 5 cm high. The lid is removed, some smoke blown into the cell, the lid replaced and the cell positioned under the microscope. Bright specks will be seen dancing around in all directions. They are the specks of smoke being struck by the air molecules at random.

8.4 DIFFUSION

Diffusion is the mixing of gases and liquids due to the motion of their molecules.

We have all experienced diffusion. Smells travel because of diffusion when the atoms of the substance causing the smell mix with the air molecules. The smell travels as the atoms move along. The speed at which a gas diffuses is greater for light molecules and this is why we very soon smell perfume after the bottle has been opened.

FIG. 8.5

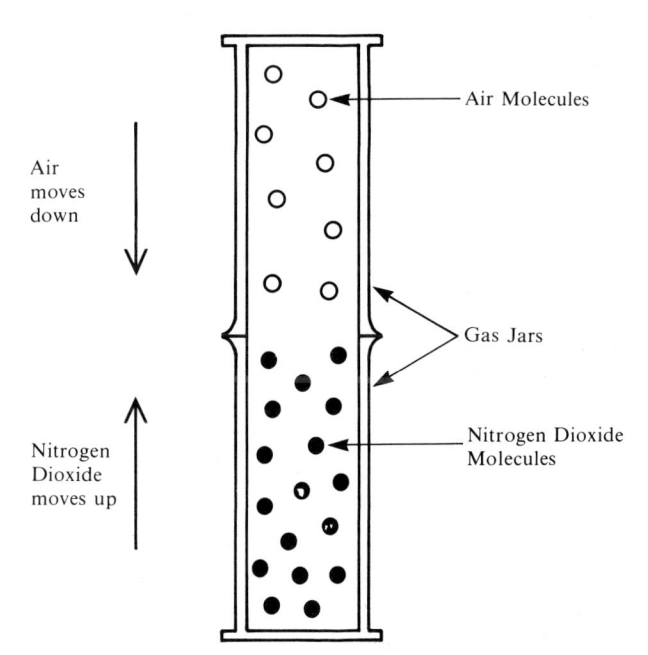

122 Matter

Diffusion can be seen in gases if a cylinder of air is placed over a cylinder of nitrogen dioxide, as shown in Fig. 8.5. The brown nitrogen dioxide will be seen spreading into the upper jar and the air will be seen spreading into the lower jar.

We can see diffusion in liquid by placing some copper sulphate solution in a jar and very gently filling the remainder of the jar with water. After about a day the blue copper sulphate will be seen to diffuse.

8.5 EVAPORATION

Not all the molecules of a liquid will have the same speed. As a result, they will not all have the same kinetic energy. There will be some molecules near the surface of the liquid which will have enough kinetic energy to overcome the attractive forces of the neighbouring molecules. They will escape from the liquid surface. This escape of molecules from a liquid surface is called evaporation and the space above the liquid becomes filled with vapour.

Because evaporation is due to the escape of high energy molecules this means that the average kinetic energy of the remaining liquid goes down and as a result the temperature of the liquid goes down. Evaporation always produces cooling.

After heavy exercise our skin becomes covered with perspiration. This evaporates from our skin and cools us as it does so. As a result, perspiring causes our bodies to keep cool.

Whenever evaporation takes place a large increase in volume occurs. Because the average molecular separation in a vapour is much greater than in a liquid, any particular volume of liquid which evaporates from a liquid surface will occupy a larger volume as a vapour.

Incidentally we have said that the space above a liquid contains vapour. A vapour is almost identical to a gas except that if a vapour is squeezed very hard it can be turned into a liquid again. A gas would have to be cooled and squeezed.

8.6 THE EFFECT OF THERMAL ENERGY ON SOLIDS, LIQUIDS AND GASES

When thermal energy or heat enters a substance, it usually causes an increase in temperature and a change in the motion of the atoms. We shall now discuss these changes in atomic motion. Other changes will be considered in later chapters.

In the case of a solid, the effect of supplying thermal energy is to cause the atoms on the lattice to vibrate over bigger distances although the time for an atom to make one complete vibration does not change.

In the case of liquid when thermal energy is supplied the molecules are made to move more rapidly and collide more often with other molecules.

When thermal energy is supplied to a gas, the speed of all the molecules of the gas increases greatly. As a result, the kinetic energy of the gas also increases. Because the speed of the molecules increases the pressure which the gas exerts increases as well.

8.7 THE ABSOLUTE ZERO OF TEMPERATURE

We have just seen that when the temperature of a gas increases so does the pressure which it exerts. The reverse case is also true, that is when the temperature of a gas is reduced, so is the pressure which it exerts.

If we could continue lowering the temperature, we would eventually reach a temperature when the pressure exerted by the gas would be zero. This temperature is called the absolute zero of temperature, denoted by 0K.

You should realise that the idea is only theoretical because it assumes that a gas has properties which no real gas has — i.e. we are considering an ideal gas. Even if we really had an ideal gas it would be impossible to cool it sufficiently to actually observe what would happen at the absolute zero.

SUPPLEMENTARY

8.8 BROWNIAN MOTION AND INERTIA

In the case of Brownian motion, it was stated that the small invisible water molecules were able to move the large pollen grains. This happens despite the large inertia of the grains.

The reason for this is that, although the water molecules have a small mass, they are rapidly decelerated when they collide with the pollen particles. They therefore exert quite a large force on the particles and despite the large mass of these particles they still experience a significant acceleration causing them to reach a high velocity after the collision.

8.9 FACTORS AFFECTING EVAPORATION

There are three factors which affect the rate at which a liquid evaporates.

Firstly, temperature. If the temperature of a liquid rises then the kinetic energy of the molecules will increase. This will provide more of them with enough energy to escape from the liquid surface, that is, it will increase the rate of evaporation.

Secondly, the surface area of the liquid. If the surface area is increased, there will be more molecules near the surface and so more will be able to escape, causing the rate of evaporation to increase.

Finally, providing a draught. Without a draught, some of the escaping liquid molecules would collide with the air molecules and some of them would be bounced back downwards into the liquid. The draught will cause escaping molecules to be blown away before this has time to happen and will therefore increase the rate of evaporation. You can observe the effect of a draught very easily. Do some strenuous exercise and then stand in a draught by an open window and notice how rapidly you cool down. Be careful not to catch a cold!!

8.10 BOYLE'S LAW

Boyle's Law, named after the discoverer, applies to changes in the pressure and volume of a constant mass of an ideal gas at constant temperature.

Robert Boyle observed that if the pressure of such a gas was doubled, its volume was halved, if the pressure was trebled, its volume was reduced to one third.

In fact he found that whenever the pressure was multiplied by the volume, the same result was obtained.

In other words, the product of pressure and volume is a constant
or $pV = $ constant
where $p = $ pressure and $V = $ volume.

If we are involved with a calculation, we often use the subscript 1 to indicate the original conditions and the subscript 2 to indicate the final conditions and then
$$p_1 V_1 = p_2 V_2$$

PROBLEM

A QUANTITY OF GAS HAS A VOLUME OF 20 cm³ AT A PRESSURE OF 1×10^5 Pa. WHAT WILL ITS VOLUME BE WHEN THE PRESSURE IS 5×10^5 Pa?

Use $\quad p_1 V_1 = p_2 V_2$
Here $\quad p_1 = 1 \times 10^5$ Pa, $V_1 = 20$ cm³
$\quad\quad\; p_2 = 5 \times 10^5$ Pa, $V_2 = V_2$.

So
$$1 \times 10^5 \times 20 = 5 \times 10^5 \, V_2$$
or therefore, $V_2 = 4 \, cm^3$

ANSWER: FINAL VOLUME OF GAS = $4 \, cm^3$.

NOTE TO STUDENT: We assume the gas is ideal and at constant temperature. We have also left the volume in cm^3 so that the answer will be in the same units.

Boyle's Law is an example of inverse proportion. If we plot a graph of p against V we obtain Fig. 8.6 and if we plot p against $\frac{1}{V}$ we obtain Fig. 8.7

FIG. 8.6 **FIG. 8.7**

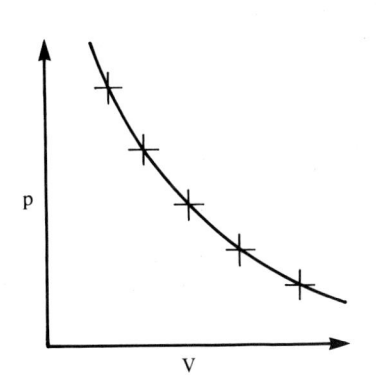

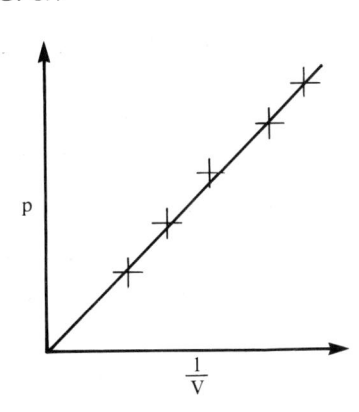

In terms of kinetic theory, a smaller volume causes more impacts with the wall causing a greater pressure.

8.11 THE PRESSURE LAW

This law applies to changes in pressure and temperature of constant mass of an ideal gas at constant volume.

The law states that the pressure of a constant mass of ideal gas at constant volume is directly proportional to its absolute temperature, or

$$\frac{p}{T} = \text{constant}$$

where p = pressure and T = absolute or Kelvin temperature.

As with Boyle's Law we may use subscripts, i.e.

$$\frac{p_1}{T_1} = \frac{p_2}{T_2}$$

PROBLEM

A CONTAINER AT CONSTANT VOLUME HOLDS GAS AT A TEMPERATURE OF 280K. WHAT WILL THE TEMPERATURE HAVE TO BE TO DOUBLE THE PRESSURE?

Use
$$\frac{p_1}{T_1} = \frac{p_2}{T_2}$$

Here
$p_1 = p_1$
$T_1 = 280K$ (this means 280 on the Kelvin scale)
$p_2 = 2p_1$
$T_2 = T_2$
$$\frac{p_1}{280} = \frac{2p_1}{T_1}$$

So
$$T_1 = 2 \times 280 = 560K$$

ANSWER: TEMPERATURE WILL BE 560K.

If we plot a graph of p against T we obtain Fig. 8.8

FIG. 8.8

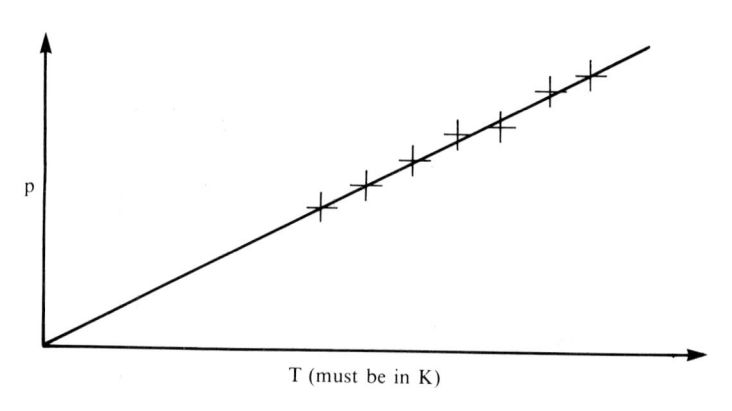

T (must be in K)

In terms of kinetic theory, an increase in temperature causes greater molecular speed causing an increase in pressure.

QUESTIONS

CORE

1. Name the three states of matter.

3. What is meant by Brownian motion?
4. Suggest why we never usually smell mercury. (Mercury is a safety hazard.)

5. Small particles of smoke in air in a well-lit glass box are seen making small jerky movements. These movements are due to
   A   energy from the light source causing the particles to expand.
   B   energy from the light source causing convection currents in the box.
   C   static electricity on the particles.
   D   the motion of the molecules of the air in the box.
   (S.E.G.)

6. Which of the following describes particles in a solid at room temperature?
   A   close together and stationary.
   B   close together and vibrating.
   C   close together and moving around at random.
   D   far apart and moving at random.
   (L.E.A.G.)

SUPPLEMENTARY

7. List three factors affecting the rate of evaporation of a liquid.
8. The diagram represents a piston and cylinder. The trapped air cannot pass the piston.

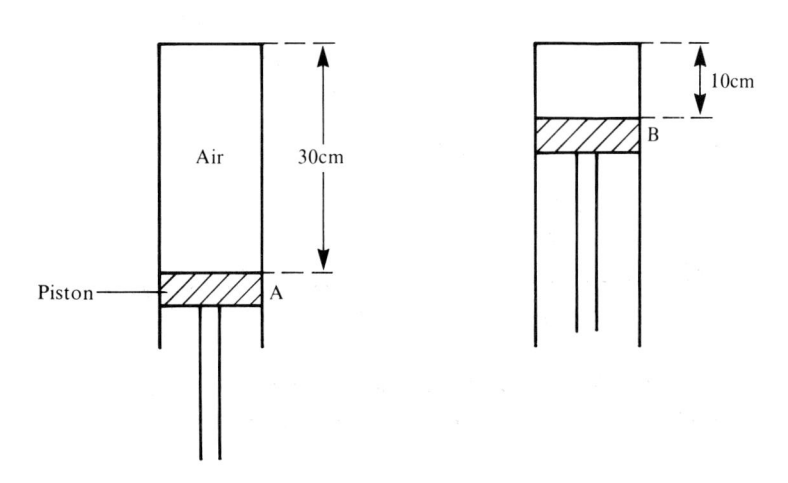

The top of the piston moves from position A to position B without changing the temperature of the enclosed air. This causes the air pressure in the cylinder to be:
   A   reduced to a third.
   B   unchanged.
   C   doubled.
   D   trebled.
   (L.E.A.G.)

9. The outlet of a bicycle pump is sealed so that the air cannot escape.

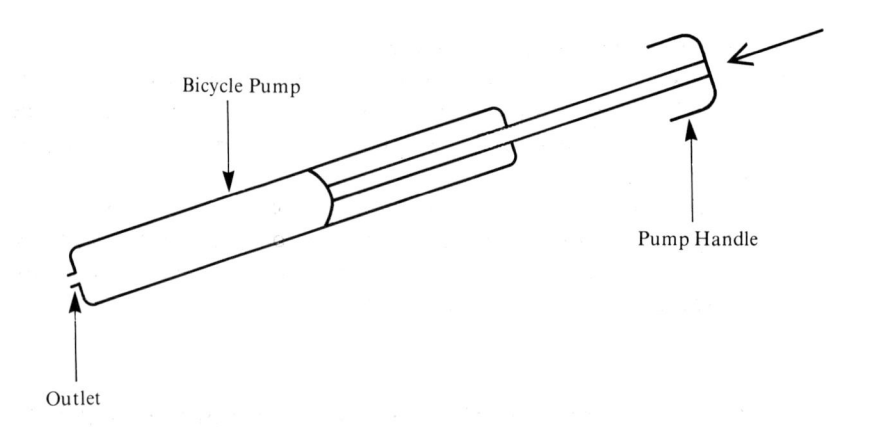

When the pump handle is pushed in, what happens to
(a) the pressure of the trapped air?
(b) the average spacing of the molecules?
(c) the density of the trapped air? (L.E.A.G.)

Chapter 9
THERMAL EXPANSION OF SOLIDS, LIQUIDS AND GASES

At the end of this chapter you will know:
CORE: that all substances expand when heated and contract when cooled; what happens to the molecules to cause the expansion; about applications of thermal expansion and how strangely water behaves when it is cooled.
SUPPLEMENTARY: the relative sizes of the expansion of solids, liquids and gases; an equation relating the volume of a gas to its temperature at constant pressure; the general gas law and what is meant by standard temperature and pressure.

CORE

9.1 THE EFFECT OF THERMAL ENERGY ON SOLIDS, LIQUIDS AND GASES

(i) The volume of most substances increases when thermal energy is given to them, that is when heat is supplied causing their temperature to rise. When their temperature falls, their volume decreases. This effect is known as thermal expansion. If substances are not allowed to move freely in these circumstances large forces develop.

(ii) When the temperature of a solid increases, the atoms on the lattice vibrate over bigger distances. Because of the forces involved between the atoms this increased vibration causes the average separation of the atoms to increase and we observe this as a thermal expansion.

(iii) When the temperature of a liquid increases, the speed of the atoms increases and their average separation increases also. It is very difficult to see the thermal expansion of a liquid because it always has to be heated in a container and the container will also expand.

(iv) When the temperature of a gas increases, at constant pressure, its volume increases, that is, it expands. This is due to the fact that the speed of the atoms increases and they bombard the container walls more violently causing them to move outwards.

(v) In order to compare the thermal expansion of different substances we need to begin with equal amounts of substances and increase their temperatures by the same amount. We would then observe that different substances expand by different amounts. This fact means that sometimes thermal expansion can be a useful effect or a hindrance and we shall consider this next. For any particular substance the expansion is more if we begin with a bigger amount or if we increase its temperature more.

9.2 APPLICATIONS OF THERMAL EXPANSION

(i) Thermal expansion causes problems on bridges and railway lines. Gaps are always left where a bridge joins the main road, as shown in Fig. 9.1.

FIG. 9.1

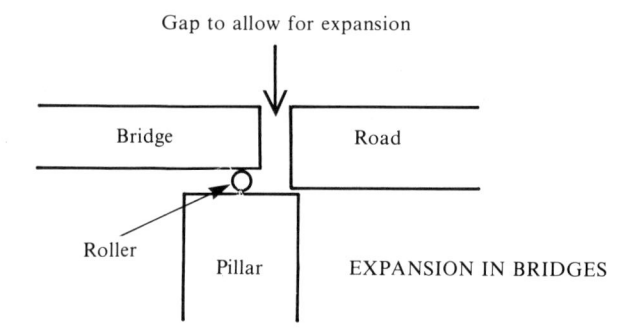

```
                  Gap to allow for expansion
                            ↓
     ─────────────────┐   ┌──────────────
         Bridge       │   │    Road
     ─────────────┐   │   │
                  │   ○   │
           Roller╱        │
                  Pillar  │      EXPANSION IN BRIDGES
                  │       │
                  │       │
```

In summer the bridge expands and moves over the roller, closing up the gap. In winter the reverse happens and the gap expands. On older railway lines, gaps were left between lengths of rail to allow for expansion in summer. On modern tracks the rails are about 1 km long and are welded into concrete sleepers which can withstand the large forces developed when the rails expand.

(ii) Glass stoppers can always be removed from jars by warming them gently underneath the hot water tap. The stopper and the jar top both expand but because the jar top is bigger than the stopper it expands more, enabling us to pull out the stopper.

(iii) The fact that different substances expand by different amounts is made use of in the bi-metallic strip, shown in Fig. 9.2.

FIG. 9.2

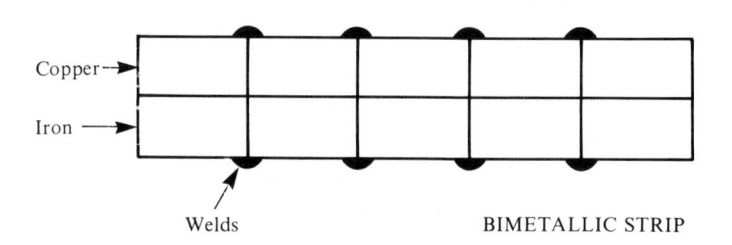

```
         Copper →┌───●───●───●───●───┐
                 │                   │
         Iron  → ├───────────────────┤
                 └───●───●───●───●───┘
                     ↗
                  Welds              BIMETALLIC STRIP
```

This consists of two identically sized strips of metal — one copper, one iron, riveted together. When they are heated, the copper expands more than the iron causing the strip to bend, as shown in Fig. 9.3.

FIG. 9.3

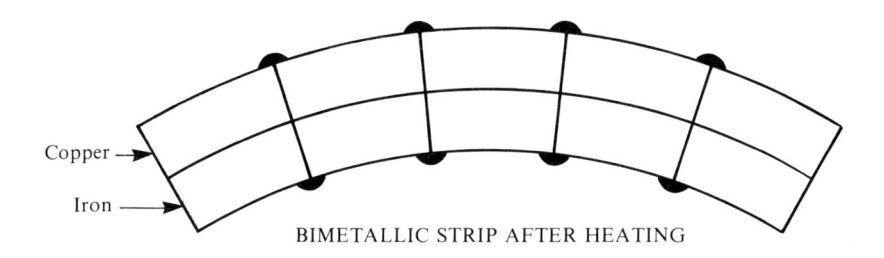

Copper →
Iron →

BIMETALLIC STRIP AFTER HEATING

(iv) A bi-metallic strip is used in a thermostat, as seen in Fig. 9.4.

FIG. 9.4

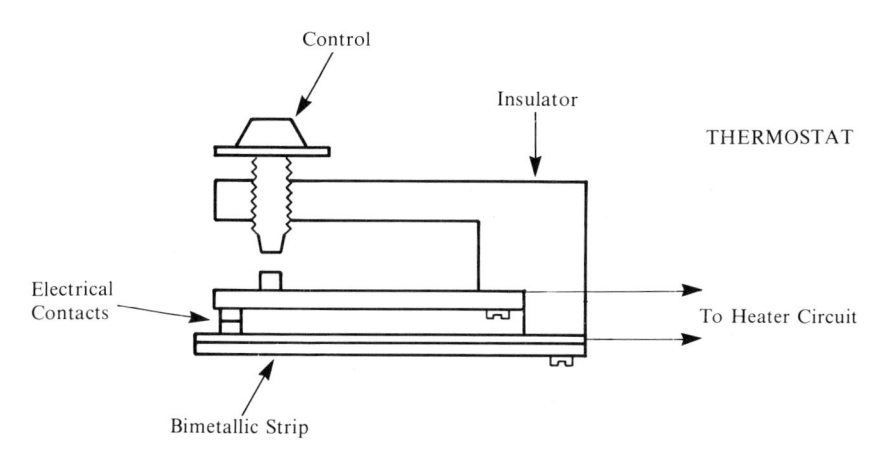

Control

Insulator

THERMOSTAT

Electrical Contacts

To Heater Circuit

Bimetallic Strip

A thermostat is used to keep the temperature of an appliance constant. As the temperature of the device increases the bi-metallic strip bends down, breaks the contacts and switches off the circuit. The strip then cools, straightens out and completes the circuit again. As a result the temperature only changes by a small amount. If the control knob is turned down the top contact is pushed down and the strip has to bend more in order to break the circuit. A higher temperature can then be reached.

(v) In the gas oven thermostat we make use of the fact that an alloy of nickel and steel, known as invar has a very small expansion. It is shown in Fig. 9.5.

FIG. 9.5

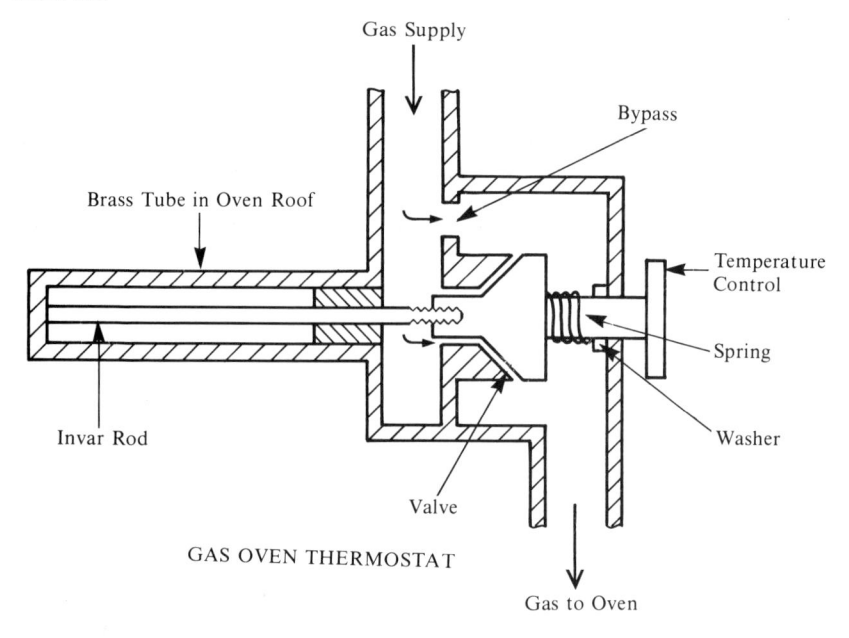

```
                    Gas Supply
                        ↓
                                    Bypass
   Brass Tube in Oven Roof
                ↓                          Temperature
                                           Control
                                           
                                           Spring
   
   Invar Rod                               Washer
                    Valve
         GAS OVEN THERMOSTAT
                                    ↓
                              Gas to Oven
```

When the temperature of the oven rises the brass tube expands to the left and drags the invar rod with it. Because invar does not expand as much the invar rod does not effectively expand to the right to compensate for this. As a result the valve is made to be less open and the gas supply is reduced. The temperature control sets the original position of the valve.

9.3 THE BEHAVIOUR OF WATER

When water is cooled its volume decreases as would be expected. This only continues until the water reaches 277K. If further cooling takes place, the volume begins to increase until 273K is reached when there is a large increase in volume when the water changes into ice. This large increase in volume when water freezes is the reason why water pipes burst in winter.

SUPPLEMENTARY

9.4 THE RELATIVE EXPANSION OF SOLIDS, LIQUIDS AND GASES

Solids expand only very little when they are heated. As we have already noted, the expansion of liquids is more difficult to observe because of the expansion of the container. However, if we make an allowance for this expansion, we find that the true expansion of the

Thermal Expansion of Solids, Liquids and Gases

liquid is greater than that of a solid. On average the expansion of a liquid is about ten times greater than that of a solid. Gases expand most of all. We find that for every 1K rise in temperature the volume of a gas increases by $\frac{1}{273}$ of its volume at 273K.

Notice that with a solid we can measure the expansion in length but with liquids and gases we measure changes in volume.

9.5 THE VARIATION IN VOLUME AND TEMPERATURE OF A GAS

If we increase the temperature of a fixed mass of an ideal gas at constant pressure we find that the volume, V, and the Kelvin temperature, T, are related by

$$\frac{V}{T} = \text{constant}$$

For calculation purposes we indicate the initial conditions with a subscript 1 and the final conditions with the subscript 2 and so

$$\frac{V_1}{T_1} = \frac{V_2}{T_2}$$

We may express this relationship as: For a fixed mass of an ideal gas at constant pressure, its volume is directly proportional to the Kelvin temperature. This is known as Charles' Law.

PROBLEM
2m³ OF GAS INITIALLY AT 300K IS HEATED TO 450K AT CONSTANT PRESSURE. CALCULATE ITS FINAL VOLUME.

Use
$$\frac{V_1}{T_1} = \frac{V_2}{T_2}$$
$V_1 = 2m^3$, $T_1 = 300K$, $V_2 = V_2$, $T_2 = 450K$
$$\frac{2}{300} = \frac{V_2}{450}$$
so $V_2 = 3m^3$

ANSWER: FINAL VOLUME = $3m^3$.

A graph of volume against temperature is shown in Fig. 9.6.

134 Thermal Expansion of Solids, Liquids and Gases

FIG. 9.6

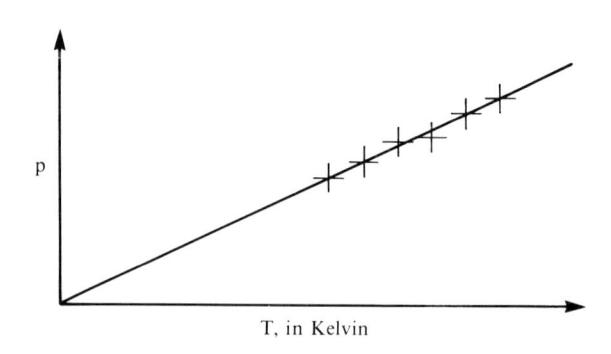

[Graph showing p versus T, in Kelvin — a straight line through the origin with data points marked by crosses.]

9.6 THE GENERAL GAS LAW

We have seen in Chapter 8 that

$$\frac{p}{T} = \text{constant}$$

where p is the pressure of a gas at temperature T, in Kelvin. We can combine this with

$$\frac{V}{T} = \text{constant}$$

to obtain

(i) $$\frac{pV}{T} = \text{constant}$$

or using subscript 1 for initial conditions and 2 for final conditions.

(ii) $$\frac{p_1 V_1}{T_1} = \frac{p_2 V_2}{T_2}$$

Equations (i) and (ii) are known as equivalent statements or equations of the General Gas Law.

Often we are interested in calculations when a gas starts or finishes at 273K and 1 atmosphere pressure. A gas under these conditions is said to be at standard temperature and pressure denoted by s.t.p.

PROBLEM

A FIXED MASS OF GAS AT A TEMPERATURE OF 300K AND A PRESSURE OF 1 ATMOSPHERE HAS A VOLUME OF 200 cm³. CALCULATE ITS FINAL VOLUME IF ITS TEMPERATURE CHANGES TO 400K AND ITS PRESSURE TO 1½ ATMOSPHERES.

Use $\dfrac{p_1 V_1}{T_1} = \dfrac{p_2 V_2}{T_2}$

$p_1 = 1$ atm, $V_1 = 200\text{cm}^3$, $T_1 = 300\text{K}$, $p_2 = 1\tfrac{1}{2}$ atm, $T_2 = 400\text{K}$, $V_2 = V_2$

So $\dfrac{1 \times 200}{300} = \dfrac{1.5 \times V_2}{400}$

$V_2 = 178\,\text{cm}^3$

ANSWER: FINAL VOLUME $= 178\,\text{cm}^3$.

QUESTIONS

CORE

1. State what happens to the separation of the atoms in a solid as thermal energy is supplied.
2. In Fig. 9.3 what would happen to the heated strip if the iron were on top?
3. State what device could be used in an iron to keep its temperature constant.
4. Jane could not unscrew a metal bottle top because it was too tight but, after she ran it under a hot tap for a few minutes, she found she could unscrew it. This was because

    A   the hot water acted like oil between the glass and the bottle.
    B   the increased pressure of the air in the bottle caused the cap to expand.
    C   the glass in the neck of the bottle contracted.
    D   the metal cap expanded more than the glass.   *(L.E.A.G.)*
5. A metal block is heated. Which line in the following table shows what happens to its volume, density and mass?

Result	Volume	Density	Mass
A	increases	decreases	same
B	increases	increases	increases
C	increases	increases	same
D	same	decreases	same

    (L.E.A.G.)

6.

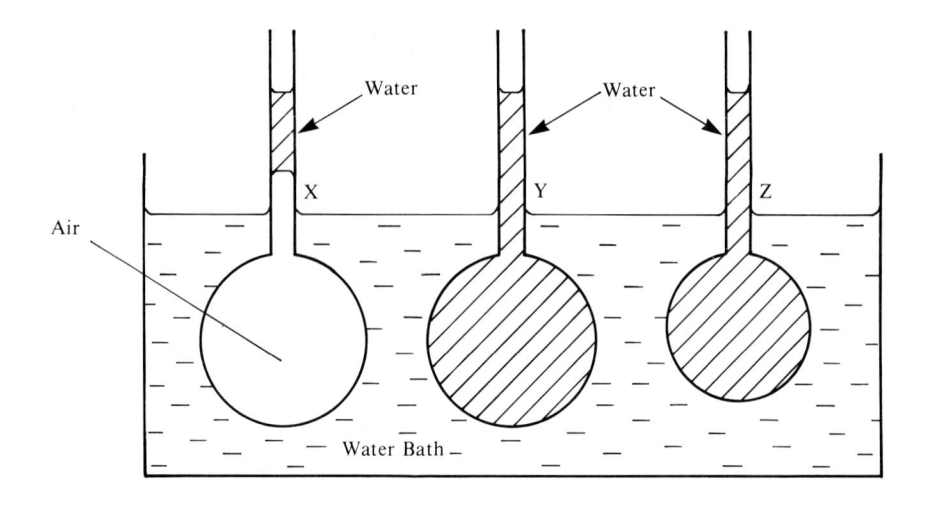

[Diagram: Three glass containers X, Y, and Z in a water bath. X contains air in a bulb with water in the tube above; Y is a solid (shaded) bulb with water in the tube above; Z is a solid (shaded) bulb with water in the tube above. Labels: Water, Air, Water Bath.]

The diagram shows three glass containers, X, Y and Z in a water bath. The water bath is gently heated.
(a) Which tube will overflow first? Explain your answer.
(b) Which tube will overflow last? Explain your answer.

SUPPLEMENTARY
7. Explain which gas equation you would use to calculate the pressure in a tyre after a long journey assuming all known quantities concerning the tyre at the start of the journey.
8. A gas has a volume of 70m^3 at 2 atmospheres pressure and a temperature of 546K. Calculate its volume at s.t.p.

Chapter 10
TEMPERATURE

At the end of this chapter you will know:
CORE: what is meant by temperature and internal energy; how temperature is measured using thermometers; what is meant by a temperature scale and fixed points; how to change from centigrade to Kelvin temperatures and what type of thermometers we use.
SUPPLEMENTARY: the requirements of a property variation so that it may be used to measure temperature; how temperature can be calculated by measuring variations and the advantages of a thermocouple.

CORE

10.1 TEMPERATURE AND INTERNAL ENERGY

The temperature of a substance is a measure of the kinetic energy of its molecules and so the higher its temperature the greater is the kinetic energy of its molecules.

If two objects at different temperatures are placed in contact, as shown in Fig. 10.1, thermal energy or heat flows from the object at the higher temperature to the one at the lower temperature until their

FIG. 10.1

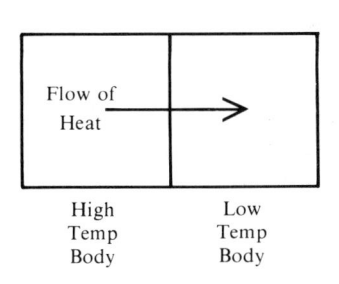

```
        ┌──────────┬──────────┐
        │ Flow of  │          │
        │   Heat   │    →     │
        │          │          │
        └──────────┴──────────┘
           High        Low
           Temp        Temp
           Body        Body
```

FLOW OF HEAT FROM HIGH TEMP TO LOW TEMP

temperatures are equal. So, the temperature of a body determines whether it will gain or lose heat from or to another body.

When heat has entered a body it increases the internal energy of that body. In solids and liquids the internal energy is made up of the kinetic energy and the potential energy of the molecules but in gases the internal energy is mostly made up of kinetic energy. We can see then that when heat enters a body, causing the internal energy to increase, the temperature rises as a result.

10.2 THE MEASUREMENT OF TEMPERATURE

(i) We measure temperature with a thermometer. Thermometers make use of some physical property of a substance which changes with temperature.

We need to express a temperature as a number. It is not good enough to say that one body has a higher temperature than a second body and a much higher temperature than a third body! In order to do this we use a scale of temperature.

(ii) On the centigrade or Celsius temperature scale we use two fixed points to define the scale.

The lower fixed point is the temperature of pure melting ice and is defined to be 0 degrees Celsius denoted 0°C.

The upper fixed point is the temperature of the steam above water boiling at normal atmospheric pressure. This is defined as 100°C.

A temperature exactly half way between these values would be taken as 50°C.

We shall see later how a Celsius temperature scale can be applied to a mercury in glass thermometer in Section 10.5.

(iii) In all modern scientific work, we use the absolute or Kelvin scale of temperature. Only one fixed point is used to define the scale. It is called the triple point and is 273.16 Kelvin denoted 273.16K. Because we use only one fixed point, we do not use the term degrees K.

(iv) We represent a Celsius temperature by the symbol θ and a Kelvin temperature by T. In order to change from one to the other we do the following sums:

to change °C to K we add 273 so
$$T = \theta + 273$$
to change K to °C we subtract 273 so
$$\theta = T - 273.$$

(v) A temperature change of 1°C is equal to a temperature change of 1K.

PROBLEM
CHANGE 50°C TO K AND 300K TO °C.

Use $\quad$ T = θ + 273
θ = 50°C
So $\quad$ T = 50 + 273 = 323 K
Use $\quad$ θ = T - 273
T = 300 K
So $\quad$ θ = 300 - 273 = 27°C

ANSWERS: 50°C = 323 K; 300 K = 27°C.

We can see that the boiling point of water is 373 K and the melting point of ice is 273 K.
Also the absolute zero of temperature 0 K is
θ = 0 - 273
or $\quad$ -273°C.

Sometimes when we are dealing with problems on temperature changes in gases, we are given temperatures in degrees Celsius. We must remember to convert them to Kelvin.

10.3 TYPES OF THERMOMETER

(i) In the liquid in glass thermometer the volume of a liquid in a glass bulb expands when the bulb is heated. As a result of this expansion the liquid rises up a capillary tube.

The liquid used must expand or contract by a large amount over a large range of temperature. It must not stick to the tube walls and it must be easily seen. The glass bulb should be thin so that the device reacts quickly to the temperature it is measuring.

Two liquids are often used. One is mercury which freezes at –39°C and boils at 357°C. It is used for high temperature measurement. The other is alcohol which is colourless but is dyed red or blue. It boils at 78°C but freezes at –115°C and so we use it for low temperature measurement.

Suppose we have an uncalibrated mercury in glass thermometer, that is one with no temperature scale.

Firstly we would use the apparatus in Fig. 10.2 to mark on it the lower fixed point or ice point.

We would then use the apparatus in Fig. 10.3 to mark on it the upper fixed point or steam point.

FIG. 10.2

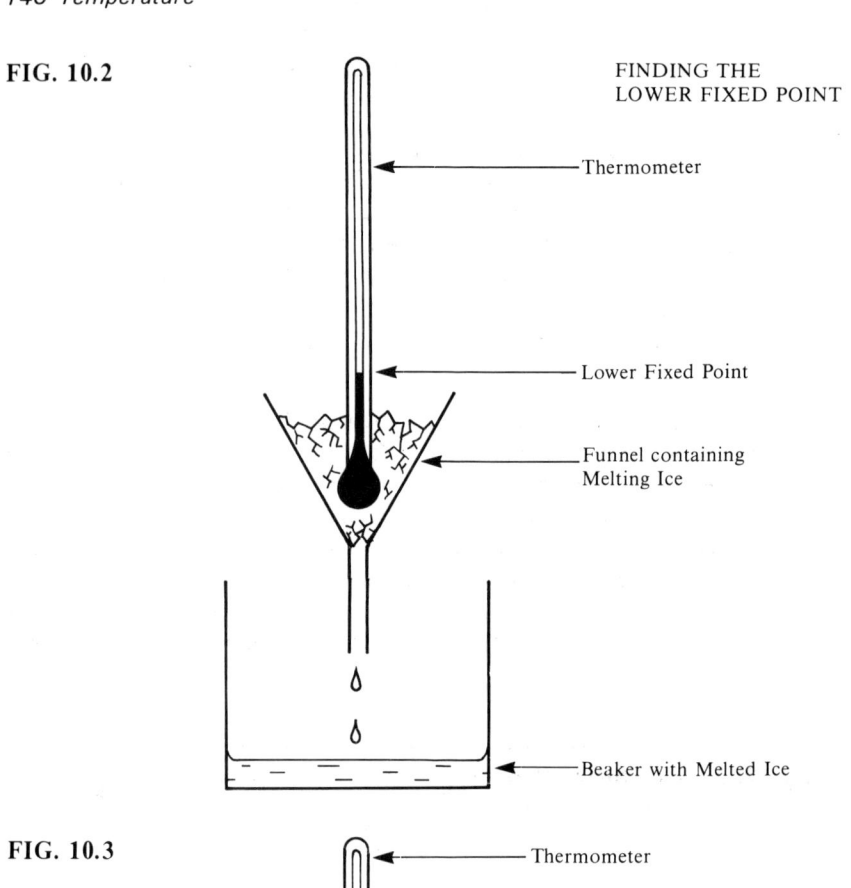

FINDING THE LOWER FIXED POINT

- Thermometer
- Lower Fixed Point
- Funnel containing Melting Ice
- Beaker with Melted Ice

FIG. 10.3

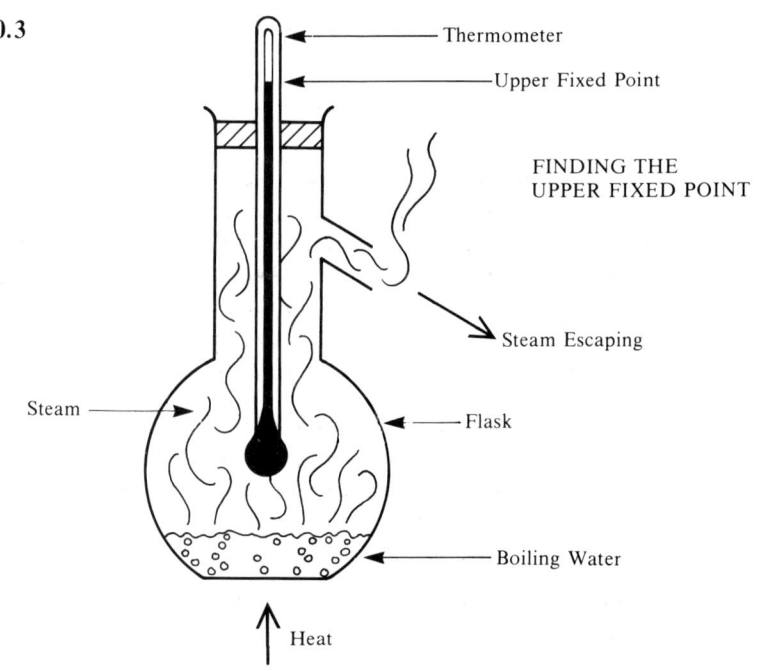

- Thermometer
- Upper Fixed Point

FINDING THE UPPER FIXED POINT

- Steam Escaping
- Steam
- Flask
- Boiling Water
- Heat

The distance between the marks is then divided into 100 equal degrees.

(ii) A clinical thermometer is a special type of mercury in glass thermometer which is used in medicine to measure the temperature of the human body. It only measures a few degrees on either side of the normal body temperature of 37°C. If our bodies go above this to about 41°C, we would die as a result of the overheating and equally if our temperature fell to about 35°C hypothermia would set in resulting in death. In winter, old people in particular are susceptible to hypothermia.

The tube has a kink or constriction after the bulb. In order to take a temperature the thermometer bulb is placed under the tongue for a minute. The mercury expands past the constriction in the tube. When we remove the thermometer, the constriction stops the mercury contracting back into the bulb and allows the temperature to be read. The thermometer is then given a quick shake by flicking the wrist in order to return all the mercury to the bulb. After sterilisation it is then ready for re-use. A clinical thermometer is shown in Fig. 10.4.

FIG. 10.4

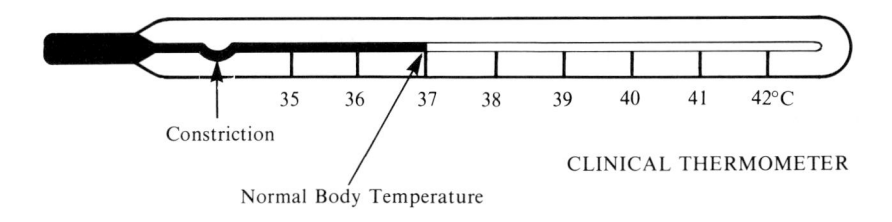

35 36 37 38 39 40 41 42°C

Constriction

Normal Body Temperature

CLINICAL THERMOMETER

(iii) A thermocouple is a thermometer which consists of two wires made from different metals. One junction of the wires is kept cold usually by placing it in melting ice. The other junction is used to measure an unknown temperature. When the wires are connected to a galvanometer the deflection obtained will depend upon the temperature of the hot junction. The galvanometer manufacturer calibrates the meter in °C. The apparatus is shown in Fig. 10.5.

(iv) A thermistor is an electronic thermometer. It is made of a material known as a semi-conductor. When its temperature rises it offers less resistance to electricity and so allows bigger electrical currents through it. The current passing through is a measure of the temperature of the device.

Thermistors are often used to prevent overloading in an electrical circuit.

FIG. 10.5

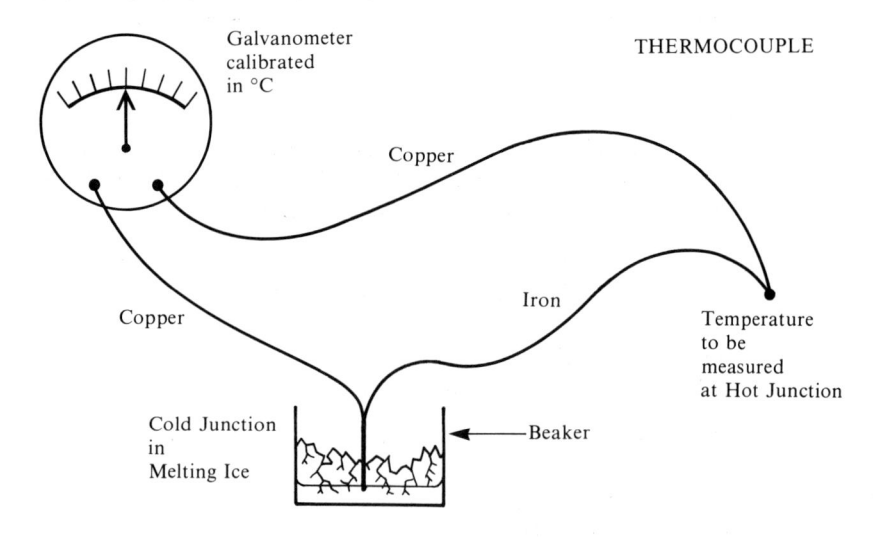

```
                    Galvanometer
                    calibrated              THERMOCOUPLE
                    in °C

                              Copper


                                    Iron
      Copper                                  Temperature
                                              to be
                                              measured
                                              at Hot Junction
         Cold Junction
         in                    ←— Beaker
         Melting Ice
```

SUPPLEMENTARY

10.4 THE REQUIREMENTS OF A THERMOMETRIC PROPERTY

In order that a change in the physical property of a substance may be used to measure temperature, it must meet three requirements:

1. The property must vary over a large range of temperature.
2. The variation must be linear — that is, it must vary by equal amounts for equal changes in temperature.
3. The variation should be as large as possible. Large variations enable us to measure very small changes in temperature, that is, they enable the thermometer to be more sensitive.

When we are using a change in some physical property to measure temperature we say that the property is behaving as a thermometric property.

10.5 CALIBRATION OF THE TEMPERATURE SCALE ON A MERCURY IN GLASS THERMOMETER

The above three requirements are met by the expansion of mercury and so it is used in a mercury in glass thermometer.

Suppose we have marked the lower and upper fixed points on an uncalibrated mercury in glass thermometer, as described in Section 10.2, and the distance between them is 150mm. This corresponds to a temperature difference of 100°C.

Each degree marking on the scale must be placed $^{150}/_{100}$mm apart. The sensitivity of this thermometer can be increased by making the capillary tube narrower. A given increase in volume of the mercury in the bulb then causes the mercury to rise further up the tube for any given rise in temperature.

PROBLEM
THE DISTANCE BETWEEN THE FIXED POINT ON A MERCURY IN GLASS THERMOMETER IS 170mm. HOW FAR FROM THE 0°C MARK IS THE 30°C MARK?

A temperature difference of 100°C is represented by 170mm.
So a difference of 1°C is represented by $\frac{170}{100} = 1.7$mm
A difference of 30°C is represented by $30 \times 1.7 = 51$mm
So the 30°C mark is 51mm away from the 0°C mark

ANSWER: THE 30°C MARK IS 51mm FROM THE 0°C MARK.

10.6 THE USE OF A THERMOCOUPLE

Because a thermocouple has such a small mass, it absorbs negligible heat from the body whose temperature it is actually measuring and therefore more accurate readings can be made. The small mass also means that it is able to measure a temperature very quickly and this enables it to be used to measure fluctuating temperatures. It is therefore used in industry to measure fluctuating temperatures up to about 1500°C.

QUESTIONS

CORE
1. What is meant by the temperature of a substance?
2. Two bodies are placed in contact. What decides whether heat will flow from one to the other?
3. State the two fixed points used in the centigrade temperature scale.
4. A metal container has two compartments, X and Y and each of these compartments contains oil at different temperatures.

FIG. 10.6

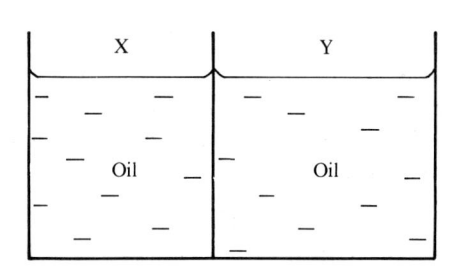

Energy flows from Y to X.
Which line in the table shows possible values for the temperatures?

	temperature of X (°C)	temperature of Y (°C)
A	25	0
B	50	10
C	10	70
D	50	25

5. Change −50°C to K.
6. Change 173K to 0°C.
7. The temperature of pure melting ice is
   A   −273K
   B   0K
   C   100K
   D   273K *(S.E.G.)*
8. State two dangers associated with the breaking of a clinical thermometer in a patient's mouth.

SUPPLEMENTARY
9. State three requirements of a thermometric property.
10. The distance between the fixed points on a mercury in glass thermometer is 150mm. What temperature will a mark 30mm along from the 0°C mark represent?

Chapter 11
THERMAL CAPACITY

At the end of this chapter you will know:
CORE: how the heat supplied to a body is related to its temperature rise; what is meant by thermal capacity and why certain hot objects burn while others do not.
SUPPLEMENTARY: what is meant by specific heat capacity and how it is measured; how heat may be stored by bodies and how to find the final temperature when two bodies at different temperatures are joined together.

CORE

11.1 THERMAL CAPACITY

Whenever heat is supplied to a body, the temperature of the body increases. If heat leaves a body, its temperature falls.

We find that if we supply different amounts of heat to different bodies we do not always see the same rise in temperature.

We can write down an expression relating the energy supplied to the change in temperature produced.

$$\text{Energy supplied} = \text{Thermal capacity} \times \text{Temperature rise}.$$

From this we see that

$$\text{Thermal capacity} = \frac{\text{Energy supplied}}{\text{Temperature rise}}$$

(If energy left the body, we would change rise to fall).

Energy is measured in joules, J, and temperature rise in degrees centigrade, °C, or Kelvin, K. Remember that a particular temperature change measured in °C is the same in K.

So, thermal capacity is measured in J/°C or J/K.

11.2 WHY SOME HOT OBJECTS BURN

If a hot object falls upon your skin it will cool down and release heat, causing a burning sensation. Some hot objects though can cool down by the same amount and yet they do not burn. This is because they release far less heat.

Objects which burn have a higher thermal capacity than those which do not. This is why hot sparks do not burn but hot water, at the same temperature does.

SUPPLEMENTARY

11.3 SPECIFIC HEAT CAPACITY

If heat is supplied to equal masses of different substances, we will find that the same amount of heat will give rise to different increases in temperature.

This is because each substance has its own value of specific heat capacity.

Energy supplied = Mass × Specific Heat Capacity × Temperature rise
or
$$W = mc\Delta\theta = mc\Delta T$$
where W = energy supplied to a mass m of specific heat capacity, c. The rise in temperature is denoted by $\Delta\theta$ in degrees centigrade and ΔT in Kelvin and is numerically the same on each scale.

W is measured in joules, J, mass in kilograms, kg, and the temperature rise in degrees centigrade, °C, or Kelvin, K.

So specific heat capacity is measured in J/kg°C or J/kgK and is the same in both sets of units.

The energy supplied, W, goes to increase the internal energy of the substance. Obviously if the temperature falls, the energy is given out.

Some values of specific heat capacities are shown below:

Material	Specific Heat Capacity (J/kgK)
Brass	380
Brick	800
Copper	385
Iron	460
Steel	460
Water	4200

PROBLEM

USING THE VALUES ABOVE, CALCULATE HOW MUCH HEAT IS NEEDED TO RAISE THE TEMPERATURE OF 2 kg OF WATER FROM 20°C TO 80°C.

Use $W = mc\Delta\theta$,
$m = 2\,kg$, $c = 4200\,J/kg°C$, $\Delta\theta = 60°C$
So $W = 2 \times 4200 \times 60 = 504{,}000\,J$

ANSWER: HEAT NEEDED = $5.04 \times 10^5\,J$.

11.4 MEASUREMENT OF SPECIFIC HEAT CAPACITY

To measure the specific heat capacity of a liquid we use the apparatus shown in Fig. 11.1.

FIG. 11.1 MEASUREMENT OF SPECIFIC HEAT CAPACITY OF A LIQUID

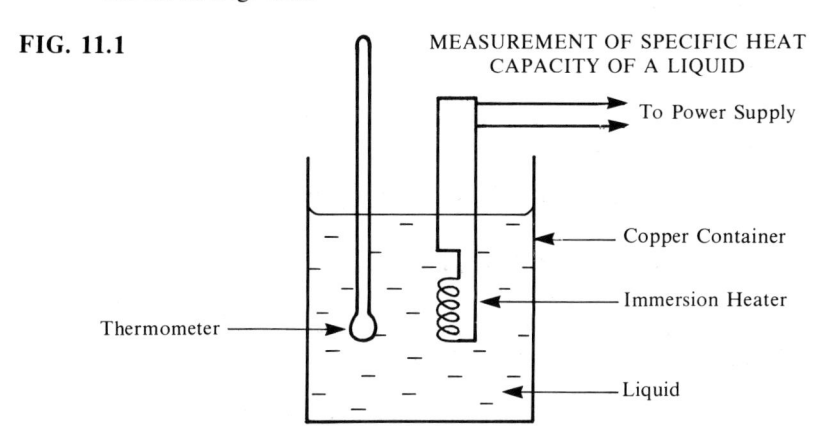

A known mass of liquid is placed in a copper container together with a thermometer and a 40 watt immersion heater. The temperature is noted and the heater switched on. A clock is started. After a suitable time has elapsed, about 5 minutes, the temperature is read again, the heater switched off and the clock read.

From the definition of specific heat capacity we have

$$\text{Specific Heat Capacity} = \frac{\text{Energy supplied}}{\text{Mass} \times \text{Temperature rise}}$$

The energy supplied is the heater wattage × time it is switched on, in seconds, and we may calculate the specific heat capacity using the

FIG. 11.2 MEASUREMENT OF SPECIFIC HEAT CAPACITY OF A SOLID

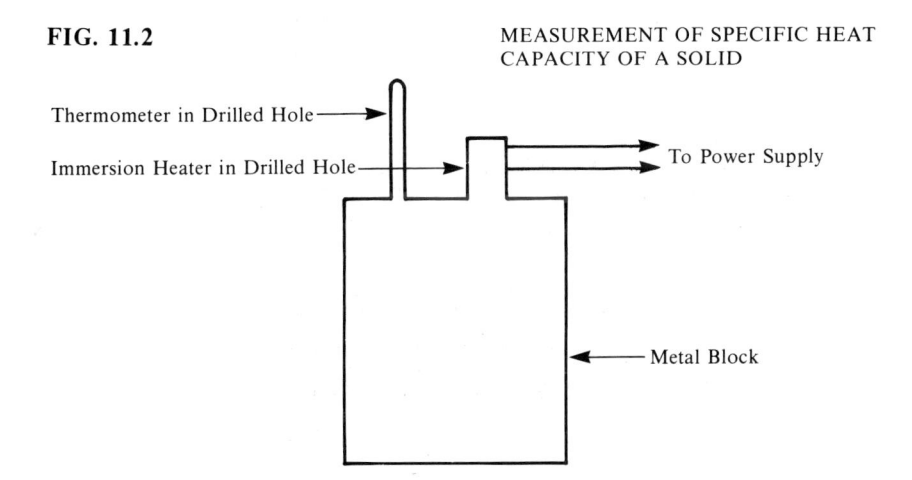

148 Thermal Capacity

equation above. We have ignored any heat supplied to the copper container.

In order to find the specific heat capacity of a solid such as a metal we use the apparatus shown in Fig. 11.2.

The specific heat capacity is calculated using the same procedure and equation as in the case of a liquid.

11.5 THE STORAGE OF HEAT BY BODIES

If the same amount of heat is supplied to identical masses of different substances, the largest temperature rise will occur in the substance with the lower specific heat capacity.

This is useful when we consider the storage of heat by bodies. During the daytime, as the temperature of the sea rises because of the sun, a large amount of energy is absorbed by the sea since water has a large specific heat capacity. It takes a long time for the sea to cool down at night as it loses the stored energy. In a similar way storage heaters are filled with material of high specific heat capacity, such as bricks, in order that they can store a large amount of energy which they can later release.

11.6 TO CALCULATE THE FINAL TEMPERATURE WHEN TWO BODIES AT DIFFERENT TEMPERATURES ARE JOINED OR MIXED

If two such bodies are joined or mixed, the hot body will lose heat and the cold body will gain heat.
In fact
Heat lost by hot body = Heat gained by cold body.

Suppose the mass of the hot body is m_1, its specific heat capacity is c_1 and its original temperature is $\theta_1°C$. The mass of the cold body is m_2, its specific heat capacity is θ_2 and its original temperature is $\theta_2°C$.

Let the final temperature of both bodies be $\theta_F°C$

The temperature fall of the hot body is $\theta_1 - \theta_F$
The temperature rise of the cold body is $\theta_F - \theta_2$

So $$m_1 c_1 (\theta_1 - \theta_F) = m_2 c_2 (\theta_F - \theta_2)$$

Removing the brackets and re-arranging gives

$$\theta_F = \frac{m_1 c_1 \theta_1 + m_2 c_2 \theta_2}{m_2 c_2 + m_1 c_1}$$

If $m_1 = m_2$ and $c_1 = c_2$, that is equal masses of the same substance are mixed then

$$\theta_F = \frac{\theta_1 + \theta_2}{2}$$

i.e. the final temperature is the average of the two temperatures. This is the principle of adding cold water to hot water in the bath when we change the final temperature by adding more cold water.

PROBLEM
80kg OF WATER IS AT A TEMPERATURE OF 80°C. HOW MUCH WATER AT 20°C WILL NEED TO BE ADDED TO BRING THE FINAL TEMPERATURE TO 60°C?

Re-arranging the equation for θ_F with $c_1 = c_2$ gives

$$m_2 = \frac{m_1(\theta_1 - \theta_F)}{(\theta_F - \theta_2)}$$

$m_1 = 80$kg
$\theta_1 = 80°C$, $\theta_2 = 20°C$, $\theta_F = 60°C$

So $m_2 = \frac{80(80 - 60)}{(60 - 20)} = \frac{80 \times 20}{40} = 40$kg

ANSWER: 40kg OF WATER MUST BE ADDED.

QUESTIONS

CORE
1. State the units of thermal capacity.
2. Explain why you are not burned if you snuff a candle out quickly.

SUPPLEMENTARY
3. 500J of energy is needed to raise the temperature of 0.5kg of paraffin through 0.5°C. In order to heat 2kg through 10°C how much energy is needed?
   A. 2,500J   B. 10,000   C. 24,000   D. 40,000J
4. How much heat is needed to increase the temperature of an iron ball of mass 2kg from 200°C to 300°C if the specific heat capacity of iron is 440 J/kg°C?

Chapter 12
MELTING AND BOILING

At the end of this chapter you will know:
CORE: what happens when substances melt and boil; the meaning of melting and boiling points and how they are affected by impurities; what is meant by condensation and solidification; what is meant by latent heat and what happens to it; what a cooling curve is and how a melting point may be found from it and how a refrigerator works.
SUPPLEMENTARY: the difference between boiling and evaporation; the definition of specific latent heats and how they may be measured in the laboratory.

CORE

12.1 WHAT HAPPENS WHEN SUBSTANCES MELT AND BOIL

If we heat some ice which is below 0°C, then its temperature will increase as we would expect. The temperature will continue to rise until it reaches 0°C when its temperature will not change but it will begin to melt, that is, change into a liquid. When all the ice has melted, the temperature of the water formed will begin to increase and this will continue until the water reaches a temperature of 100°C when, once again, its temperature will not change but it will begin to boil, that is, change into a vapour. During this stage there will be a very large increase in volume as the liquid changes into a vapour. When all the water has boiled, the temperature of the vapour will begin to increase at which point the vapour is termed a gas.

Melting and boiling are two processes when an energy input to a substance does not cause a change in temperature.

12.2 MELTING POINTS AND BOILING POINTS

The temperature at which a solid changes into a liquid is called the melting point of the substance.

The temperature at which a liquid changes into a vapour is called the boiling point of the substance.

If a substance is not pure, that is, it contains impurities, its melting point is lowered. This is why we use anti-freeze in car radiators and why salt is spread on roads in winter. The impurity lowers the melting point of the mixture. This means that the mixture will melt or become a liquid at a much lower temperature than it would do if the substance were pure.

As well as lowering the melting point of a pure substance, an impurity also increases the boiling point. If salt is added to water the boiling point of the mixture will be above 100°C.

12.3 CONDENSATION AND SOLIDIFICATION

We have discussed what happens when heat is supplied to very cold ice in order to change it into a gas. We may carry out the process in reverse. If a gas is cooled by extracting heat when it reaches its boiling point, it will condense to a liquid. In the same way, when the liquid reaches its melting point, it will freeze or turn into a solid.

Because of this, we may refer to the boiling point as the condensation point and we may refer to the melting point as the freezing point.

It is usual then to say that impurities lower the freezing point rather than the melting point of a substance. As an example, salt lowers the freezing point of water.

12.4 LATENT HEAT

The heat which is used to melt or boil a substance does not produce the temperature rise which heat usually does. From this point of view the heat is hidden or latent.

The heat needed to melt or vaporize a substance is known as latent heat. In order to melt a substance we must supply latent heat of fusion and in order to vaporize a substance we must supply latent heat of vaporization.

What happens to this latent heat? In the case of fusion, it enables the atoms to break free from the regular lattice structure. The heat enables them to break free from the intermolecular forces and it therefore increases their potential energy. In the case of vaporization, the latent heat enables the molecules to escape from the intermolecular forces and allows them to move around independently. Once again their potential energy is increased. Additionally the vapour has to do work in pushing back the atmosphere as a result of the expansion.

A melting or boiling process is known as a change of phase. In such a change of phase, the heat supplied increases the molecular potential energy. When heat is usually supplied to a substance, it increases the molecular kinetic energy and causes an increase in temperature.

Large amounts of latent heat are required to melt or boil substances. This is why ice is very effective at cooling drinks and kettles, once they are hot, take a long time to boil dry.

12.5 COOLING CURVES

The melting point of a substance may be found from a cooling curve.

If a liquid is cooled, the heat loss will cause the temperature to fall until it reaches its freezing point. Its temperature will remain steady then until it has all solidified. During this process it will lose its latent heat but its temperature stays the same. When all the substance has solidified, it will continue to lose heat but its temperature will now begin to fall.

In order to find the melting point, which is the same as the freezing point, of a substance such as acetamide, we would place some solid in a test tube which is then placed in a beaker of water. The water is gently heated until all the solid has melted and its temperature has risen slightly.

The tube is then removed from the water and inserted in a clamp. The thermometer is firmly clamped in the liquid, as shown in Fig. 12.1.

FIG. 12.1

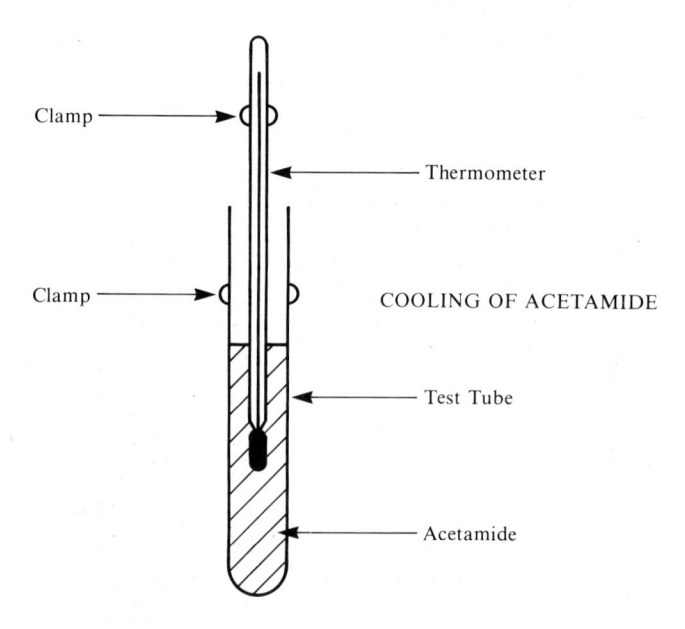

COOLING OF ACETAMIDE

A clock is started and the temperature is taken every minute until it has fallen to about 70°C.

A graph is then drawn of temperature versus time, as in Fig. 12.2.

FIG. 12.2

```
TEMPERATURE (°C)
   |
   |\
   | \
   |  \
   M.P.◄---_____
   |              \
   |               \_____
   |_____►
              TIME (min)
```

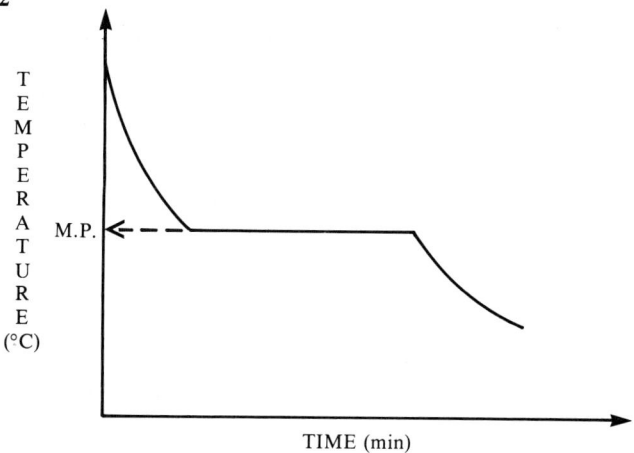

The melting point is read off from the horizontal part of the graph, shown by M.P.

12.6 THE REFRIGERATOR

Usually heat flows from a warm place to a cold place. The refrigerator makes heat move in the opposite direction.

A refrigerator is shown in Fig. 12.3.

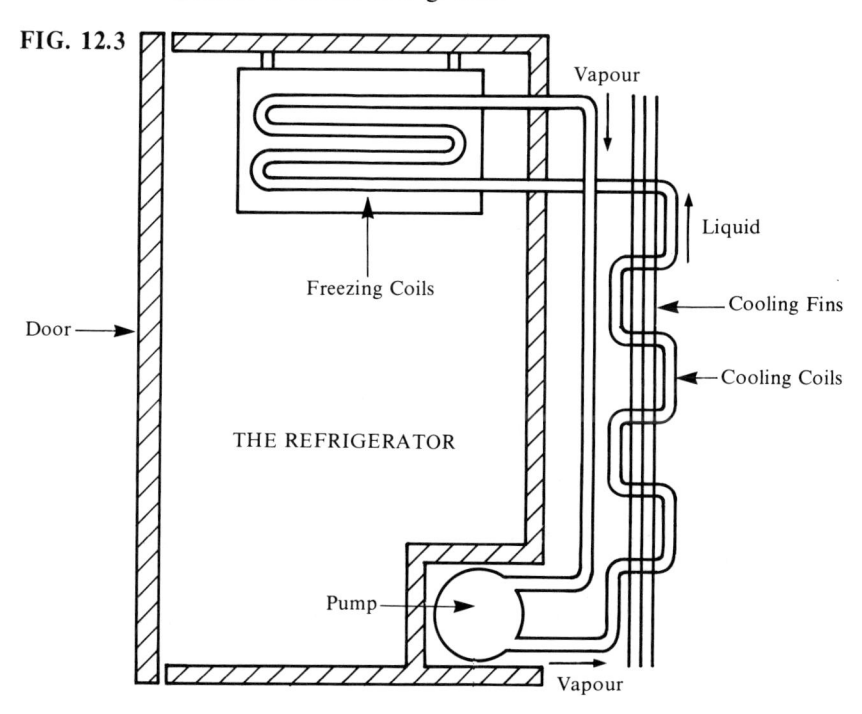

FIG. 12.3

THE REFRIGERATOR

Labels: Door, Freezing Coils, Vapour, Liquid, Cooling Fins, Cooling Coils, Pump, Vapour

The freezing coils contain a volatile liquid that is one which has a low boiling point and evaporates easily at room temperature. This liquid vaporizes and takes latent heat from its surroundings, causing the air at the top to cool. A cold convection current is set up (see Chapter 13). The electric pump removes this vapour and forces it through the cooling coils. Here the vapour is compressed and liquefied giving out latent heat of vaporization to the surroundings. The cooling fins help the cooling coils to cool. The liquid returns to the freezing coils and the cycle is repeated.

The temperature is controlled by a thermostat.

SUPPLEMENTARY

12.7 BOILING AND EVAPORATION

In both boiling and evaporation, molecules escape from a liquid. However, there are important differences between the two processes.

Evaporation occurs at all temperatures, involves a loss of surface molecules only and results in a cooling of the remaining liquid.

Boiling only occurs at the boiling point, involves a loss of molecules from the bulk of the liquid and does not involve a cooling of the liquid since heat is being supplied. At the boiling point the pressure exerted by the vapour is equal to the atmospheric pressure and so the temperature of the boiling point varies with atmospheric pressure. As the atmospheric pressure increases so does the temperature of the boiling point.

12.8 SPECIFIC LATENT HEATS

(i) We have seen that latent heat of fusion is needed to melt a substance and latent heat of vaporization is needed to vaporize a substance.

(ii) The amount of heat needed to change 1kg from the solid to the liquid state, with no change in temperature, is known as the specific latent heat of fusion of the substance.

So, for a given mass of substance:

Heat required = Mass of substance × Specific latent heat of fusion

We use the symbol L for specific latent heat of fusion and so the heat needed W to melt m is given by

$$W = mL$$

W is measured in joules, J, and mass is measured in kilograms, kg, and so specific latent heat of fusion is measured in joules/kilogram or J/kg.

PROBLEM
CALCULATE THE AMOUNT OF HEAT NEEDED TO MELT 10g OF ICE IF $L = 3.4 \times 10^5$ J/kg.

Use $\quad\quad\quad\quad W = mL$
$\quad\quad\quad\quad\quad\quad m = 10g = 10^{-2}$ kg, $L = 3.4 \times 10^5$ J/kg
So $\quad\quad\quad\quad W = 10^{-2} \times 3.4 \times 10^5 = 3.4 \times 10^3$ J

ANSWER: AMOUNT OF HEAT REQUIRED = 3.4 kJ.

The high value of the specific latent heat of fusion of ice is the reason why it is far more effective to add ice at 0°C to a drink instead of water at 0°C.

(iii) The amount of heat needed to change 1 kg from the liquid to the vapour state, with no change in temperature, is known as the specific latent heat of vaporization of the substance.
So, for a given mass of substance

Heat required = Mass of substance × Specific latent heat of vaporization

As in the case of specific latent heat of fusion, we use the symbol L. The units are also the same, joules/kilogram or J/kg.

PROBLEM
CALCULATE THE AMOUNT OF HEAT NEEDED TO VAPORIZE 0.5 kg OF WATER IF $L = 2.3 \times 10^6$ J/kg.

Use $\quad\quad\quad\quad W = mL$
$\quad\quad\quad\quad\quad\quad m = 0.5$ kg, $L = 2.3 \times 10^6$ J/kg
So $\quad\quad\quad\quad W = 0.5 \times 2.3 \times 10^6 = 1.15 \times 10^6$ J

ANSWER: AMOUNT OF HEAT REQUIRED = 1.15 MJ.

The high value of the specific latent heat of vaporization of water is the reason why steam will burn you far more severely than boiling water at 100°C.

In order to change ice at 0°C into vapour at 100°C, the heat required, W, is given by

$\quad\quad\quad\quad\quad W = mL_F + mc \times 100 + mL_V$
where $\quad\quad\quad m$ = mass of ice or water
$\quad\quad\quad\quad\quad c$ = specific heat capacity of water
$\quad\quad\quad\quad\quad L_F$ = specific latent heat of fusion
$\quad\quad\quad\quad\quad L_V$ = specific latent heat of vaporization.

12.9 MEASUREMENTS OF SPECIFIC LATENT HEATS IN THE LABORATORY

In order to measure the specific latent heat of fusion of ice we use the apparatus shown in Fig. 12.4.

FIG. 12.4

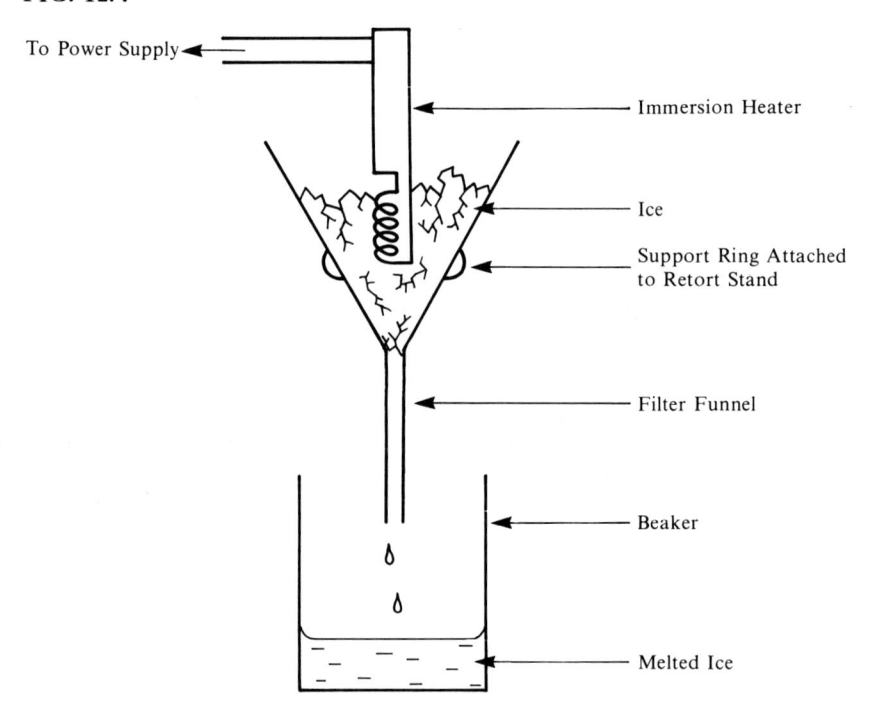

DETERMINATION OF THE SPECIFIC LATENT HEAT OF FUSION OF ICE

The empty beaker of known mass is placed under the funnel, the heater is switched on and the clock started. After a suitable amount of time, say 5 minutes, the heater is switched off, the clock stopped and the new mass of beaker and water obtained in order to give the mass of the water formed by the ice melting, m.

We use $\quad W = mL$
with $\quad\quad W = Pt$
where $\quad\;$ P = wattage of heater, t = time of heating in seconds.

In order to measure the specific latent heat of vaporization of water use the apparatus shown in Fig. 12.5.

FIG. 12.5

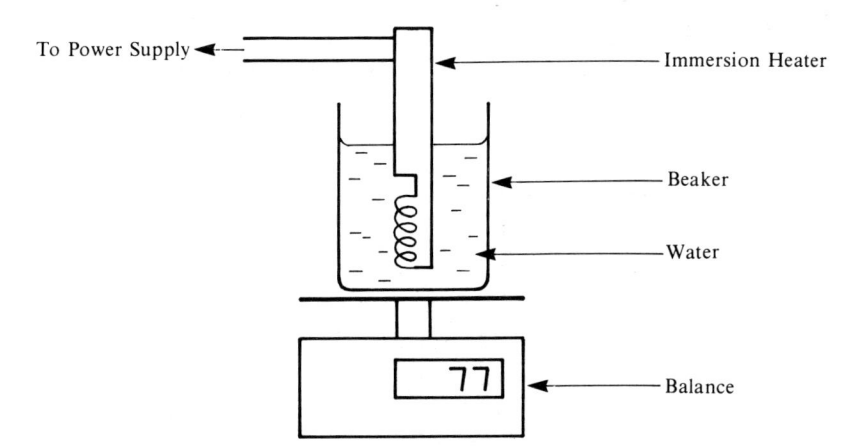

DETERMINATION OF THE SPECIFIC LATENT HEAT
OF VAPORIZATION OF WATER

When the water is boiling steadily, the balance reading is noted and the clock started. After a suitable amount of time, depending on the power of the heater, the heater is switched off and the new balance reading noted. The difference between the balance readings gives the mass of water vaporized, m.

We use W = mL
with W = Pt
where P = wattage of heater, t = time of heating in seconds.

QUESTIONS

CORE

1. Alcohol freezes at −115°C. What state would you expect it to be in at −120°C?
2. Mercury boils at 357°C. What state would you expect it to be in at 101°C?
3. The temperature of pure melting ice is
   A   −273K
   B   0K
   C   100K
   D   273K   *(S.E.G.)*
4. Some water freezes at −5°C. What would you expect the boiling point to be?
5. Explain how the cooling curve of salt water differs from that of pure water.

SUPPLEMENTARY

6. State two reasons why the boiling point of water may be higher than 100°C.
7. A 2kW electric kettle is left on for 3 minutes. What mass of water is boiled off in this time if $L = 2.3 \times 10^6$ J/kg?
8. Calculate the amount of heat given out when 10^{-2} kg of steam at 100°C condenses and the water formed cools to 50°C. Assume $L = 2.3 \times 10^6$ J/kg, $c = 4200$ J/kg°C.

Chapter 13
THE TRANSFER OF HEAT

At the end of this chapter you will know:
CORE: the three methods and mechanisms of heat transfer; applications of conduction, convection and radiation and the principle of operation of the heat engine.
SUPPLEMENTARY: about the molecular theory of conduction.

CORE

13.1 CONDUCTION

(i) If we place a teaspoon in a hot cup of coffee, the handle of the spoon very quickly becomes hot. The heat travels along the spoon to the handle by a method known as conduction.

When heat travels through a substance by conduction, the substance itself does not move.

(ii) Conduction occurs in solids, liquids and gases. Solids are better conductors than liquids and gases with metals being better conductors than other solids.

If two objects, both at the same temperature less than body temperature, with one being a metal and the other a non-metal, are touched, the metal will feel colder. This is because the metal will conduct heat away from the body more quickly than the non-metal.

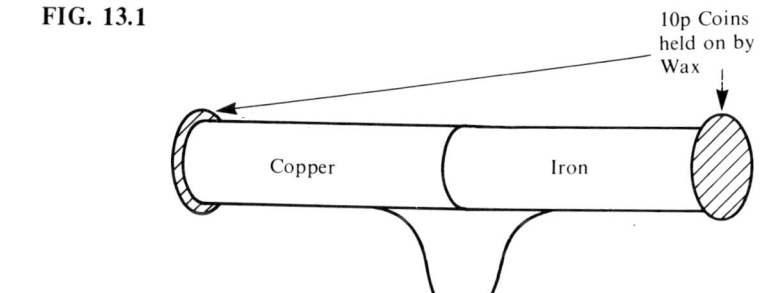

FIG. 13.1

DEMONSTRATION OF CONDUCTING PROPERTIES

160 The Transfer of Heat

In the following list, some substances are arranged with the best conductor first and the worst last: copper, aluminium, iron, brick, glass, water, polythene, air, plaster, expanded polystyrene.

(iii) In order to compare the conducting properties of a solid, we can use the apparatus shown in Fig. 13.1.

We use two metal rods, here copper and iron. They are both the same size and are joined together. At the other end of each rod, a 10p coin is held by wax. A bunsen burner is used to heat the rods at their join. The coin stuck to the better conductor will drop off first. Here it would be the copper.

(iv) In order to show that water is a poor conductor, we use the experiment shown in Fig. 13.2.

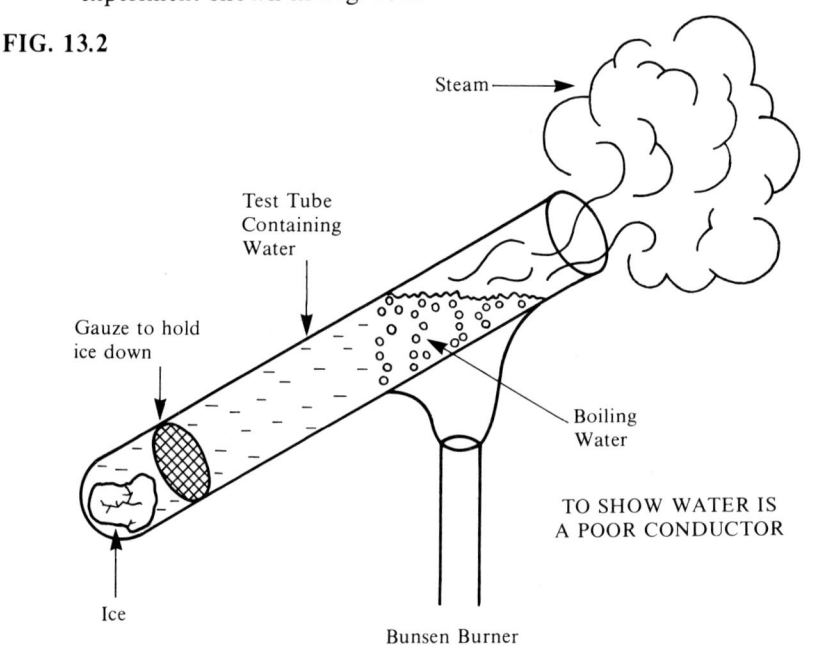

FIG. 13.2

TO SHOW WATER IS A POOR CONDUCTOR

The water at the top of the tube is boiling but the ice remains at the bottom. This shows that very little heat is conducted through the water.

13.2 THE RATE AT WHICH HEAT IS CONDUCTED THROUGH A SUBSTANCE

The amount of heat conducted every second through a substance depends upon four things:
1) the type of material — whether or not it is a good conductor.

2) the thickness of the material, x.
3) the temperature difference across the thickness, $\theta = \theta_1 - \theta_2$, and
4) the area of the substance, A.

These dimensions are shown in Fig. 13.3.

FIG. 13.3

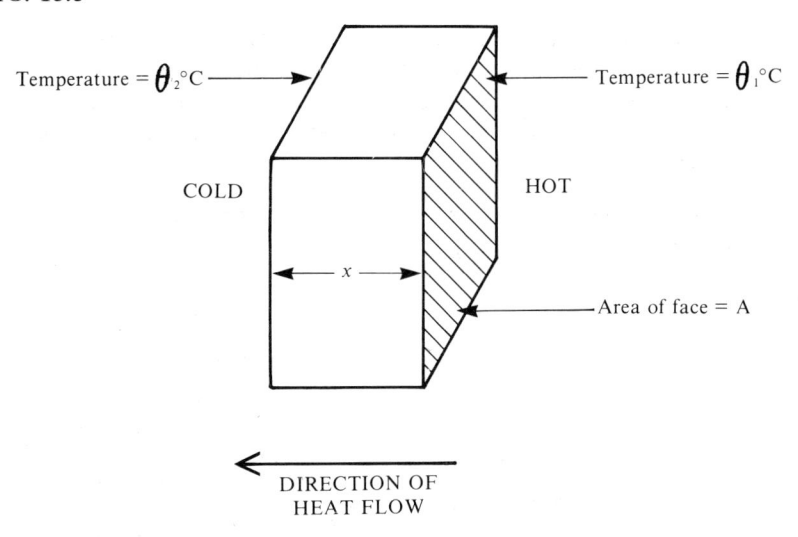

Temperature = θ_2°C

Temperature = θ_1°C

COLD

HOT

x

Area of face = A

DIRECTION OF HEAT FLOW

For any particular material, the heat conducted every second will be increased by having large A and Θ and small x.

13.3 CONVECTION

(i) Convection is the movement of heat through a substance by movement of the substance itself.

Obviously because a solid is rigid and cannot move, convection can only take place in liquids and gases, i.e. fluids.

(ii) To demonstrate convection in a liquid we use the apparatus shown in Fig. 13.4.

The flask containing a crystal of potassium permanganate in water is gently heated. Heat travels through the liquid by convection and this can be seen by the purple streaks. In fact the warmer liquid expands and becomes less dense. The surrounding denser liquid then pushes it upwards, just like denser water pushes up a cork which is held under its surface.

These fluid movements are called convection currents. In order for convection to take place we need these differences in density.

FIG. 13.4

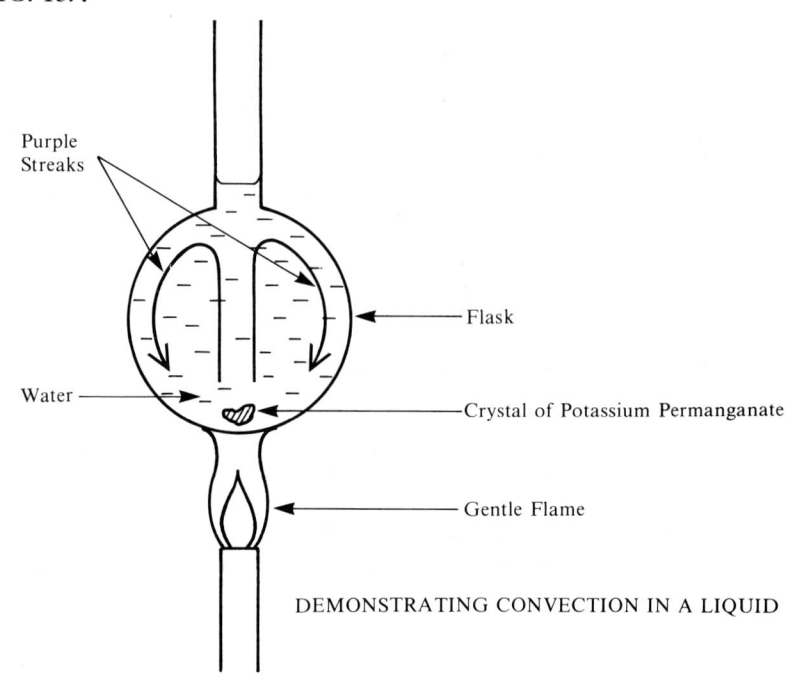

```
                    Purple
                    Streaks

                                          Flask

         Water                            Crystal of Potassium Permanganate

                                          Gentle Flame

              DEMONSTRATING CONVECTION IN A LIQUID
```

13.4 RADIATION

(i) Radiation is the transfer of heat from one place to another by means of electromagnetic waves known as infra-red waves.

We have seen that we need a substance in order that conduction and convection can take place. However, we do not need a substance in order that radiation can take place. Radiation, in fact, can travel through a vacuum and this is the way in which heat travels to the earth from the sun.

(ii) Radiation can be detected in three ways:
1) by our body — it makes us feel warm.
2) by a thermocouple — it generates a current.
3) by a thermistor — it lowers its electrical resistance.

13.5 EMITTERS AND ABSORBERS OF RADIATION

Dull black surfaces are better absorbers of radiation than shiny white surfaces. This can be shown using the experiment in Fig. 13.5.

We use two metal plates one with a side painted shiny white and one with a side painted dull black. A coin is stuck on each of these

FIG. 13.5

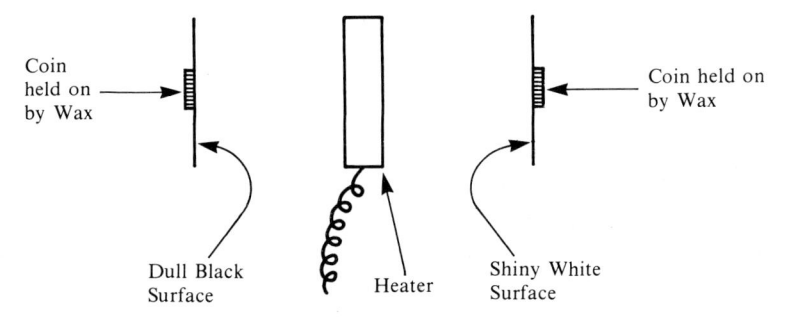

```
Coin                                              Coin held on
held on  →                           ←            by Wax
by Wax

         Dull Black        Heater    Shiny White
         Surface                     Surface

              COMPARISON OF ABSORBERS
```

surfaces with wax. A heater is placed half way between the plates. We find that the first coin to fall off is the one on the dull black surface.

Dull black surfaces are also better emitters of radiation than shiny white ones. To see this we use the experiments shown in Fig. 13.6.

FIG. 13.6

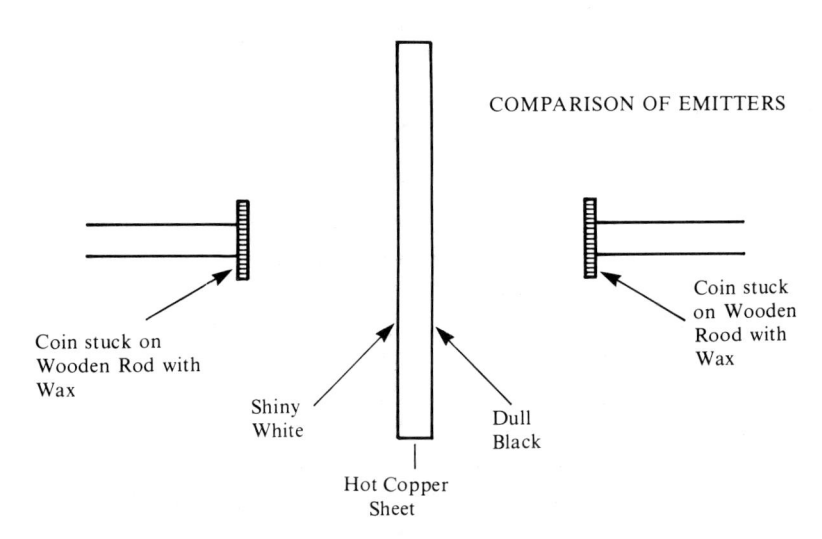

COMPARISON OF EMITTERS

```
                                                  Coin stuck
Coin stuck on                                     on Wooden
Wooden Rod with                                   Rood with
Wax                                               Wax
           Shiny           Dull
           White           Black
                Hot Copper
                Sheet
```

The coin facing the dull black surface falls first.

We can see, then, that good absorbers are also good emitters and poor absorbers are poor emitters.

164 The Transfer of Heat

13.6 APPLICATIONS OF CONDUCTION, CONVECTION AND RADIATION

(i) CONDUCTION

Woollen clothes keep us warm because they trap a layer of poorly conducting air next to our bodies.

Pan handles should be made out of plastic so heat is not conducted to our hands. The pans themselves should be made of thin metal. Photographs 12 and 13 show some modern pans. The shiny ones will radiate less heat.

PHOTOGRAPH 12 *Acknowledgement: Swan Housewares.*

PHOTOGRAPH 13 *Acknowledgement: Swan Housewares.*

In double glazing we make an air-glass sandwich, as shown in Fig. 13.7.

FIG. 13.7

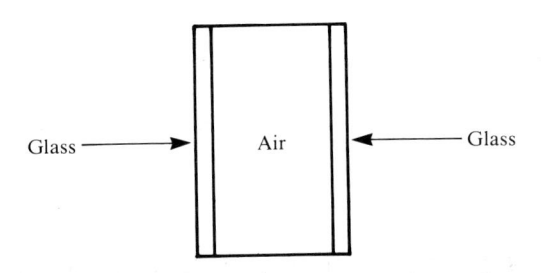

Glass → | Air | ← Glass

The air inside prevents conduction of heat to the outside. In a normal window more heat is conducted through the single sheet of glass. You should note that only about 15% of the heat lost from a house is through the windows.

In roof insulation, layers of poorly conducting glass wool are laid between the joists in the loft. This prevents the main heat loss mechanism.

Heat loss through house walls is reduced by having a layer of air between the outside and inside wall. It is reduced even more by filling the space with plastic foam because convection currents are eliminated.

(ii) CONVECTION

A domestic hot water system makes use of convection. A typical system is shown in Fig. 13.8.

Hot water rises from the top of the boiler to the top of the hot water tank. Cold water from the bottom of the hot tank flows to the bottom of the boiler to replace it. A convection current is set up. Hot water is drawn off from the top of the hot tank and is replaced by cold water entering at the bottom.

The expansion pipe allows the escape of dissolved air and the escape of steam if the water boils. The ballcock allows water from the mains to enter the cold tank.

Gliders and hand-gliders make use of convection currents in air known as thermals.

Extractor fans should always be positioned as high as possible in a room.

FIG. 13.8

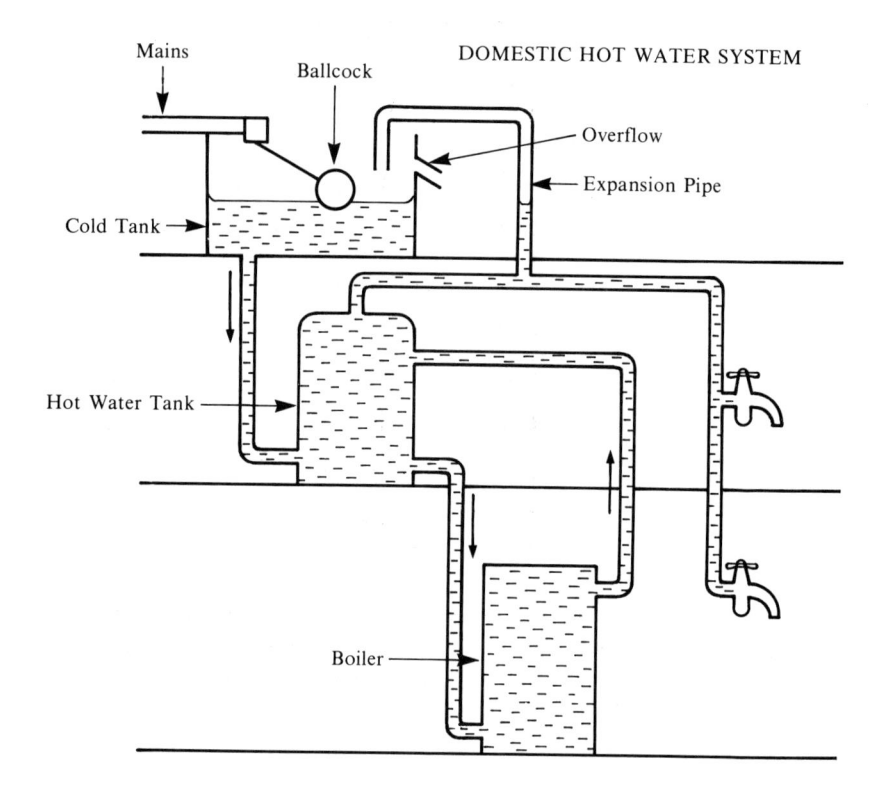

Mains
Ballcock
DOMESTIC HOT WATER SYSTEM
Overflow
Expansion Pipe
Cold Tank
Hot Water Tank
Boiler

(iii) RADIATION

Buildings in hot countries are painted white to reflect heat. Most heaters called radiators are in fact convectors. They should really be painted black. Reflectors in electric fires are made from shiny metal.

In greenhouses, radiation from the sun enters and raises the temperature. The plants absorb radiation and re-radiate the radiation in a different form which cannot escape from the glass. Glass does not allow ultra-violet light from the sun to pass through it and so you cannot get a sun-tan in a greenhouse.

A vacuum or Thermos flask keeps hot liquids hot and cold liquids cold. A flask is shown in Fig. 13.9.

FIG. 13.9

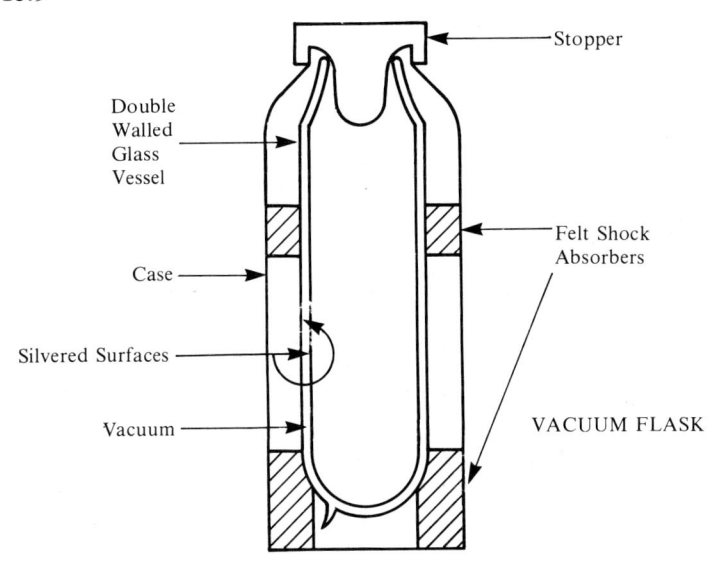

```
                    Stopper
Double
Walled
Glass
Vessel
                    Felt Shock
                    Absorbers
Case

Silvered Surfaces

Vacuum              VACUUM FLASK
```

Conduction and convection are reduced by the double walls with a vacuum between them. Radiation is reduced by silvering both walls on the inside. Slight conduction takes place up the walls.

13.7 THE HEAT ENGINE

In a heat engine mechanical work is extracted from a high temperature gas which is then discharged from the engine at a lower temperature. The four stroke petrol engine or internal combustion engine, is a good example.

A four stroke petrol engine is shown in Fig. 13.10.

On the intake stroke shown, the piston moves down, reducing the pressure in the cylinder. The inlet valve opens allowing in a petrol-air mixture from the carburettor.

On the compression stroke, both valves close and the cylinder moves up and compresses the mixture.

On the power stroke, a spark from the plug explodes the mixture, generating a high temperature and forces the piston down.

On the exhaust stroke, the outlet valve opens and the piston rises, forcing the cooler exhaust gases out of the cylinder.

The motion of the piston is passed to the driving system via the crankshaft.

FIG. 13.10

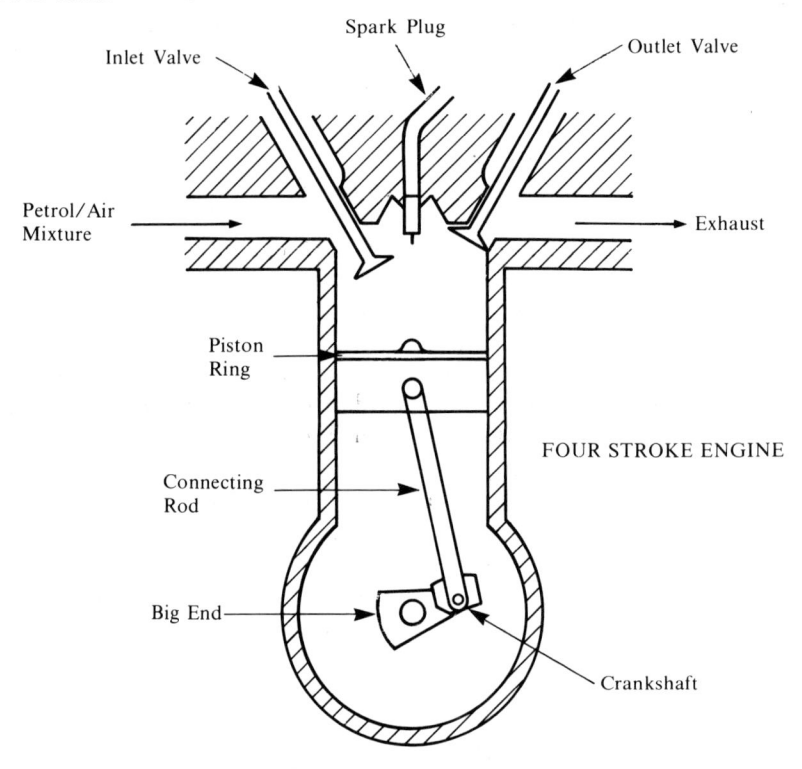

Spark Plug, Inlet Valve, Outlet Valve, Petrol/Air Mixture, Exhaust, Piston Ring, Connecting Rod, Big End, Crankshaft

FOUR STROKE ENGINE

SUPPLEMENTARY

13.8 THE MOLECULAR THEORY OF CONDUCTION

In solids which are good conductors, i.e. metals, the heat is conducted by hot electrons moving through the metal. A small amount of heat is carried by the lattice atoms being made to vibrate over greater distances.

In solids which are poor conductors only the small amount of heat carried by the lattice atoms is able to be transferred.

QUESTIONS

CORE

1. Energy may be transferred through a vacuum by
    - A conduction only
    - B convection only
    - C radiation only
    - D convection and radiation.

(S.E.G.)

2. Two liquids are spilt on the hand. One is alcohol, the other is water, and both are at the same temperature. The alcohol feels colder because alcohol
   - A has a higher boiling point than water
   - B is a worse conductor of heat than water
   - C has a higher specific latent heat of vaporization than water
   - D evaporates more readily than water *(S.E.G.)*
3. In cold weather the metal handlebars of a bicycle feel colder to the hands than the plastic handgrips. This is because
   - A the metal is at a colder temperature than the plastic
   - B the plastic contains more heat energy than the metal
   - C the metal conducts heat better than the plastic
   - D the plastic is a good radiator of heat. *(L.E.A.G.)*
4. (a) (i) Name three ways by which heat energy can be transferred.
    (ii) Which is the main method of heat transfer in each of the following cases?
      - (A) Heat energy reaching us from the sun
      - (B) Heating water in an electric kettle
      - (C) Heating a room using central heating radiators.
   (b) Fig. 3 shows a pudding which has been cooked in an oven at 200°C for a time of fifteen minutes.

FIG. 3

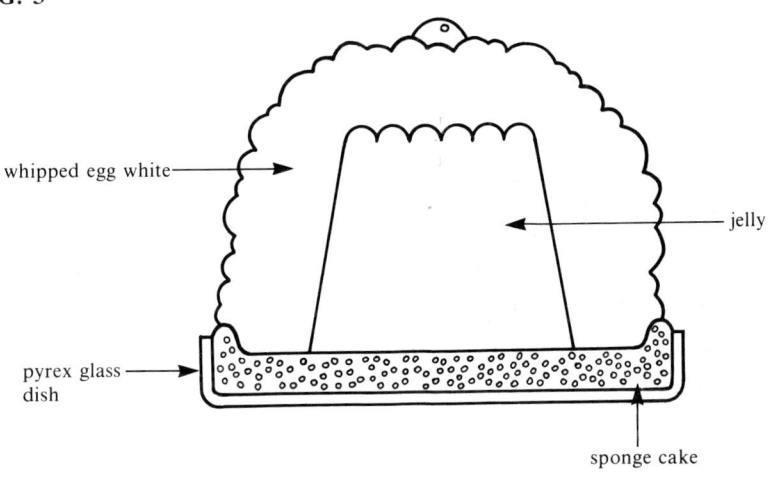

whipped egg white

jelly

pyrex glass dish

sponge cake

(i) Explain why the jelly has not melted.
(ii) The oven elements have a total power of 2kW. The elements are switched on for a total time of 15 minutes. If the cost of electricity is 6p per kilowatt hour, calculate the cost of cooking the pudding. *(N.E.A.)*

(The student is recommended to leave b(ii) until Chapter 24).

SUPPLEMENTARY
5. In Fig. 13.2, why is the water heated at the top?
6. Name a metal in which heat could be transferred by convection.

Chapter 14
WAVES

At the end of this chapter you will know:

CORE: what is meant by wave motion and that waves transfer energy; what is meant by the speed, frequency, wavelength and amplitude of waves; the relationship between speed, frequency and wavelength, what is meant by plane waves, circular waves and wavefronts; how a ripple tank may be used to show reflection and refraction at a plane boundary, interference and diffraction and the difference between transverse and longitudinal waves.

SUPPLEMENTARY: how plane waves are reflected from a circular boundary and circular waves from a plane boundary; how the refraction of plane wavefronts at a plane boundary results from a change in speed and how diffraction may be explained.

CORE

14.1 WAVE MOTION

FIG. 14.1

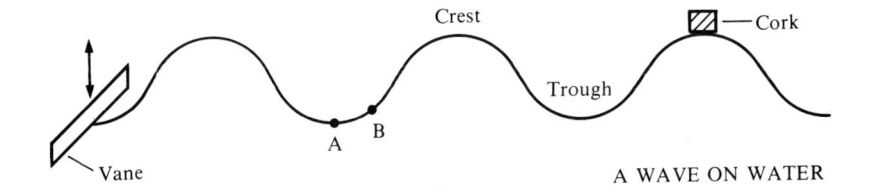

A WAVE ON WATER

Suppose that a vane is gently dipped in and out of a pool of water, as shown in Fig. 14.1. We will see a series of troughs and crests on the water surface.

The water surface is moving up and down but each bit of the surface is slightly out of step with the next bit. As an example of this consider position A. An instant later it will have moved up a little. Position B will have moved down a little and as a result the trough will have moved along from A to B. All the other troughs and crests will have moved along by the same amount and so the shape of the water surface appears to move along. This disturbance of the surface which is moving along is known as a wave.

As the vane moves up and down its potential energy changes. The wave which it makes will cause a cork on the water surface to also

172 Waves

move up and down, changing its potential energy. We can see that a wave transfers energy from one place to another. Obviously, because they transfer energy, waves such as this can sometimes do damage.

The water surface is just moving up and down, with its average position being its normal rest position when the water surface is left alone. The wave is moving along to the right. It is called a transverse wave. In a transverse wave, the substance or medium being disturbed moves at right angles to the direction of travel or propagation of the wave.

We can represent the motion of a transverse wave using the equipment shown in Photograph 14.

PHOTOGRAPH 14   *Acknowledgement: Philip Harris Ltd.*

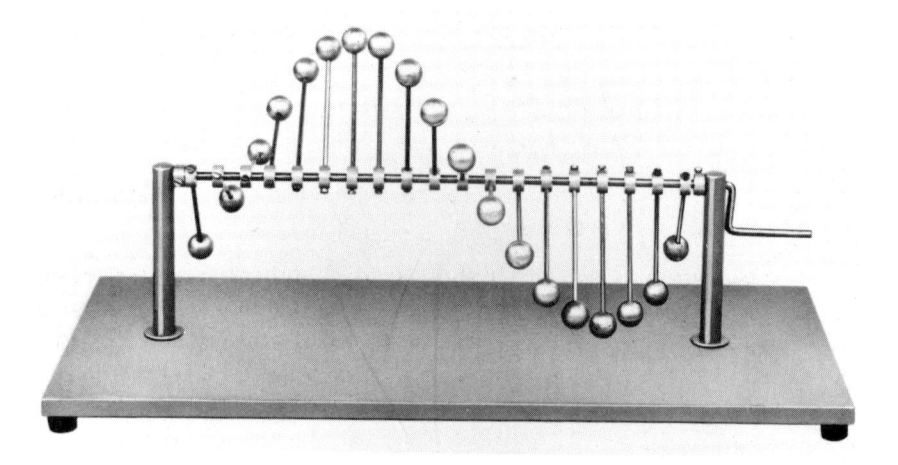

The balls are at the end of equal length rods, but the rods are rotated on the spindle so that at both ends the rods are pointing downwards with all the others being displaced by about 20°. When the handle is turned we see the rods edge-on. They all appear to move up and down but each slightly out of step with their neighbours. We will see a transverse wave move along.

Other examples of transverse waves are light and a rope being shaken up and down.

14.2 SPEED, WAVELENGTH, FREQUENCY, AMPLITUDE AND PERIOD

(i) The speed of a wave is the distance which it travels in one second. We represent it with the symbol v.

(ii)

FIG. 14.2

WAVELENGTH AND AMPLITUDE

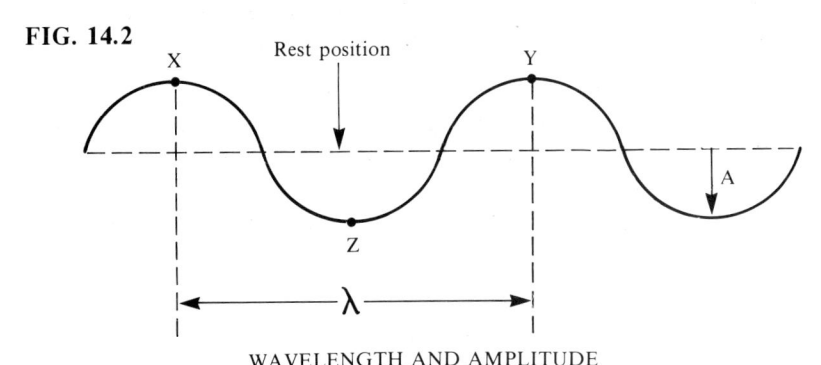

On Fig. 14.2, X and Y are in step. They are both at the top of their motion and will now begin to move downwards. We say that they are in-phase.

But Z is at the bottom of its motion and is about to move upwards. We say that Z is out of phase or in anti-phase with X and Y.

If two points are neither in phase nor out of phase we say that a phase difference exists between them.

Now as well as X and Y being in phase with each other, they will be in phase with all other points at the top of the crests. The shortest distance between two in-phase points, such as X and Y, is called the wavelength of the wave. We represent it with the Greek letter lambda, λ. The actual wave is made up of a repeated pattern of wavelengths.

(iii) The number of complete wavelengths passing by a particular position in one second is called the frequency of the wave. It is measured in hertz, symbol Hz, and we represent it with the letter f.

If we consider Fig. 14.1 again, we can see that each time the vane makes one complete vibration it will generate one wavelength. So the frequency of the wave, which is the number of waves passing a point every second, will also be the same as the number of vibrations made every second by the vibrating object.

(iv) The distance from the trough to the rest position, or from the crest to the rest position is called the amplitude of the wave, shown by A in Fig. 14.2. The amplitude of a wave is the maximum displacement of the particles from the rest position.

(v) The time for one wave to pass is its period, T.

14.3 THE RELATIONSHIP BETWEEN SPEED, FREQUENCY AND WAVELENGTH

Each time an object vibrates, the wave it generates moves forward by one wavelength, as shown in Fig. 14.3.

FIG. 14.3

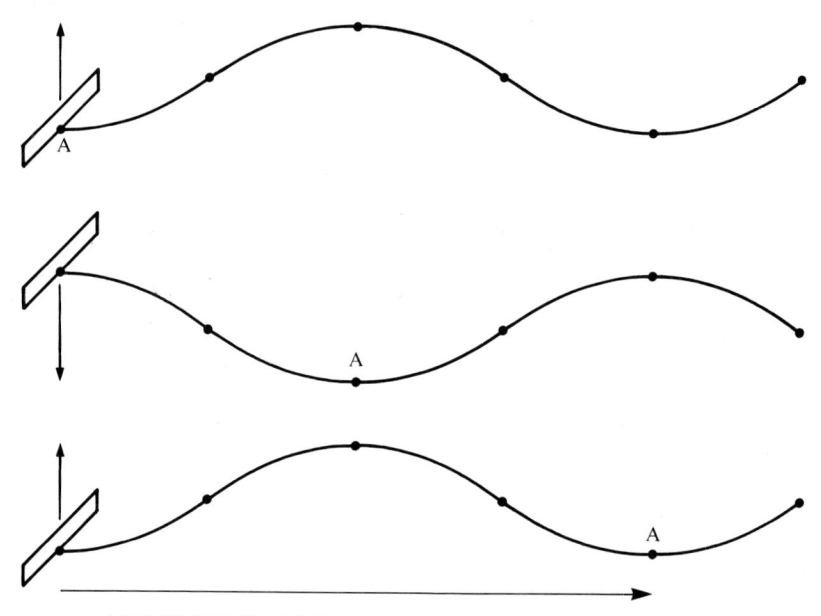

THE TROUGH 'A' HAS MOVED FORWARD BY ONE WAVELENGTH

If the object makes f vibrations every second, that is its frequency is f Hz then the distance moved by the waves will be $f\lambda$.

But this distance is moved in one second and so it must be the wave speed, v.

So wave speed = frequency × wavelength
or $v = f\lambda$

PROBLEM

A WAVE HAS A FREQUENCY OF 4 Hz. IF ITS WAVELENGTH IS 0.5m, CALCULATE ITS SPEED.

Using $v = f\lambda$
 $f = 4Hz$ $\lambda = 0.5m$
 $v = 4 \times 0.5 = 2m/s$

ANSWER: WAVE SPEED = 2m/s.

14.4 PLANE WAVES, CIRCULAR WAVES AND WAVEFRONTS

The waves which have been considered so far are called plane waves because they travel in straight lines.

If we replaced the vane in Fig. 14.1 with a round object, such as a ball bearing, circular waves would spread out from it.

It is often easier to represent waves by what are called wavefronts.

If we look at Fig. 14.1 from a different viewpoint we see Fig. 14.4.

FIG. 14.4

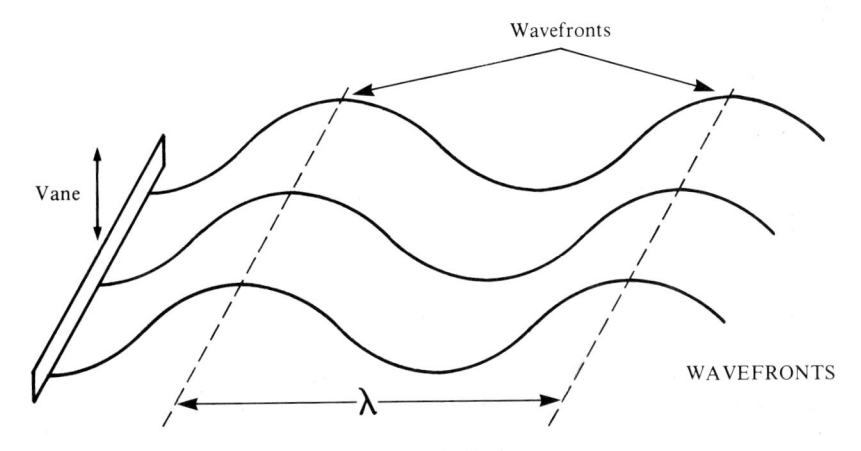

We can see waves starting out from each point on the vane. The wavefronts are the lines drawn through the waves at right angles to the direction of the waves and one wavelength apart. Waves do not need to be drawn, but can be completely represented by wavefronts.

In the case of circular waves, the wavefronts are a series of concentric circles, each one wavelength apart, as shown in Fig. 14.5.

14.5 THE RIPPLE TANK

(i) In order to investigate waves, we can use a ripple tank, as shown in Fig. 14.6.

This is a clear glass tray on legs. Below it is a screen and above it is a lamp.

The tray contains water. Suspended above the tray, from a support, is a vane and motor. Two adjustable balls are attached to the vane. When the motor is switched on and the balls are twisted sideways, as in Fig. 14.6, the vane dips in and out of the water and generates

176 Waves

FIG. 14.5

CIRCULAR WAVEFRONTS — Wavefronts

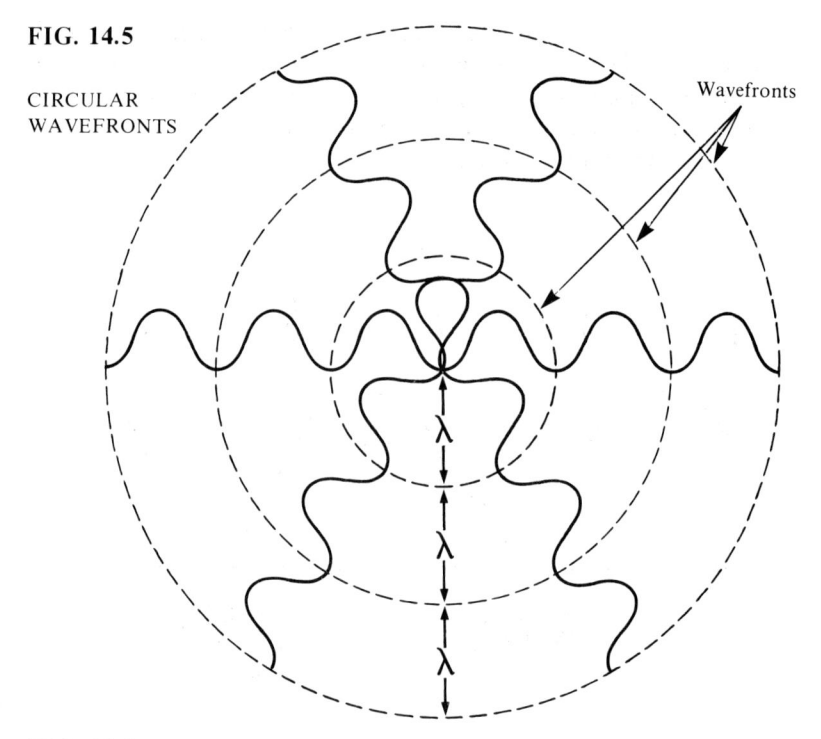

λ

FIG. 14.6

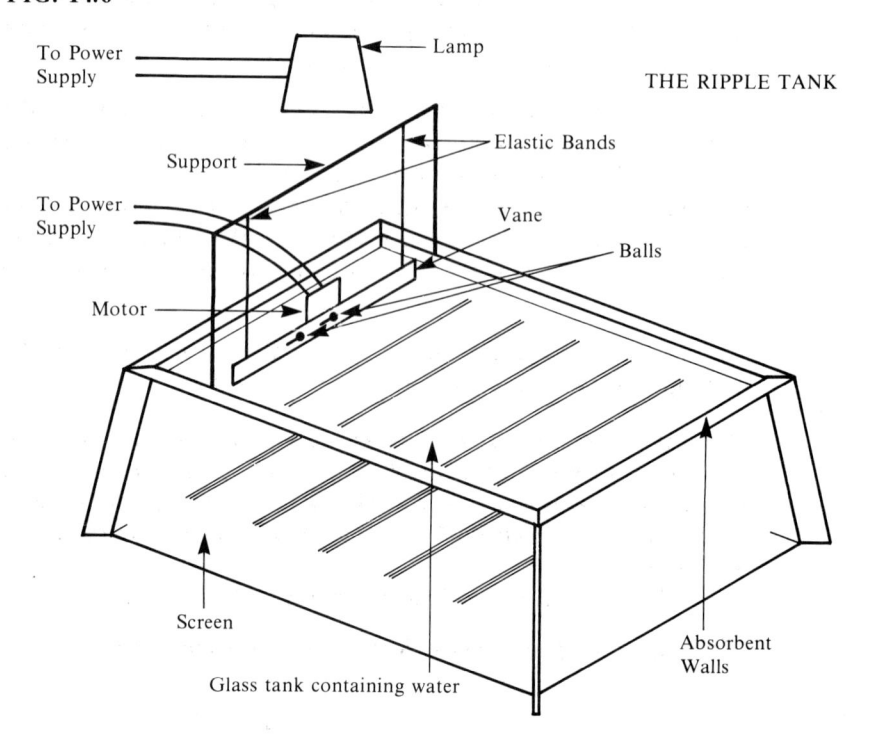

THE RIPPLE TANK

To Power Supply — Lamp
Support — Elastic Bands
To Power Supply
Motor
Vane
Balls
Screen
Glass tank containing water
Absorbent Walls

transverse waves on the water. A pattern of light and dark bands will be seen on the screen. Where there are troughs, the water will be shallower, more light will pass through and so we will see bright bands. Where there are crests, the water will be deeper, less light will pass through and we will see dark bands. This is shown in Fig. 14.7.

FIG. 14.7

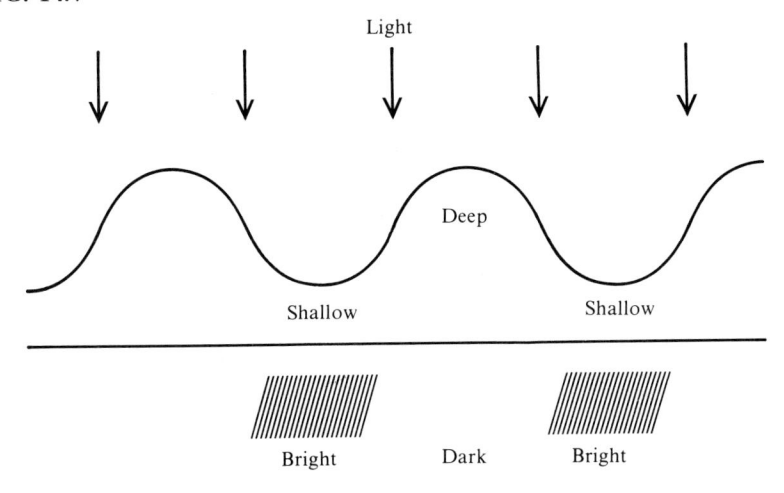

Light

Deep

Shallow   Shallow

Bright   Dark   Bright

We can see from this diagram that the bright bands are one wavelength apart and are at right angles to the direction in which the wave is moving — in other words they are wavefronts.

We can find the frequency of the vane by reading the frequency of the motor drive. If we use a special flashing light called a stroboscope we can "freeze" the waves. They will appear to be stopped when the frequency of the light is the same as the waves. We can, then, find the frequency of the waves. We would find that the frequency of these waves would be the same as the frequency of the vane, just as we would expect.

(ii) We can investigate reflection at a flat or plane boundary by placing a barrier in the tank, as shown in Fig. 14.8.

The dotted line at 90° to the barrier is called the normal. The angle between the direction of travel of the incident waves and this normal is called the angle of incidence, i. The angle between the normal and the direction of the reflected waves is called the angle of reflection, r. We find that

angle of incidence, i = angle of reflection, r.

(iii) Suppose we place a glass block in the tank, as shown in Fig. 14.9.

FIG. 14.8

Incoming or Incident Waves

Barrier or Boundary

Outgoing or Reflected Waves

REFLECTION AT A PLANE BOUNDARY

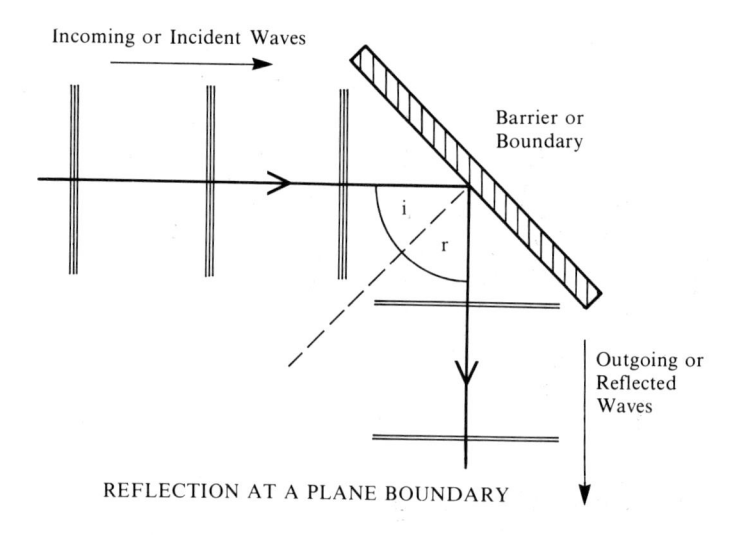

FIG. 14.9

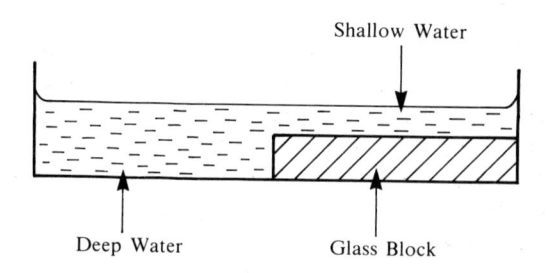

Shallow Water

Deep Water   Glass Block

REFRACTION AT A PLANE BOUNDARY (1)

Obviously the water over the glass block will be shallower than elsewhere. If we arrange for waves to strike the boundary between the deep and the shallow water at same angle of incidence, i, as shown in Fig. 14.10, we find two things:

1. When the waves pass into the shallow region they change direction.
2. In this shallow region, their wavelength is less.

This change of direction is called refraction. The angle between the normal to the boundary and the direction of travel of the refracted waves is called the angle of refraction, r.

FIG. 14.10

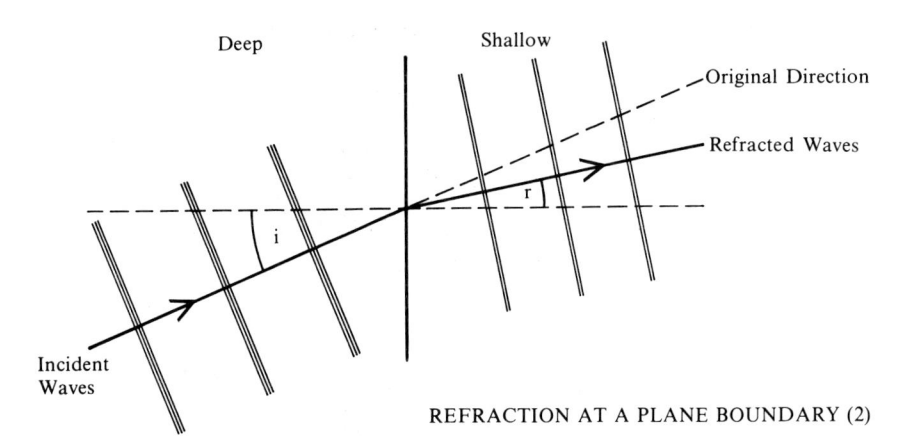

(Diagram: Refraction at a plane boundary showing incident waves in Deep region, refracted waves in Shallow region, with angles i and r, and original direction indicated by dashed line.)

REFRACTION AT A PLANE BOUNDARY (2)

14.6 INTERFERENCE AND DIFFRACTION

(i) Using the ripple tank we can investigate interference. We shorten the elastic bands to raise the vane and twist the balls so that they hang down.

When the motor is switched on, the balls generate circular waves which start out in phase. In some directions, the waves from one ball will have travelled extra distances of 1, 2, 3, 4 etc. wavelengths. The waves will combine and will be in phase and so they will add together to make a wave of double the amplitude. We say that they interfere constructively. In other directions, the waves from one ball will have travelled extra distances of $\frac{1}{2}$, $1\frac{1}{2}$, $2\frac{1}{2}$, $3\frac{1}{2}$ etc. wavelengths. The waves will now combine out of phase and will cancel each other out. We say that they interfere destructively. We will see an interference pattern, as shown in Fig. 14.11.

FIG. 14.11

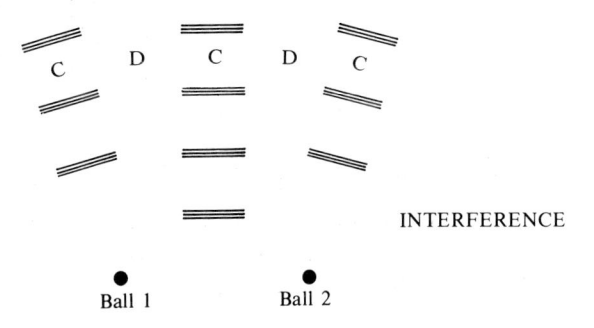

(Diagram showing Ball 1 and Ball 2 as two point sources with alternating directions labeled C, D, C, D, C for constructive and destructive interference.)

INTERFERENCE

C = Directions of Constructive Interference
D = Directions of Destructive Interference

180 Waves

The directions of constructive interference are the ones in which crests coincide and the directions of destructive interference are the ones in which a crest coincides with a trough.

(ii) If the waves are incident on a slit in a barrier, as in Fig. 14.12

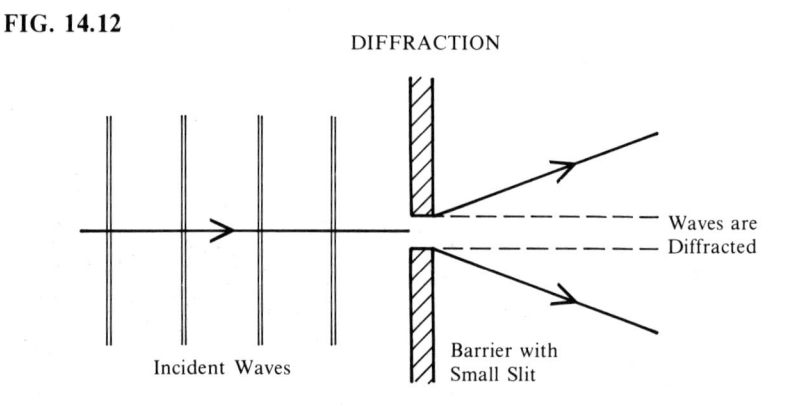

FIG. 14.12

DIFFRACTION

Incident Waves — Barrier with Small Slit — Waves are Diffracted

we would only expect those not blocked by the slit to carry on — that is we would only expect waves between the dotted lines. Everywhere else would be in "shadow". In fact if the slit is very narrow, that is only about the width of a few wavelengths at most, we find that the waves spread out into the shadow area. This bending or spreading out of waves into the shadow region after passing through a small opening, is called diffraction.

14.7 LONGITUDINAL WAVES

If a spring is fixed at one end and pulled in and out at the other end, as in Fig. 14.13, a wave travels down the spring.

FIG. 14.13

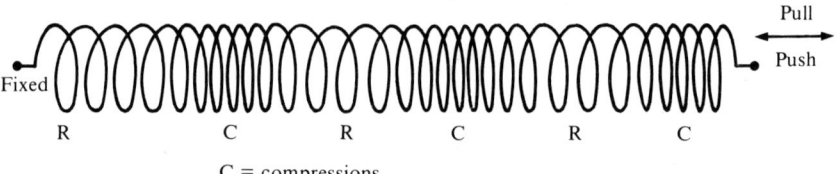

Fixed — R C R C R C — Pull / Push

C = compressions
R = rarefactions

LONGITUDINAL WAVES

The wave is not a series of troughs and crests but a series of squeezed coils, known as compressions, and stretched coils, known as rarefactions. Both compressions and rarefactions move along the length of the spring. This is an example of a longitudinal wave. In a longitudinal wave the direction of travel, or propagation, of the wave is the same direction as that of the disturbance of the medium. On the spring, the coils move horizontally and so does the wave motion.

We can represent the motion of a longitudinal wave using the equipment shown in Photograph 15.

PHOTOGRAPH 15 *Acknowledgement: Philip Harris Ltd.*

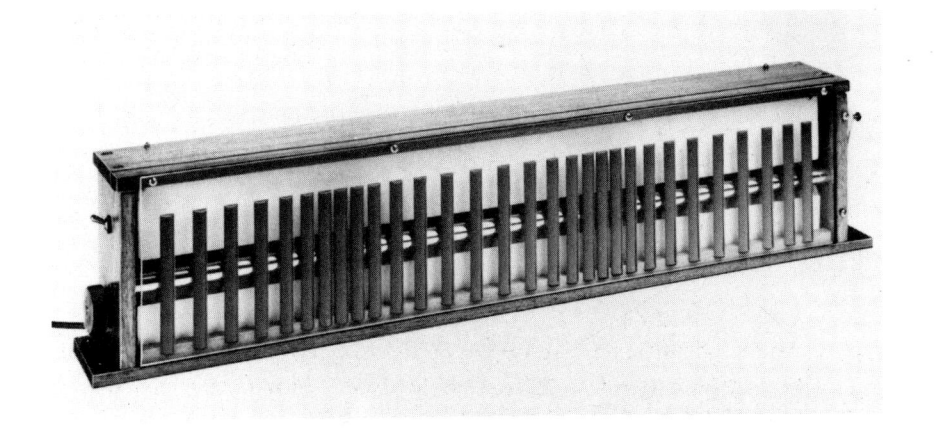

The rods move closer together in some regions and further apart in others and these regions themselves move along in the same direction in which the rods move. We will see a longitudinal wave move along.

Sound is a very important type of naturally occuring longitudinal wave.

All the characteristics of transverse waves — speed, wavelength, frequency and amplitude — apply to longitudinal waves, with a wavelength being the distance from the middle of one compression to the next.

SUPPLEMENTARY

14.8 REFLECTION OF PLANE WAVES FROM A CIRCULAR BOUNDARY

(i) Suppose in a ripple tank the vane is used to generate plane waves. If these are reflected from a concave barrier, as shown in Fig. 14.14, their shape is changed.

They are reflected as circular waves which converge to a point F, the focus of the barrier.

FIG. 14.14

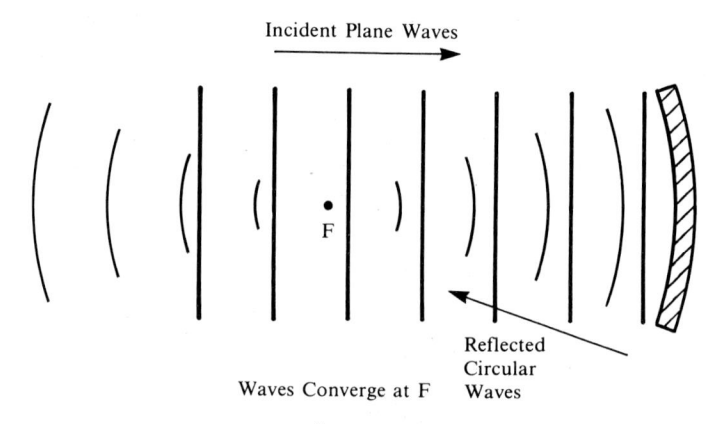

Incident Plane Waves →

· F

Waves Converge at F   Reflected Circular Waves

REFLECTION OF PLANE WAVES
FROM A CONCAVE BARRIER

The focus of a concave barrier is the point at which circular waves meet after reflection of plane waves from the barrier.

(ii) If the barrier is now replaced with a convex barrier, as shown in Fig. 14.15, the plane waves are reflected as circular waves which

FIG. 14.15

REFLECTION OF PLANE WAVES
FROM A CONVEX BARRIER

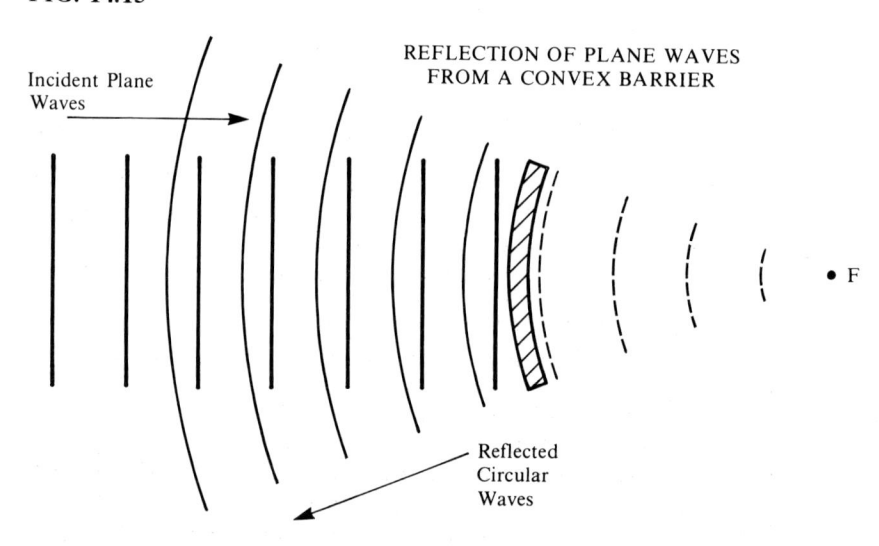

Incident Plane Waves →

· F

Reflected Circular Waves

Waves Appear to Diverge from F

are diverging. They appear to have come from a point F behind the barrier. This is the focus of the convex barrier and is the point from which incident plane waves appear to come after reflection from the barrier. Notice that we use dotted wavefronts after the barrier to show the fact that the wavefronts are not actually there but only appear to be there.

(iii) Suppose that we now use one of the balls on the vane to generate circular waves and we allow them to strike a plane boundary. They will be reflected off the barrier, as shown in Fig. 14.16.

FIG. 14.16

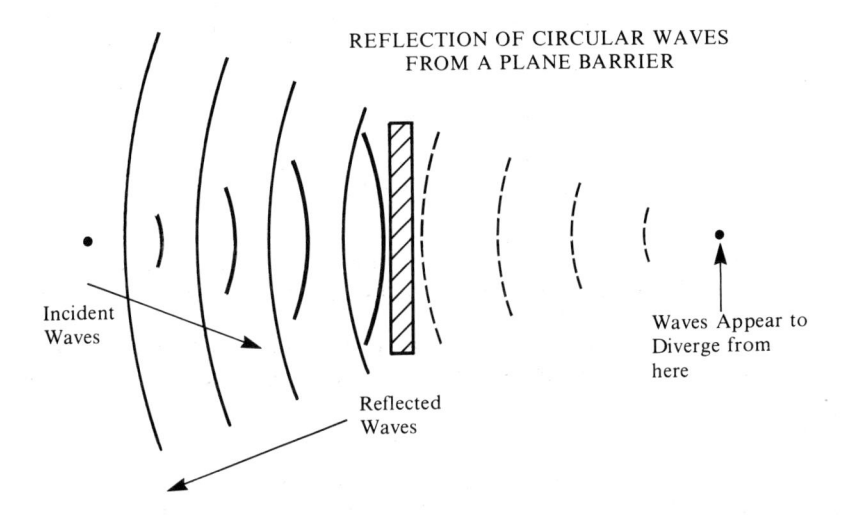

REFLECTION OF CIRCULAR WAVES FROM A PLANE BARRIER

Incident Waves

Reflected Waves

Waves Appear to Diverge from here

The barrier will reverse the curvature of the waves. They will diverge after reflection and will appear to come from a point which is as far behind the barrier as the ball is in front. We use dotted wavefronts behind the barrier to show that they only appear to be there.

14.9 REFRACTION DUE TO A CHANGE IN SPEED

Consider again refraction of waves as discussed earlier, using the deep and shallow water, as shown in Fig. 14.9.

If we illuminate the water with a stroboscope we shall see that the frequencies of the incident and refracted waves are identical. We know that the wavelength of the refracted waves is less than that of the incident waves. It follows then that the speed of the refracted waves is less than that of the incident waves because

$$\text{wave speed} = \text{frequency} \times \text{wavelength}.$$

It is this slowing down of the waves that is responsible for the change in direction. Consider Fig. 14.17.

184 Waves

FIG. 14.17

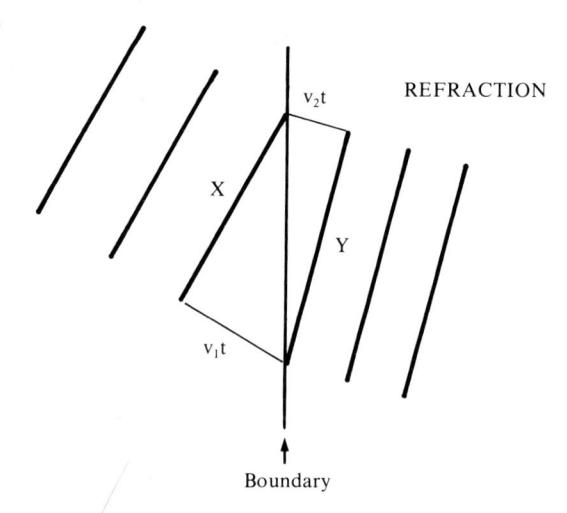

REFRACTION

(diagram showing incident wavefront labelled X with distance $v_1 t$ to boundary, and refracted wavefront labelled Y with distance $v_2 t$, meeting at the Boundary)

The top of the incident wavefront, X, is just striking the boundary. If its speed is v_1 and the time taken for the bottom of the wavefront to reach the boundary is t then the bottom of the wavefront is a distance $v_1 t$ from the boundary. When the wave enters the shallow region, its speed will slow down to v_2. In the same time, t, that it takes the bottom of the incident wavefront to reach the boundary, the top of the refracted wavefront, Y, will only travel $v_2 t$. As a result, the wavefront, and therefore the wave, has changed direction.

We define the refractive index of the shallow region with respect to the deep region as

$$\frac{\sin i}{\sin r} \text{ or } \frac{v_1}{v_2}$$

We represent it with the symbol n.

PROBLEM
A WAVE TRAVELS ACROSS THE SURFACE OF SOME DEEP WATER AT A SPEED OF 0.14 m/s. IT THEN PASSES OVER SHALLOW WATER WHEN ITS SPEED DROPS TO 0.10 m/s. CALCULATE THE REFRACTIVE INDEX OF THE SHALLOW WATER WITH RESPECT TO THE DEEP WATER.

Use $\quad n = \dfrac{v_1}{v_2}$

$v_1 = 0.14$ m/s, $\quad v_2 = 0.10$ m/s

So $\quad n = \dfrac{0.14}{0.10} = 1.4$

ANSWER: REFRACTIVE INDEX = 1.4.

14.10 AN EXPLANATION OF DIFFRACTION

We have seen that when waves strike a small slit in a barrier they are diffracted.

The reason for this is shown in Fig. 14.18.

FIG. 14.18

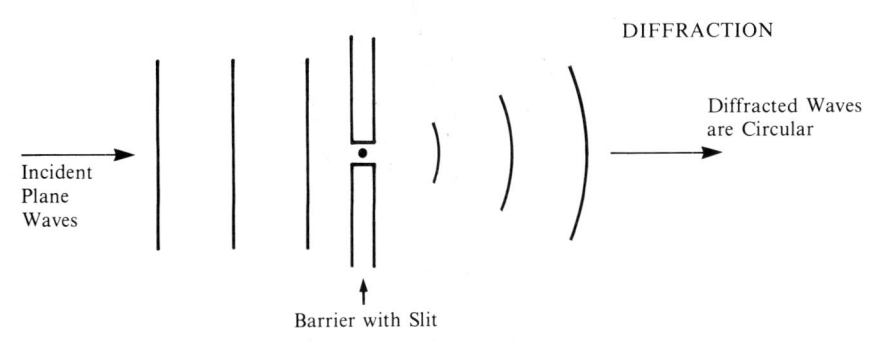

DIFFRACTION

Incident Plane Waves → | Barrier with Slit | → Diffracted Waves are Circular

The barrier stops most of the waves passing through. Only a tiny amount of the wavefront is allowed to continue. Now this portion is so small that it behaves like a point source of waves and it generates circular waves. Some of these are blocked off by the forward edges of the barrier and so only a narrow cone of waves moves forward.

If the slit is made wider we then have more point sources which generate more waves. But these interfere with each other and the effect is destroyed leaving us with waves which just move forward with no diffraction taking place.

QUESTIONS

CORE

1. Make a drawing of photograph 14 and label a crest, a trough, a wavelength and the amplitude.
2. Make a drawing of photograph 15 and label a compression, a rarefaction and a wavelength.
3. State what is transferred by a wave.
4. A wave travels 2m in 10s. Calculate its speed.
5. A wave passes under a boat. If the boat rises a total distance of 0.50m due to the wave, what is the amplitude of the wave?
6. A wave on water has a frequency of 2Hz. If its wavelength is 0.5m, calculate its speed.
7. A wave in a ripple tank strikes a plane boundary at an angle of incidence of 40°. What is the angle of reflection?

186 Waves

8. When a wave in a ripple tank moves from deep to shallow water, its direction of travel changes. What is this effect called?
9. In Fig. 14.19 (a) and (b) mark on the position of the wavefronts after passing through the barrier.

FIG. 14.19

(a)   (b)

10. a) Waves can be used to carry energy. Some waves are described as being transverse and others are longitudinal. How do transverse waves differ from longitudinal ones?
    b) Which of the following are transverse waves and which are longitudinal? (i) Ripple tank waves on water (ii) Sound waves (iii) Light waves (iv) Radio waves. *(L.E.A.G.)*
11.

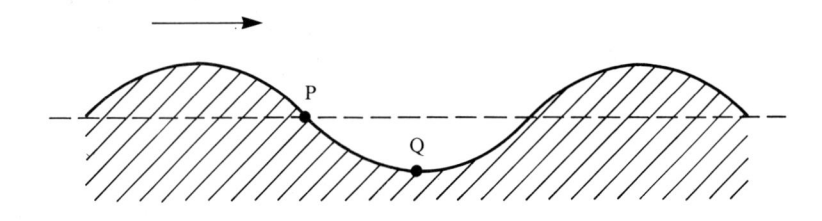

The diagram shows a water wave travelling in the direction of the arrow. As the wave moves forward
 A   P will go up, Q will go down
 B   P will go down, Q will go up
 C   P will go up, Q will go up
 D   P will go down, Q will go down. *(S.E.G.)*

SUPPLEMENTARY

12. The speed of water waves in deep water is 15m/s and in shallow water it is 10m/s. Calculate the refractive index of the shallow water with respect to the deep water.
13. The diagram represents parallel plane waves approaching a semi-circular barrier in a ripple tank.

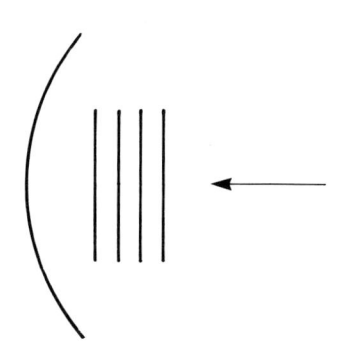

Which of the following diagrams best show how the waves are reflected by the barrier?

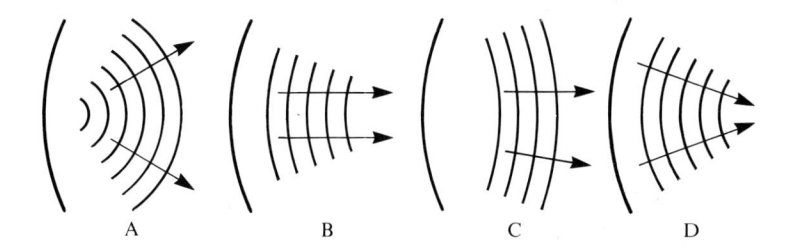

A　　　B　　　C　　　D

(L.E.A.G.)

Chapter 15
REFLECTION OF LIGHT

At the end of this chapter you will know:
CORE: that light is a wave motion; the laws of reflection and how they may be verified; how an image is formed in a plane mirror; the nature of the image formed in a plane mirror; what is meant by real and virtual images; how parallel light rays behave when they strike curved mirrors and some examples of plane and curved reflectors.
SUPPLEMENTARY: how to perform calculations using the laws of reflection; and the difference between regular and diffuse reflection.

CORE

15.1 LIGHT AS A WAVE MOTION

We can design experiments to show that light undergoes reflection, refraction, interference and diffraction. Interference and diffraction are effects which only waves undergo. We conclude that light itself is a wave motion. Luminous objects emit light, other objects reflect it.

In fact, light is an electromagnetic wave and is part of the electromagnetic spectrum which we shall consider in more detail in Chapter 18.

The path which a light wave follows is called a ray. It is the direction in which the energy of the wave travels. We represent a ray by a straight line, with an arrow marked on it to show its direction, as in Fig. 15.1. The rays travel in straight lines.

FIG. 15.1

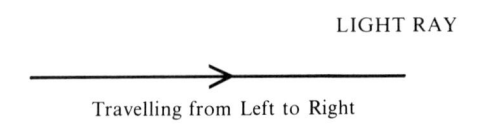

LIGHT RAY

⎯⎯⎯⎯⎯⎯⎯→

Travelling from Left to Right

A beam of light is made up of a number of rays.

15.2 THE LAWS OF REFLECTION OF LIGHT

(i) In the same way that waves in a ripple tank reflect off a barrier, light waves reflect from a barrier. The barrier used must be flat. We call it a plane mirror and it consists of a thin film of silver on a flat piece of glass. The front surface of the silver reflects the light and its back surface is painted to avoid scratching.

Reflection of Light

We represent a plane mirror by the symbol shown below:

FIG. 15.2   PLANE MIRROR SYMBOL

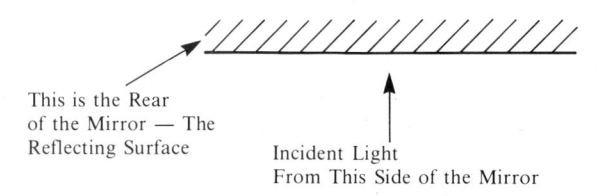

This is the Rear of the Mirror — The Reflecting Surface

Incident Light From This Side of the Mirror

(ii) As with waves in a ripple tank, the line at 90° to the mirror is called the normal. The angle between the incident ray and the normal is the angle of incidence, i, and the angle between the normal and the reflected ray is the angle of reflection, r.

The Laws of Reflection are:
1. The incident ray, the normal and the reflected ray all lie in the same plane — that is, they are all level.
2. The angle of incidence equals the angle of reflection.

$$i = r$$

These are shown in Fig. 15.3.

FIG. 15.3

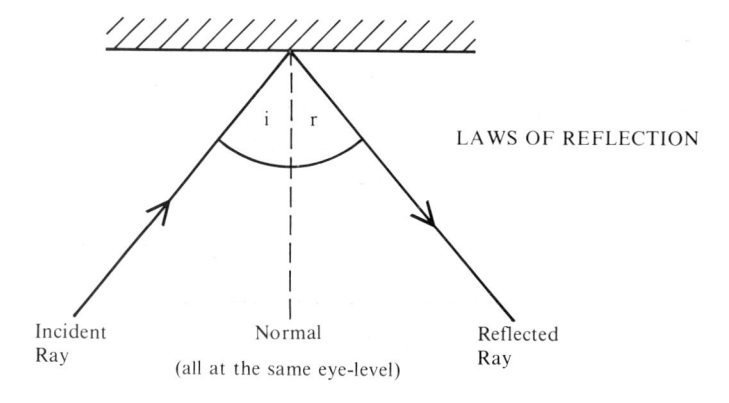

LAWS OF REFLECTION

Incident Ray   Normal   Reflected Ray
(all at the same eye-level)

(iii) In order to prove the laws of reflection, we use the experiment shown in Fig. 15.4.

A mirror is placed on a clean sheet of drawing paper lying on a cork mat. The position of the front of the mirror is drawn with a pencil. Two pins, P_1 and P_2 are positioned on one side of the normal, as shown. We then move our head to the other side of the normal until

FIG. 15.4

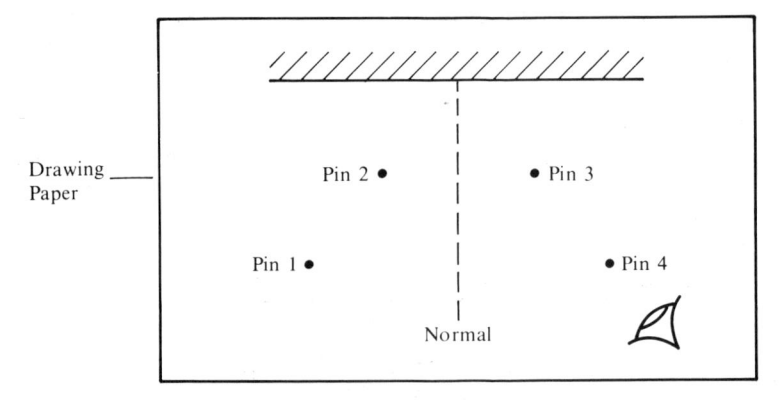

```
                    ////////////////
                           |
                           |
      Pin 2 •              |        • Pin 3
                           |
                           |
                           |
      Pin 1 •              |        • Pin 4
                           |
                         Normal
```

Drawing Paper

TO PROVE THE LAWS OF REFLECTION

pins P_1 and P_2 are in line with each other and so we only see one pin. Two more pins P_3 and P_4 are then positioned so that all four pins are in line and we still only see one pin. The position of P_1, P_2, P_3 and P_4 are marked. We remove the pins and repeat this process five more times for different angles of incidence. To reduce confusion we now identify the pins as P_5, P_6, P_7 and P_8 etc.

Finally we remove the mirror and draw lines through pins P_1 and P_2 to the mirror — giving us the incident ray — and through pins P_3 and P_4 to the mirror — giving us the reflected ray. The angle of incidence and the angle of reflection are then measured and the process repeated for the other five angles of incidence.

We then draw up a table showing the angles of incidence and the corresponding angles of reflection, as shown.

Angle of incidence	Angle of reflection

We find that in each case the angles are equal.

15.3 HOW AN IMAGE IS FORMED IN A PLANE MIRROR

Consider an object in front of a plane mirror, as shown in Fig. 15.5.

FIG. 15.5

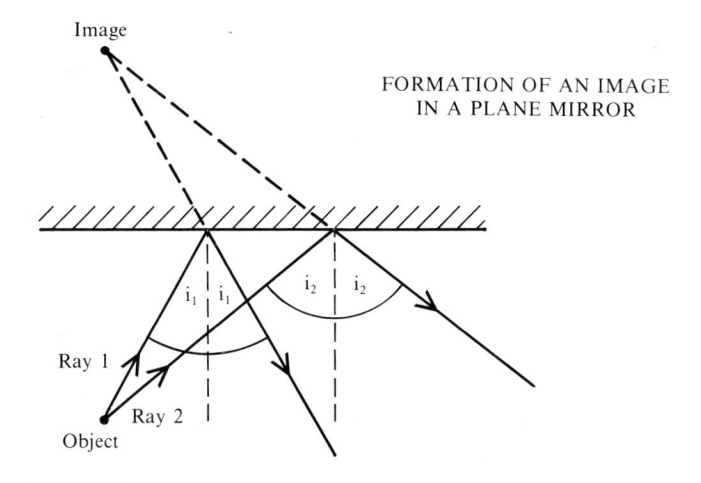

FORMATION OF AN IMAGE IN A PLANE MIRROR

In order to find the image, we consider two of the rays from the object, Ray 1 and Ray 2. Suppose the angle of incidence of Ray 1 is i_1. It will be reflected at the same angle, i_1. Now the eye thinks that light always travels in a straight line and it thinks that the ray has actually come from behind the mirror, as shown by the left dotted line. A similar thing will happen to Ray 2. If its angle of incidence is i_2, it will be reflected at this angle. The eye thinks that it came from behind the mirror, as shown by the right dotted line. The image appears to be where these two dotted lines meet.

In an identical way, every point on the object gives rise to its own image.

15.4 THE NATURE OF THE IMAGE FORMED IN A PLANE MIRROR

The image which is formed in a plane mirror has the following properties:
1. It is the same size as the object.
2. It is the right way up.
3. It is as far behind the mirror as the object is in front.
4. It is laterally inverted.

In order to understand what is meant by lateral inversion, consider a person facing you. Their left hand side is on your right. This changing of sides always takes place. However, if you look at yourself in a mirror, your image faces you but your left hand side stays on the left hand side. The changing of sides does not take place and this is known as lateral inversion.

It causes difficulty when we try to read letters or numbers reflected in a mirror.

As an example, consider the word **POLICE**. If this is reflected in a mirror it will appear as ƎƆIJOԀ.

You may often now see police cars with the word ƎƆIJOԀ on the front. When this is seen through a driver's mirror it is laterally inverted and so appears as normal.

For similar reasons we now see ambulances with ambulance written on their fronts laterally inverted.

15.5 VIRTUAL AND REAL IMAGES

In the case of a plane mirror, the rays only appear to come from the image although they do not actually do so. They are called virtual rays and the image is a virtual image. Such an image can never be formed on a screen.

If the rays actually came from the image, the rays and the image would be called real. An important property of a real image is that it can be formed on a screen.

15.6 PARALLEL LIGHT RAYS STRIKING CURVED MIRRORS

There are two types of curved mirror. In one type, the concave mirror, the reflecting surface of the mirror curves inwards and in the other type, the convex mirror, the reflecting surface of the mirror curves outward. Both types of mirror reflect light according to the laws of reflection.

FIG. 15.6

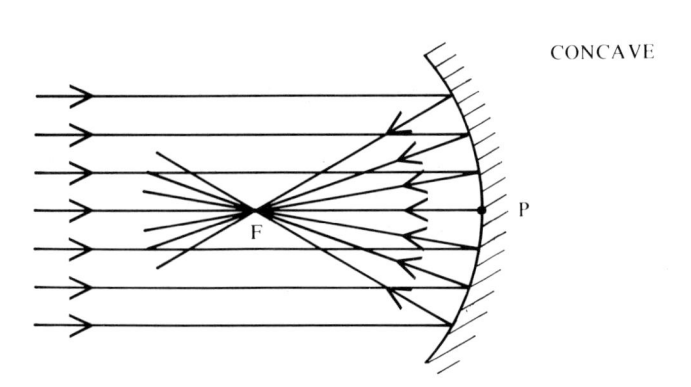

If parallel rays of light are incident on a concave mirror they are brought together to meet at a point, F, known as the focus. This is in front of the mirror and it is a real focus because light rays actually meet there, as shown in Fig. 15.6.

Although the incident rays are parallel, the reflected rays are not because each has a different angle of incidence because of the curvature of the mirror.

When the parallel rays strike the mirror horizontally, F is called the principal focus and the distance to F from the centre of the mirror, P, is called the focal length of the mirror. It is real.

If parallel rays of light are incident upon a convex mirror they are spread out and appear to come from a point, F, known as the focus. This is behind the mirror and it is a virtual focus because light rays only appear to come from there, as shown in Fig. 15.7.

FIG. 15.7

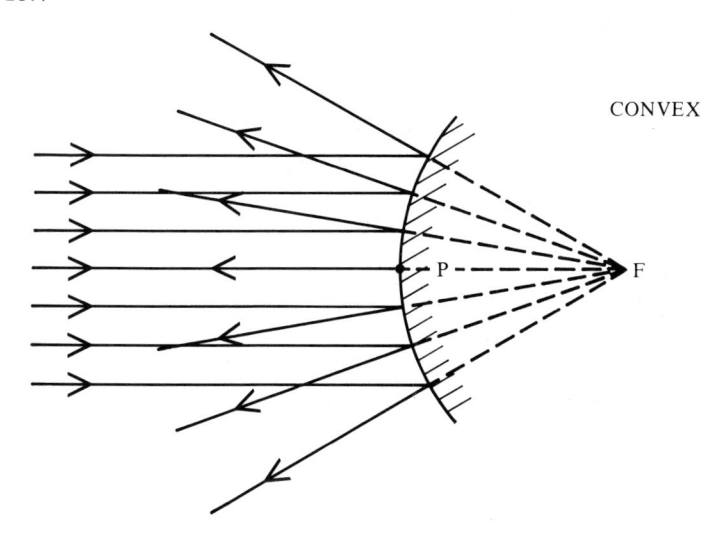

Once again the reflected rays are not parallel because each strikes the mirror at a different angle of incidence.

When the incident rays are horizontal, F is called the principal focus and the distance from F to the centre of the mirror, P, is the focal length of the mirror. In this case it is virtual.

194 Reflection of Light

15.7 EXAMPLES OF THE USES OF PLANE MIRRORS, CURVED MIRRORS AND CURVED REFLECTORS

(i) Plane mirrors are used in everyday life for a variety of purposes. In science they can be used in periscopes, as shown in Fig. 15.8. These are used to look over obstacles.

FIG. 15.8

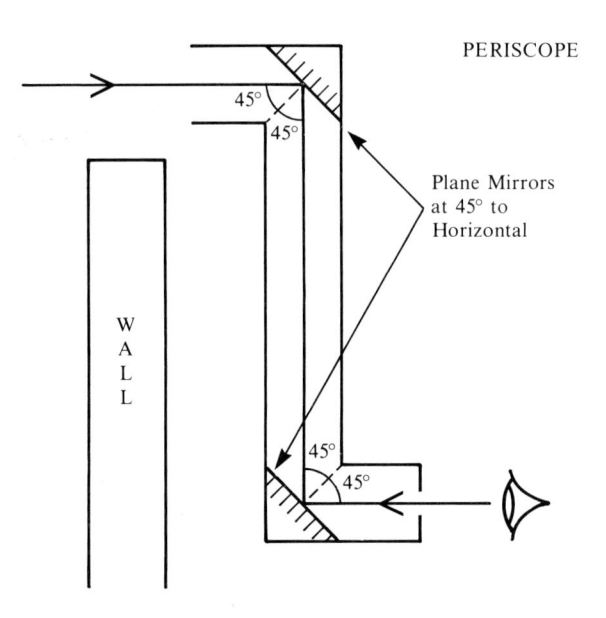

PERISCOPE

Plane Mirrors at 45° to Horizontal

They may also be used to help us read the scales of instruments and increase our accuracy. When the eye is directly over the pointer, the image of the pointer will be directly behind the pointer and so only one pointer will be seen, as in Fig. 15.9(a). If the eye is to one side, 2 pointers will be seen — the actual pointer and its image in the mirror, as in Fig. 15.9(b).

FIG. 15.9(a)

Correct Reading — No image can be seen.

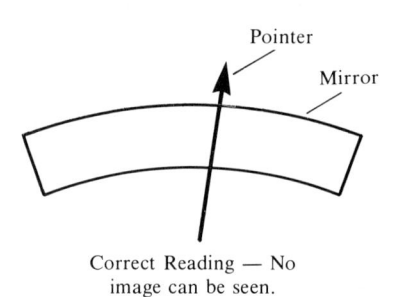

FIG. 15.9(b)

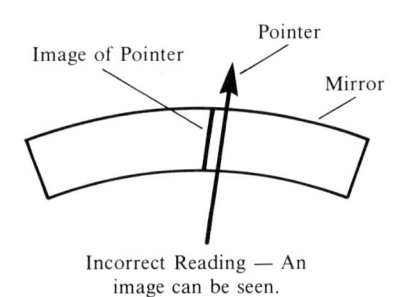

Incorrect Reading — An image can be seen.

Reflection of Light

In the correct reading no parallax takes place but in the incorrect reading, parallax does take place.

(ii) Convex mirrors are used when we want to see more, that is, when we wish to increase our field of view. This is shown in Fig. 15.10(a) and Fig. 15.10(b).

FIG. 15.10(a)

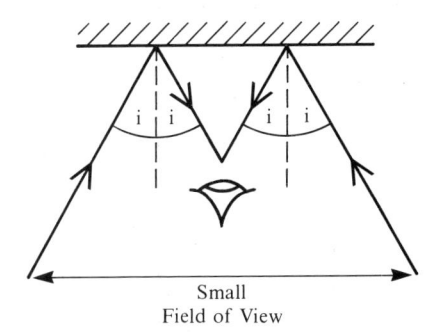

Small Field of View

FIG. 15.10(b)

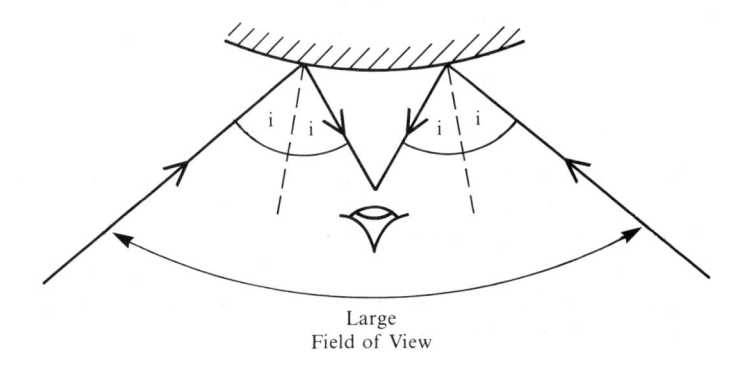

Large Field of View

They are used to do this when they are used as driving mirrors and security mirrors. The image is always the right way up but it is smaller than the object.

(iii) Concave mirrors are used in telescopes to reflect light to a focus. Such a telescope is shown in Photograph 16.

196 Reflection of Light

PHOTOGRAPH 16

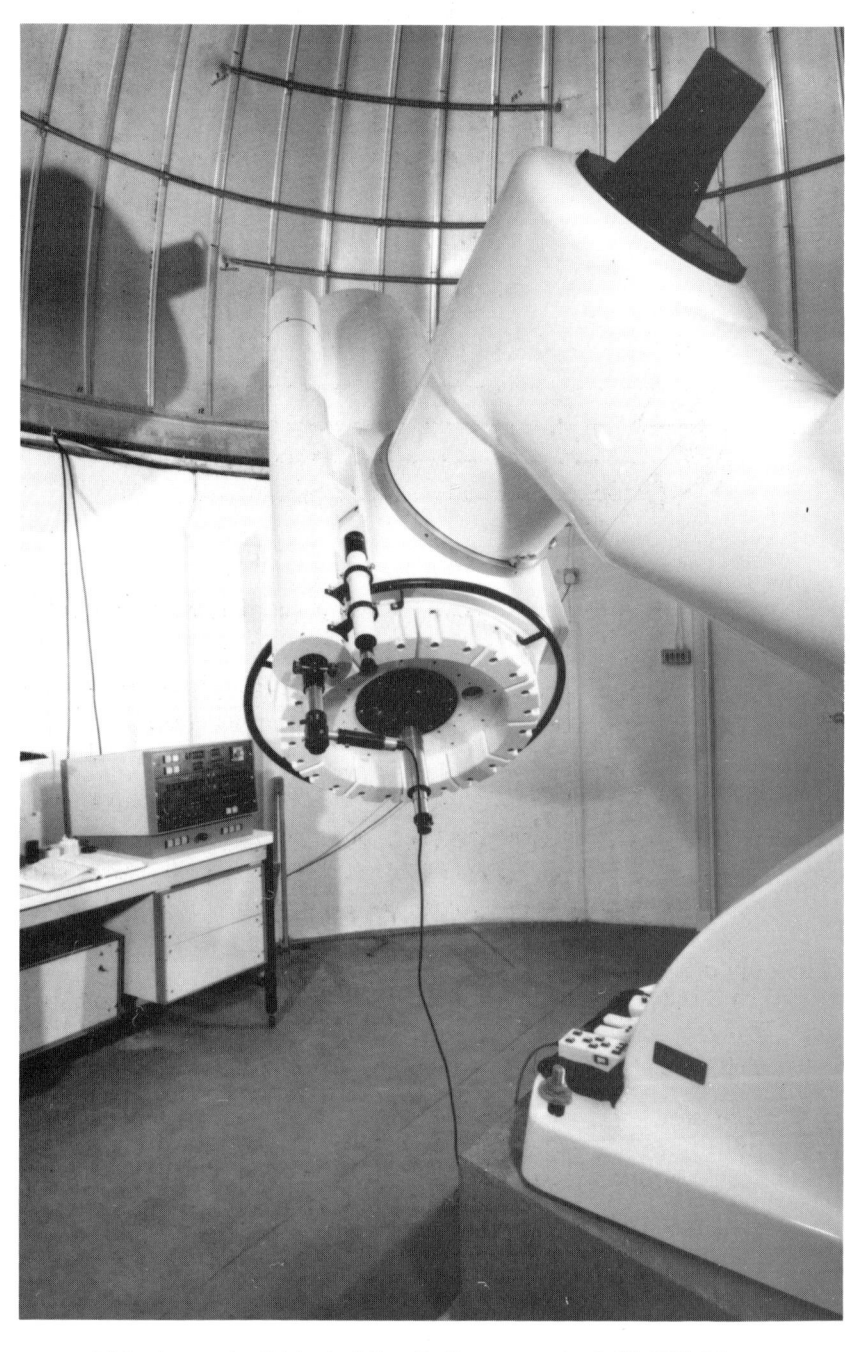

This shows the 24 inch Allen Reflector at the Mill Hill Observatory.

Concave reflectors are also used in radar scanners and radio-telescopes. This will be considered in Chapter 18.

Concave mirrors are used:
as reflectors in car headlamps and torches. A small lamp at their focus causes a beam of parallel light rays to be reflected. In order to avoid distortion we need to use a parabolic curved mirror, as shown in Fig. 15.11.

FIG. 15.11

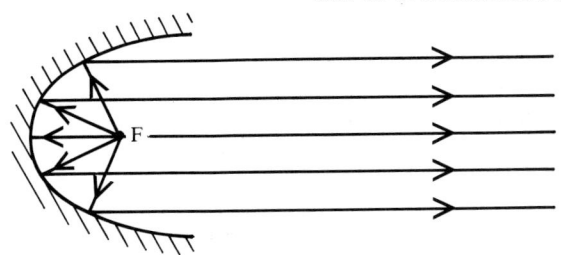

USE OF A PARABOLIC MIRROR

as shaving, cosmetic and dental mirrors. The virtual image which is formed is the right way up and magnified.

(iv) Concave reflectors of shiny metal rather than mirrors are used in electric fires to reflect parallel radiation from the element.

SUPPLEMENTARY

15.8 CALCULATIONS USING THE LAWS OF REFLECTION

We may use the laws of reflection to calculate the paths of rays after they have been reflected from plane mirrors.

PROBLEM
A RAY OF LIGHT STRIKES A PLANE MIRROR AT AN ANGLE OF INCIDENCE OF 30°. WHAT IS THE ANGLE BETWEEN THE INCIDENT RAY AND THE REFLECTED RAY?

Now here $i = 30°$
so $r = 30°$
But the angle between the incident and the reflected ray is
$i + r = 30 + 30 = 60°$

ANSWER: THE ANGLE BETWEEN THE INCIDENT AND REFLECTED RAYS IS 60°.

PROBLEM

A RAY OF LIGHT STRIKES A MIRROR AT AN ANGLE OF INCIDENCE OF 15°. IF THE MIRROR IS ROTATED ABOUT ITS MID POINT BY AN ANGLE OF 25°, WHAT ARE THE POSSIBLE ANGLES BETWEEN THE INCIDENT AND REFLECTED RAYS?

THE ORIGINAL POSITION IS AS SHOWN IN FIG. 15.12(a).

FIG. 15.12(a)

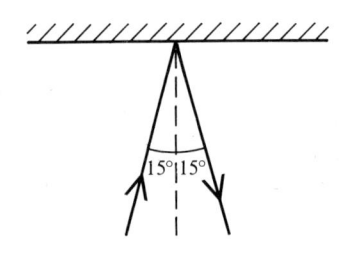

SUPPOSE THE MIRROR IS ROTATED 25° ANTI-CLOCKWISE AS SHOWN IN FIG. 15.12(b).

FIG. 15.12(b)

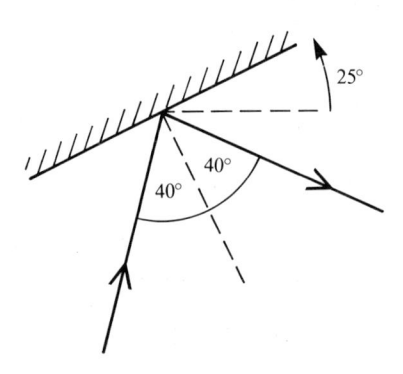

THE ANGLE OF INCIDENCE IS NOW 15° + 25° = 40°. THE NEW ANGLE OF INCIDENCE IS THUS 40°.

THE ANGLE BETWEEN THE INCIDENT AND REFLECTED RAYS IS
$$40 + 40 = 80°$$

SUPPOSE THE MIRROR IS ROTATED 25° CLOCKWISE, AS SHOWN IN FIG. 15.12(c).

FIG. 15.12(c)

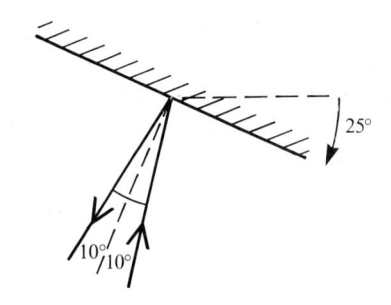

THE ANGLE OF INCIDENCE IS NOW 25 − 15 = 10°.
i.e. THE INCIDENT RAY IS NOW ON THE OTHER SIDE OF THE NORMAL.
THE NEW ANGLE OF REFLECTION IS THUS 10°.
THE ANGLE BETWEEN THE INCIDENT AND REFLECTED RAYS IS
$$10 + 10 = 20°.$$

ANSWER: POSSIBLE ANGLES = 80° AND 20°.

15.9 REGULAR AND DIFFUSE REFLECTION

In all our work on reflection we have been concerned with reflection from smooth surfaces. This is known as regular reflection. Parallel incident rays are reflected as parallel rays. Images are obtained as we know when we look in a mirror.

However, if the surface is not smooth, parallel light rays which are incident all strike the surface at different angles of incidence and are reflected as non-parallel rays. They are scattered in all directions. This is known as diffuse reflection and no images can be seen. Most objects are seen by diffusion reflection. The difference between regular and diffuse reflection is shown in Fig. 15.13(a) and Fig. 15.13(b).

FIG. 15.13(a)

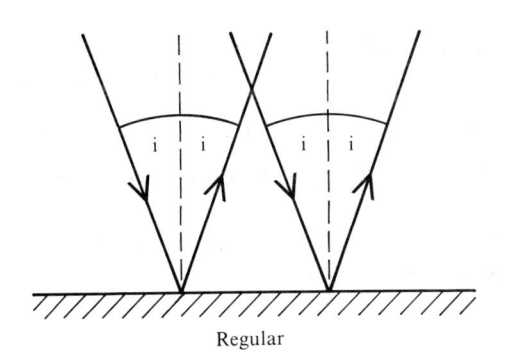

Regular

FIG. 15.13(b)

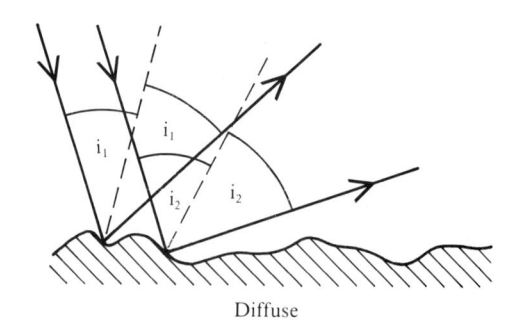

Diffuse

QUESTIONS

CORE
1. State the laws of reflection.
2. Explain the difference between virtual and real images.
3. A girl sits 3m in front of an optician's mirror. The eye chart is 1m behind her. What is the distance from the girl to the image of the eye chart?
5. Why is a convex mirror positioned at the top of the stairs on a double decker bus?
6. The word **AMBULANCE** appears on one of those vehicles but is laterally inverted. Write down how it appears.
7. An object O is placed in front of a plane mirror XY. At which of the points A—D will someone looking from Z see the image of the object?

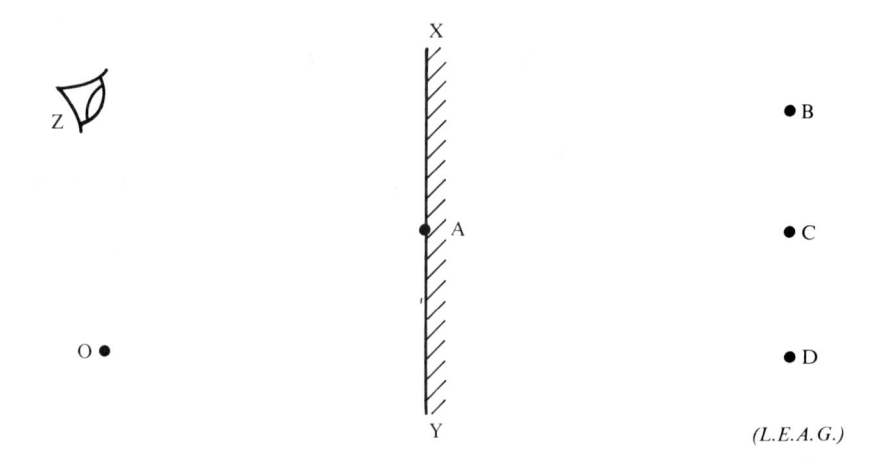

(L.E.A.G.)

8. (a) Fig. 3 shows two rays of light leaving an object O and striking a plane mirror.

FIG. 3

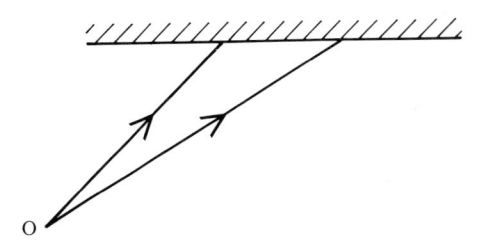

Draw the two reflected rays and use them to find the position of the image.

(b) Fig. 4 shows a side view of an electric fire.

FIG. 4

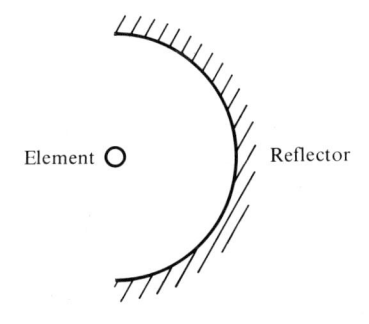

(i) What type of electromagnetic waves are given out by the element?
(ii) What name is given to the shape of the reflector?
(iii) The reflector is made of metal. Describe its surface and explain why metal is used. *(N.E.A.)*

SUPPLEMENTARY

9. Explain why a white painted wall reflects light but images cannot be seen in it.
10. A ray of light strikes a plane mirror. The mirror is then turned through an angle of 30°.

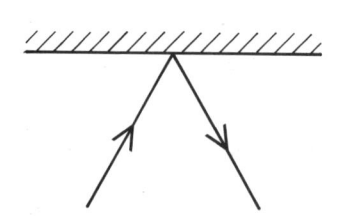

What angle will the reflected ray be turned through?
A. 15° B. 30° C. 60° D. 90°. *(L.E.A.G.)*

Chapter 16
REFRACTION OF LIGHT

At the end of this chapter you will know:
CORE: how light is refracted, some effects of refraction and how the effect may be demonstrated; what is meant by angle of incidence and angle of refraction; how light travels through a parallel sided glass block and a glass triangle, or prism; what is meant by critical angle and total internal reflection; how total internal reflection occurs in prisms, semi-circular blocks and thick glass mirrors; how optical fibres are used and what is meant by dispersion.
SUPPLEMENTARY: more about optical fibres, the constancy of sin i/sin r and what is meant by refractive index.

CORE

16.1 LIGHT IS REFRACTED

(i) Suppose a ray of light travels from air into glass. When it reaches the glass, a small amount of light will be reflected, obeying the laws of reflection. But most of the light will travel into the glass. As it enters the glass, its direction will change. We say that it is refracted. The situation is shown in Fig. 16.1.

FIG. 16.1

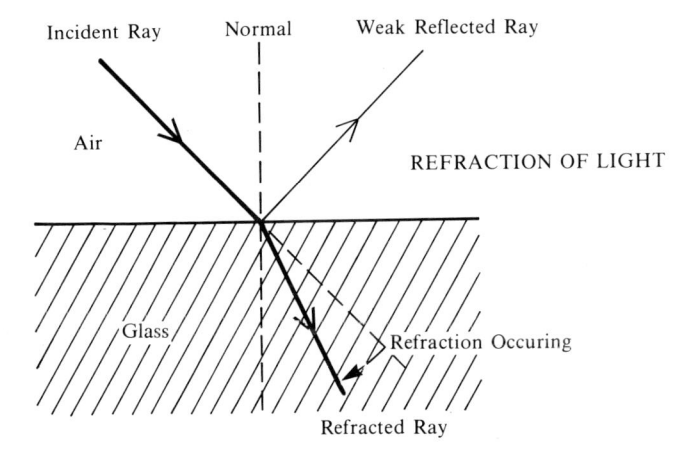

Incident Ray — Normal — Weak Reflected Ray

Air

REFRACTION OF LIGHT

Glass — Refraction Occuring

Refracted Ray

When the light ray is travelling in the glass it is known as a refracted ray.

If the light is travelling from air to glass, that is, from a less optically dense medium to a more optically dense medium, it is refracted

204 Refraction of Light

towards the normal. If it travels in the reverse direction from glass to air, it is refracted away from the normal.

(ii) The effect of refraction is due to the fact that light slows down when it enters a more optically dense medium. Its frequency remains the same and so its wavelength must decrease.

Refraction can be seen when we look through poor quality panes of glass whose sides are not parallel. It causes distortion.

Refraction also makes pools appear less deep than they really are. This effect of apparent depth is shown in Fig. 16.2.

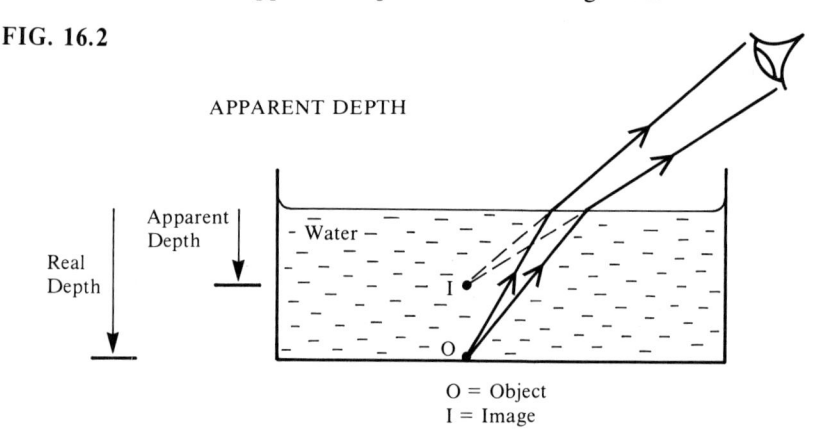

FIG. 16.2

APPARENT DEPTH

O = Object
I = Image

Because of refraction, if water is observed like this it only appears to be $\frac{3}{4}$ of its real depth.

(iii) Refraction in glass may be seen using the experiment shown in Fig. 16.3.

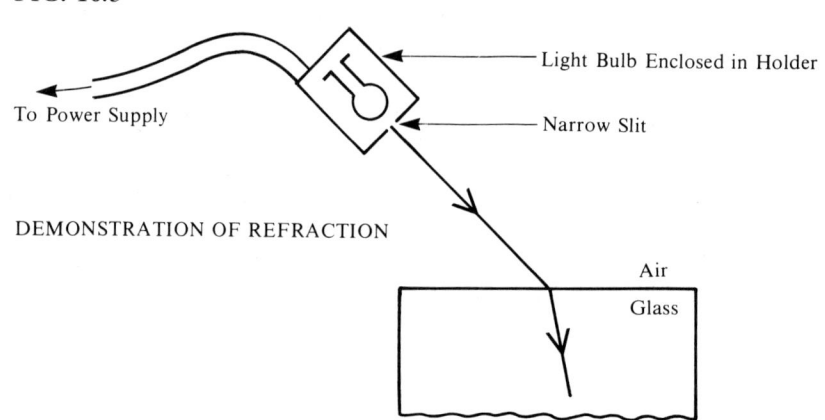

FIG. 16.3

DEMONSTRATION OF REFRACTION

16.2 ANGLE OF INCIDENCE AND ANGLE OF REFRACTION

The narrow slit enables a narrow ray of light to strike the glass. We see that the light is refracted. If the angle of the light ray falling on the glass is changed then so too is the refraction which occurs.

The angle between the normal and the incident ray is called the angle of incidence, represented by i.

The angle between the normal and the refracted ray is called the angle of refraction, represented by r.

These angles are shown in Fig. 16.4.

FIG. 16.4

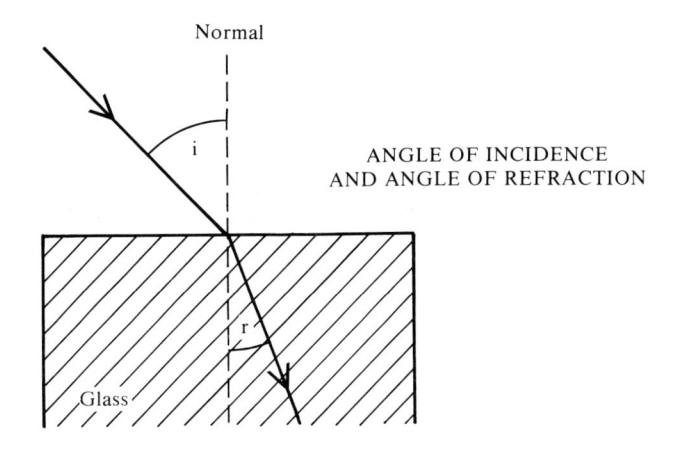

ANGLE OF INCIDENCE AND ANGLE OF REFRACTION

PROBLEM

THE TABLE BELOW SHOWS VALUES OF ANGLES OF INCIDENCE AND CORRESPONDING VALUES OF ANGLES OF REFRACTION. FOR EACH PAIR OF ANGLES, CALCULATE THE REFRACTION PRODUCED.

ANGLE OF INCIDENCE, i	22°	28°	33°
ANGLE OF REFRACTION, r	15°	18°	21°
DEVIATION, i - r	7°	10°	12°

THE REFRACTION PRODUCED IS MEASURED BY THE DEVIATION WHICH IS THE DIFFERENCE BETWEEN i AND r. THIS IS THE THIRD LINE IN THE TABLE.

16.3 THE PASSAGE OF LIGHT THROUGH PARALLEL SIDED GLASS BLOCKS AND PRISMS

(i) The passage of a light ray through a parallel sided glass block is shown in Fig. 16.5.

FIG. 16.5

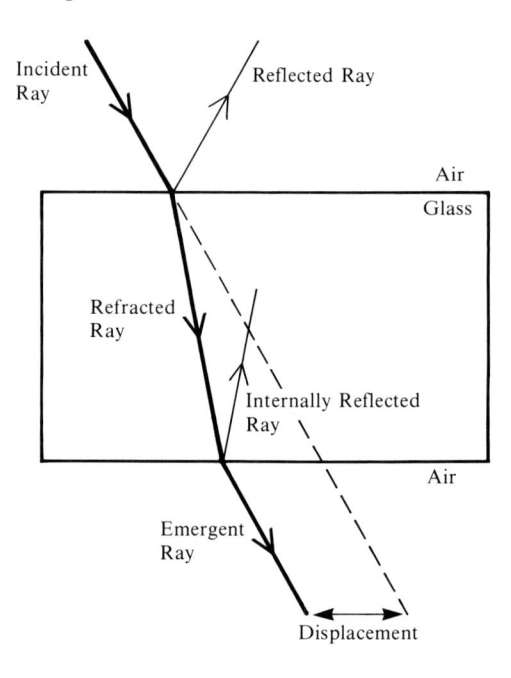

A small amount of light is reflected when it strikes the glass but most passes into the glass and is refracted. A little of this is internally reflected when it reaches the other edge of the block but most leaves the glass and is refracted but this time away from the normal.

The emergent ray is parallel to the incident ray, but it is displaced, as shown.

If the angle of incidence is zero, that is, the ray strikes the block at right angles, it passes straight through with no refraction and no displacement.

(ii) The passage of a light ray through a glass prism is shown in Fig. 16.6.

The light is refracted when it enters and leaves the prism and the total angle of deviation is as shown.

FIG. 16.6

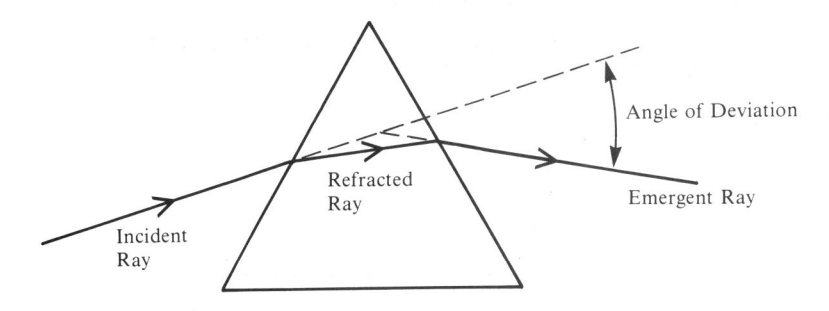

Figure: Light ray passing through a triangular prism showing Incident Ray, Refracted Ray, Emergent Ray, and Angle of Deviation.

16.4 CRITICAL ANGLE AND TOTAL INTERNAL REFLECTION

Suppose a ray of light is travelling in glass towards air, as shown in Fig. 16.7.

FIG. 16.7

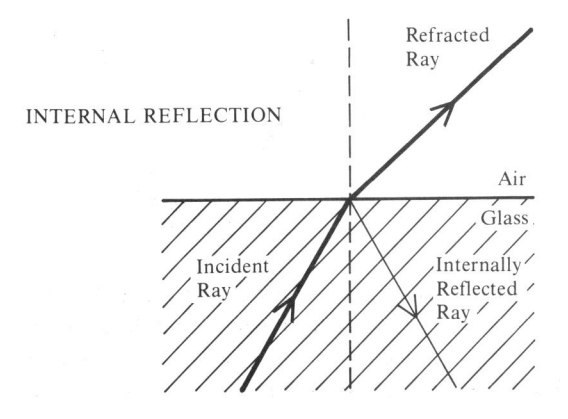

Figure: Internal reflection diagram showing Incident Ray in glass, Refracted Ray in air, and Internally Reflected Ray.

Most of the incident ray would be refracted, but some would be internally reflected.

If the angle of incidence in the glass is increased, eventually we reach the situation when the angle of refraction is 90° and the refracted ray travels along the surface of the glass. The angle of incidence is now called the critical angle, symbol c. This is shown in Fig. 16.8(a).

If the angle of incidence is increased beyond the critical angle, all the light is reflected. This is known as total internal reflection and is shown in Fig. 16.8(b).

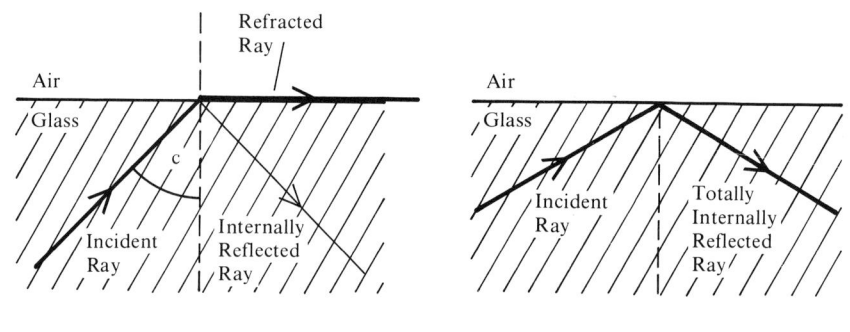

FIG. 16.8(a)   **FIG. 16.8(b)**

CRITICAL ANGLE   TOTAL INTERNAL REFLECTION

16.5 TOTAL INTERNAL REFLECTION IN PRISMS, SEMI-CIRCLES AND THICK GLASS MIRRORS

(i) The critical angle of ordinary glass is about 42°. If a light ray is travelling in glass and strikes a face at a greater angle than this, then total internal reflection will occur.

In Fig. 16.9, a ray hits face AB at 45°. Total internal reflection takes place and the ray is turned through 90°. Glass prisms are used in place of mirrors in high quality periscopes.

FIG. 16.9

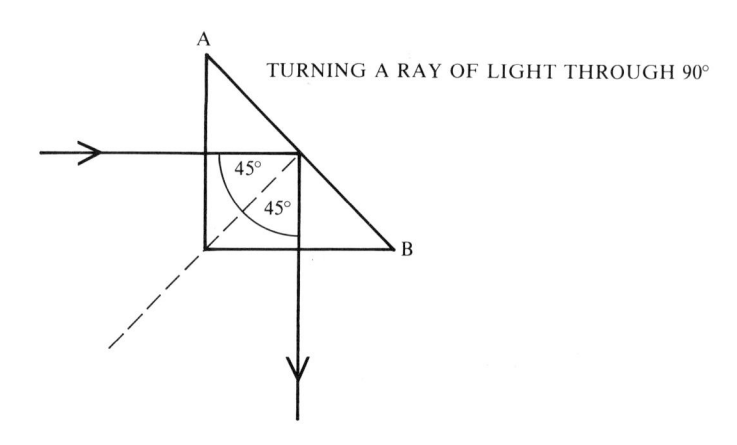

TURNING A RAY OF LIGHT THROUGH 90°

In Fig. 16.10 the ray strikes face AB at 45° where it is turned through 90°. It next strikes face BC at 45° where it is turned through another 90°. In total it is turned through 180°. Glass prisms are used like this in binoculars.

FIG. 16.10

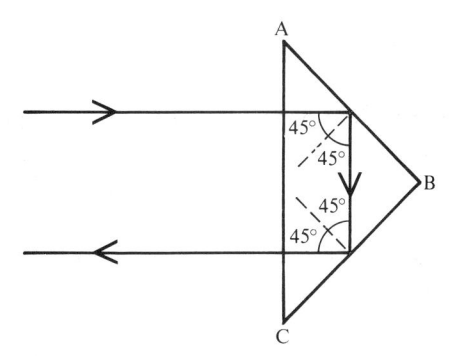

TURNING A RAY OF LIGHT THROUGH 180°

(ii) Whenever a ray of light enters a glass block along a radius such as AO or CO in Fig. 16.11, it is not refracted at the curved surface.

Consider a ray along AO. This is striking the plane surface at an angle less than the critical angle and so most of the light is refracted along OB.

A ray along CO strikes the plane surface at an angle greater than the critical angle. Total internal reflection takes place and the ray travels along OD.

FIG. 16.11

TOTAL INTERNAL REFLECTION
IN A SEMI-CIRCULAR GLASS BLOCK

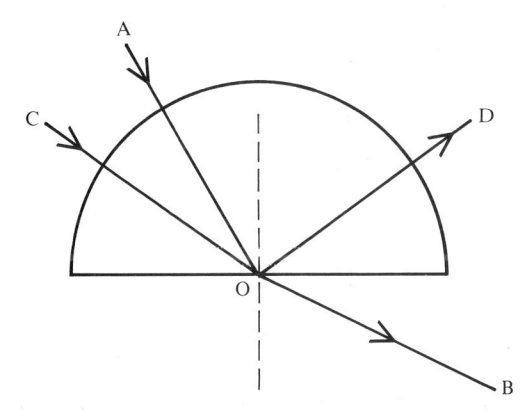

(iii) Ordinary thick glass mirrors which are silvered at the back form several images of an object because of multiple reflection inside the glass, as shown in Fig. 16.12.

210 Refraction of Light

FIG. 16.12

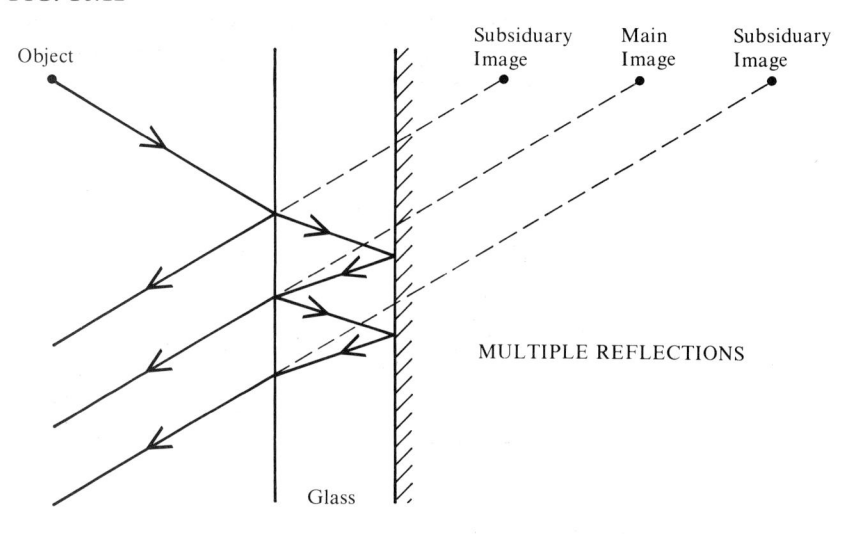

MULTIPLE REFLECTIONS

In addition to the main image there are subsiduary images. The effect is reduced if the glass is very thin and it is eliminated altogether if the mirror is front-silvered. These are expensive and are easily damaged.

16.6 OPTICAL FIBRES

Light can be trapped inside long glass fibres by total internal reflection. This is shown in Fig. 16.13.

FIG. 16.13

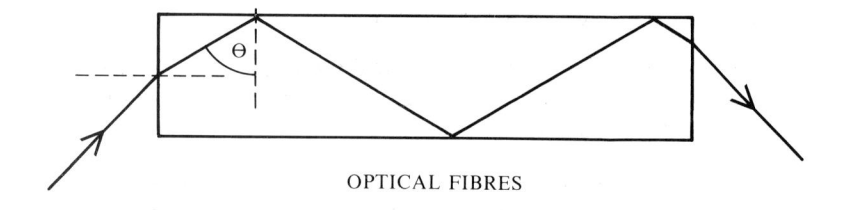

OPTICAL FIBRES

Providing angle Θ is greater than c, all the light is multiply reflected down the fibre.

The effect still takes place when the fibre is curved.

If large numbers of fibres are grouped together, a flexible light pipe is formed. This can be used by doctors to inspect the body internally, by engineers to form illuminated motorway signs and by the security services in coding devices when the fibres are intertwined in a bundle to scramble an image.

Refraction of Light 211

16.7 DISPERSION

If a ray of white light falls on a glass prism, as shown in Fig. 16.14, a band of colours is formed on the screen. The band is called a spectrum and the effect is called dispersion.

FIG. 16.14

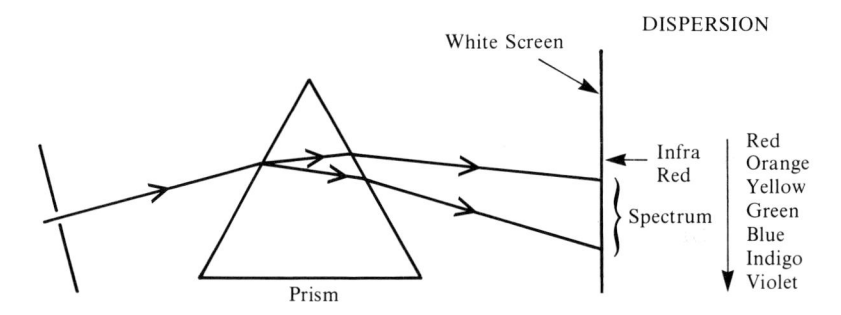

[Diagram showing white light passing through a prism, dispersing into a spectrum on a white screen. Labels: White Screen, DISPERSION, Infra Red, Spectrum, Prism, and colours Red, Orange, Yellow, Green, Blue, Indigo, Violet.]

From this experiment we see that white light is made up of many colours — the colours of the rainbow — and also that the blue end of the spectrum is deviated more than the red end of the spectrum.

SUPPLEMENTARY

16.8 MORE ABOUT OPTICAL FIBRES

It is important that the walls of optical fibres are kept clean because serious light losses occur if they are dirty. Some light will be lost at each reflection. Now in a glass optical fibre of diameter 25μ m, light entering at an angle of incidence of 10° makes 40 reflections per cm and so the losses soon become very large.

In general the fibres can be bent without any serious effects. Serious light losses only occur if the radius of curvature of the fibre is less than $\frac{1}{20}$th of its diameter.

Images can be conveyed using a bundle of such fibres, such as in cystoscopes used by doctors for internal body examination. The outer fibres are used to carry light to illuminate the object, a lens is used to form an image and the inner fibres are used to carry the image to the other end.

16.9 THE CONSTANCY OF SIN i AND SIN r

In Fig. 16.4 we find that if i, the angle of incidence increases then r, the angle of refraction increases also.

212 Refraction of Light

In fact we find that
$$\frac{\sin i}{\sin r} \text{ always has the same value.}$$

16.10 REFRACTIVE INDEX

The refractive index of a medium, symbol n, is defined as

$$n = \frac{\text{speed of light in air (or a vacuum)}}{\text{speed of light in medium}}$$

If c_a = speed of light in air
c_m = speed of light in medium
then
$$n = \frac{c_a}{c_m}$$

We can also show that when light passes from air to glass
$$n = \frac{\sin i}{\sin r}$$

i = angle of incidence
r = angle of refraction.

The change in speed causes a change in direction.

PROBLEM

THE SPEED OF LIGHT IN AIR IS 3×10^8 m/s AND IN GLASS ITS SPEED IS 2×10^8 m/s. CALCULATE THE REFRACTIVE INDEX OF GLASS.

Use
$$n = \frac{c_a}{c_m}$$
$c_a = 3 \times 10^8$ m/s, $c_m = 2 \times 10^8$ m/s

$$n = \frac{3 \times 10^8}{2 \times 10^8} = 1.5$$

ANSWER: REFRACTIVE INDEX OF GLASS = 1.5.

Refractive indices are always greater than 1.

QUESTIONS

CORE
1. What happens to light when it passes from air to glass?
2. Which one of the diagrams correctly shows the path of a ray of light through a rectangular glass block?

A

B

C

D

(S.E.G.)

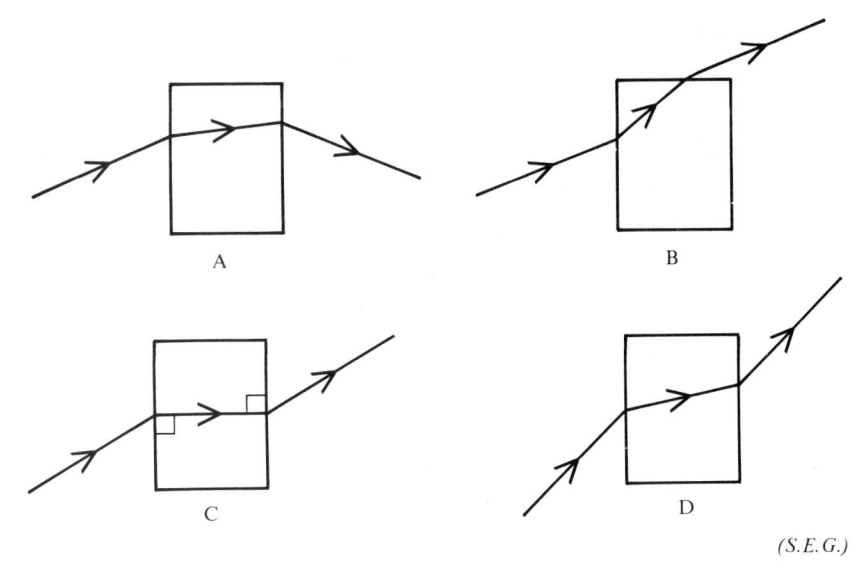

Question 3 and 4.
The diagram shows a narrow beam of white light passing through a glass prism and forming a spectrum on a screen. The points X and Y are on the screen and the rays drawn show the limits of the visible spectrum.

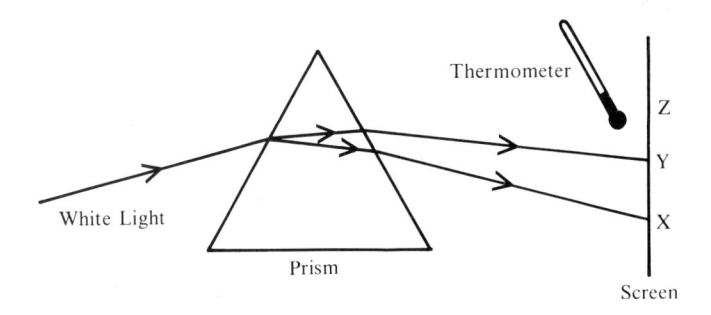

3. The colour of the light appearing at X will be
   A. red   B. white   C. violet   D. blue.
4. A thermometer placed at Z will show a rise in temperature from the radiation produced. The correct name for the radiation arriving at Z is
   A. ultra-violet   B. X-rays   C. gamma rays   D. infra red.
   (3 and 4: L.E.A.G.)
5. (a) Fig. 1 shows a long block of glass over an object O. Light from O reaches the top surface of the glass at X, Y and Z.

214 Refraction of Light

FIG. 1

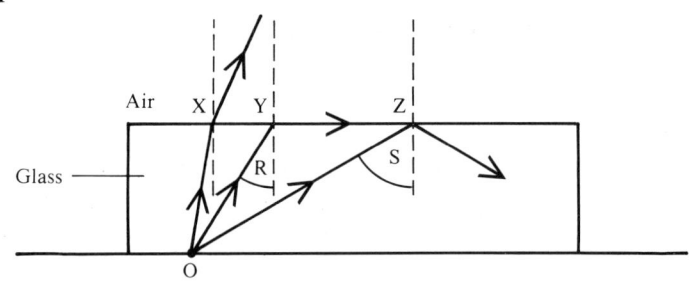

(i) The name given to the bending of the light at X is ----------
(ii) Fill in the two missing words in the following sentence. At Z light is ---------- ---------- reflected.
(iii) The angle marked R is called ----------
(iv) Light is reflected as shown at Z because ----------
(b)

FIG. 2

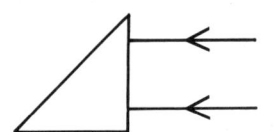

Fig. 2 shows two 45°, 45°, 90° glass prisms with two rays of light incident on a face of one of them.
(i) Complete the path of both rays through both prisms.
(ii) A practical use for such a device would be ----------

(N.E.A.)

SUPPLEMENTARY

6. If the speed of light in air is 3×10^8 m/s and the speed of light in water is 2.25×10^8 m/s, calculate the refractive index of water.

Chapter 17
THIN CONVERGING LENSES

At the end of this chapter you will know:
CORE: the action of a thin converging lens on a light beam; what is meant by principal focus and focal length; how focal length may be found; how a ray diagram may be used to show the formation of a real image and how thin converging lenses are used in projectors, cameras and telescopes.
SUPPLEMENTARY: how a ray diagram may be used to show the formation of a virtual image and how a converging lens may be used as a magnifying glass.

CORE

17.1 THE ACTION OF A THIN CONVERGING LENS ON A LIGHT BEAM

A thin converging lens is shown in Fig. 17.1.

FIG. 17.1

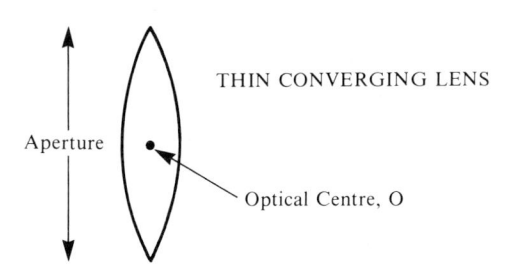

THIN CONVERGING LENS

Aperture

Optical Centre, O

It is a piece of glass or plastic with convex surfaces and is thicker in the middle than it is at the edges. We can think of it as a series of prisms, whose tops have been sliced off, stacked on top of each other. It therefore refracts light rays which pass through it. Rays at the edge are refracted most and those passing through the optical centre are not refracted at all. The refraction which it produces causes it to converge a light beam.

The bigger the aperture of the lens, the more light is allowed through. Sometimes the lens is also known as a thin convex lens.

17.2 PRINCIPAL FOCUS AND FOCAL LENGTH

If parallel rays of light are incident on a thin converging lens, they are brought together at a point, F, behind the lens, known as the focus. It is a real focus because the rays actually meet there.

216 Thin Converging Lenses

When the incident rays strike the lens horizontally, as shown in Fig. 17.2, F is called the principal focus of the lens.

FIG. 17.2

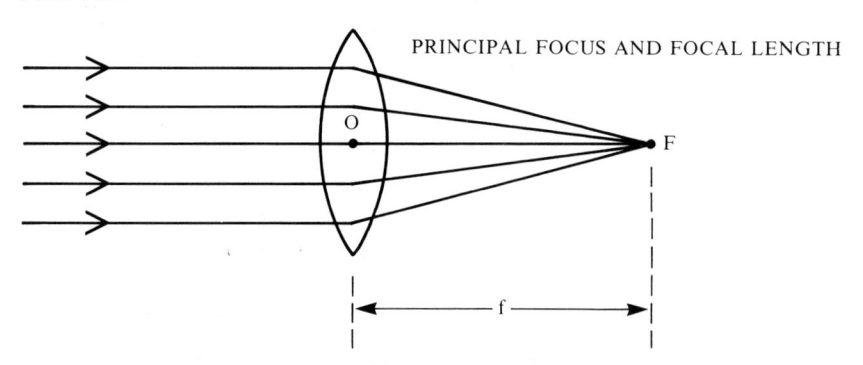

PRINCIPAL FOCUS AND FOCAL LENGTH

The distance from F to the optical centre of the lens is called the focal length, symbol f.

In fact the light rays are continually refracted as they travel through the lens, but in diagrams we represent the refraction by one single change of direction half way through the lens.

The diagram in Fig. 17.2 shows light incident from the left. Of course, the light may be incident from the right in which case the light would converge to a point F on the left. In other words, a lens has a principal focus and a focal length on each side.

The more a lens bulges in the middle, the greater the refraction which it produces and the shorter the focal length.

17.3 AN EASY WAY TO FIND FOCAL LENGTH

An easy and quick way to find the focal length of a thin converging lens is shown in Fig. 17.3.

FIG. 17.3

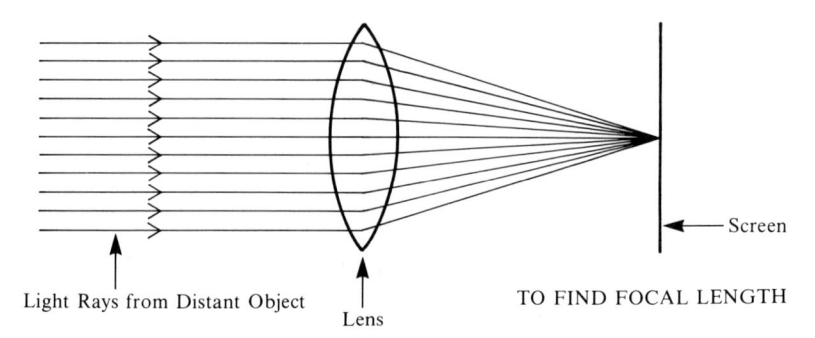

Light Rays from Distant Object — Lens — Screen

TO FIND FOCAL LENGTH

A screen is positioned behind the lens as shown. Light rays from a distant object are allowed to fall on the lens. Such rays will almost certainly be parallel as we require. Usually, in a school there will be a distant sports hall from which the rays will travel! We move the lens until a sharp image is formed on the screen and the distance from the screen to the middle of the lens is the focal length.

The reason why this method is slightly inaccurate is that the rays we use are not parallel but are diverging very slightly.

17.4 THE USE OF RAY DIAGRAMS TO LOCATE A REAL IMAGE

If light rays which are not parallel strike a thin converging lens, they are converged or brought to a focus further away from the lens than the focal length. They still meet, though, to produce a real image.

In practice light rays from objects which are reasonably close to a lens are not parallel but actually diverge.

In order to locate images in these cases we use ray diagrams, in which we represent light rays by straight lines, as usual.

There are three rays we can use:
(1) an incident ray which is horizontal and which is refracted through the principal focus.
(2) an incident ray through the principal focus which is refracted horizontally, and
(3) a ray through the optical centre which is not refracted.

These rays are shown in Fig. 17.4(a), (b) and (c).

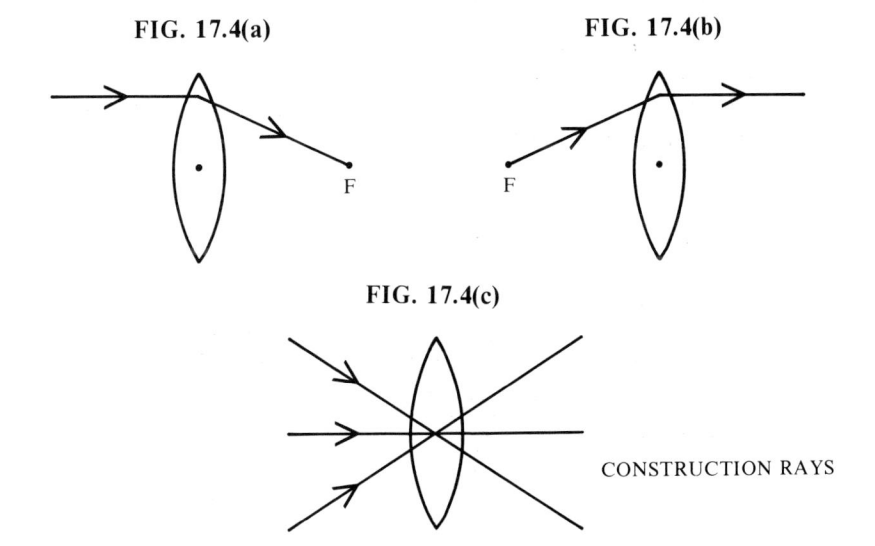

FIG. 17.4(a)   FIG. 17.4(b)

FIG. 17.4(c)

CONSTRUCTION RAYS

218 Thin Converging Lenses

These three rays are called construction rays and the first two are more commonly used than the third.

A thin converging lens always forms a real, upside down or inverted image whenever the object is further away than the focal length.

If the object is between F and 2F the image is magnified, as shown in Fig. 17.5.

FIG. 17.5

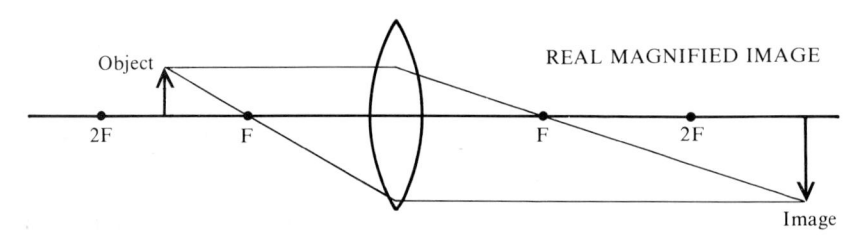

[Ray diagram: Object between F and 2F on left side of lens; REAL MAGNIFIED IMAGE formed beyond 2F on right side, inverted.]

If the object is further away than 2F the image is now reduced, as shown in Fig. 17.6.

FIG. 17.6

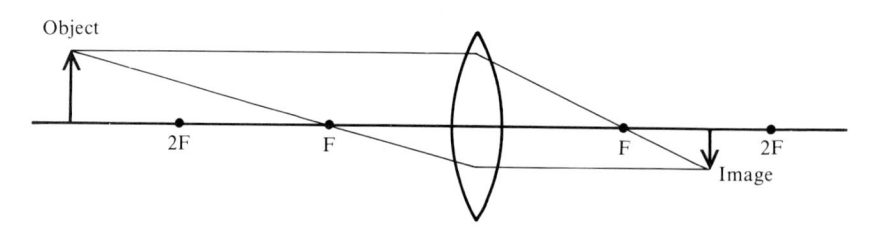

[Ray diagram: Object beyond 2F on left side of lens; reduced inverted Image formed between F and 2F on right side.]

We can see that as the object moves away from the lens, the image moves nearer to the lens on the other side.

Each point on the object generates its own point on the image.

17.5 THE USE OF THIN CONVERGING LENSES IN PROJECTORS, CAMERAS AND TELESCOPES

(i) In a projector, a thin converging lens is used to produce a magnified real image. A diagram is shown in Fig. 17.7.

A concave mirror is placed a distance 2F behind the bulb. Any light travelling backwards from the bulb is then reflected back along its path. The light goes forward from the bulb to strike a condenser. This consists of a thin converging lens sliced in half and re-arranged.

FIG. 17.7

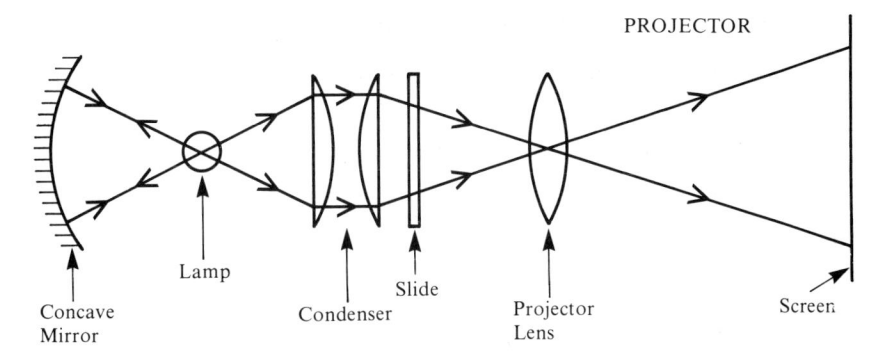

Lamp · Slide · Projector Lens · Screen · Concave Mirror · Condenser · PROJECTOR

It acts to concentrate all the light through the slide. The light from the slide is focussed by the projector lens onto the screen.

The slide is placed in the projector upside down. The lens inverts it to appear the correct way up. The position of the lens can be adjusted so that a sharp image may be focussed on the screen over a range of distances.

(ii) In a camera, a thin converging lens is used to produce a reduced real image. A diagram is shown in Fig. 17.8.

FIG. 17.8

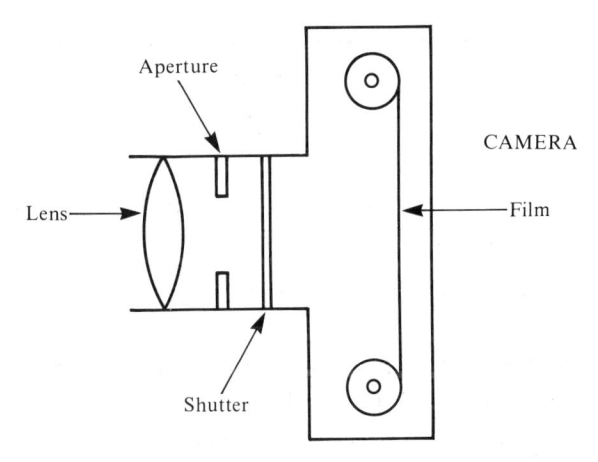

Aperture · Lens · Shutter · Film · CAMERA

The thin converging lens forms an image on the film. The lens can be moved forwards and backwards in order to give a sharp focussed image on the film of objects which may be near or far from the camera. The lens will be focussed for distances as shown on the focussing ring around the lens.

220 Thin Converging Lenses

The amount of light reaching the film is controlled by the aperture and shutter speed. The aperture is a hole whose diameter can be changed. To photograph a fast moving object we need to use a fast shutter speed and a big aperture. To obtain sharp focus over a large range of distances we need a small aperture and a slow shutter speed. Slow shutter speeds are between $\frac{1}{30}$th and $\frac{1}{120}$th of a second and fast shutter speeds less than $\frac{1}{500}$th of a second. Big apertures have values of f numbers between f2.8 and f8 and small apertures have values between f11 and f22.

(iii) Thin converging lenses are used in telescopes, together with prisms. The lenses bring light to a focus. Such a telescope is shown in Photograph 17. It shows the 24 inch Radcliffe telescope at the Mill Hill Observatory.

PHOTOGRAPH 17

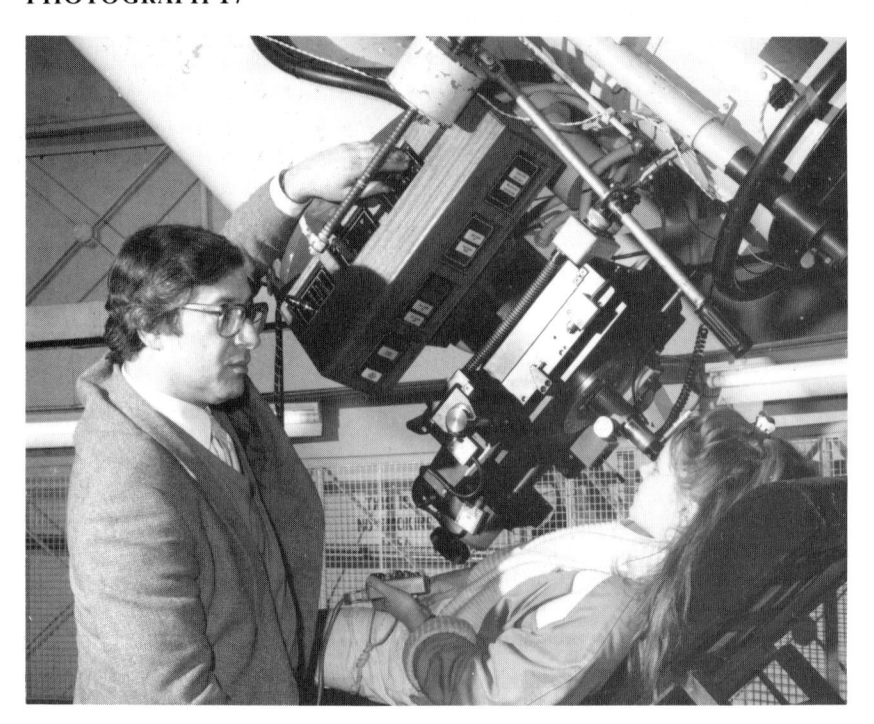

SUPPLEMENTARY

17.6   THE USE OF RAY DIAGRAMS TO LOCATE A VIRTUAL IMAGE
If an object is nearer a thin converging lens than the principal focus then a virtual image is formed. The rays only appear to meet at the image.

As well as being virtual, the image is the right way up or erect, on the same side of the lens as the object and is magnified, as shown in Fig. 17.9.

FIG. 17.9

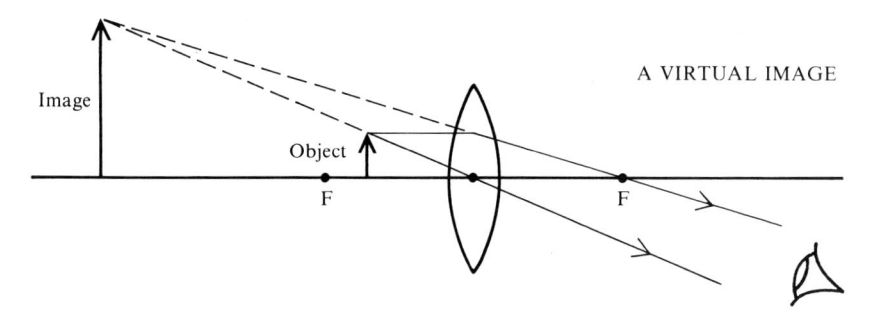

A VIRTUAL IMAGE

17.7 THE MAGNIFYING GLASS

We use a lens, as above, as a magnifying glass when we require a very large image which we do not require to focus on a screen.

The nearer an object is brought to the eye, the bigger it seems to be because it subtends a greater angle to the eye. The magnifying glass causes an object to subtend such a greater angle without being brought nearer to the eye, as shown in Fig. 17.10.

FIG. 17.10

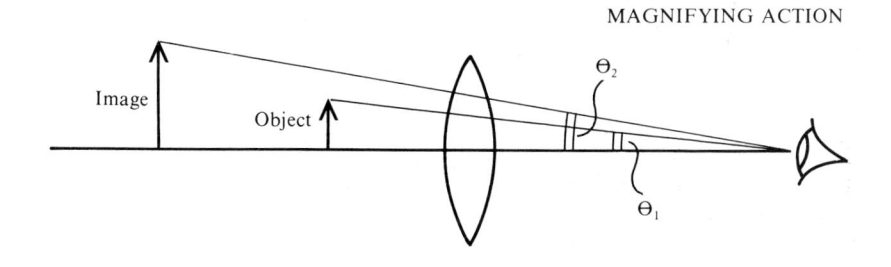

MAGNIFYING ACTION

The object subtends an angle Θ_1 at the eye. When the lens is used as a magnifying glass, the virtual image formed subtends a much larger angle Θ_2.

QUESTIONS

CORE
1. Why should a camera to be used in poor lighting conditions have a wide lens?

2. A ray of light is incident on a thin convex lens as shown below.

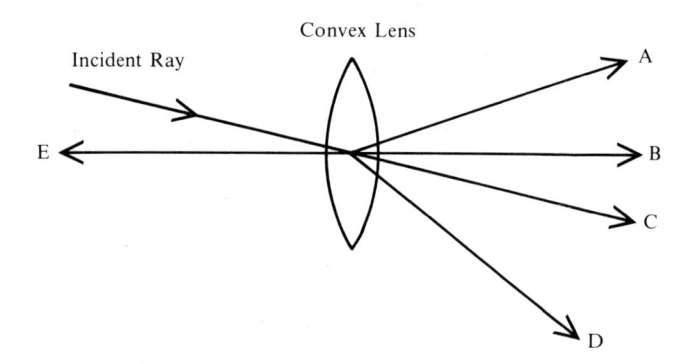

In which direction will the ray emerge? *(M.E.G.)*

3. Lens Q has the same focal length as lens P, but only half the diameter. Both lenses are used, separately, to form two images of a tree on a screen. Which statement about the images is correct?
   A. The image Q forms is smaller than the image P forms.
   B. The image Q forms is not as sharply focussed as the image P forms.
   C. The image Q forms is closer to the lens than the image P forms.
   D. The images are both upside-down.
   E. The images are the same brightness. *(M.E.G.)*
4. Draw a ray diagram to show the formation of a real inverted reduced image.
5. Draw a ray diagram to show the formation of a real inverted magnified image.

SUPPLEMENTARY
6. If an object is located at 2F, how big will the image be?
7. Our eyes contain a lens. What will the nature of the image be?
8. A thin converging lens can produce two types of magnified image. Distinguish between them.

Chapter 18
ELECTROMAGNETIC WAVES

At the end of this chapter you will know:
CORE: the properties of electromagnetic waves; the types of electromagnetic waves in the electromagnetic spectrum and their ordering in terms of wavelength and frequency; how the colour and deviation of light is related to wavelength and brightness is related to amplitude and important uses of electromagnetic waves.
SUPPLEMENTARY: what is meant by monochromatic waves; the speed of electromagnetic waves in air and the order of magnitude of the wavelength of members of the electromagnetic spectrum.

CORE

18.1 PROPERTIES OF ELECTROMAGNETIC WAVES

Electromagnetic waves consist of changing magnetic forces and changing electric forces which travel along. Both the magnetic forces and the electric forces propagate as transverse waves. The magnetic changes occur at right angles to the direction of motion and so do the electric changes — and also the magnetic changes and the electric changes are at right angles to each other.

All electromagnetic waves:
1. transfer energy.
2. do not need a medium to travel through — they can pass through a vacuum.
3. travel at the same speed in vacuum or air.

Like all waves they undergo reflection, refraction, interference and diffraction.

18.2 THE ELECTROMAGNETIC SPECTRUM

There are various types of electromagnetic waves. When they are arranged in order, they form the electromagnetic spectrum.

The electromagnetic spectrum is shown in the following table:

In order of increasing wavelength we have gamma rays, X rays, ultra violet, visible light, infra red and radio-waves. Radio waves cover microwaves, radar, television and radio broadcast waves. Notice that visible light is only a tiny part of the spectrum.

The frequency and wavelength increases in the opposite direction as shown.

224 Electromagnetic Waves

WAVELENGTH INCREASING ⟶

γ RAYS	X RAYS	ULTRA VIOLET	V I S I B L E	INFRA RED	RADIO		
					MICROWAVES RADAR	T.V.	RADIO BROAD- CASTS

⟵ FREQUENCY INCREASING

18.3 LIGHT — ITS COLOUR, DEVIATION AND BRIGHTNESS

In the visible part of the electromagnetic spectrum, the wavelength increases as we go from violet through indigo, blue, green, yellow, orange to red.

As will be seen in Fig. 16.14, the shorter wavelength light is deviated more than the longer wavelength light.

The greater the amplitude of a light wave then the brighter it appears.

18.4 USES OF ELECTROMAGNETIC WAVES

(i) γ rays are emitted by certain radioactive substances and are used in the treatment of cancer and the sterilisation of food.

(ii) X rays are used to see through the flesh to the bones and so are used to detect broken bones. They are also used to locate cracks in metal.

(iii) U.V. rays are emitted by the sun and various lamps They are responsible for sun tanning and in excess cause skin cancer. They also cause certain substances to fluoresce or glow brightly giving out light of various colours.

(iv) I.R. rays are thermal radiation.

(v) Microwaves are used in ovens, where they agitate the food molecules and cause heating. The wavelength used can cause cataracts on the eyes and it is important to ensure that the oven does not leak. They are also used in communications to send information from one place to another.

(vi) Radar waves are used to locate objects. Radar waves generated by a transmitter are beamed at an object. This reflects them back to the transmitter. The speed of the waves is known so by timing how long it takes for the waves to travel out to the object and back again we

Electromagnetic Waves 225

can calculate the distance of the object. Radar is used in this way to locate aircraft.

The radar is transmitted and received by an antenna, as shown in Photograph 18.

PHOTOGRAPH 18

The radar information is displayed on a television screen, as shown in Photograph 19.

226 Electromagnetic Waves

PHOTOGRAPH 19

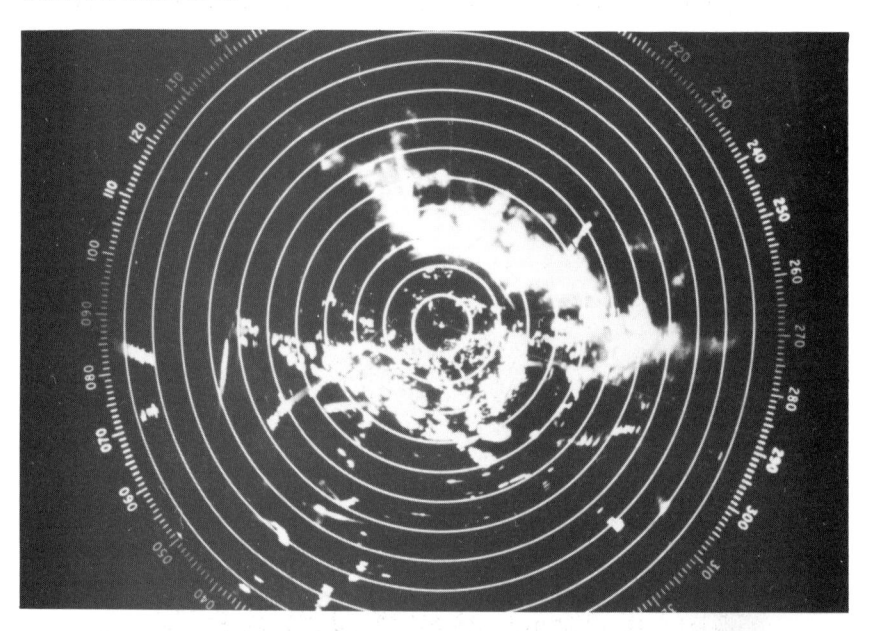

As well as the aircraft reflecting the radar, it is also reflected by rain, clouds and buildings on the ground giving what is known as clutter. This can be removed electronically to give a display of the aircraft only, as shown in Photograph 20.

PHOTOGRAPH 20

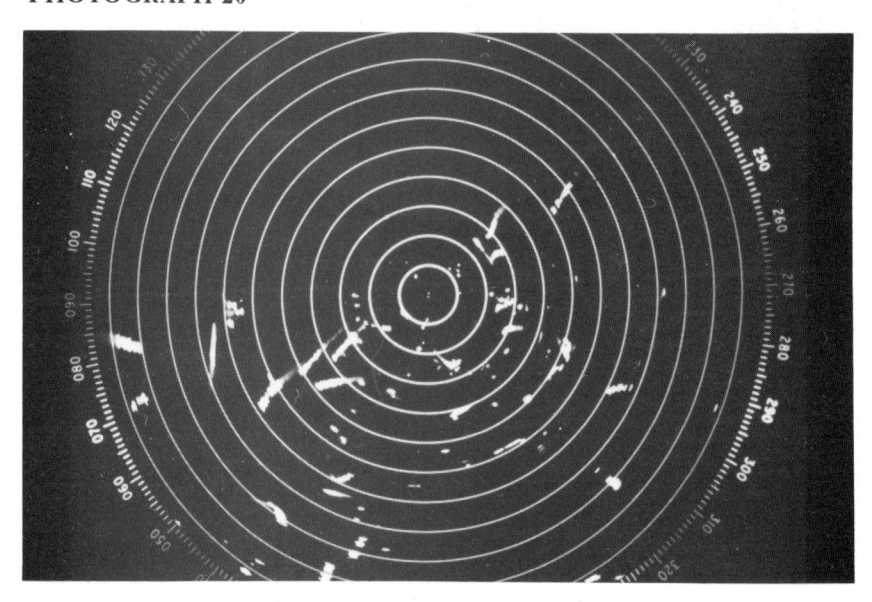

Electromagnetic Waves 227

(vii) T.V. and radio waves are used by commercial broadcasting stations.

(viii) Radio waves are also emitted by hot bodies including stars. Radioastronomy is the branch of physics concerned with their detection and the waves are received by radiotelescopes such as those at the Nuffield Radioastronomy Laboratories at Jodrell Bank, Cheshire.

Photograph 21 shows the Mark IA telescope at Jodrell Bank.

PHOTOGRAPH 21

Radio or radar waves may also be used in security systems when they are reflected off objects.

SUPPLEMENTARY

18.5 MONOCHROMATIC WAVES

Monochromatic waves are those consisting of one wavelength, and therefore one frequency, only. If they are visible then they will have the same colour.

228 Electromagnetic Waves

18.6 THE SPEED OF ELECTROMAGNETIC WAVES IN AIR
All electromagnetic waves travel in vacuum or air at a speed of 3×10^8 m/s. We represent it by the symbol c.

We can therefore specify them in terms of their wavelength or frequency and if given one find the other using $c = f\lambda$. Sometimes a radio station is specified in terms of wavelength or frequency.

18.7 WAVELENGTHS IN THE ELECTROMAGNETIC SPECTRUM
The wavelengths in the electromagnetic spectrum are very small. They are measured in nanometres, nm where
$$1 \text{nm} = 10^{-9} \text{m}.$$
or micrometers, μm where
$$1\mu \text{m} = 10^{-6} \text{m}.$$
Approximate wavelengths are
γ rays, 0.01nm
X rays, 1nm
U.V., 0.2 μm
Visible, 0.4 to 0.7 μm
I.R., 0.01mm
Microwaves, 1cm
Radar, 10cm
T.V., 1m
Radio, 1km.

QUESTIONS

CORE
1. State three properties of electromagnetic waves.
2. Which light has the higher frequency, red or blue?
3. Which colour is deviated most by a prism?
4. Explain the differences between bright red light and dim blue light.
5. The diagram below shows the main regions of the electromagnetic spectrum.

GAMMA RAYS	X RAYS			VISIBLE		RADIO WAVES

(a) On the diagram write in the names of the two blank regions.
(b) Which radiation shown in the table has the shortest wavelength?
(c) Which radiation shown in the table has the highest frequency?
(d) In a vacuum, is the speed of gamma rays greater than, the same as or less than the speed of radio waves?
(e) State one use of gamma rays. *(S.E.G.)*

6. Fig. 1. shows the electromagnetic spectrum.

FIG. 1

RADIO		VISIBLE	ULTRA VIOLET		γ RAYS

(a) On Fig. 1 fill in the names of the two missing regions.
(b) Which region
   (i) has the longest wavelength
   (ii) has the highest frequency
   (iii) causes a sun tan
   (iv) is used in burglar alarms?
(c) Some washing powders contain a chemical which is sensitive to ultra-violet radiation. State and explain what you see when clothes washed in such a powder are put in sun light. *(N.E.A.)*

SUPPLEMENTARY

7. Are yellow and green light waves monochromatic?
8. Calculate the wavelength of radio-waves of frequency 150 MHz if the speed of electromagnetic waves is 3×10^8 m/s.

Chapter 19
SOUND

At the end of this chapter you will know:
CORE: the properties of sound; the frequencies which we can hear; that a substance is needed to carry sound; how loudness and pitch can be shown on a cathode ray oscilloscope; how materials reflect or absorb sound; what is meant by an echo and how it can be used to measure the speed of sound in air and how sonar is used.
SUPPLEMENTARY: how compressions and rarefactions in sound waves arise; some values of the speed of sound in gases, liquids and solids; what is meant by the quality of sound and how a cathode ray oscilloscope may be used to measure the frequency of sound.

CORE

19.1 PROPERTIES OF SOUND

Sound is a longitudinal wave motion. All vibrating objects including our vocal chords and loudspeakers produce sound waves. As an object vibrates in air it disturbs the air molecules and causes a sound wave to travel along. The air molecules are pushed together, stretched apart and then pushed together etc. and these movements take place in the same direction in which the wave is travelling. When the wave reaches our ear it makes our eardrum vibrate and we hear the sound.

Like all other waves, sound undergoes inteference and diffraction. Also like all other waves sound waves transfer energy from the vibrating source to our eardrum. The energy given out every second or power of a vibrating object such as a loudspeaker can be measured in a special room known as an anechoic chamber. An anechoic chamber is shown in Photograph 22.

We shall discuss why the walls have such a strange shape later in the chapter.

PHOTOGRAPH 22

19.2 AUDIBLE FREQUENCIES

Human beings are only able to detect sounds in a particular frequency range. As the frequency of sound increases, it appears more shrill.

We can detect sound waves above a frequency of 20 Hz. The highest frequency which we can hear depends upon our age. Young children can hear up to 18 kHz, teenagers up to 15 kHz and people 50 years old can only hear up to 12 kHz.

Sounds above 20 kHz obviously cannot be heard — we say they are inaudible. Such sounds are said to be ultrasonic. These waves can be detected by certain animals including bats and dogs. Dog whistles, some T.V. remote controls and sonar detectors all use ultrasonic waves.

19.3 THE NEED FOR A MEDIUM

A sound wave needs a substance or medium to travel through. It can travel through solids, liquids and gases.

We can demonstrate that a medium is needed, using the experiment shown in Fig. 19.1.

FIG. 19.1

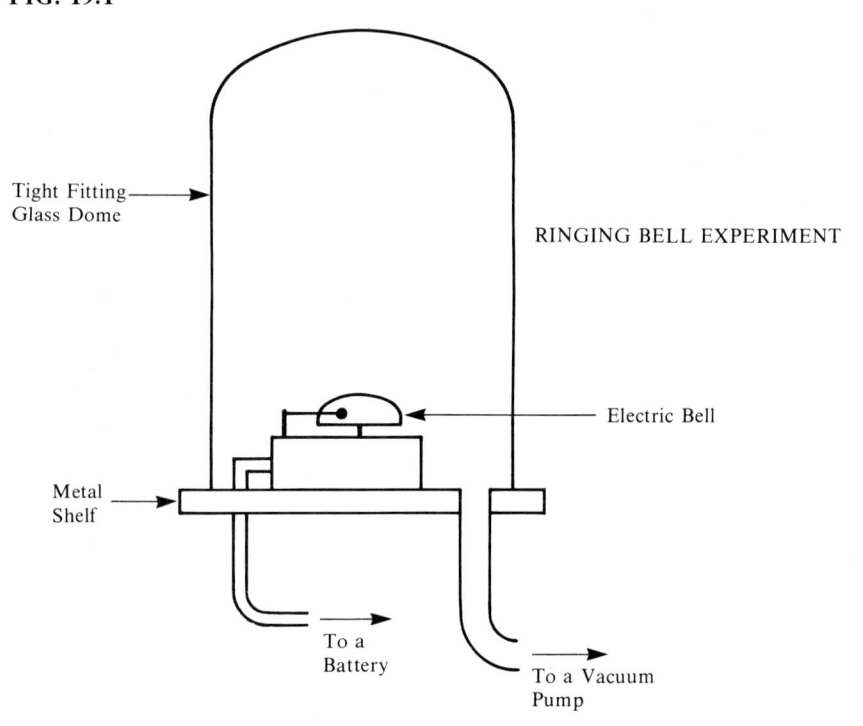

RINGING BELL EXPERIMENT

Tight Fitting Glass Dome

Electric Bell

Metal Shelf

To a Battery

To a Vacuum Pump

The bell is switched on and can be both seen and heard to be ringing. The vacuum pump is then switched on. As it removes the air from underneath the glass dome the sound of the bell dies away even though it can be still seen to be ringing.

The sound dies away because the medium is being removed and so the wave has nothing through which to move.

19.4 USE OF A CATHODE RAY OSCILLOSCOPE TO SHOW LOUDNESS AND PITCH

The louder a sound wave is, the greater is its amplitude and the shriller it sounds, the greater is its frequency or pitch.

We can demonstrate these facts using a cathode ray oscilloscope or C.R.O. The C.R.O. will be discussed in detail in Chapter 28. For now we can think of it as a special type of television screen which can be used to display transverse waves. On the screen there are horizontal and vertical lines just as there are on graph paper.

A microphone is connected to the C.R.O. and this converts sound energy to electrical energy which is converted to light energy on the C.R.O. screen.

If a loudspeaker generating a particular frequency is brought up to the microphone, the C.R.O. screen will display a transverse wave representation of the sound wave. This is shown in Fig. 19.2.

FIG. 19.2

DISPLAYING A SOUND WAVE ON A C.R.O.

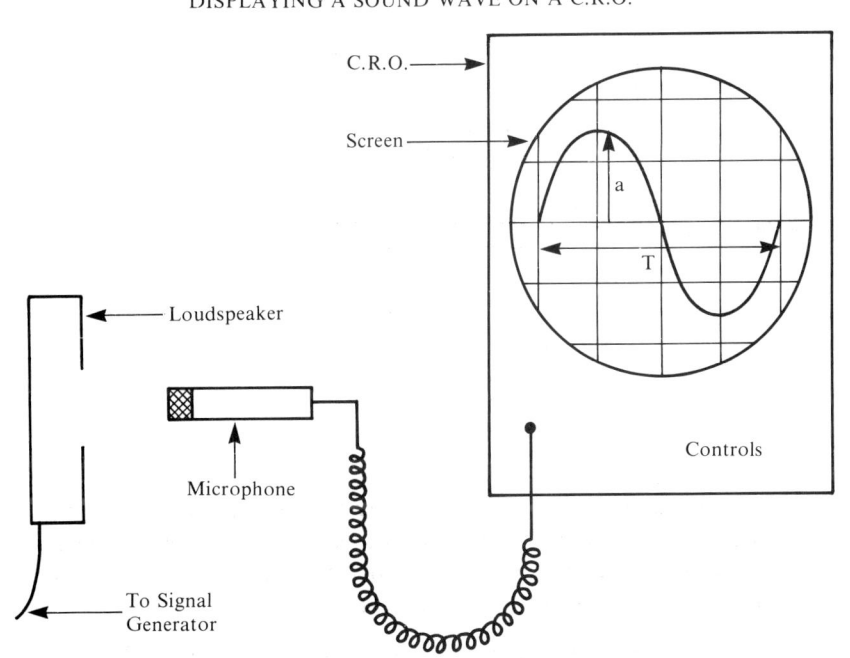

The amplitude of the sound wave is represented by a. The actual period of the sound wave is shown by T.

The loudspeaker is attached to a signal generator which can be adjusted to make the loudspeaker generate sound waves of varying loudness and frequency.

If the signal generator is adjusted to make the loudspeaker generate louder sounds at the same frequency we see that the height, a, of the wave on the screen increases. This means that the amplitude of the sound wave is also increasing.

If the signal generator is now adjusted to make the loudspeaker generate higher frequencies or higher pitched sounds at the same loudness we see that the period of the wave on the screen decreases and if we started with only one complete wave on the screen, as shown in Fig. 19.2, we will now have more than one. The period of the wave on the screen has decreased and as this is the period of the sound wave, it too has decreased. We would expect a decrease in wavelength as the frequency rises because: wave speed = frequency × wavelength and period = 1/frequency.

19.5 ABSORPTION AND REFLECTION OF SOUND

Materials can either absorb or reflect sound. A good absorber is a poor reflector and vice versa.

Good reflectors include a water surface, brick, concrete, tiled floors, parquet floors and hard seats.

Good absorbers include glass wool, foams, hardboard, carpets, curtains and upholstered seats.

The walls, floors and ceilings of anechoic chambers are covered with specially shaped pieces of foam to eliminate the reflection of sound.

Concert halls are well upholstered and curtained to reduce reflections which create unpleasant effects.

19.6 ECHOES AND THE SPEED OF SOUND IN AIR

Reflected sound forms an echo and echoes can be used to measure the speed of sound in air.

You need to stand about 100m from a concrete wall, clapping your hands together. The clapping rate is adjusted until each clap co-incides with the echo of the last one. The sound has therefore travelled to the wall and back in the time interval between two claps. Thirty time intervals are measured with a stop watch so that one time interval may be found.

If the time interval is t s and the distance from your hands to the wall is s m then

$$\text{speed of sound in air} = \frac{2s}{t} \text{ m/s}$$

19.7 SONAR

Ships use an echo-sounding system called sonar to measure the depth of the sea and of shoals of fish. Ultrasonic waves are transmitted by the ship, reflected from the sea bottom or the fish and are detected by a receiver, as shown in Fig. 19.3.

FIG. 19.3

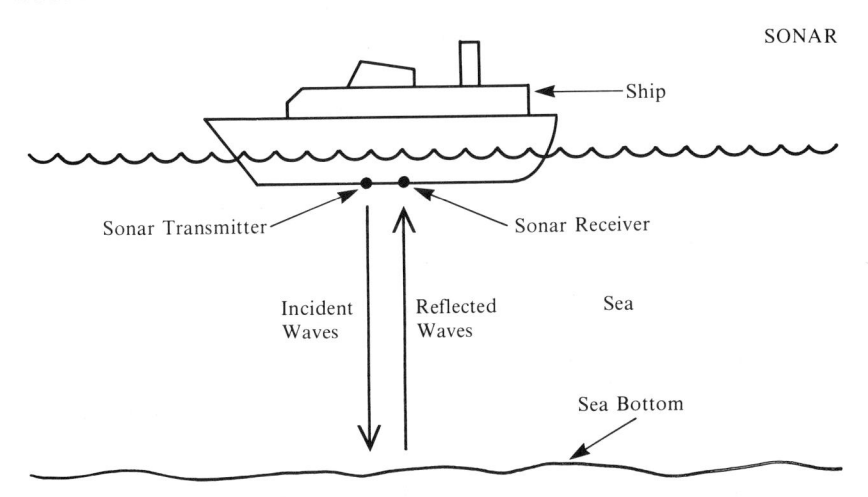

SONAR

[Diagram: Ship on sea surface with Sonar Transmitter and Sonar Receiver labelled, showing Incident Waves going down and Reflected Waves coming up from the Sea Bottom]

If the speed of sound in water is v, the sea depth s and the time between transmission and receipt of sound is t then we can re-arrange the echo formula of Section 19.6 to obtain

$$s = \frac{vt}{2}$$

Often the transmitted and received signals are displayed on a C.R.O. with the horizontal scale calibrated in distance.

The device is able to tell if the sound has been reflected from fish or the sea bottom because the energy of the reflected wave is different in each case.

Ultrasound is also used in medicine. It is used to examine a mother's unborn baby because unlike X rays it does not present a health hazard. It is also used to watch the beating heart. X rays, as well as being a health hazard, could not be used to do this because they are not emitted continuously but in short bursts.

SUPPLEMENTARY

19.8 COMPRESSIONS AND RAREFACTIONS IN SOUND WAVES

We have seen that sound waves push together and stretch apart the molecules of the medium through which they travel. The regions where the molecules are squeezed together are compresions and those where the molecules are stretched out are rarefactions, as shown in Fig. 19.4.

FIG. 19.4

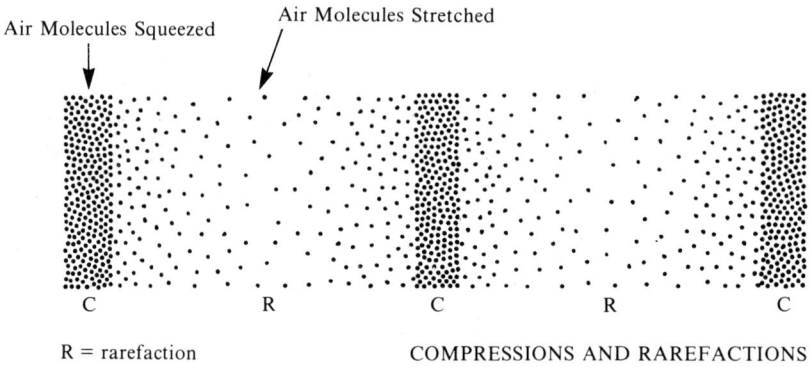

Air Molecules Squeezed Air Molecules Stretched

C   R   C   R   C

R = rarefaction
C = compression

COMPRESSIONS AND RAREFACTIONS
IN A SOUND WAVE IN AIR

19.9 SPEED OF SOUND IN GASES, LIQUIDS AND SOLIDS

The speed of sound increases as temperature increases. In air, for example, its speed is 330 m/s at 0°C but 343 m/s at 20°C.

The speed of sound is least in gases, greater in liquids and greatest of all in solids, as can be seen below:—

Material	Speed of sound at 20°C (m/s)
Carbon Dioxide	267
Air	343
Pure Water	1483
Sea Water	1522
Sea Water	1522
Aluminium	5100
Mild Steel	5200

19.10 THE QUALITY OF SOUND

If two musical instruments are playing sounds of the same frequency, we are able to tell the difference between the sound from each instrument. This is because each sound has a different quality or timbre. The reason for this is that each instrument emits a sound wave with a different wave form.

We can show this using a microphone connector to a C.R.O. A pure sound wave generated by a tuning fork is a sin curve, as shown in Fig. 19.5(a). The waves generated by a violin and a piano at the same wavelength are not as smooth giving a difference in quality.

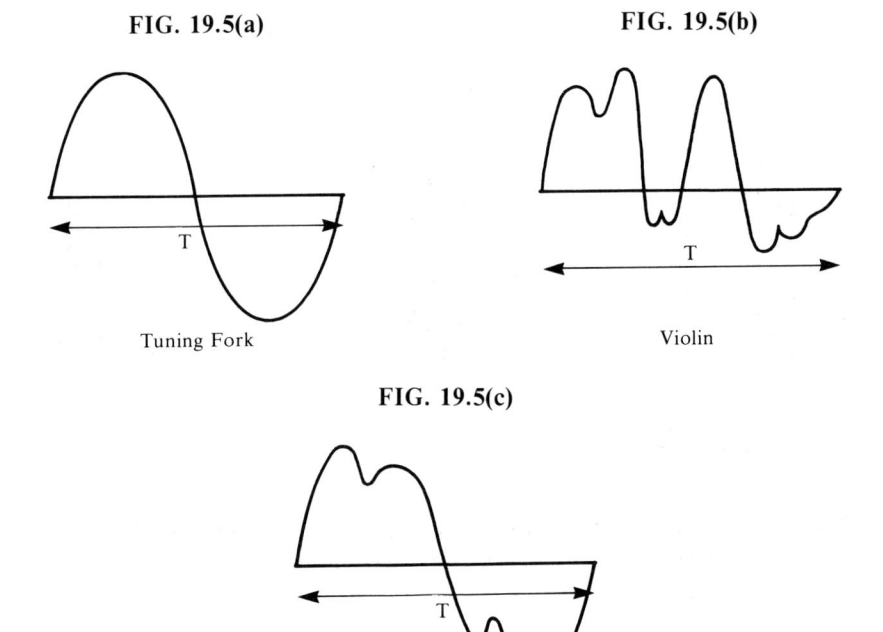

FIG. 19.5(a)

Tuning Fork

FIG. 19.5(b)

Violin

FIG. 19.5(c)

Piano

19.11 DETERMINATION OF THE FREQUENCY OF SOUND USING A C.R.O.

Using the apparatus shown in Fig. 19.2 we can find the frequency of sound.

We adjust a control on the device called the timebase until we obtain two or three complete waves on the screen.

The wavelength is measured — suppose it is x cm. We read the timebase calibration — suppose it is 1 ms/cm; this means that each cm on the screen corresponds to 1 ms of time.

We multiply the wavelength by the timebase calibration. Here one complete wave corresponds to x ms; in other words the time for one complete wave is x ms. The frequency of the sound — the time for one complete wavelength is the reciprocal of this, in seconds.

$$\text{Here the frequency is } \frac{1}{x/1000} = \frac{1000}{x} \text{ Hz}$$

PROBLEM
A C.R.O. IS USED TO MEASURE THE FREQUENCY OF A SOUND. THE TIMEBASE IS SET AS 1ms/cm AND ONE COMPLETE WAVELENGTH OCCUPIES 2cm. CALCULATE THE FREQUENCY OF THE SOUND.

1 wavelength occupies 2cm
Since the timebase setting is 1ms/cm, the time for one complete wavelength is $2 \times 1 = 2$ ms
The frequency is $\frac{1}{2/1000} = \frac{1000}{2} = 500$ Hz

ANSWER: FREQUENCY OF THE SOUND = 500 Hz.

QUESTIONS

CORE
1. Which of the following is/are longitudinal waves?
   A. water waves; B. waves on a stretched spring; C. sound waves; D. light waves.
2. A whistle emits a sound of frequency 17 kHz. Could it be heard by an old aged pensioner? Explain.
3. Explain why certain television remote control units could disturb a dog.
4. Explain why we can see the sun but we cannot hear it.
5. A microphone is connected to a cathode ray oscilloscope. Three sounds are made in turn in front of the microphone. The traces A, B and C produced on the screen are shown below. (The controls of the oscilloscope are not altered during the experiment.

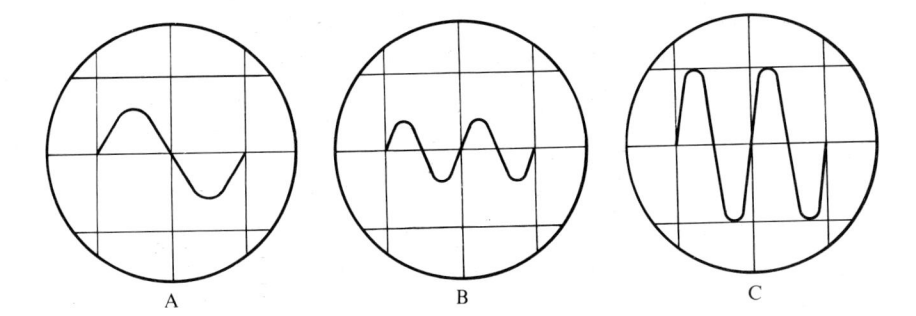

(a) Which trace is due to the loudest sound? Explain your answer.
(b) Which trace is due to the sound with the lowest pitch? Explain your answer. *(M.E.G.)*
6. Explain why concert halls are well upholstered.
7. A person stands in front of a tall cliff and claps her hands. If she hears an echo 1.2s later and the speed of sound is 330m/s, calculate her distance from the cliff.
8. Fig. 5 shows a beam of sonar waves sent out to a shoal of fish directly underneath a fishing boat.

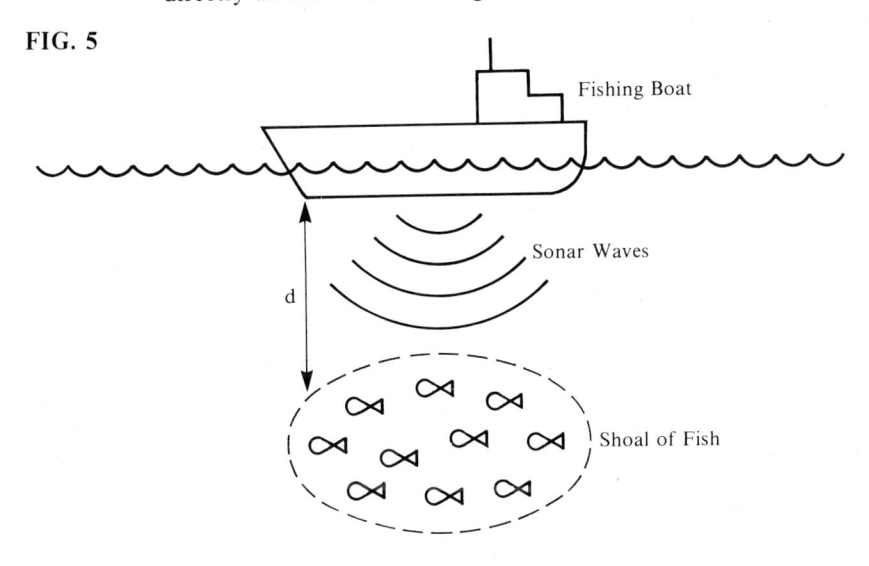

FIG. 5

(a) The speed of the sonar waves in water is 1400m/s and the echo returns after 0.1 seconds. Use the equation
$$\text{distance} = \text{speed} \times \text{time}$$
to calculate the depth of the shoal of fish (d).
(b) Explain why the returning pulse lasts for a longer time than the pulse sent out. *(N.E.A.)*

SUPPLEMENTARY
9. Explain why sound travels faster in summer than winter.
10. A stick is used to hit a steel fence. If the ear is held close to the other end of the fence, two sounds are heard when the stick hits the fence. Explain why and state which sound is heard first.
11. A C.R.O. is used to determine the frequency of a sound. Two complete waves occupy 4cm and the timebase setting is 10ms/cm. Calculate the frequency of the sound.

Chapter 20
MAGNETISM

At the end of this chapter you will know:
CORE: the properties of a magnet; the law of magnetic poles; methods of making and destroying magnets; what is meant by induced magnetism; the difference between hard and soft magnetic materials with examples and uses of each; what is meant by magnetic fields and how they may be observed; that there is a magnetic field associated with the earth and what is meant by magnetic screening.
SUPPLEMENTARY: examples of paramagnetic substances; the field pattern due to a U shaped magnet with curved pole-pieces and how to identify the poles of a magnet made by a solenoid.

CORE

20.1 PROPERTIES OF MAGNETS

(i) If a magnet is dipped into iron filings and then removed we will find that the iron filings will be attracted to it, gathering in large clusters around its ends.

Magnets are made from iron, cobalt and nickel and their alloys.

We find that magnets will attract unmagnetised pieces of iron, cobalt and nickel and their alloys. Because these metals and alloys can be made into strong magnets they are said to be ferromagnetic. We can think of all other substances as being non-magnetic.

Magnetism arises as a result of the motion of charged particles called electrons, in the substance. In most substances the effects of this motion cancel out, but in ferromagnetic substances, they do not.

(ii) The iron filings cluster around the ends of a magnet because a magnet behaves as if all its magnetism were concentrated near its ends. These places where the magnetism appears to be concentrated are called the poles of the magnet.

If we suspend a magnet by a fine thread, arranged to form a stirrup, as shown in Fig. 20.1, we find that it comes to rest in an approximate north-south direction.

The pole which is pointing north is called the north seeking or simply the north pole, identified by an N. The other pole pointing south is called the south pole, identified by an S. The shape of magnet shown in this diagram is called a bar magnet.

242 Magnetism

FIG. 20.1

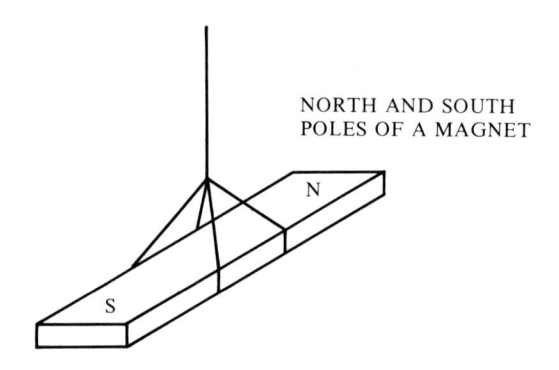

NORTH AND SOUTH POLES OF A MAGNET

20.2 THE LAW OF MAGNETIC POLES

(i) Suppose a bar magnet is suspended as in Fig. 20.2(a). If the south pole of another magnet is brought up to the south pole of the suspended magnet, the suspended magnet is repelled.

If we change round both poles by bringing up the north pole of the magnet to the north pole of the suspended magnet, we find that repulsion also takes place.

Suppose now we bring the north pole of a magnet up to the south pole of the suspended magnet, as in Fig. 20.2(b). The suspended magnet will now be attracted.

This attraction will again occur if we change round both poles and bring up the south pole of the magnet up to the north pole of the suspended magnet.

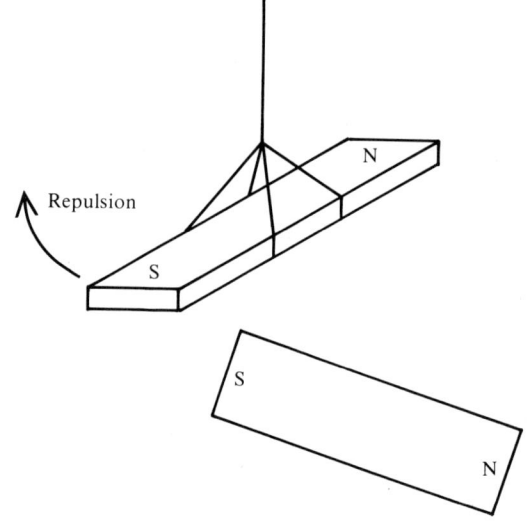

FIG. 20.2(a)

FIG. 20.2(b)

LAW OF MAGNETIC POLES

Attraction

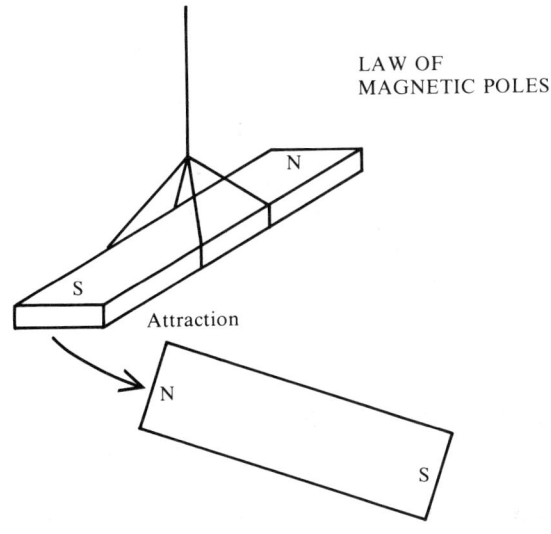

From this experiment we can see that:
1) a north pole repels another north pole
2) a south pole repels another south pole
3) a north pole attracts a south pole and
4) a south pole attracts a north pole.

Writing this in another way we have the Law of Magnetic Poles: Like poles repel, unlike poles attract.

(ii) The Law of Magnetic Poles enables us to decide whether or not a material is a magnet. Attraction will occur between any pole of a magnet and a piece of ferromagnetic material which is not a magnet. Obviously attraction will also occur between the pole of a magnet and the unlike pole of another magnet. However, repulsion will only occur between one pole of a magnet and the like pole of another magnet. Repulsion is therefore the only test for a magnet.

20.3 MAKING AND DESTROYING MAGNETS

We can use non-electrical and electrical methods to magnetise and demagnetise substances.

(i) In order to make a ferromagnetic substance into a magnet non-electrically, we stroke it with a magnet. In the single stroke method shown in Fig. 20.3, the substance is stroked from end to end between 20 to 30 times in the same direction by the same pole of a magnet. The pole produced at the end where the stroking ends is the opposite type to the stroking pole.

244 Magnetism

FIG. 20.3

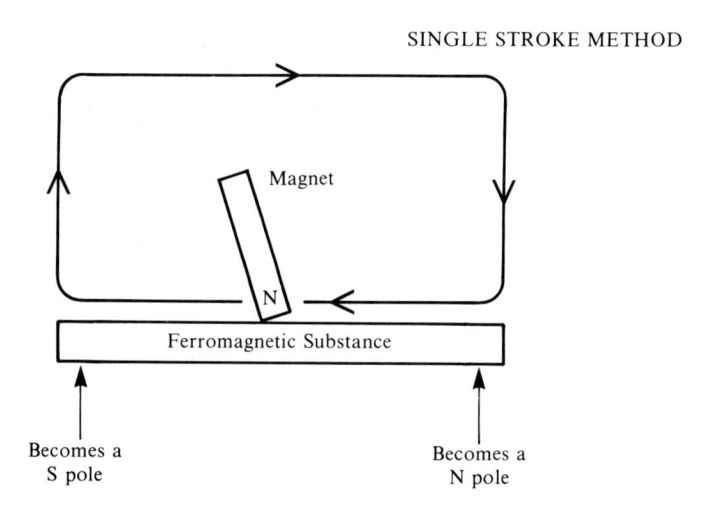

SINGLE STROKE METHOD

Magnet

Ferromagnetic Substance

Becomes a S pole

Becomes a N pole

In the double stroke method shown in Fig. 20.4, the stroking is done from the centre to the ends with the opposite poles of two magnets at the same time. This is a better method because the poles are the same distance from each end.

FIG. 20.4

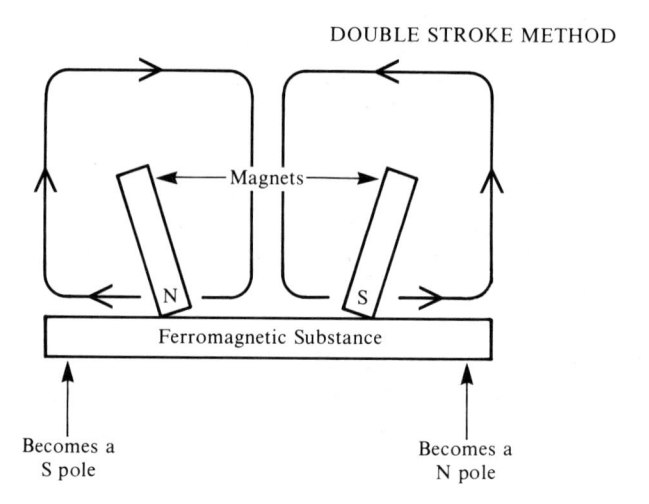

DOUBLE STROKE METHOD

Magnets

Ferromagnetic Substance

Becomes a S pole

Becomes a N pole

In order to make a ferromagnetic substance into a magnet by an electrical method, we use a solenoid as shown in Fig. 20.5.

FIG. 20.5 MAKING A MAGNET USING A SOLENOID

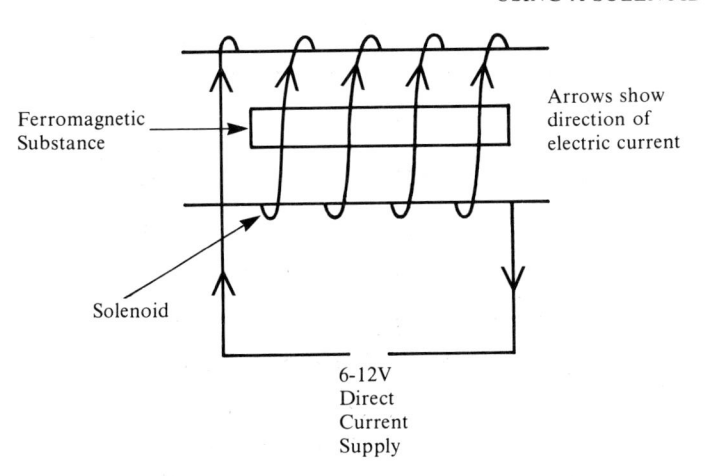

Ferromagnetic Substance

Arrows show direction of electric current

Solenoid

6-12V Direct Current Supply

The solenoid is a coil with a large number of insulated copper turns. The solenoid is connected to a 6-12V direct current supply after the ferromagnetic substance has been placed in it. After a few seconds the substance will be magnetised and the current can be switched off and the new magnet removed. All modern magnets are made in this way.

(ii) To demagnetise a magnet non-electrically, it is heated to a very high temperature — until it glows red — and it is then allowed to cool down lying in an east-west direction. The disadvantage of this method is that the substance is damaged physically. Dropping a magnet also destroys some of its magnetism.

To demagnetise a magnet electrically, we use a solenoid as shown in Fig. 20.5. This time the solenoid is connected to a 12V alternating current supply and the magnet is slowly pulled out of the solenoid away to a distance of a few metres, while the current is still flowing through the solenoid.

20.4 INDUCED MAGNETISM

If a piece of ferromagnetic substance is made to touch or brought near to the pole of a magnet, it becomes a magnet itself. This is called induced magnetism.

The end of the substance nearest to the inducing pole has an opposite pole induced in it, as shown, in Fig. 20.6.

A chain of pins can be attached to a bar magnet, as shown in Fig. 20.7, with each induced pole inducing an opposite pole next to it.

FIG. 20.6

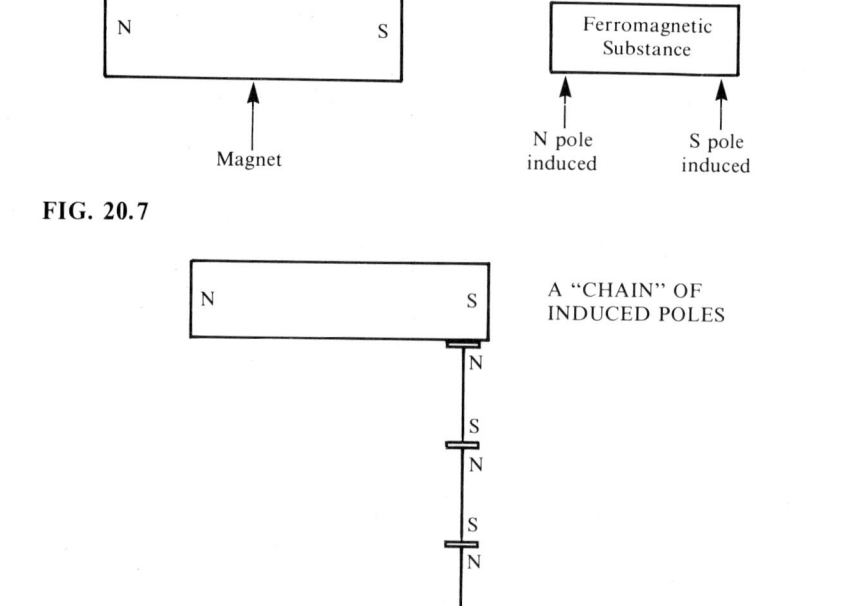

```
┌─────────────────────┐                    INDUCED POLES
│ N               S   │              ┌──────────────────┐
└─────────────────────┘              │  Ferromagnetic   │
           ↑                         │    Substance     │
           │                         └──────────────────┘
         Magnet                          ↑           ↑
                                         │           │
                                      N pole      S pole
                                      induced     induced
```

FIG. 20.7

```
┌─────────────────────┐
│ N               S   │        A "CHAIN" OF
└─────────────────────┘        INDUCED POLES
                  │N
                  │
                  │S
                  │N
                  │
                  │S
                  │N
                  │
                  │S
```

If the south pole of a magnet is brought near the bottom of the lowest pin in Fig. 20.7, the pin will be repelled showing that it is a south pole.

20.5 HARD AND SOFT MAGNETIC MATERIALS

Suppose we hang some steel pins from one pole of a magnet and some iron pins from the other pole as shown in Fig. 20.8.

Even though the weight of a steel pin is the same as the weight of an iron pin, we find that we are able to hang more iron pins than steel pins. Iron magnetizes more easily than steel.

We notice a more interesting effect if we gently remove the magnet from the top of each chain. The iron chain collapses immediately but the steel one does not. This shows that the magnetism induced in iron is temporary but that induced in steel is permanent.

Ferromagnetic substances which magnetize easily but temporarily are called "soft" magnetic materials. Those which are harder to magnetize but are permanently magnetized are called "hard" magnetic materials. It is co-incidence that iron is also "soft" in the sense that it can easily be bent and hammered.

FIG. 20.8

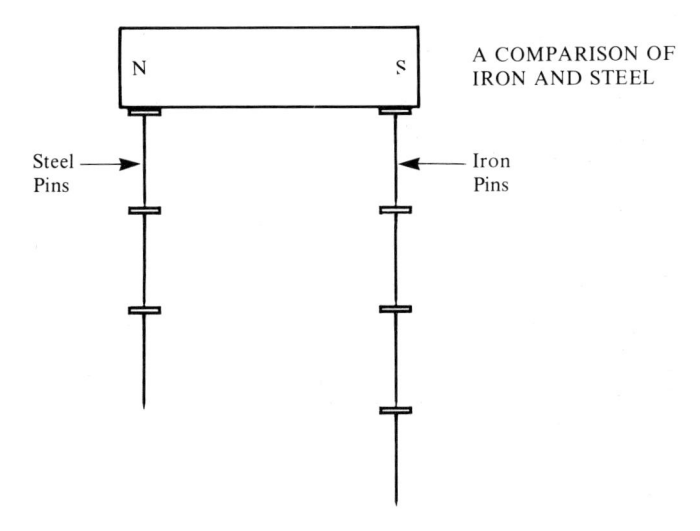

A COMPARISON OF IRON AND STEEL

Examples of soft magnetic materials are obviously iron, silicon-iron alloy, Permalloy (78% nickel, 22% iron) and Mumetal (77% nickel, 14% iron, 5% copper and 4% molybdenum).

Examples of hard magnetic materials are carbon steel (99% iron and 1% carbon), tungsten steel (0.3% chromium, 0.7% carbon, 6% tungsten and 93% iron) and Alnico (6% copper, 10% aluminium, 12% cobalt, 17% nickel and 55% iron). These are all alloys. Another one is a powder or ceramic material known as Magnadure, a compound of barium, iron and oxygen.

Hard magnetic materials are used to make permanent magnets. These types of magnets are used in moving coil meters and loudspeakers.

Soft magnetic materials are used to make temporary magnets. The electrical industry owes its existence to these substances. They are used in electromagnets which are powerful and can be used for delicate tasks such as removing metal splinters from the eyeball to such heavy duty work as moving scrap metal.

Soft magnetic materials are also used in precision electrical apparatus such as the recording heads on tape and video-recorders and audio tapes and videotapes themselves consist of a layer of soft magnetic material on a plastic backing. Thin films of the material are also used in some computer memories.

20.6 MAGNETIC FIELDS

(i) The space surrounding a magnet where it produces a magnetic force is called a magnetic field. The field contains a quantity called magnetic flux. The greater the magnetic force, the stronger the magnetic field and the greater is the magnetic flux.

We can represent the field by drawing field lines or lines of flux.

We say that the direction of the magnetic field is the direction in which a free north pole would move. We can watch the motion of such a free north pole using the experiment shown in Fig. 20.9.

FIG. 20.9

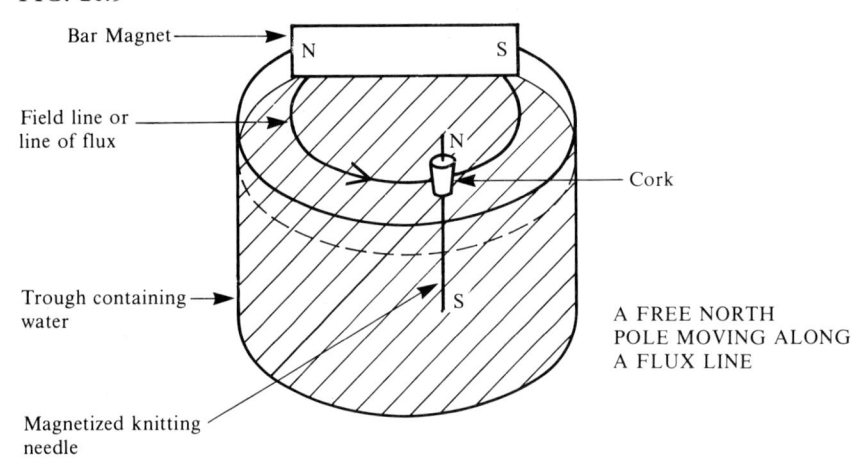

- Bar Magnet
- Field line or line of flux
- Cork
- Trough containing water
- A FREE NORTH POLE MOVING ALONG A FLUX LINE
- Magnetized knitting needle

A bar magnet is positioned on the rim of a trough of water. A magnetized knitting needle is pushed through a cork with the N pole at the top. The cork keeps the needle afloat and the water cancels out any magnetic forces from the S pole of the needle. The needle is held next to the N pole of the magnet and released. It will follow the line of flux to the S pole. We can then put an arrow on the flux line from N to S as shown, indicating the direction of the magnetic field.

(ii) In order to investigate the magnetic fields due to magnets we use a plotting compass, as shown in Fig. 20.10.

FIG. 20.10

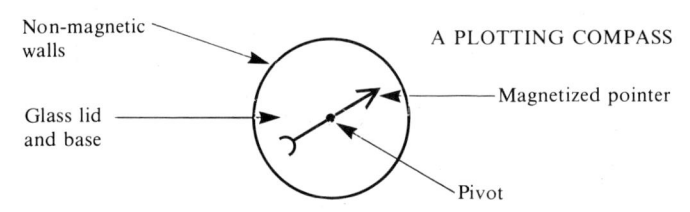

- Non-magnetic walls
- Glass lid and base
- A PLOTTING COMPASS
- Magnetized pointer
- Pivot

The arrowhead of the pointer is a N pole and the tail is a S pole. The arrowhead will therefore point in the direction of the magnetic field at a point.

To plot the magnetic field line or flux lines due to a bar magnet we place the magnet on a sheet of paper. We place a plotting compass at a point A near the N pole, as shown in Fig. 20.11.

FIG. 20.11

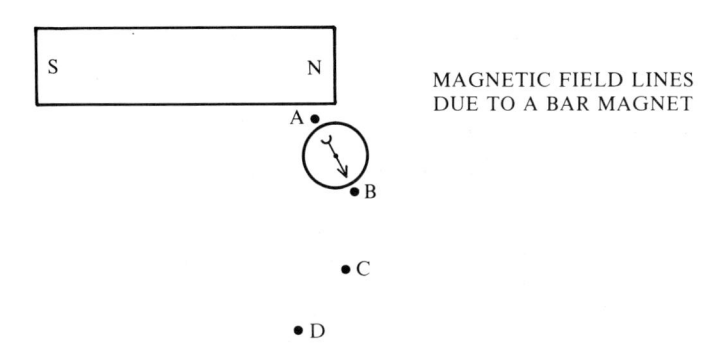

MAGNETIC FIELD LINES
DUE TO A BAR MAGNET

We mark the direction of the arrowhead at B. The plotting compass is then moved along so that its tail lies at B and the arrowhead at C which is marked, the tail placed there and the arrowhead position at D marked. We carry on doing this until we reach the S pole.

The field lines which we get are shown in Fig. 20.12.

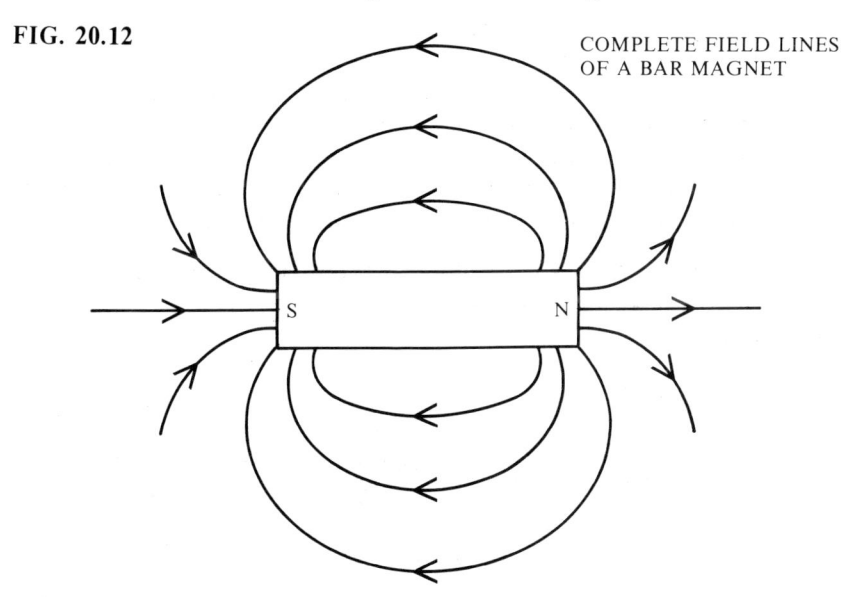

FIG. 20.12

COMPLETE FIELD LINES
OF A BAR MAGNET

250 Magnetism

The arrows on the field lines or flux lines give the direction of the magnetic field.

We may plot the field between two near magnets using the same method. Fig. 20.13(a) shows the field between two unlike poles and Fig. 20.13(b) shows the field between two like poles — at the point O we have a neutral point because the fields cancel out.

FIG. 20.13(a)

FIELD LINES DUE TO UNLIKE POLES

Unlike poles

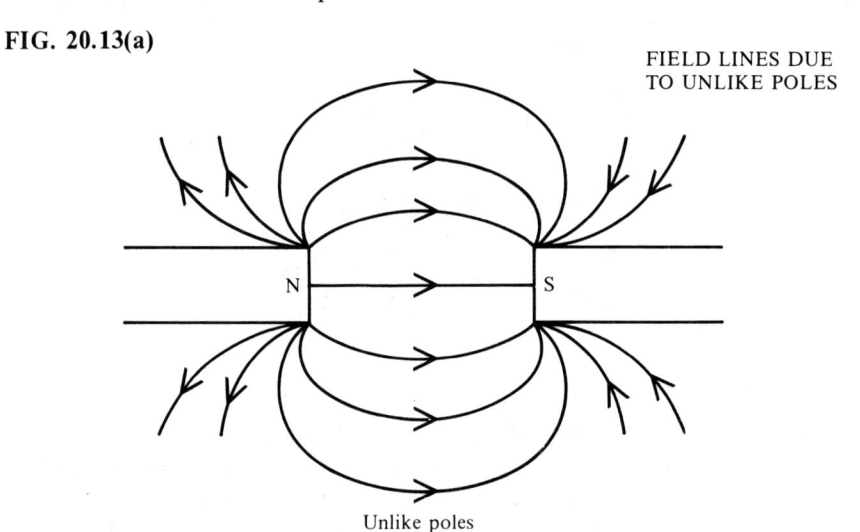

FIG. 20.13(b)

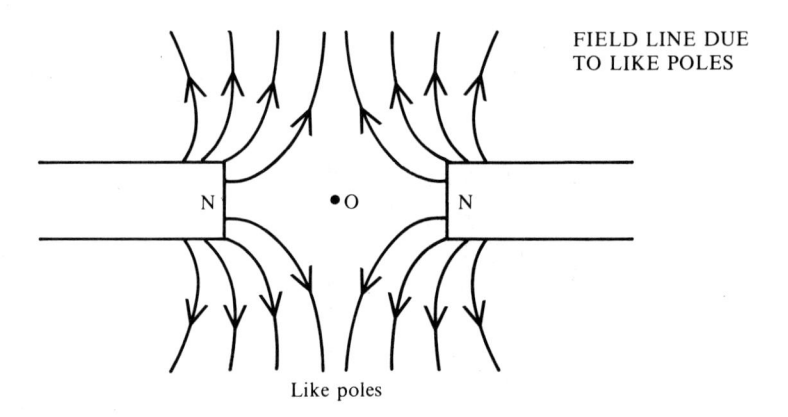

FIELD LINE DUE TO LIKE POLES

Like poles

The field pattern due to a U shaped magnet are shown in Fig. 20.14.

FIG. 20.14

FIELD LINES DUE TO A U SHAPED MAGNET

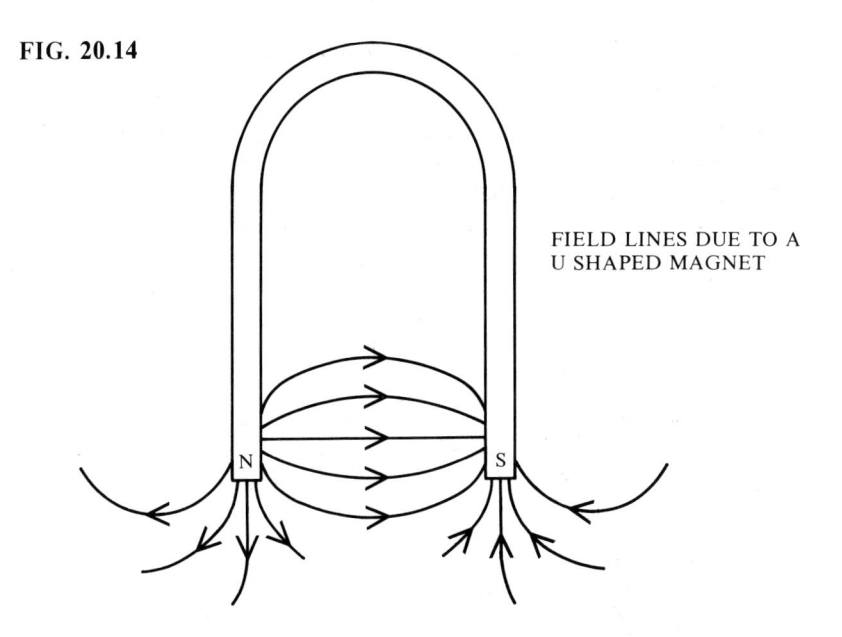

20.7 THE MAGNETIC FIELD DUE TO THE EARTH

(i) If some field lines are plotted on a sheet of paper with no magnets nearby, we obtain a series of parallel straight lines. They point to the magnetic north pole which is not quite in the same direction as the true geographic north pole, as can be seen in Fig. 20.15.

FIG. 20.15

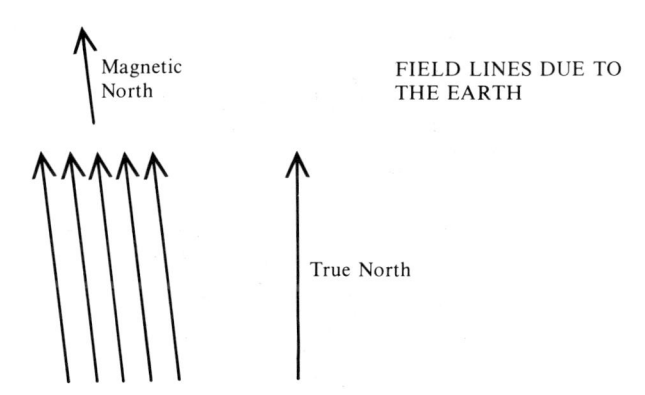

Magnetic North

FIELD LINES DUE TO THE EARTH

True North

The earth behaves just as if it contains a huge bar magnet at a slight angle to the axis of rotation of the earth and with the S pole in the northern hemisphere and vice versa. The magnetism created by the earth is due to the movement of molten liquid in the core of the earth.

252 Magnetism

The direction in which this "magnet" points varies and sometimes it changes direction completely on a timescale of millions of years. This fact is of importance to geologists.

A compass at the earth's north pole will want to point downwards towards the south pole of the earth's "magnet" and it is for this reason that aircraft cannot navigate using their compasses whenever they are near the magnetic north pole.

(ii) The total field due to a bar magnet with its N pole pointing N and the field due to the earth is shown in Fig. 20.16. The neutral points, O, are marked.

FIG. 20.16

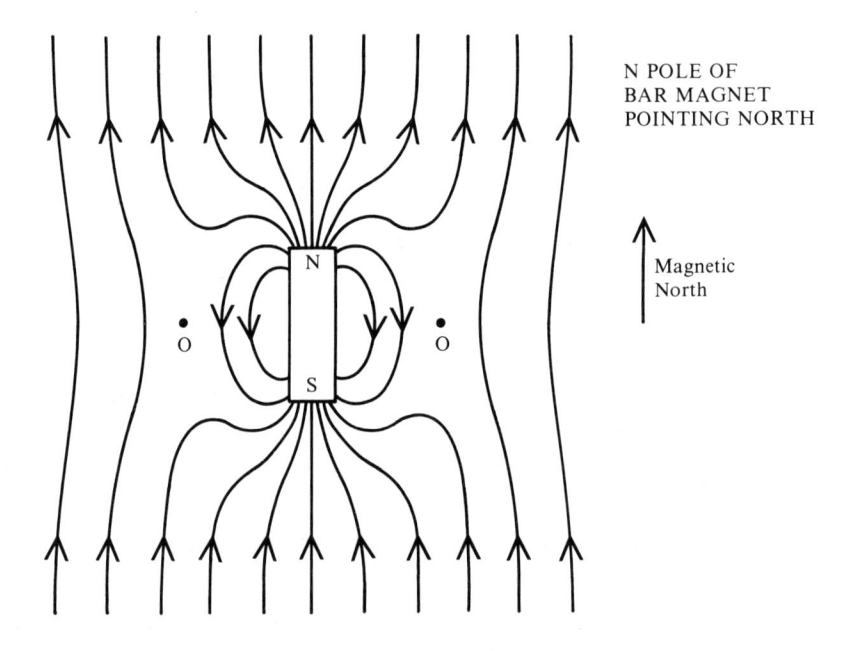

Nearer the magnet its field is stronger than the earth. Further away than the neutral point, the earth's field is stronger.

If the direction of the magnet is reversed, the neutral points are as shown in Fig. 20.17.

FIG. 20.17

S POLE OF
BAR MAGNET
POINTING NORTH

↑ Magnetic North

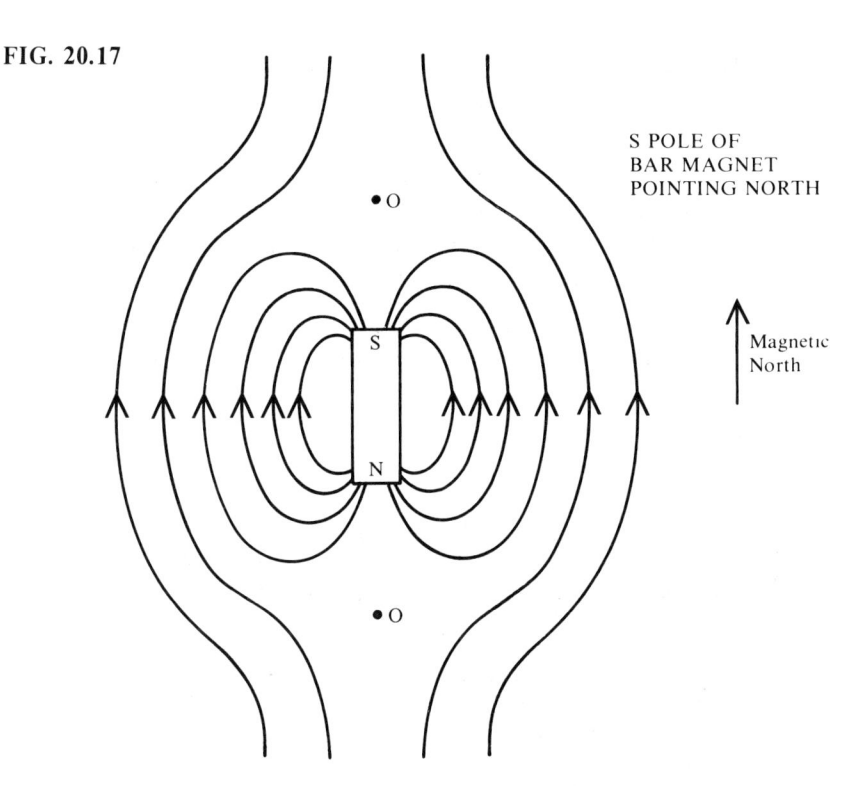

20.8 MAGNETIC SCREENING

If a soft iron ring is placed in a magnetic field, we find that the field does not pass inside the ring. The inside of the ring is screened from the field. Although the ring is magnetized, it does not have a south or a north pole.

Delicate instruments which may be damaged by magnetic fields are screened by placing them inside soft iron boxes.

A similar principle is used with keepers. Bar magnets are stored in pairs with keepers between them, as shown in Fig. 20.18. The whole arrangement becomes magnetized with there being no exposed N or S poles at the ends of the magnets. This enables the magnets to remain strong magnets.

FIG. 20.18

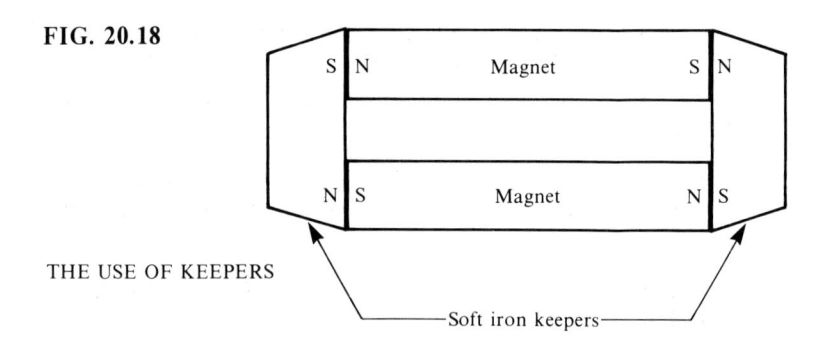

THE USE OF KEEPERS

[Diagram: Two bar magnets arranged in parallel with soft iron keepers at each end. Top magnet: S|N ... S|N. Bottom magnet: N|S ... N|S. Soft iron keepers connect the ends.]

SUPPLEMENTARY

20.9 PARAMAGNETIC SUBSTANCES

Earlier, it was mentioned that substances which are not ferromagnetic are non-magnetic. This is not quite the case because some substances are very weakly magnetic. These materials are called paramagnetic and, on average, they are only 10^{-9} as strongly magnetic as ferromagnetic substances.

Paramagnetic substances include aluminium, manganese, platinum and air.

20.10 THE FIELD PATTERN DUE TO A U MAGNET WITH CURVED POLE PIECES

Suppose we have a U magnet with curved pole pieces as shown in Fig. 20.19.

FIG. 20.19

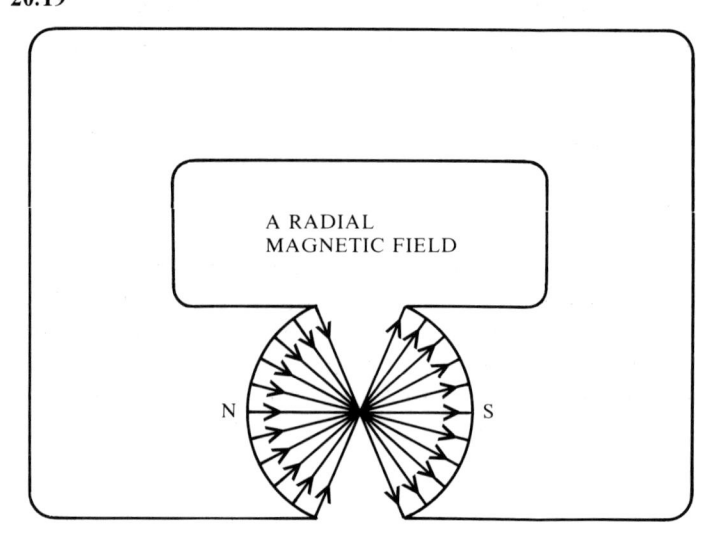

[Diagram: A U magnet with curved pole pieces labelled N and S, showing a radial magnetic field between them.]

A RADIAL MAGNETIC FIELD

The flux lines are as shown and they tell us that the field is directed along lines passing through the centre of the circle which the pole pieces are part of. Because it passes along the radii, it is called a radial field.

A radial field is an important type of field and the scales on moving coil meters are uniform or linear because the devices use such a field.

20.11 IDENTIFYING THE POLES OF A MAGNET MADE BY A SOLENOID

Using the equipment shown in Fig. 20.5, we can always decide which end of the substance will become an N pole and which will become an S pole.

If we look at the end of the substance and the current is flowing round the coil in a clockwise direction then that end will be an S pole; if the current is flowing in an anti-clockwise direction then that end will be a N pole. Using this rule we can see that the left hand side of the substance becomes a N pole and the right hand side a S pole. An easy way to remember this rule is to use the diagrams shown in Fig. 20.20(a) and Fig. 20.20(b).

FIG. 20.20(a)   **FIG. 20.20(b)**

N Pole — Current anti-clockwise   S Pole — Current clockwise

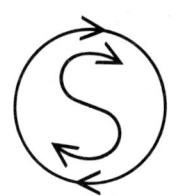

QUESTIONS

CORE
1. A magnet attracts:
   A. plastic B. platinum C. aluminium D. steel.
2. To test if a substance was a magnet, we would see if it
   A. repelled a metal bar B. attracted a metal bar C. repelled a magnet D. attracted a magnet.
3. A material is magnetized using the double stroke method, as shown in Fig. 20.21.

256 Magnetism

FIG. 20.21

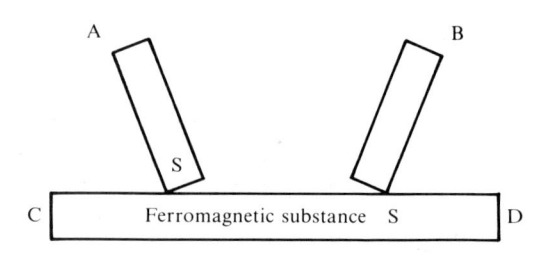

A and B are two bar magnets and the bottom pole of A is a S pole. Identify the bottom pole of B and the poles produced at C and D.

4. Which one of the following materials is most suitable for the core of the electromagnet?
   A. air   B. aluminium   C. brass   D. copper   E. iron   *(M.E.G.)*
5. The diagram shows some plotting compasses around a bar magnet. One of the compass needles has been drawn in.

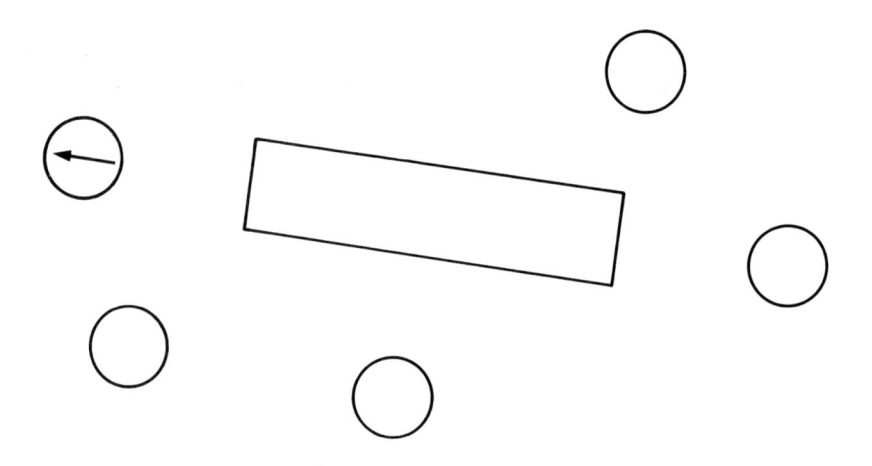

Use your knowledge of the magnetic field to
(a) label the poles of the magnet.
(b) draw the other compass needles in the blank circles. *(L.E.A.G.)*

6. Explain what is meant by a neutral point.

SUPPLEMENTARY
7. Which of the following substances is paramagnetic?
   A. aluminium   B. cobalt   C. nickel   D. steel.
8. Where would a radial magnetic field be used and what would happen if the field were not radial in these circumstances?

9.

Solenoid

V

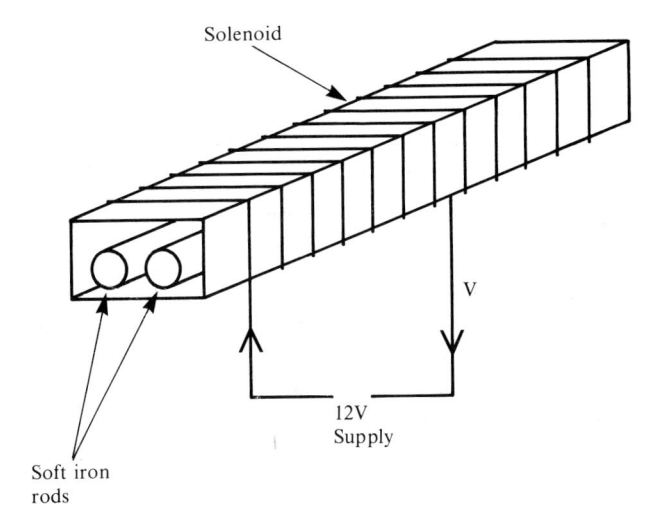

12V Supply

Soft iron rods

Explain what will happen to the near ends of the rods when the current is switched on and how the rods will behave as a result.

Chapter 21
ELECTROSTATICS

At the end of this chapter you will know:
CORE: what is meant by electrostatic charging and how it may be explained; how charges behave with other charges; what is meant by an electric field and the difference between conductors and insulators in terms of electrostatic charging.
SUPPLEMENTARY: the units in which electrical charge is measured; what is meant by electric lines of force and their direction; how the difference between conductors and insulators may be explained in terms of electron movements and how we may charge bodies by induction.

CORE

21.1 ELECTROSTATIC CHARGING
(i) Suppose a rod of cellulose acetate is rubbed with a cloth and hung in a stirrup, as shown in Fig. 21.1.

FIG. 21.1

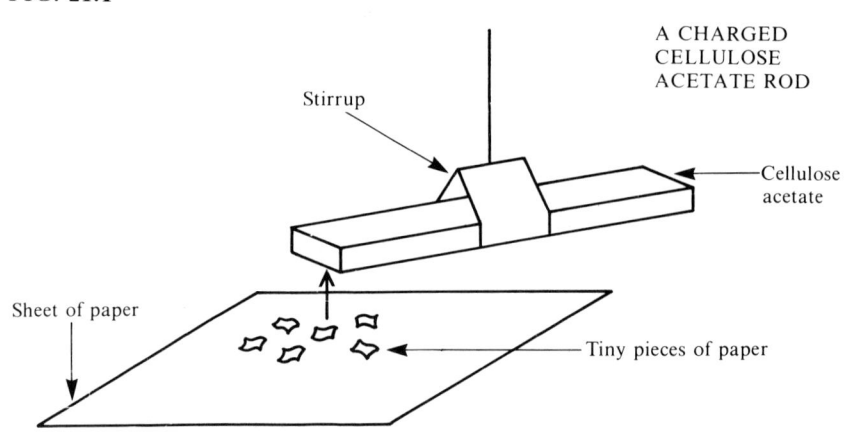

A CHARGED CELLULOSE ACETATE ROD
Stirrup
Cellulose acetate
Sheet of paper
Tiny pieces of paper

If a sheet of paper, on which are tiny pieces of paper, is brought near to it as shown, some pieces will jump onto the rod.

This happens because the rod is electrostatically charged. If we bring another charged rod of the same material close to it we notice that they repel each other.

We say that the cellulose acetate rods are positively charged.

(ii) The experiments can be done again but this time using a rod of polythene which has been rubbed with a cloth. Again, tiny pieces of paper will jump onto the rod. The rod is electrostatically charged. If another charged polythene rod is brought close to it, repulsion will occur.

We say that the polythene rods are negatively charged.

(iii) If a positively charged cellulose acetate rod is brought up to a negatively charged polythene rod, attraction will occur between them.

(iv) The reason why the rods become charged can be explained in terms of the movement of charged particles.

We saw in Chapter 8 that all substances are made up of atoms.

Each atom consists of a tiny central core called the nucleus surrounded by electrons which are in orbit around it. The nucleus carries a positive charge and the electrons carry a negative charge. The positive charge of the nucleus is exactly equal to the negative charge of the electrons. Now in some substances, some of the orbiting electrons can be freed from the atoms by rubbing. The electrons cannot move around from where the rubbing occurs — they are known as static. However, they can move onto the rubbing material. The substance loses electrons and the material which does the rubbing gains them. This is shown in Fig. 21.2.

FIG. 21.2

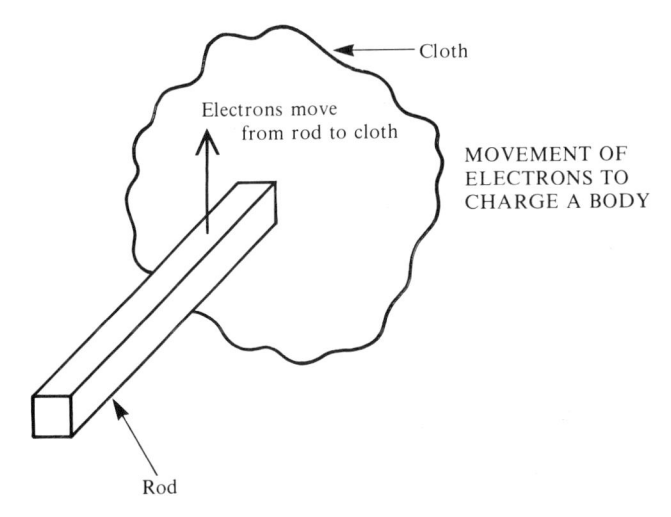

Cloth

Electrons move from rod to cloth

MOVEMENT OF ELECTRONS TO CHARGE A BODY

Rod

Here the rod loses electrons — it now has more positive charges than negative ones and so has a net positive charge. The cloth gains

260 Electrostatics

electrons — it now has more negative charges than positive ones and so has a net negative charge.

It is important to understand that we have not created any new charges but we have simply moved them from one place to another.

The process we have just described is what happens when the cellulose acetate rod is rubbed with the cloth — electrons leave the rod and move to the cloth, leaving the rod positively charged and the cloth negatively charged.

The opposite thing happens when we rub the polythene rod with a cloth. Electrons leave the cloth and go to the rod. The cloth becomes

FIG. 21.3(a)

Cloth

CHARGING A ROD POSITIVELY

Electrons move from rod to cloth

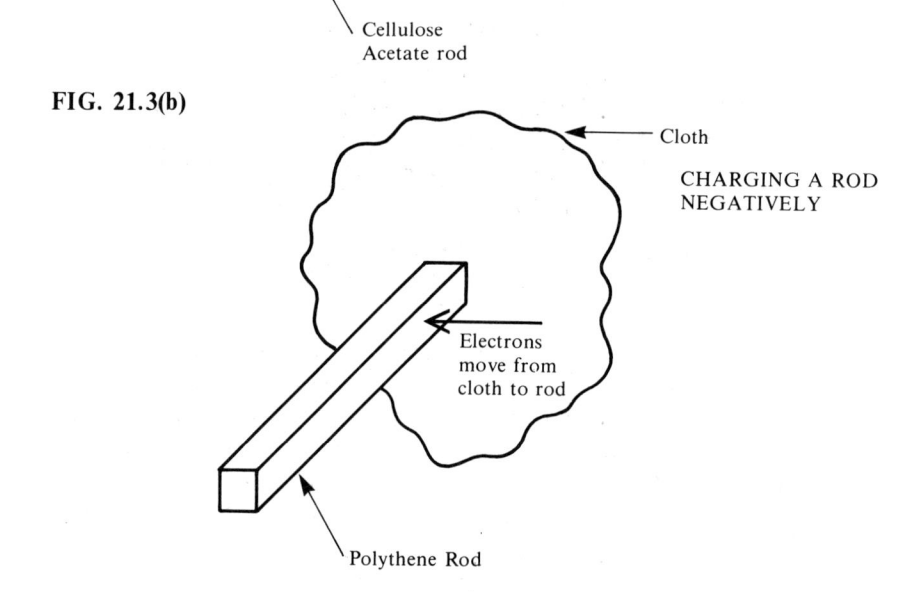

Cellulose Acetate rod

FIG. 21.3(b)

Cloth

CHARGING A ROD NEGATIVELY

Electrons move from cloth to rod

Polythene Rod

positively charged and the rod negatively charged. Both of these situations are shown in Fig. 21.3(a) and Fig. 21.3(b).

21.2 THE FORCES BETWEEN CHARGES

(i) We have seen that two positively charged cellulose rods repel each other.

Also, two negatively charged polythene rods repel each other.

Attraction occurs between a positively charged cellulose rod and a negatively charged polythene rod.

We can conclude that:
1) a positive charge repels another positive charge
2) a negative charge repels another negative charge
3) a positive charge attracts a negative charge.

Writing this in another way, we arrive at the law of charged bodies: Like charges repel, unlike charges attract.

(ii) We can use this law to decide whether or not a substance is electrostatically charged.

Attraction will occur between a charged rod and an unknown substance which is not charged. The reason for this can be seen in Fig. 21.4.

FIG. 21.4

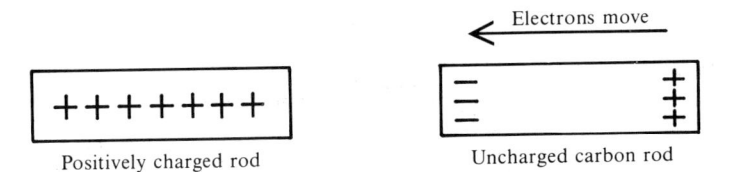

```
     +++++++              ← Electrons move
  [+++++++]            [ −        + ]
                       [ −        + ]
                       [ −        + ]
  Positively charged rod    Uncharged carbon rod
```

ATTRACTION BETWEEN A CHARGED ROD
AND AN UNCHARGED CARBON ROD

The positively charged rod will attract electrons in the uncharged carbon to the end nearest to it. Now although the uncharged rod has equal numbers of positive and negative charges, the attraction between the positive rod and the negative charges is bigger than the repulsion between the positive rod and the positive charges because the negative charge are nearer to the positive rod. The resultant effect is one of attraction.

262 Electrostatics

Attraction would also occur between a charged rod and a substance carrying the opposite charge.

Repulsion would occur only between a charged rod and a substance carrying the same charge.

Repulsion then, is the only way to test if an unknown substance is charged. When it happens, the charge on the unknown substance is the same as the charge of the rod used to perform the test.

We have already met a similar situation in magnetism when we saw that the only test for a magnet was repulsion.

21.3 ELECTRIC FIELDS

Around a charged body there is an electric field. This is a region in which another charged body will feel a force.

The field can be attractive, as shown in Fig. 21.5(a) or repulsive, as in Fig. 21.5(b).

FIG. 21.5(a)

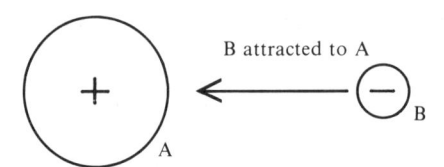

FIG. 21.5(b)

As the distance between A and B, or A and C, increases the force decreases. This is because the electric field becomes weaker.

The direction of the electric field is the direction in which a positive charge would move when in the field.

21.4 CONDUCTORS, INSULATORS AND ELECTROSTATIC CHARGING

Cellulose acetate and polythene are known as insulators. They can be charged by rubbing because the electrons produced do not move, as we have already mentioned.

On the other hand, all metals and carbon are known as conductors. In these substances electrons can move freely from atom to atom. A conductor will only become charged if we hold it in an insulating handle — otherwise the charge will pass through our body to the earth. We have already considered the motion of electrons in conductors in Fig. 21.4.

21.5 OCCURRENCE AND USES OF ELECTROSTATIC CHARGING IN EVERYDAY LIFE

(i) Very often our bodies may become charged by friction, particularly when we are wearing man-made clothing or are walking over man-made floor covering such as carpet tiles. If we are wearing rubber or synthetic soled shoes and the atmosphere is dry, this charge cannot escape and it will build up. If we then touch a metal object, such as shelving if we are in a library, we discharge ourselves suddenly and often we feel a slight electric shock and may see lightning sparks. When walking around a library in such situations you should often discharge yourselves by touching the metal shelving.

On a dry day if we are wearing synthetic soled shoes and we comb our hair with a nylon comb, our hair becomes charged.

(ii) Spark discharging can sometimes be very dangerous, particularly if fuel vapour or other inflammable vapour is present. The nozzles of petrol tankers become charged by friction as they pump fuel. In order to prevent this situation becoming dangerous, metal chains are connected between the nozzle and the earth to allow the charge to leak away. Aircraft become charged as they move through the air. The charge is allowed to leak away effectively from discharge spikes, as shown in Fig. 21.6, which are located at the end of the leading edge of the wing and the top of the tail.

FIG. 21.6

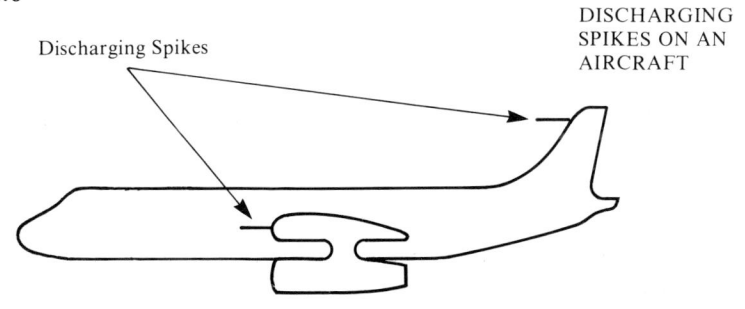

Discharging Spikes

DISCHARGING SPIKES ON AN AIRCRAFT

In hospitals, operating trolleys can become charged and this is not able to leak away from the rubber tyres. Metal chains are trailed to

264 Electrostatics

ground to allow a constant discharge. A spark discharge in the operating theatre could cause the anaesthetic gases to explode. Clouds can become electrically charged. When they discharge, we see lightning. In order to avoid being struck by lightning you should never stand under a tree but should stand in the open, wearing rubber soled shoes. You would also be safe in a car. Most public buildings have a metal spike on their roof, connected by metal to the ground. This has the effect of neutralising any charged clouds which pass over.

In the laboratory we can investigate spark discharges using a Van de Graaff Generator, as shown in Fig. 21.7.

FIG. 21.7

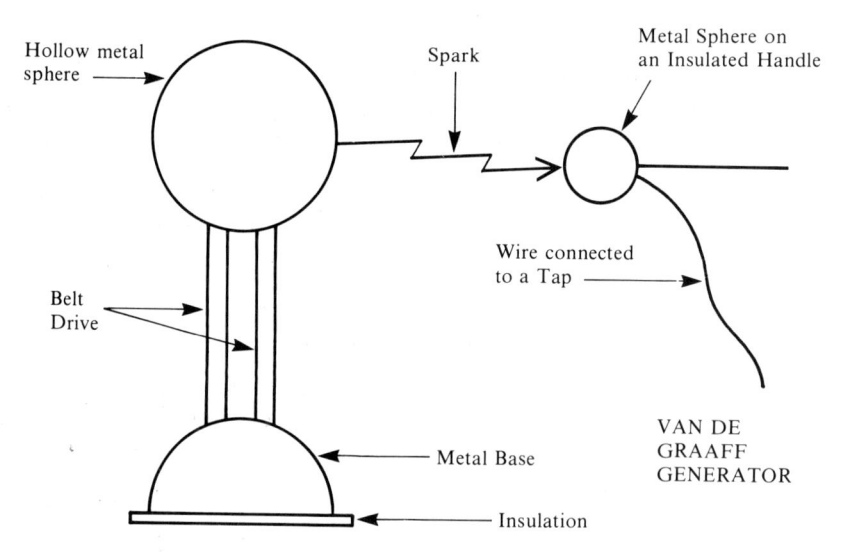

![Diagram of a Van de Graaff Generator showing: Hollow metal sphere at top, Spark jumping to Metal Sphere on an Insulated Handle, Wire connected to a Tap, Belt Drive inside column, Metal Base, and Insulation at bottom. Labelled VAN DE GRAAFF GENERATOR.]

The belt drive carries a large electric charge to the hollow metal sphere at the top. If a metal sphere on an insulated handle, connected by a wire to a tap is held nearby, a spark will jump from the generator to the sphere and through the wire to the earth.

(iii) Sometimes electrostatic charging can be useful. Photocopiers depend on it for their operation. It is also used in the chemical industry.

SUPPLEMENTARY

21.6   MEASUREMENT OF ELECTRIC CHARGE

We have considered the electrostatic charge on a body. If two identical but unequally charged bodies are connected by a conductor, charges in the form of electrons will flow from one body to the other. Moving electrons are known as an electric current.

Whether charges are static or moving we measure them in the same units. The unit of charge is the coulomb, symbol C.

We would represent an unknown charge by Q coulombs, QC and we would indicate whether it was positive or negative by writing either +QC or −QC.

If, in Fig. 21.4, a charge of −9C appears on the left hand side of the carbon rod, one of +9C appears on the right hand side in order that the total charge is zero
that is $(+9) + (-9) = 0$.

21.7 ELECTRIC LINES OF FORCE

In the same way that we can represent a magnetic field by field lines, we can represent an electric field by field lines or lines of force.

An electric field is a vector quantity. Its direction is that in which a positive charge would move if placed in the field. We represent the field direction by means of an arrow on the field line.

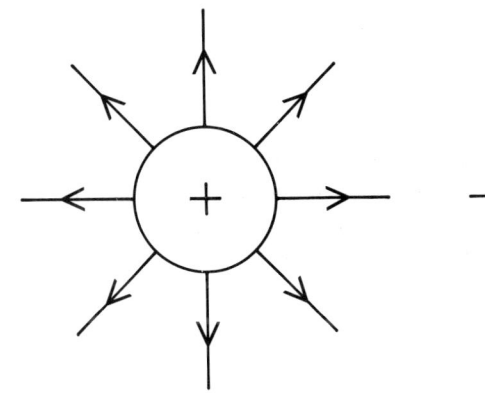

The field lines due to a positive charge and a negative charge are shown in Fig. 21.8(a) and Fig. 21.8(b).

FIG. 21.8(a) **FIG. 21.8(b)**

FIELD LINES DUE TO A POSITIVE CHARGE

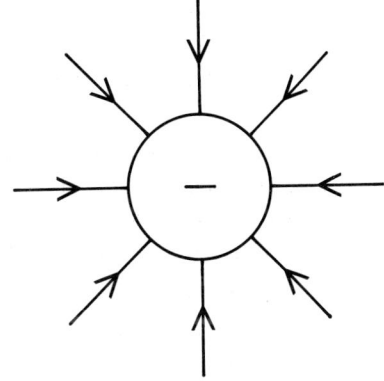

FIELD LINES DUE TO A NEGATIVE CHARGE

Important points about electric lines of force are:
1) the stronger the field the closer the lines are and
2) the lines repel each other sideways.

21.8 DIFFERENCES BETWEEN INSULATORS AND CONDUCTORS IN TERMS OF ELECTRON MOVEMENT

In insulators, the electrons liberated by charging cannot move through the substance but stay on the surface leading to a build up of charge which can escape to the rubbing material.

If a conductor is isolated and charged, the charge appears on its surface, as shown in Fig. 21.9(a) and Fig. 21.9(b).

FIG. 21.9(a) **FIG. 21.9(b)**

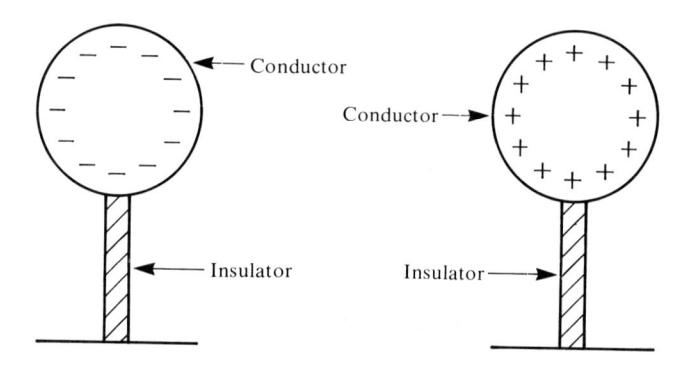

CHARGE RESIDES ON SURFACE   CHARGE RESIDES ON SURFACE

If a charged conductor is not isolated but connected to earth, electrons will flow to or from the earth until the body is uncharged, as shown in Fig. 21.10(a) and Fig. 21.10(b).

FIG. 21.10(a)

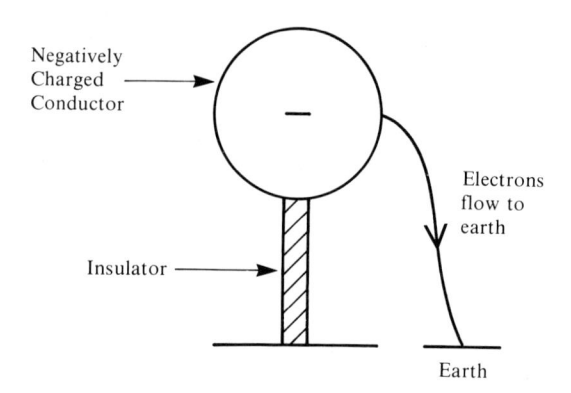

NEGATIVELY CHARGED CONDUCTOR
CONNECTED TO EARTH

FIG. 21.10(b)

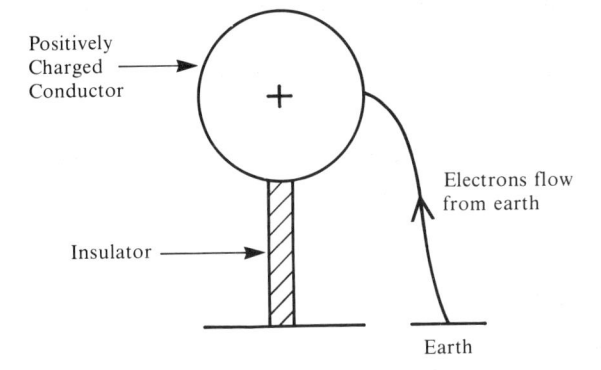

Positively Charged Conductor

Electrons flow from earth

Insulator

Earth

POSITIVELY CHARGED CONDUCTOR
CONNECTED TO EARTH

The process of connecting a charged conductor to earth is known as earthing.

21.9 CHARGING BY INDUCTION

(i) Suppose an insulated negatively charged rod is brought up to two uncharged insulated conductors in contact as shown in Fig. 21.11.

FIG. 21.11

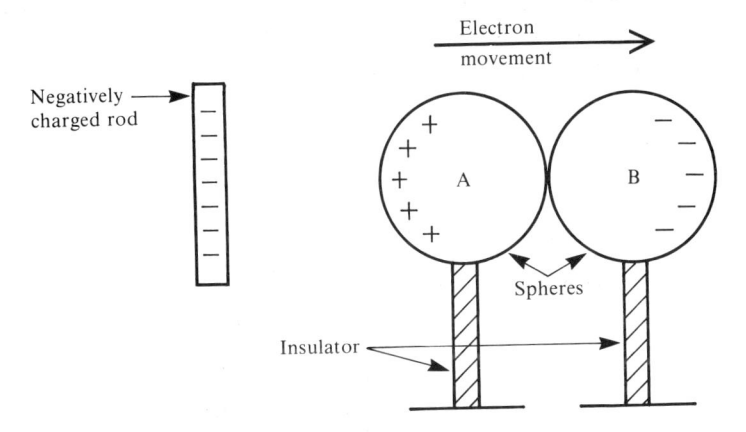

Negatively charged rod

Electron movement

A   B

Spheres

Insulator

CHARGING BY INDUCTION

The charged rod will repel electrons from sphere A to sphere B. As a result A will be left positively charged and B will be left negatively charged. If the spheres are now separated they will remain charged — A positively and B negatively.

268 Electrostatics

We have caused this charging without any physical contact between the spheres and the charged rod. The process is known as charging by induction.

If the rod had been removed with the spheres still in contact the electrons would return from B to A leaving each sphere uncharged.

If we repeated the process, replacing the negatively charged rod with one positively charged then electrons would be attracted to A leaving A negatively charged and B positively charged.

(ii) A single conductor may be charged by induction as follows. In order to charge the conductor negatively, a positively charged rod is brought near the conductor and the conductor earthed. Electrons flow from earth to the conductor, charging it negatively. The earth connection is broken and then the charged rod is removed. The situation is shown in Fig. 21.12.

FIG. 21.12

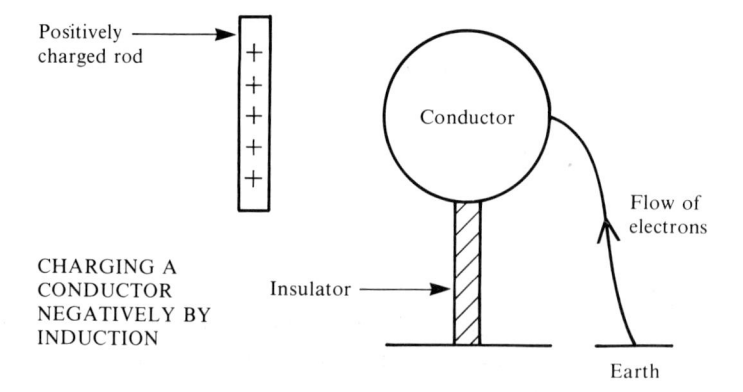

CHARGING A CONDUCTOR NEGATIVELY BY INDUCTION

To charge the conductor positively, we use a negatively charged rod and repeat the procedure. This time electrons flow from the conductor to the earth, leaving the conductor positively charged. The situation is shown in Fig. 21.13.

Electrostatics

FIG. 21.13

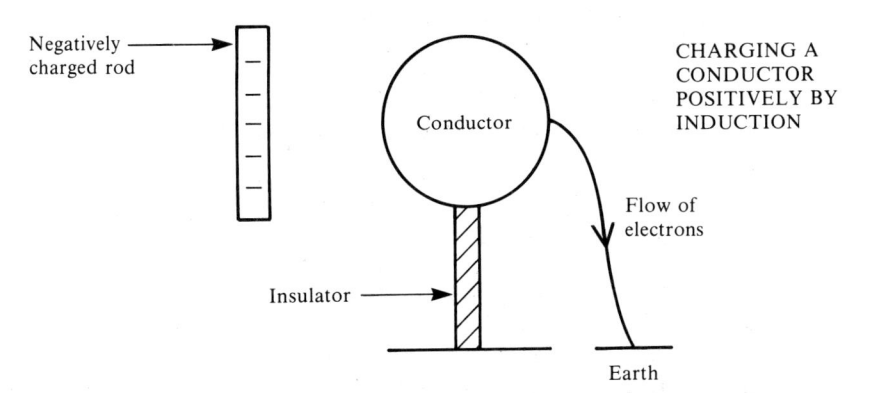

```
Negatively ──────▶  │ −          CHARGING A
charged rod         │ −          CONDUCTOR
                    │ −          POSITIVELY BY
                    │ − Conductor INDUCTION
                    │ −
                    │ −          Flow of
                    │            electrons
         Insulator ──▶
                                 Earth
```

Usually we represent an earth connection by the symbol shown in Fig. 21.14.

FIG. 21.14

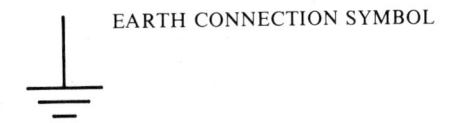

EARTH CONNECTION SYMBOL

QUESTIONS

CORE
1. Explain in terms of electron movement what happens when a cellulose acetate rod becomes charged positively by being rubbed with a cloth.
2. A positively charged rod is brought up to a rod A. Attraction occurs between them. A negatively charged rod is then brought up to A and attraction occurs again. What can you say about A?
3. Explain what is meant by the term electric field.
4. Explain the difference between insulators and conductors.
5. A plastic pen is rubbed on your sleeve and it is then found that it can pick up small pieces of paper. Explain why this happens.

SUPPLEMENTARY
6. State the units of electric charge.
7. A negatively charged conductor is connected to earth. Explain what happens.
8. Two spheres are charged by induction as shown in Fig. 21.11. If B carries a charge of $-10C$, what is the charge on A?

270 Electrostatics

9. A positively charged rod is brought close to an uncharged metal sphere held on an insulated stand.

FIG. 21.15

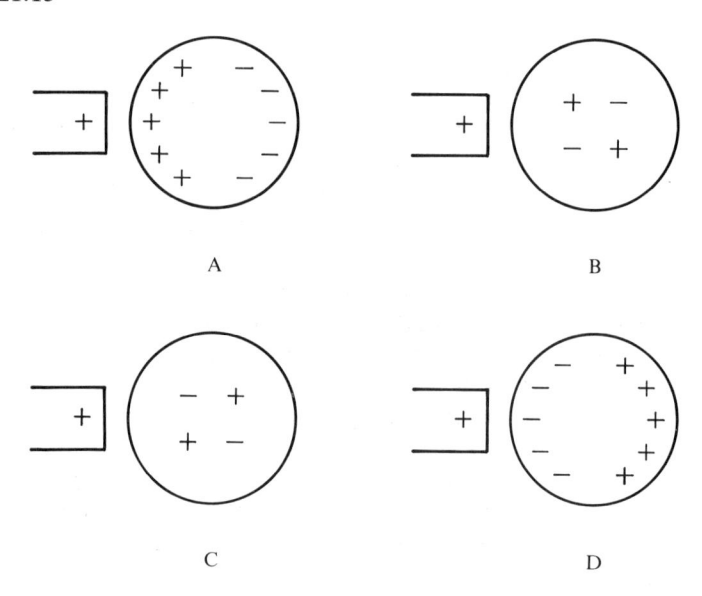

A

B

C

D

(a) Which of the diagrams in Fig. 21.15 shows the distribution of charge on the sphere when the charged rod is held near?
(b) What would happen if the sphere was earthed while the positively charged rod was near?
(c) What would happen if the sphere was earthed without the charged rod being near?

Chapter 22
ELECTRIC CURRENTS

At the end of this chapter you will know:
CORE: what an electric current is, its units and how it is measured; the two types of electric current; what is needed to make a current flow; what is meant by electromotive force and its units; what is meant by potential difference, its units and how it is measured; the meaning of resistance and its units; what a rheostat is, Ohm's Law for a metallic conductor and how it may be demonstrated; how the resistance of a metal wire depends upon its length and area and changes with temperature; the difference between conductors, semi-conductors and insulators and how the current through a filament lamp and a diode varies with the voltage across them.
SUPPLEMENTARY: the relationship between the amp and the coulomb; that energy is lost by a cell when it drives current around a complete circuit; the definition of the volt; that when the temperature of a metallic conductor increases so does its resistance; that the resistance of a metal wire increases when its length increases and its area decreases and why voltage varies with current as it does for a filament lamp and a diode.

CORE

22.1 ELECTRIC CURRENT

(i) An electric current is made up of moving charges. Current is measured in amperes, often abbreviated to amps. We use the symbol A. Sometimes we are interested in measuring very small currents and so sometimes we see currents given in milliamps, mA, or microamps, μA.

(ii) Electric current is measured with a device known as a moving coil meter. If it is designed to measure very small currents it will be known as a milliammeter or microammeter. A typical microammeter is shown in Photograph 23. It is calibrated in 2μA divisions up to 50μA. You will notice a scale on either side of the central zero but we shall say more about this later.

272 Electric Currents

PHOTOGRAPH 23 *Acknowledgement: Philip Harris Ltd.*

The symbols for an ammeter, a milliammeter and a microammeter are shown in Fig. 22.1(a), Fig. 22.1(b) and Fig. 22.1(c).

FIG. 22.1(a) **FIG. 22.1(b)** **FIG. 22.1(c)**

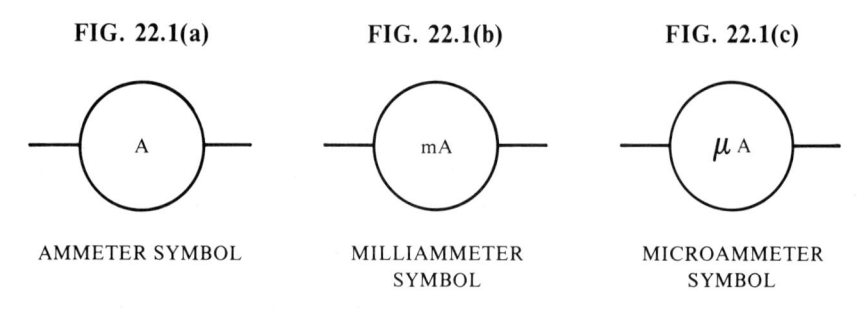

AMMETER SYMBOL   MILLIAMMETER SYMBOL   MICROAMMETER SYMBOL

FIG. 22.2

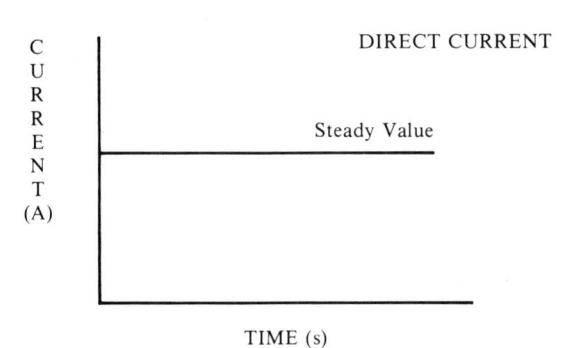

CURRENT (A)

DIRECT CURRENT

Steady Value

TIME (s)

Electric Currents 273

(iii) There are two types of electric current. In one type, known as direct current (d.c.), the charges flow in one direction only and the current has a steady value as time goes by. Fig. 22.2 shows a graph of current against time for a direct current.

In the other type, known as alternating current (a.c.), the charges direction of flow regularly reverses. Fig. 22.3 shows a graph of current against time for an alternating current.

FIG. 22.3

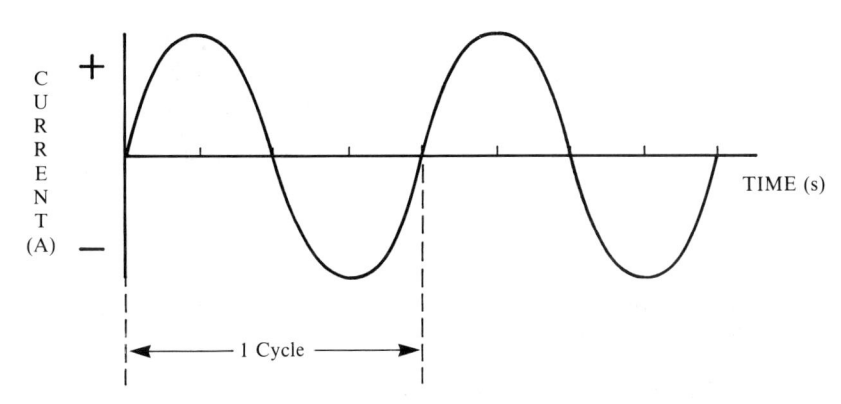

ALTERNATING CURRENT

[Graph showing sinusoidal alternating current: CURRENT (A) on vertical axis with + and − regions, TIME (s) on horizontal axis, with one full cycle marked]

The number of complete cycles every second is the frequency of the a.c. The mains supply in Britain is a.c. of frequency 50Hz.

The moving coil meters we have mentioned cannot be used to measure a.c. because it would cause the needle to move to and fro about zero.

Batteries and generators can give d.c. but only generators give a.c.

The sign for a.c. is $\sim$ and a.c. generators will be discussed in Chapter 25.

(iv) In order that current can flow through a device such as a bulb, we need two things: a source of electrical energy and conducting pathways or wires to connect the source to the bulb. When the bulb is connected by wires to the source, we say that we have an electrical circuit.

FIG. 22.4(a)   **FIG. 22.4(b)**

A cell   A battery of cells

A cell is a source of electrical energy. It converts chemical energy to electrical energy. A collection of cells is called a battery. The symbols for a cell and a battery are shown in Fig. 22.4(a) and Fig. 22.4(b).

In these diagrams the long thin line represents the positive terminal and the short wide line represents the negative terminal.

The bulb or lamp converts the electrical energy supplied by the cell into light and heat. The symbol for a lamp is shown in Fig. 22.5.

FIG. 22.5

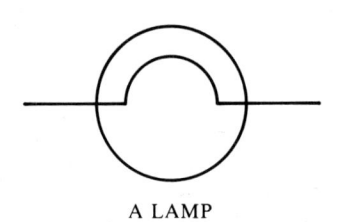

A LAMP

The symbol for connecting wire is shown in Fig. 22.6(a). The symbol for joined wires is shown in Fig. 22.6(b) and the symbol for wires which cross but do not join (in other words, the insulating covering has not been removed) is shown in Fig. 22.6(c).

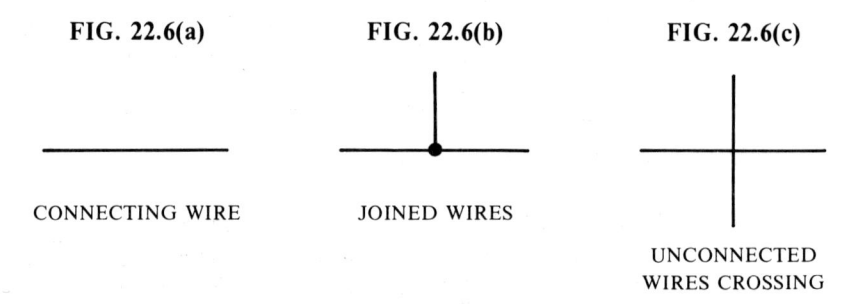

FIG. 22.6(a)   **FIG. 22.6(b)**   **FIG. 22.6(c)**

CONNECTING WIRE   JOINED WIRES

UNCONNECTED WIRES CROSSING

The complete circuit is shown in Fig. 22.7.

FIG. 22.7

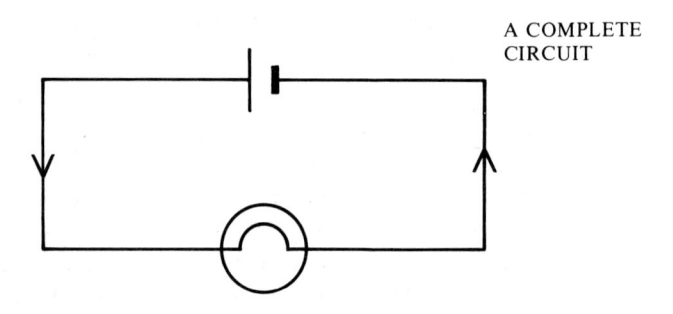

A COMPLETE CIRCUIT

Now an electric current is a flow of negatively charged particles. They flow from the negative terminal of the cell, through the bulb to the positive terminal of the cell. However, when electricity was first discovered it was thought to be a movement of positive charges which would flow in the opposite direction, from positive to negative. By the time it was actually discovered that an electric current consisted of negative charges, a lot of rules connected with currents had been worked out and it would have been very complicated to change them. So, when we talk about electrical circuits we talk in terms of a conventional current — that is one made up of positive charges, flowing from positive terminal to negative terminal. We indicate the direction of this conventional current on circuit diagrams by arrows, as shown on Fig. 22.7.

The direction of the conventional current (and also the electronic current) in a circuit can be reversed by turning the cell round or reversing its terminals. It is important to connect an ammeter the correct way round in a circuit otherwise it may be damaged. The meter shown in Photograph 23 has a centre zero and can be used to measure current flowing in both directions.

22.2 ELECTROMOTIVE FORCE

A cell provides electrical energy. The electromotive force or e.m.f. of such a source is a measure of the electrical energy which it provides.

e.m.f. is measured in volts, symbol V.

We shall consider e.m.f. again in the next chapter.

22.3 POTENTIAL DIFFERENCE

In order that a current should flow through a device such as a lamp there must be a potential difference across it. It is a measure of the electrical energy which is converted into other forms of energy as the current flows through the device. The potential difference is provided by the cell.

Potential difference or p.d. is measured in volts, symbol V. Because of the unit in which it is measured we sometimes refer to p.d. as voltage.

Potential difference is measured with a device known as a moving coil voltmeter. A typical voltmeter is shown in Photograph 24. It is used to measure a d.c. supply and has two scales — one reading to 5V, calibrated in 0.1V and another reading to 15V, calibrated in 0.5V. For the first scale we connect to the 5V+ and C− terminal and for the second scale we connect to the 15V+ and C− terminal. In each case the + terminal is connected on the side of the positive terminal of the cell and the − terminal is connected on the side of the negative terminal of the cell.

PHOTOGRAPH 24 *Acknowledgement: Philip Harris Ltd.*

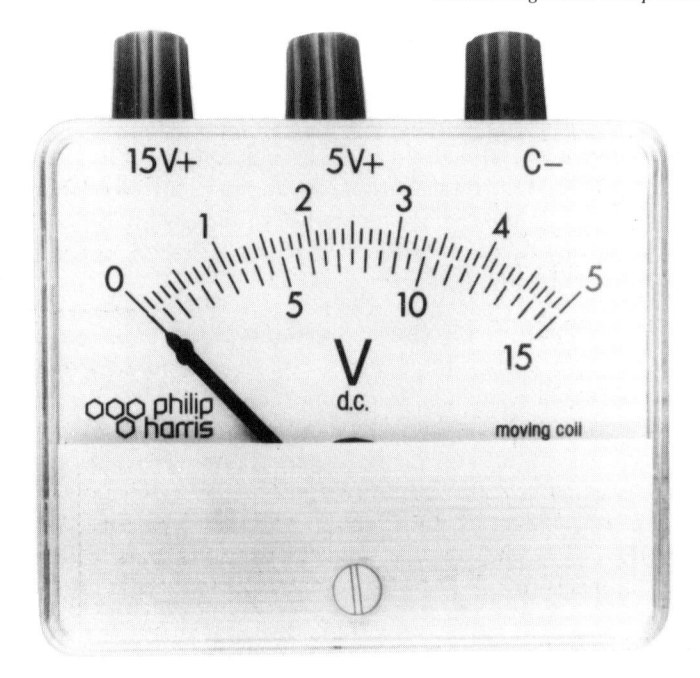

Meters with many different scales are available and both ammeters and voltmeters are available in digital form. The symbol for a voltmeter is shown in Fig. 22.8.

FIG. 22.8

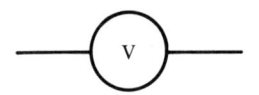

VOLTMETER SYMBOL

22.4 RESISTANCE

An electric current moves more easily through some conductors than others when a p.d. is applied. The opposition which a conductor offers to a current is called its resistance.

A good conductor has a low resistance and a poor conductor has a high resistance.

Resistance is measured in ohms, symbol Ω.

In any particular circuit, the greater the resistance of the circuit, the lower the current.

22.5 RESISTORS AND RHEOSTATS

Some conductors are specially made to have resistance and are called resistors. They are made from alloy wires or carbon. Fig. 22.9(a) shows a resistor and Fig. 22.9(b) its symbol.

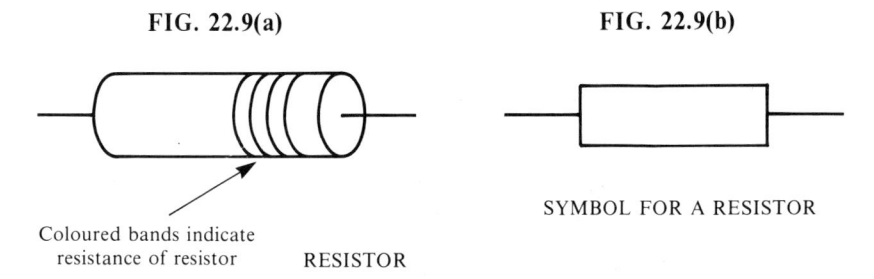

FIG. 22.9(a) **FIG. 22.9(b)**

Coloured bands indicate resistance of resistor

RESISTOR

SYMBOL FOR A RESISTOR

A rheostat is a variable resistor and it is used for changing the current in a circuit. Fig. 22.10(a) shows a variable resistor used in electrical devices, Fig. 22.10(b) shows a variable resistor used in laboratory experiments and Fig. 22.10(c) shows the symbol for them.

FIG. 22.10(a)

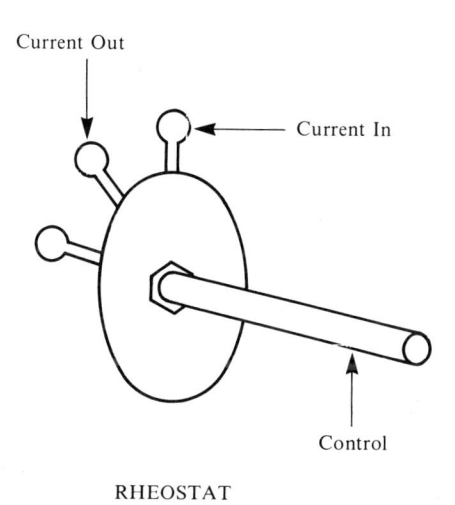

Current Out

Current In

Control

RHEOSTAT

In Fig. 22.10(b), the resistance of the rheostat is zero when the sliding contact is on the left so that the current can pass through the metal

FIG. 22.10(b)

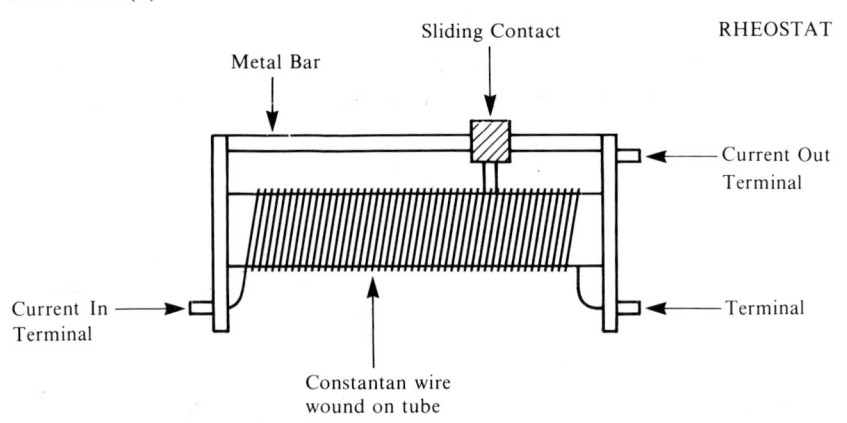

Diagram labels: Metal Bar, Sliding Contact, RHEOSTAT, Current Out Terminal, Current In Terminal, Terminal, Constantan wire wound on tube

FIG. 22.10(c)

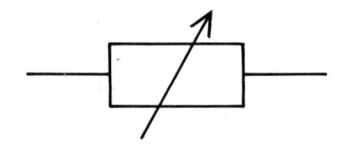

RHEOSTAT SYMBOL

and the resistance is a maximum when the sliding contact is on the right and the current has to go through all the constantan wire.

Rheostats like the one shown in Fig. 22.10(a) are used in electrical apparatus as volume controls and also in dimming lightswitches.

22.6 OHM'S LAW FOR A METALLIC CONDUCTOR

(i) The resistance of a metallic conductor at constant temperature is given by

$$\text{resistance} = \frac{\text{voltage across conductor}}{\text{current through conductor}}$$

or $\quad R = \dfrac{V}{I}$

where R = resistance
V = voltage across conductor
I = current through conductor.

This relationship is Ohm's Law. From it we define the ohm, the unit of resistance.

The resistance of a conductor is 1 Ω if the current flowing through it is 1A when the p.d. across it is 1V.

(ii) Ohm's Law for a metallic conductor can be demonstrated using the circuit shown in Fig. 22.11. This circuit includes a switch.

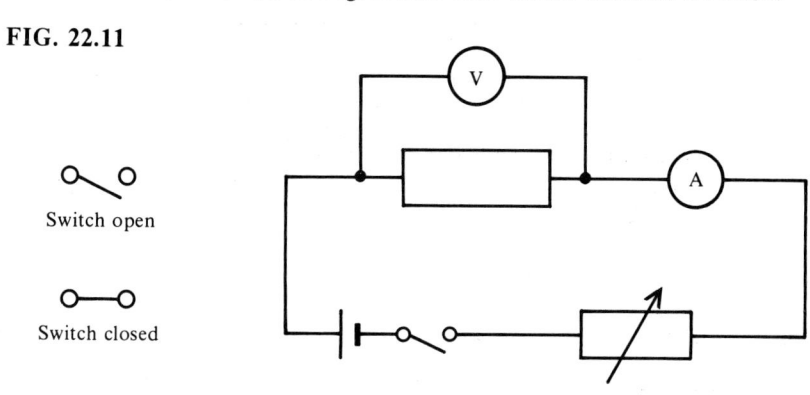

FIG. 22.11

Switch open

Switch closed

DEMONSTRATION OF OHM'S LAW

The ammeter is connected in the main circuit and a connection is made from each terminal on the voltmeter to each side of the resistor.

The rheostat is adjusted to give a small current and the values on the voltmeter and ammeter are recorded. The rheostat is adjusted to give five more values of current and voltage. A graph is then plotted of voltage (vertical axis) against current (horizontal axis). A straight line graph verifies Ohm's Law and its gradient is equal to the resistance of the resistor. Representing current by I and voltage by V we obtain the graph shown in Fig. 22.12.

FIG. 22.12

V AGAINST I
FOR A METALLIC CONDUCTOR

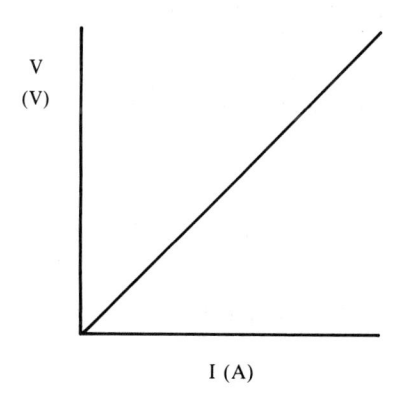

V (V)

I (A)

PROBLEM
CALCULATE THE RESISTANCE OF A LAMP WHEN A p.d. OF 6V ACROSS IT CAUSES A CURRENT OF 2A THROUGH IT.

Using $R = \dfrac{V}{I}$

$V = 6V, \quad I = 2A$

So $R = \dfrac{6}{2} = 3\,\Omega$

ANSWER: RESISTANCE $= 3\,\Omega$.

Because a metallic conductor obeys Ohm's Law, it is said to behave ohmically.

22.7 FACTORS AFFECTING THE RESISTANCE OF A METAL WIRE
The resistance of a metal wire depends upon
1. its length — the greater the length, the greater the resistance
2. its cross-sectional area — the greater the area, the less the resistance
3. its temperature — the higher the temperature, the greater the resistance.

The long thin wire on a rheostat means that it has a large resistance.

22.8 CONDUCTORS, SEMI-CONDUCTORS AND INSULATORS
Conductors have a low resistance which increases as its temperature rises. Insulators have so high a resistance that they do not conduct currents.

Semiconductors are inbetween these. Germanium and silicon are the best known examples. Pure semiconductors at very low temperatures are insulators but they rapidly become conductors as their temperature increases. They become better conductors if impurities are added and above room temperature the conducting properties of such doped semiconductors increase very noticeably.

When the pure germanium or silicon is doped with phosphorus we have an n type semiconductor; when the pure germanium or silicon is doped with boron we have a p type semiconductor. A junction diode is made from a region of p type semiconductor joined to a region of n type semiconductor.

22.9 VARIATION OF VOLTAGE AND CURRENT FOR A FILAMENT LAMP AND A JUNCTION DIODE
If we plot a graph of V against I for a metallic conductor we obtain a straight line. We also obtain a straight line if we plot I (vertically)

against V (horizontally). The steeper the line, the less the resistance when we plot the graph this way round. This is shown in Fig. 22.13.

FIG. 22.13

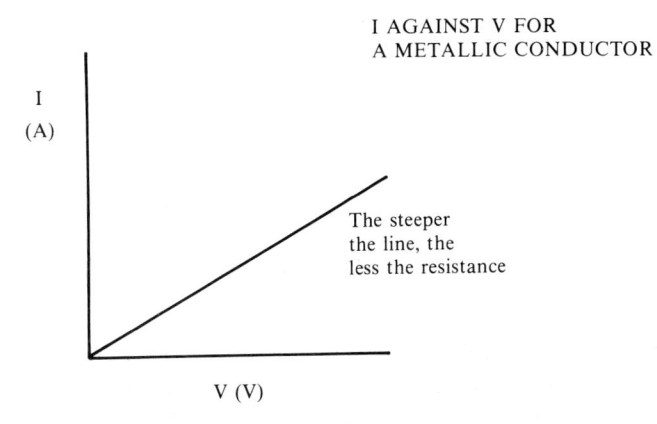

I AGAINST V FOR A METALLIC CONDUCTOR

I (A)

The steeper the line, the less the resistance

V (V)

If we plot a graph of I against V for a filament lamp, the graph bends over indicating that the resistance increases as the current increases. This is shown in Fig. 22.14.

FIG. 22.14

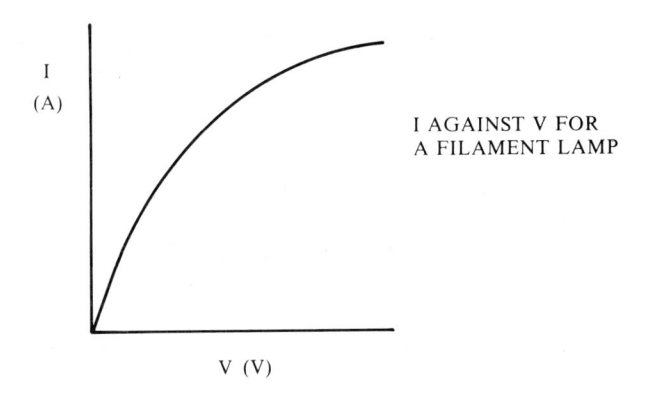

I (A)

I AGAINST V FOR A FILAMENT LAMP

V (V)

If we plot a graph of I against V for a junction diode, we find that a current passes when the p.d. is applied in one direction but only a tiny current passes when the p.d. is applied in the opposite direction. The device is behaving non-ohmically when it allows the current to pass and has a very high resistance when it only allows the tiny current to flow. Effectively the device conducts in one direction only.
This is shown in Fig. 22.15.

FIG. 22.15

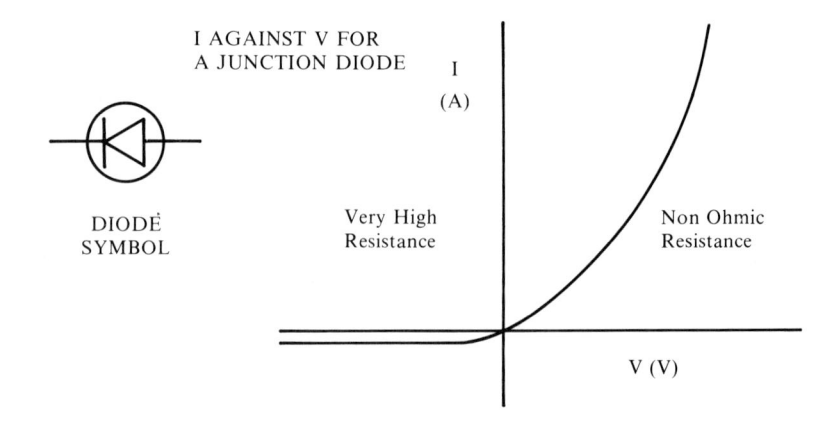

I AGAINST V FOR A JUNCTION DIODE

DIODE SYMBOL

Very High Resistance

Non Ohmic Resistance

SUPPLEMENTARY

22.10 THE AMP AND THE COULOMB

When a current flows in a circuit, a charge is transferred. An electric current is the rate of flow of charge that is

$$\text{Current} = \frac{\text{Charge}}{\text{Time}}$$

or

$$I = \frac{Q}{t}$$

where

I = current in A
Q = charge in C
t = time in s.

A current of 1A is therefore equal to a rate of flow of charge of 1C every second.

PROBLEM

WHAT IS THE CURRENT FLOWING IN A CIRCUIT IF THE CHARGE PASSING EACH POINT IS 120C IN 1 MIN?

Use

$$I = \frac{Q}{t}$$

$Q = 120C, \quad t = 1 \text{ min} = 60s$

So

$$I = \frac{120}{60} = 2A$$

ANSWER: CURRENT = 2A.

22.11 ENERGY LOST BY A CELL DRIVING CURRENT THROUGH A CIRCUIT

When a cell drives current through a circuit, it loses energy. It is supplying electrical energy to the circuit. In the circuit this electrical energy is changed into other forms of energy — in a heater the electrical energy is changed into thermal energy or heat and in a lamp it is changed into heat energy and light energy. Energy is wasted by the cell in driving the current through itself.

We can write
Energy supplied by cell = Energy changed in external circuit + Energy wasted in cell.

We shall consider this further in the next chapter.

22.12 THE VOLT

The volt is the unit of potential difference.

The p.d. between two points in a circuit is 1 volt if 1 joule of electrical energy is converted into other forms of energy when 1 coulomb of charge passes between the two points.

In general then
p.d. between two points = $\dfrac{\text{amount of electrical energy converted}}{\text{amount of charge transferred}}$

If
V = p.d. between the two points
W = amount of electrical energy converted
Q = amount of charge transferred

then
$$V = \dfrac{W}{Q}$$

PROBLEM

THE p.d. ACROSS A LAMP IS 12V. HOW MANY JOULES OF ELECTRICAL ENERGY ARE CHANGED WHEN A CHARGE OF 10C PASSES THROUGH IT?

Using $V = \dfrac{W}{Q}$

then $W = VQ$
$V = 12V$ and $Q = 10C$

So $W = 12 \times 10 = 120J$

ANSWER: ENERGY CHANGED = 120J.

22.13 RESISTANCE AND TEMPERATURE FOR A METALLIC CONDUCTOR

The resistance which a metallic conductor offers to the passage of an electric current increases as its temperature rises.

This is because as the temperature of the conductor rises the lattice atoms vibrate over greater distances. This makes it more difficult for the electrons making up the electric current to pass through the conductor because their progress is hindered by these atoms. In other words, the resistance of the conductor increases.

22.14 VARIATION IN RESISTANCE OF A METAL WIRE WITH ITS AREA AND LENGTH

For a metal wire at constant temperature we find:
1) its resistance is directly proportional to its length
   or $R \propto l$
   when R = resistance
          l = length.

   This means that if the length is doubled, then so is its resistance.
2) its resistance is inversely proportional to its area
   or $R \propto 1/A$
   where R = resistance
          A = area.

   This means that if the area is doubled, then the resistance is halved.

PROBLEM

A METAL WIRE OF LENGTH 15cm AND AREA 2cm^2 HAS A RESISTANCE OF 10Ω.

FIND THE RESISTANCE OF WIRES OF THE SAME METAL
1) OF LENGTH 45cm AND AREA 2cm^2
2) OF LENGTH 15cm AND AREA 1cm^2
3) OF LENGTH 45cm AND AREA 1cm^2

In (1) the length is trebled and so the resistance will be trebled to 30Ω.
In (2) the area is halved so the resistance will be doubled to 20Ω.
In (3) the length is trebled, trebling the resistance and the area is halved, doubling the resistance. The total effect is that the resistance is multiplied by a factor of six to 60Ω.

ANSWER: RESISTANCE = 30Ω, 20Ω and 60Ω.

22.15 VARIATION OF VOLTAGE WITH CURRENT FOR A FILAMENT LAMP AND A DIODE

We shall now consider the shape of the graphs in Fig. 22.14 and Fig. 22.15.

(i) The filament of a lamp is very fine and therefore it has a very high resistance. When the current is small, this causes no problems and the resistance is constant as indicated by the first part of the graph which is a straight line.

However, as the current increases, the resistance of the filament means that the passage of the current generates a large amount of heat which causes the filament temperature to rise. This rise in temperature causes an increase in resistance. The greater the current, the greater the rise in temperature and the greater the resistance becomes. This is why the graph, after the initial straight part, begins to bend over indicating a rise in resistance.

Because of the high temperature of such a lamp, it is important that the filament should be made of a metal with a high melting point such as tungsten. Light bulbs "go" when air enters the vacuum inside the glass envelope and allow the filament to oxidise.

(ii) In an n type semiconductor, the current travels in the form of electrons, as it does in all metallic conductors. However, in p type semiconductors, the current travels in the form of positive charges called holes. These are created because of chemical differences between the impurity and the pure semiconducting material. A junction diode consists of a layer of n type semiconductor joined to a layer of p type semiconductor.

If the diode is connected as shown in Fig. 22.16, with the p type

FIG. 22.16

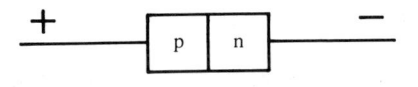

FORWARD BIASED DIODE

connected to the positive terminal of a battery and the n type to the negative terminal, the holes drift from the p type, across the junction, into the n type and the electrons drift the other way from n to p type. The diode conducts and has a very low resistance, which is non-ohmic. The diode is said to be forward biased.

If the diode is connected as shown in Fig. 22.17, with the p type

FIG. 22.17

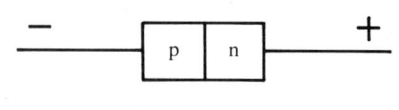

```
─────┬───┬───┬─────
  −  │ p │ n │  +
─────┴───┴───┴─────
```

REVERSE BIASED DIODE

connected to the negative terminal of a battery and the n type connected to the positive, both the holes and the electrons are repelled away from the junction. The resistance of the diode becomes very large and it hardly conducts at all. We say that the diode is reversed biased.

So, a diode behaves as a conductor when it is forward biased but an insulator when it is reverse biased — it only allows current to pass through it in one direction.

In practice, a diode is a small cylindrical device, with electrical contacts. A band is drawn near one end of it.

The circuit symbol and actual appearance of the diode in forward and reverse bias are shown in Fig. 22.18(a) and Fig. 22.18(b).

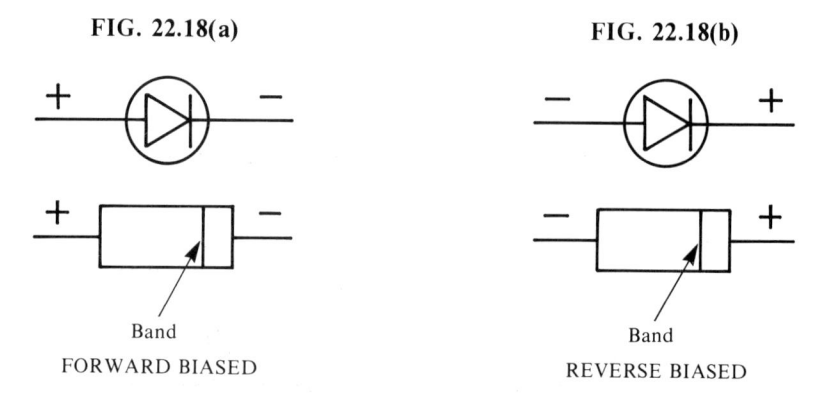

FIG. 22.18(a)   **FIG. 22.18(b)**

Band
FORWARD BIASED

Band
REVERSE BIASED

So in Fig. 22.15, the right hand side of the graph shows forward bias with a low non-ohmic resistance and the left hand side shows reverse bias with the very high resistance.

QUESTIONS

CORE
1. What are the units of current and how is current measured?
2. What device would you use to measure an extremely small current?

3. What is an alternating current?
4. Name the two things needed to make a current flow.
5. What is e.m.f. measured in?
6. What does a voltmeter measure?
7. Explain what is meant by the term resistance.
8. State the unit of resistance.
9. Which one of the following circuits would be suitable for measuring the resistance of a lamp?

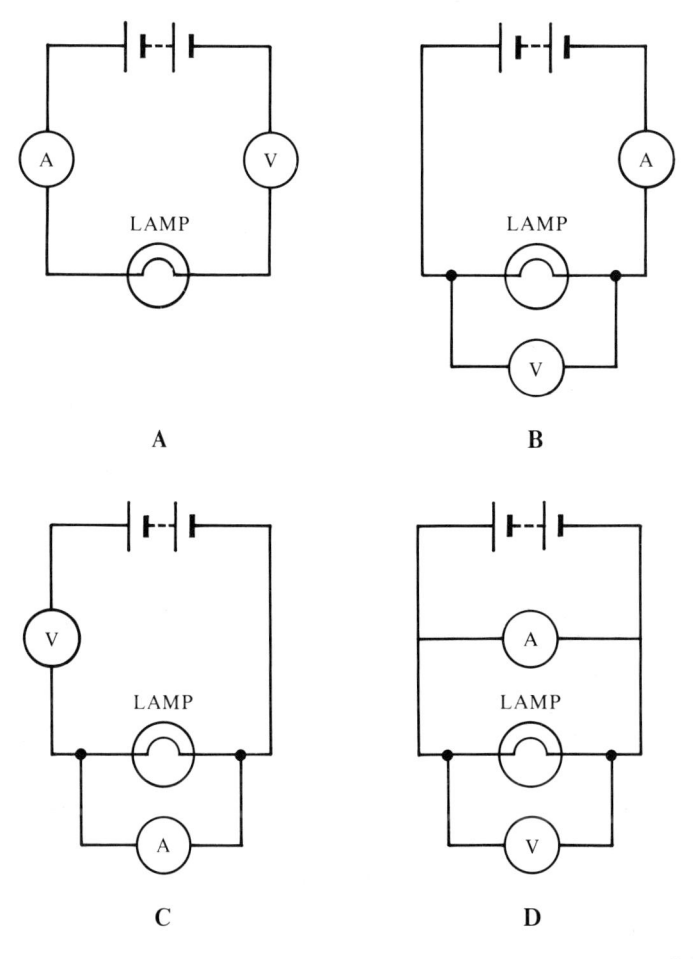

A

B

C

D

(L.E.A.G.)

10. The p.d. across a 4 Ω resistor is 8V. The current flowing is
    A. ½A   B. 2A   C. 12A   D. 32A
11. Fig. 9 shows a diagram of an electrical circuit.

FIG. 9

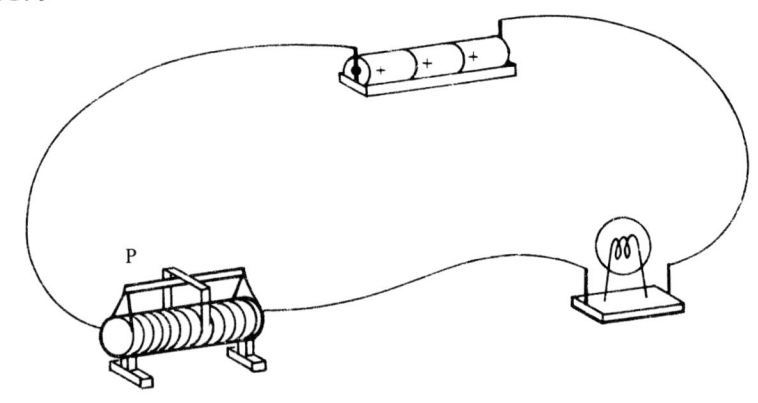

(a) Name the device P
(b) What effect does adjusting P have on the lamp?
(c) Why does P have this effect?
(d) Add to Fig. 9
  (i) an ammeter to measure the current (use the symbol (A))
  (ii) a voltmeter to measure the potential difference across the lamp (use the symbol (V)).
(e) Draw a circuit diagram of your completed circuit, including the ammeter and voltmeter.
(N.E.A.)

12. Explain why the wire on a rheostat is long and thin.

SUPPLEMENTARY

12. Calculate the charge passing through a lamp when a current of 5A flows for 10 minutes.
13. 20 joules of electrical energy are changed when a current of 2A passes through a lamp. Calculate the p.d. across the lamp.
14. The resistance of a piece of wire is 6 Ω. One third of the wire is cut off and thrown away. What is the resistance of the remaining piece?
15. The resistance of a length of wire, of area 5cm^2, is 20 Ω. What will be the area of the same length of the same type of wire if the resistance is 50 Ω?
16. Describe what happens to the voltage across a bulb as the current through it is increased steadily.
17. Would there be a current flowing in the lamp shown in Fig. 22.19?

FIG. 22.19

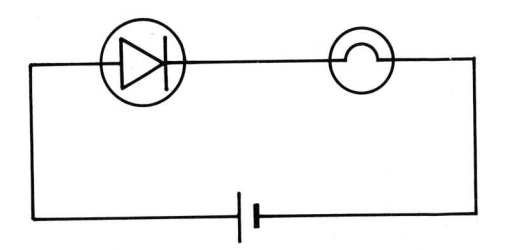

Chapter 23
ELECTRIC CIRCUITS

At the end of this chapter you will know:
CORE: what fuses are and their circuit symbol; how cells may be connected in series and in parallel; how resistors may be connected in series and what their total resistance is; that in a series circuit the current is the same everywhere; what is meant by a potential divider; how resistors may be connected in parallel and how their total resistance decreases; that in a parallel circuit the current splits up; what is meant by internal resistance and Ohm's Law for a complete circuit and an expression for e.m.f.
SUPPLEMENTARY: how a diode can be used as a rectifier; how the total resistance of resistors connected in parallel may be calculated; how the total resistance of mixed series and parallel arrangements may be calculated and a definition of e.m.f.

CORE

23.1 FUSES

A fuse is a short piece of wire with a low melting point. If a higher than normal current flows through it, it becomes hot, melts and breaks the circuit. It prevents overloading of electrical circuits which could cause fires. A typical fuse and its circuit symbol is shown in Fig. 23.1(a) and Fig. 23.1(b).

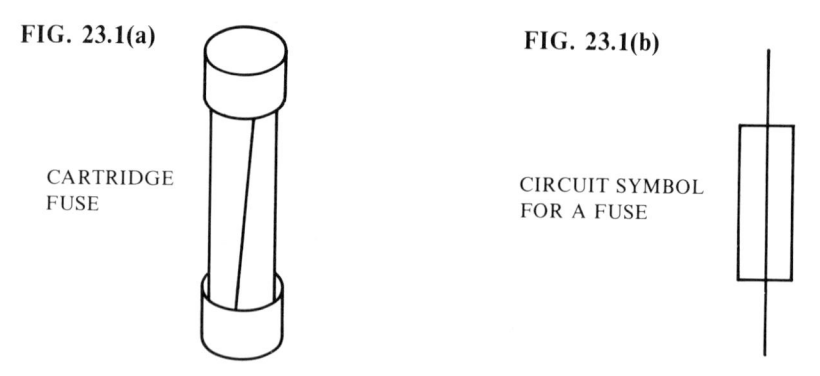

FIG. 23.1(a)

CARTRIDGE FUSE

FIG. 23.1(b)

CIRCUIT SYMBOL FOR A FUSE

The two reasons for a fuse melting or "blowing" are
1. a short circuit, caused by worn insulation on the wires and
2. too many devices used on a mains circuit or too little resistance included in a battery circuit.

23.2 CELLS IN SERIES AND PARALLEL

If two or more identical cells are connected together so that the positive terminal of one is connected to the negative terminal of the next then they are said to be connected in series as shown in Fig. 23.2.

FIG. 23.2

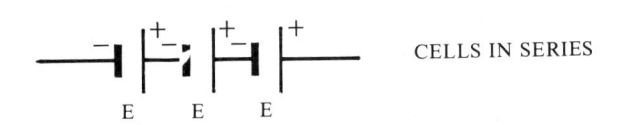

CELLS IN SERIES

The total e.m.f. when cells are connected in series is obtained by adding together all the separate e.m.f.s.

So, in Fig. 23.2, if each cell has an e.m.f. E the total is

Total e.m.f. = E + E + E = 3E volts.

If two or more identical cells are connected together so that all the positive terminals are joined together and all the negative terminals are joined together then they are said to be connected in parallel as shown in Fig. 23.3.

FIG. 23.3

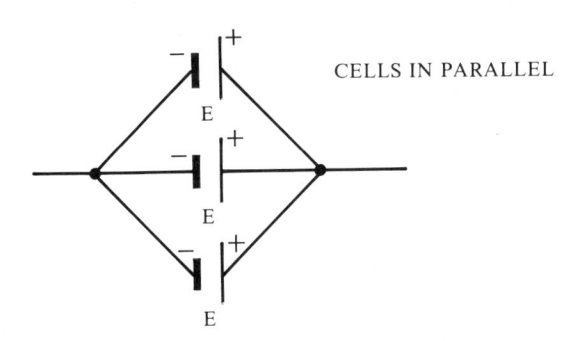

CELLS IN PARALLEL

The total e.m.f. when cells are connected in series is equal to the e.m.f. of one cell by itself.

So, in Fig. 23.3, if each cell has an e.m.f. E the total is

Total e.m.f. = E volts.

PROBLEM

CALCULATE THE TOTAL e.m.f. IF FOUR CELLS, EACH OF e.m.f. 2V ARE CONNECTED (i) IN PARALLEL, (ii) IN SERIES.

In parallel
$$\text{Total e.m.f.} = \text{e.m.f. of one cell} = 2V$$

In series
$$\text{Total e.m.f.} = \text{sum of e.m.f. of each cell} = 2 + 2 + 2 + 2 = 8V$$

ANSWER: IN PARALLEL 2V, IN SERIES 8V.

23.3 RESISTORS IN SERIES

Resistors may also be connected in series as shown in Fig. 23.4.

FIG. 23.4

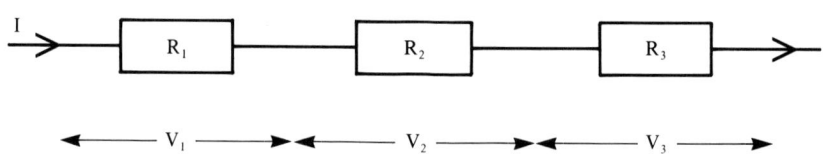

RESISTORS IN SERIES

[Circuit diagram: current I flowing through R_1, R_2, R_3 in series, with voltages V_1, V_2, V_3 across each]

In this case, the total resistance is obtained by adding the values of the separate resistances together.

So, in Fig. 23.4
$$\text{Total resistance} = R_1 + R_2 + R_3.$$

PROBLEM

THREE 5Ω RESISTORS ARE CONNECTED IN SERIES. WHAT IS THEIR TOTAL RESISTANCE?

$$\text{Total resistance} = \text{Sum of all resistances} = 5 + 5 + 5 = 15\Omega$$

ANSWER: TOTAL RESISTANCE = 15Ω.

When resistors are connected in series, the same current flows through each resistor.

The p.d. across each resistor can be found using Ohm's Law. So in Fig. 23.4
$$V_1 = IR_1$$
$$V_2 = IR_2$$
$$V_3 = IR_3$$

Electric Circuits 293

23.4 THE POTENTIAL DIVIDER

A rheostat can be used as a potential divider when a changing p.d. is needed to be applied to a device.

The two bottom terminals shown in Fig. 22.10(b) are connected to some cells in series and the variable p.d. required is obtained from one terminal and the sliding contact terminal, as shown in Fig. 23.5.

FIG. 23.5

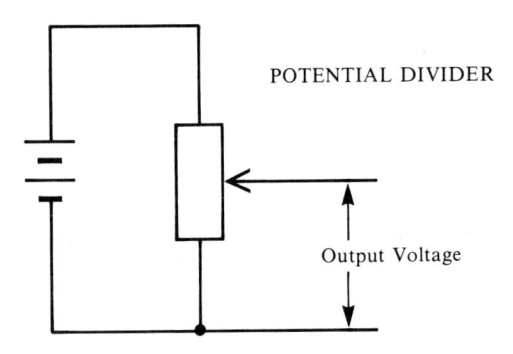

POTENTIAL DIVIDER

Output Voltage

We can think of the potential divider as consisting of lots of resistors connected in series. The further the sliding contact is from the other output terminal, the greater the resistance. Since the same current flows through the whole potential divider, then the greater is the p.d. So, if the sliding contact is half way along then the output p.d. will be exactly half of that across the whole potential divider. In Fig. 23.6, the output voltage will be 1.5V.

FIG. 23.6

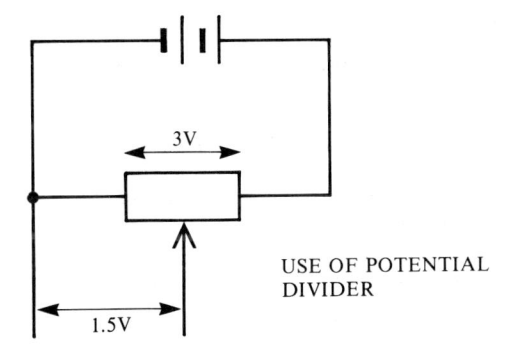

3V

USE OF POTENTIAL DIVIDER

1.5V

23.5 RESISTORS IN PARALLEL

Resistors may be connected in parallel, as shown in Fig. 23.7.

FIG. 23.7

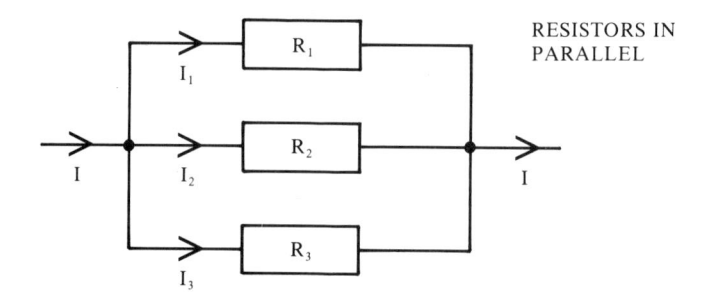

RESISTORS IN PARALLEL

Whenever resistors are connected in parallel, the total resistance is always less than the smallest individual resistor in the arrangement.

The current entering the parallel arrangement or network splits up between the resistors and joins up to leave the network. So, in Fig. 23.7 suppose the current entering and leaving the network is I. It will split up into I_1, I_2 and I_3 through the resistors. We have
$$I = I_1 + I_2 + I_3$$
The voltage across each resistor, V, is the same and so
$$V = I_1 R_1 = I_2 R_2 = I_3 R_3.$$

We can see that if one of the resistors is broken the current can still travel through the others. In the case of lamps connected in series, if one lamp is broken the current cannot get through and the lamps go out — this often happens on Christmas tree lights. If the lamps are connected in parallel, as in a house wiring circuit, all the lamps may be used independently.

PROBLEM
IN FIG. 23.7, THE CURRENT ENTERING THE NETWORK IS 10A. IF 3A FLOWS THROUGH R_1 AND 3A FLOWS THROUGH R_2, WHAT CURRENT FLOWS THROUGH R_3?

Use
$$I = I_1 + I_2 + I_3$$
$$I = 10A, \quad I_1 = 3A, \quad I_2 = 3A$$
So
$$10 = 3 + 3 + I_2$$
$$I_2 = 4A$$

ANSWER: CURRENT THROUGH $R_3 = 4A$.

23.6 INTERNAL RESISTANCE

A cell itself resists the passage of an electric current through it. We say that the cell has an internal resistance. In circuit calculation we represent internal resistance by r.

FIG. 23.8

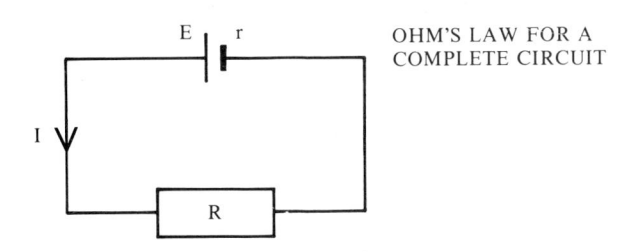

OHM'S LAW FOR A COMPLETE CIRCUIT

The advantage of connecting cells in parallel, as shown in Fig. 23.3, is that their total internal resistance is reduced.

In order to calculate the current flowing in a circuit, we use Ohm's Law for a complete circuit which says:

$$\text{Current in circuit} = \frac{\text{e.m.f. of cell}}{\text{total circuit resistance}}$$

In Fig. 23.8
- E = e.m.f. of cell
- R = resistance of resistor
- r = internal resistance of cell

then I, the current in the circuit is given by

$$I = \frac{E}{R + r}$$

Now we saw earlier

Energy supplied by cell = Energy changed in external circuit + Energy wasted in cell

Suppose a cell of e.m.f. E drives a current I around a circuit. If the resistance in the circuit is R and the internal resistance of the cell is r we can write

e.m.f. of cell = sum of p.d.s in circuit + p.d. inside cell

or $\quad E = IR + Ir$

PROBLEM

CALCULATE THE CURRENT IN THE CIRCUIT SHOWN IN FIG. 23.9.

296 Electric Circuits

FIG. 23.9

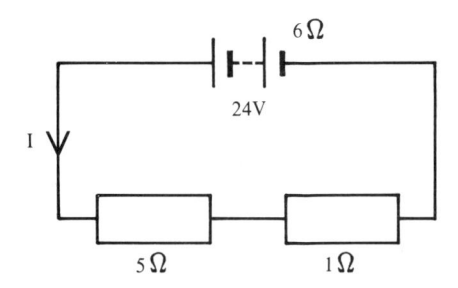

[Circuit diagram: 24V battery with 6Ω internal resistance, connected to 5Ω and 1Ω resistors in series, with current I flowing.]

Using

$$\text{Current in circuit} = \frac{\text{e.m.f. of battery}}{\text{total circuit resistance}}$$

e.m.f. of battery = 24V
total circuit resistance = 6 + 5 + 1 = 12Ω
current in circuit = $\frac{24}{12}$ = 2A

ANSWER: CURRENT IN CIRCUIT = 2A

Note to student: if the internal resistance is not given, we assume it is zero.

SUPPLEMENTARY

23.7 USE OF A DIODE AS A RECTIFIER

A diode only conducts electric current in one direction. It can be used to change alternating current into direct current. This can be shown using the circuit in Fig. 23.10.

FIG. 23.10

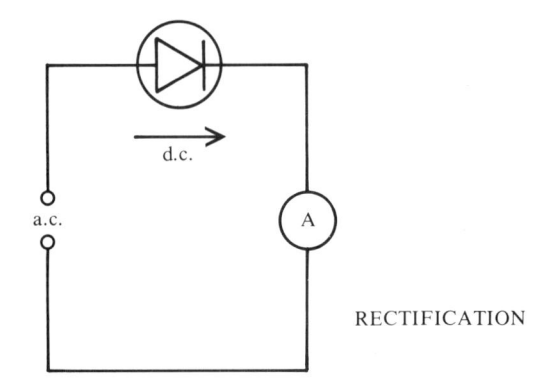

[Circuit diagram showing a diode with a.c. input, d.c. output through an ammeter A, labelled RECTIFICATION.]

The diode will only conduct on one half cycle and the output will be d.c. as shown in Fig. 23.11. It would appear like this on a C.R.O.

FIG. 23.11

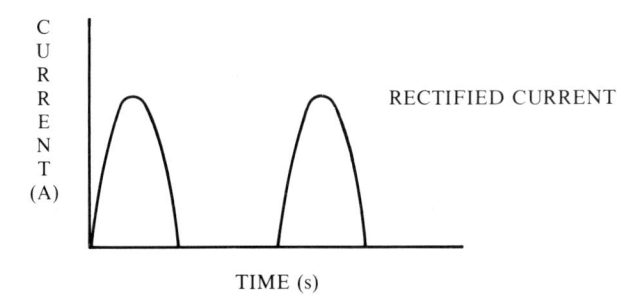

```
C
U
R
R      ∩           ∩              RECTIFIED CURRENT
E
N
T
(A)
         TIME (s)
```

The meter will deflect on each conducting half cycle. The a.c. is being rectified to d.c. and the process is called rectification.

23.8 THE TOTAL RESISTANCE OF RESISTORS CONNECTED IN PARALLEL

Suppose three resistors R_1, R_2 and R_3 are connected in parallel, as shown in Fig. 23.12.

FIG. 23.12

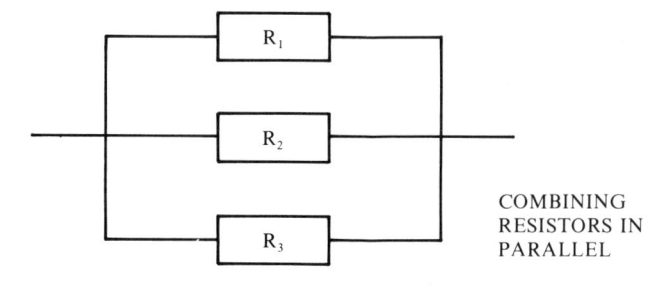

COMBINING RESISTORS IN PARALLEL

The total resistance R is given by
$$\frac{1}{R} = \frac{1}{R_1} + \frac{1}{R_2} + \frac{1}{R_3}$$

This relationship holds for any number of resistors but the formula can be simplified for only two resistors when
$$\frac{1}{R} = \frac{1}{R_1} + \frac{1}{R_2}$$
or
$$R = \frac{R_1 R_2}{R_1 + R_2},$$
that is
$$\text{Total resistance} = \frac{\text{Product of resistances}}{\text{Sum of resistances}}$$

PROBLEM
CALCULATE THE TOTAL RESISTANCE WHEN THREE RESISTORS OF RESISTANCE 6Ω, 6Ω AND 3Ω ARE CONNECTED IN PARALLEL.

Using
$$\frac{1}{R} = \frac{1}{R_1} + \frac{1}{R_2} + \frac{1}{R_3}$$
$R_1 = 6\,\Omega$, $R_2 = 6\,\Omega$ and $R_3 = 3\,\Omega$

So
$$\frac{1}{R} = \frac{1}{6} + \frac{1}{6} + \frac{1}{3} = \frac{1}{6} + \frac{1}{6} + \frac{2}{6} = \frac{4}{6}$$
$$R = \frac{6}{4} = 1.5\,\Omega.$$

ANSWER: TOTAL RESISTANCE = 1.5 Ω.

23.9 THE TOTAL RESISTANCE OF MIXED NETWORKS

In networks with series and parallel arrangements, we first find the total resistance of any parallel arrangements and then combine them with series arrangements.

PROBLEM
CALCULATE THE TOTAL RESISTANCE OF THE NETWORK SHOWN IN FIG. 23.13.

FIG. 23.13

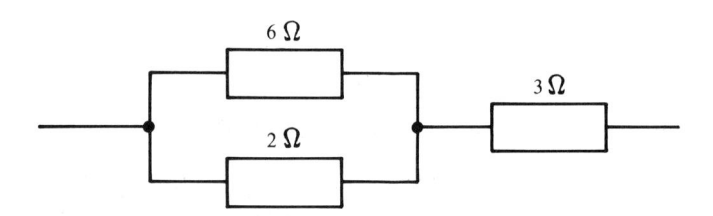

Total resistance of parallel network is given by
$$\frac{1}{R} = \frac{1}{6} + \frac{1}{2} = \frac{1}{6} + \frac{3}{6} = \frac{5}{6}$$
$$R = 1.2\,\Omega$$
Total resistance of series network is given by
$$1.2 + 3 = 4.2\,\Omega$$

ANSWER: TOTAL RESISTANCE = 4.2 Ω.

PROBLEM
IN THE CIRCUIT SHOWN IN FIG. 23.14,

FIG. 23.14

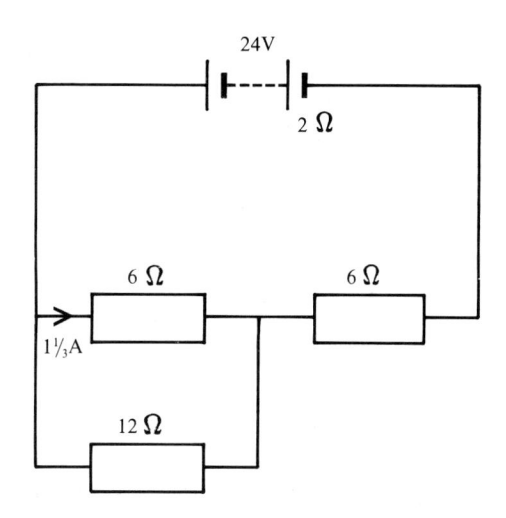

CALCULATE (i) THE TOTAL CIRCUIT RESISTANCE (ii) THE CURRENT THROUGH THE 12 Ω RESISTOR IF THE CURRENT THROUGH THE 6 Ω PARALLEL RESISTOR IS $1\frac{1}{3}$A.

Resistance of parallel network is given by

$$\frac{1}{R} = \frac{1}{R_1} + \frac{1}{R_2}$$

$$R_1 = 6\,\Omega, \quad R_2 = 12\,\Omega.$$

$$\frac{1}{R} = \frac{1}{6} + \frac{1}{12} = \frac{2}{12} + \frac{1}{12} = \frac{3}{12}$$

$$R = 4\,\Omega$$

Total circuit resistance = 4 + 6 + 2 = 12 Ω

$$\text{Circuit current} = \frac{\text{e.m.f.}}{\text{total circuit resistance}}$$

$$= \frac{24}{12} = 2\text{A}$$

If the circuit current is I and those through the 6 Ω and 12 Ω resistors are I_1 and I_2 then

$$I = I_1 + I_2$$
$$2 = 1\frac{1}{3} + I_2$$

So $\quad I_2 = \frac{2}{3}$ A.

Current through 12 Ω resistor = $\frac{2}{3}$A.

ANSWER: TOTAL RESISTANCE AND CURRENT = 12 Ω AND $\frac{2}{3}$A.

23.10 DEFINITION OF ELECTROMOTIVE FORCE

We have seen that:

e.m.f. of a cell = sum of p.d.s in circuit + p.d. inside cell.
Now from the definition of the volt we know that the p.d. between two points is the amount of electrical energy converted when unit charge passes between the two points. It therefore follows that:
the e.m.f. of a source is the energy per unit charge transferred by a source driving charge round a circuit. We obviously include the current being driven through the cell itself.

So, if a cell of e.m.f. 2V drives 3C completely around a circuit, 6J of electrical energy are transferred.

QUESTIONS

CORE

1. Calculate the total e.m.f. when two cells each of e.m.f. 2V are connected in series.
2. Why would identical cells be connected in parallel?
3. The diagram represents part of a circuit in which three resistors are connected.

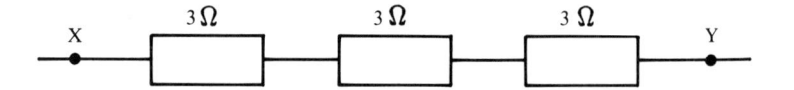

X —[3 Ω]—[3 Ω]—[3 Ω]— Y

   What is the effective resistance in ohms between the points X and Y?

   A 1 Ω   B 3 Ω   C 9 Ω   D 27 Ω   (L.E.A.G.)

4. The total resistance of the resistors in Fig. 23.15 will be

FIG. 23.15

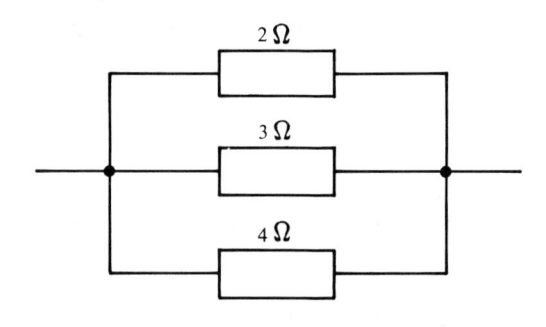

(parallel combination of 2 Ω, 3 Ω, 4 Ω)

A less than 1 Ω   B 2 Ω   C greater than 4 Ω
D exactly 9 Ω

5. In Fig. 23.15, the current entering the network is 6.5A. If the currents through the 2Ω and 3Ω resistors are 3A and 2A respectively, what is the current through the 4Ω resistor?
6. The internal resistance of a cell is 1.5Ω. Calculate the p.d. lost across the cell when a current of 2A flows through it.
7. a) An ammeter is being used to check on electrical heating element. The diagram shows a suitable circuit including the heating element with a resistance of 3Ω

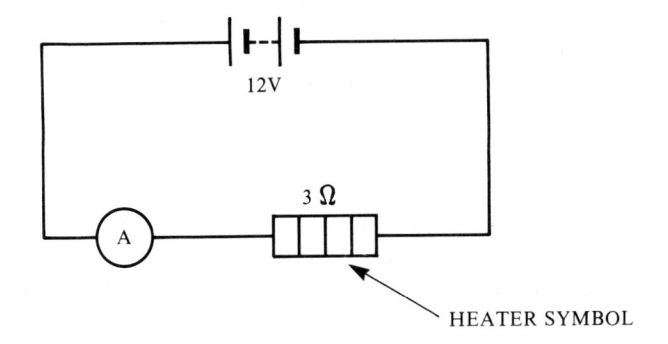

Calculate the reading of the ammeter.
b) A second identical element is added to the circuit.

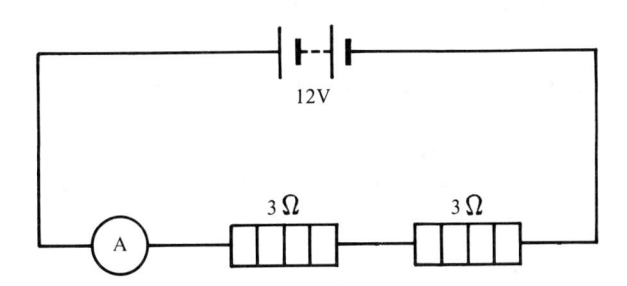

i) Calculate the total resistance of the circuit.
ii) Calculate the new reading of the ammeter. *(L.E.A.G.)*

SUPPLEMENTARY
8. Karen sets up the following circuit:

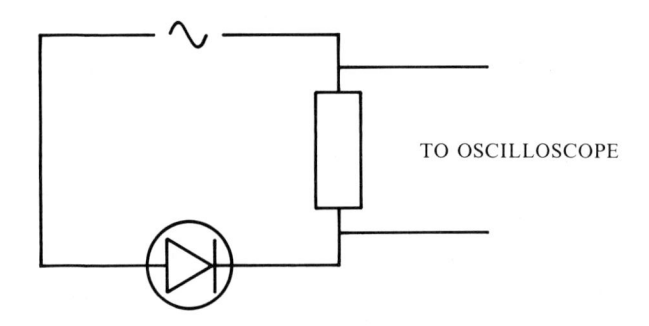

302 Electric Circuits

Which of the following traces will be seen on the oscilloscope screen?

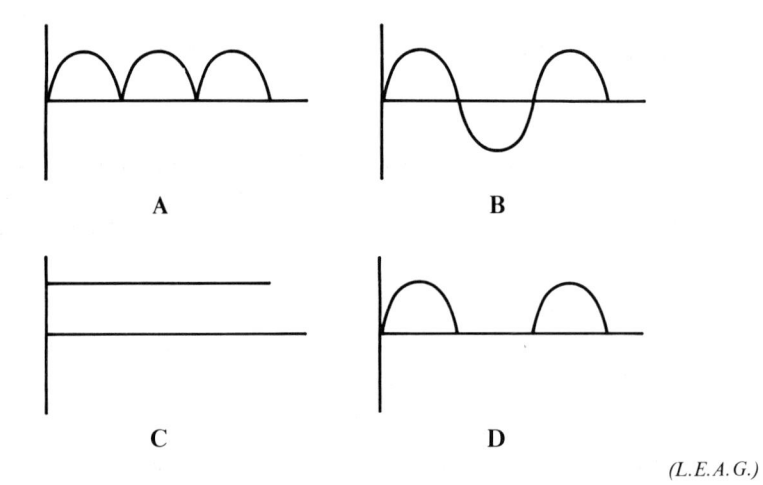

A
B
C
D

(L.E.A.G.)

9. Calculate the total resistance of three resistors of 2Ω, 5Ω and 10Ω connected in parallel.
10. Calculate the total resistance of the network of resistors shown in Fig. 23.16.

FIG. 23.16

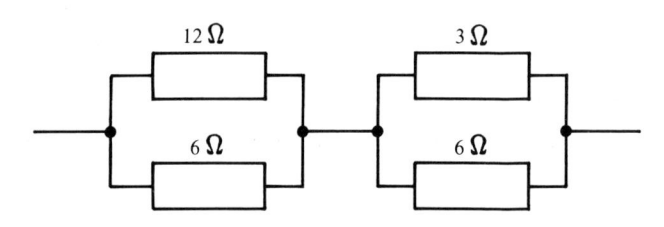

Chapter 24
PRACTICAL ELECTRIC CIRCUITRY

At the end of this chapter you will know:
CORE: the voltage and frequency of the mains supply; some uses of electricity; how to calculate power in electrical circuits and the cost of electricity used; how houses are wired; what is meant by live neutral and earth; the rating of fuses; the position of fuses and switches, why devices are earthed; what is meant by circuit breakers and double insulation; how three pin plugs should be wired and the hazards of damaged insulation, overheated cables and damp conditions.
SUPPLEMENTARY: an expression for heat energy produced per second and the total heat energy produced by an electric current and the relationship between the kilowatt hour and the joule.

CORE

24.1 THE VOLTAGE AND FREQUENCY OF THE MAINS SUPPLY
The voltage of the a.c. mains in the United Kingdom is 240V. The frequency is 50Hz and so in Fig. 22.3 there will be 50 complete cycles every second.

24.2 SOME USES OF ELECTRICITY
Electrical energy is used significantly in our houses. Outside, of course, it is used to light our streets. Street lamps are wired in parallel so that if one lamp fails the others remain lit.

Inside our homes electricity is used in lighting and heating and in many other devices including refrigerators, washing machines, irons, toasters, microwave ovens, televisions, radios, music centres, computers, video-recorders and telephones. It is a vital source of energy and some of the devices we have listed above could not operate with any other type of energy.

24.3 ELECTRICAL POWER AND COSTINGS
We know that in circuits, electrical energy is being changed into other forms of energy.

The electrical power used = $\dfrac{\text{electrical energy changed}}{\text{time taken}}$

Using the definition of the volt we find that

electrical power used = current through device $\times$ p.d. across device

or
$$P = IV$$

where P = power in watts
I = current in amps
V = p.d. in volts
So Watts = Amps × Volts.

PROBLEM

CALCULATE THE POWER USED BY A LAMP ON MAINS SUPPLY IF THE CURRENT USED IS 0.25A.

Use $P = IV$
$I = 0.25A$, $V = 240V$
So $P = 0.25 \times 240 = 60W$

ANSWER: POWER USED = 60W.

The typical power of some devices are:
Lamps   40W, 60W and 100W
Refrigerator   150W
Television   200W
Iron   750W
Electric Fire (1 bar)   1kW
Kettle   2-3kW
Immersion Heater   3kW
Cooker   8kW

In order to calculate the cost of using electrical power, we use kilowatt hours, kWh.

A device with a power rating of 1kW uses 1kWh of energy every hour. In other words
Energy in kWh = Power in kW × Time in h

1 kilowatt hour is called a unit of electricity.

In order to calculate the cost of electricity we multiply the number of units by the cost per unit. At the moment, one unit costs 5.7p.
So
Cost = Number of units × Cost per unit

PROBLEM

CALCULATE THE COST OF RUNNING A 2kW ELECTRIC HEATER FOR 10h IF ELECTRICITY COSTS 5.7p PER UNIT.

Use Number of Units = Power × Time
$= 2 \times 10 = 20$
Cost = Number of units × Cost per unit
$= 20 \times 5.7 = 114p.$

ANSWER: COST = 114p.

FIG. 24.1

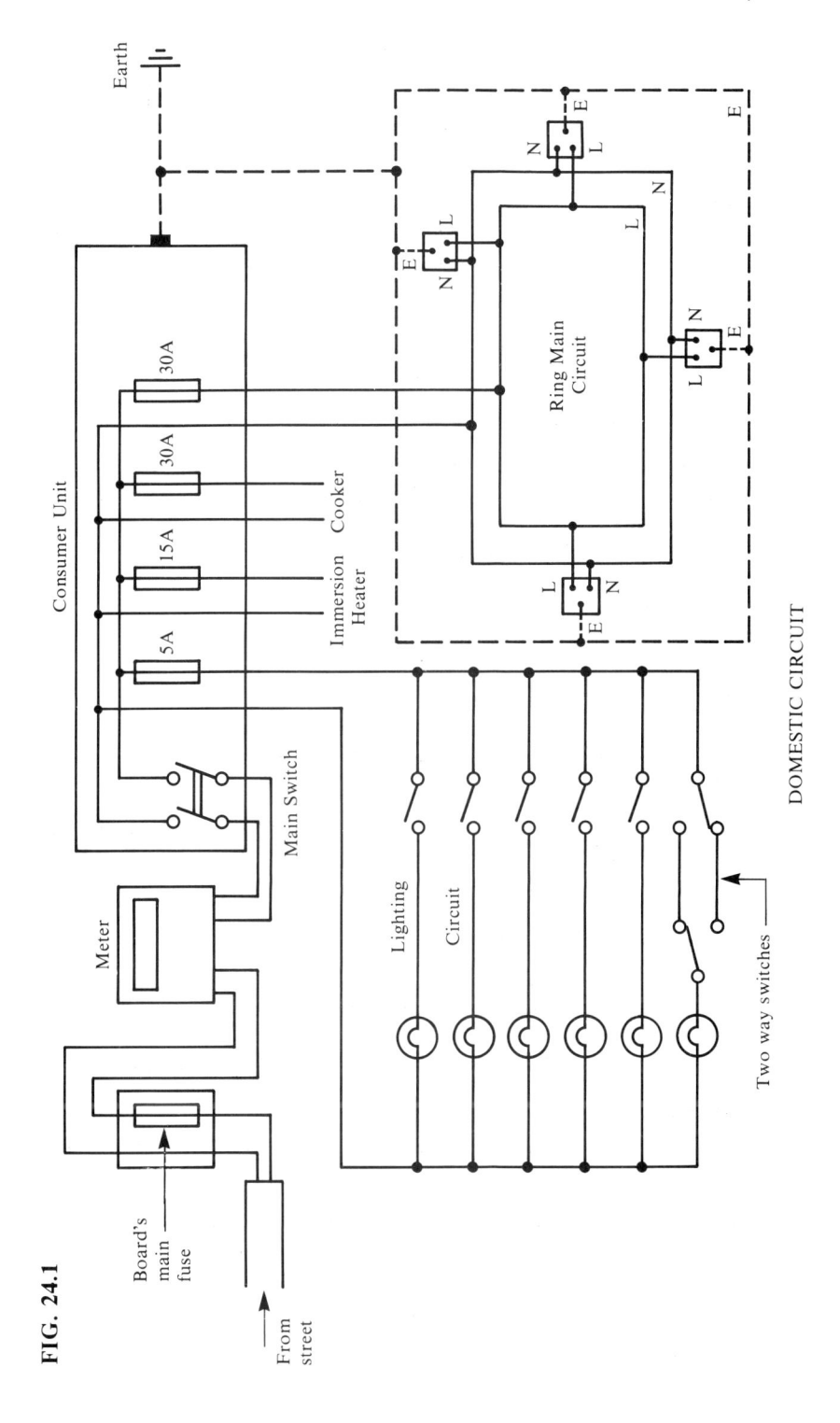

24.4 HOUSE CIRCUITS
(i) A house circuit is shown in Fig. 24.1.

The electricity supply enters from the street by means of a two core cable. This contains two wires, the live (L) and the neutral (N). The neutral wire is earthed at the local sub-station and so there is no p.d. between it and earth. The live wire is alternately positive and negative because the supply is a.c. Both of these wires pass through a sealed container where the board's main fuse is located. After that they pass through the meter which displays the number of units used. They then pass through the main switch in the consumer unit. Here the N and L wires are fed through different fuses into the main circuits of the house.

The lighting circuit supplies the light socket in each room with each socket being wired in parallel. Two-way switches are used wherever a socket needs to be operated from more than one point. Usually a two way switch is located at the top and bottom of a staircase.

Devices such as the immersion heater and the cooker are wired directly to the consumer unit.

The other major circuit in the house is the ring main circuit. The live and neutral wires each run in two rings around the house and the power sockets, all rated at 13A, are wired to them. Because current can travel in both directions around the rings, thinner wires can be used. The ring main also has a third wire which goes to the top hole of each power point. The third wire is called an earth and it is connected to a metal water pipe in the house.

(ii) A 40W lamp uses a current of 0.25A when connected to the mains, as we have already seen. Similarly a 100W lamp uses 0.42A. The lighting circuit then can be fitted with a fuse rated at 5A — that is a fuse which will melt if the current exceeds 5A. This is perfectly reasonable since it is very unlikely that 12 100W lamps will all be switched on at once.

It is very bad practice to connect appliances such as irons to light sockets since these use a current of about 3A and if other light sockets are also being used, then the fuse could easily blow. The immersion heater and the cooker take large currents and are connected via 15A and 30A rated fuses.

The ring main is fitted with a 30A fuse. This will enable a sufficient number of appliances such as irons, televisions and electric fires to be used safely without causing the fuse to blow.

(iii) Fuses and switches are always wired into the live wire. If they were in the neutral then lamp sockets and power sockets would be live, that is at a high voltage, when switches were off or fuses blown. It would then be possible for example, to get a shock by touching the bar of an electric fire, even though it was switched off.

24.5 THE EARTH WIRE

A fuse is a device which is meant to prevent damage to an appliance. An earth prevents damage to the user.

Suppose a fault develops in an electric fire and the element is in contact with the body of the fire. The body will be live and if we were to touch it we would get a possibly fatal electric shock as the current rushed through our bodies to the earth. The earth wire prevents this. It offers a low resistance route of escape enabling the current to go to earth by a wire rather than through a human body. The large current would blow the fuse in the plug.

Any appliance with a metal body could become live if a fault developed.

24.6 CIRCUIT BREAKERS AND DOUBLE INSULATION

Circuit breakers are used in some consumer units as an alternative to a fuse. They contain an electromagnet and if the current exceeds the rating of the circuit breaker, the electromagnet separates a pair of contacts and breaks the circuit. They operate much faster than fuses and can be reset by pressing a button.

Appliances such as vacuum cleaners and hair dryers are usually double insulated. The appliance is encased in an insulating plastic case and is connected to the supply by a two core insulated cable containing only a live and a neutral wire. Any metal attachments which the user might touch are fitted into the plastic case so that they do not make a direct connection with the motor or other internal electrical parts.

24.7 WIRING THREE PIN PLUGS

A three pin plug and the socket into which it fits are shown in Fig. 24.2(a) and Fig. 24.2(b).

The 3 core cable is held tight with the cord grip. The wire with the blue insulation is the neutral wire and is connected to the left hand pin. The brown insulated wire is connected to the right hand pin which has a fuse because this is the live wire. The wire with the yellow and green insulation is the earth wire and it is connected to the top pin.

308 Practical Electric Circuitry

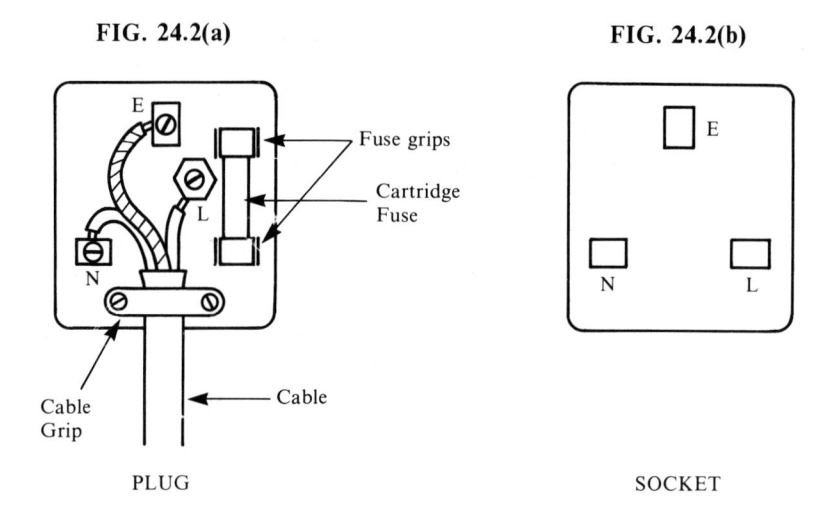

FIG. 24.2(a)

FIG. 24.2(b)

PLUG

SOCKET

Each of these wires should be wrapped around its securing screw so that it is tightened as the screw tightens.

The fuse used is either a 3A (blue) for appliances up to 720W or 13A (brown) for appliances between 720W and 3kW. If a larger than usual current flows, the fuse will blow.

The earth wire is connected to the metal case of the appliance. Some devices such as hairdryers with plastic cases do not have an earth wire but rely on double insulation.

Each pin on the plug fits into a corresponding hole in the socket. The earth pin is longer than the others so that it goes into the socket first and pushes aside safety covers which cover the rear of the neutral and live holes in the socket.

The socket is connected as shown in Fig. 24.1. If the appliance becomes live, a current flows through the earth wire and from the socket earth connection to the earth via a water pipe. During the process, the fuse in the plug will blow. Before it is replaced, the appliance should be checked by a qualified electrician.

24.8 DANGERS OF ELECTRICITY

Mains electricity is dangerous and should always be treated with care.

In particular three hazards should be avoided:
1) Insulation on wires should be regularly checked to ensure that it is in good condition. If the insulation around the live wire breaks down, anyone touching the wire could get a shock. In order to make checking easier, wires should not be laid underneath carpets and rugs.

2) Care should be taken to ensure that cables do not become overheated. Normally, overheating does not occur because the fuse would blow. However, if an incorrect fuse is fitted in a plug, larger currents could flow, causing overheating and possible fires. Equally if the wrong fuses are fitted in the consumer unit to enable larger currents to be used in lighting circuits, overheating and fires could result.

3) Electrical devices should always be used in damp-free conditions. In particular they should never be used in bathrooms. Devices falling into water will make the water live. Water conducts electricity and if a person were to touch the water she/he would be electrocuted. Electric fires must be fixed on bathroom walls; electric showers are fixed to the wall and are well earthed and doubly insulated.

SUPPLEMENTARY

24.9 ELECTRICAL POWER AND ENERGY

We have seen that electrical power P is given by

$$P = IV$$

where I = current in amps
V = p.d. in volts

We can write this in two different ways, using Ohm's Law.
Since $V = IR$
then

$$P = IV = I(IR) = I^2R$$

This expression is used if we know current and resistance.

Also $I = \dfrac{V}{R}$

So $P = IV = \left(\dfrac{V}{R}\right)V = \dfrac{V^2}{R}$

This expression is used if we know p.d. and resistance.

PROBLEM

CALCULATE THE POWER USED BY A LAMP OF RESISTANCE 6Ω TAKING A CURRENT OF 2A.

Use $P = I^2R$
$I = 2A \quad R = 6$
So $P = 2^2 \times 6 = 24W$

ANSWER: POWER USED = 24W.

Now since

$$\text{electrical power used} = \dfrac{\text{electrical energy changed}}{\text{time taken}}$$

then
> electrical energy changed = electrical power used × time taken
> or used

and so the energy used, W, is given by

$$W = VIt$$

where t = time, in seconds

Using Ohm's Law we may write
$$W = I^2Rt = \frac{V^2t}{R}$$

PROBLEM
CALCULATE THE AMOUNT OF ENERGY CHANGED PER MINUTE BY A LAMP CONNECTED TO THE MAINS AND USING A CURRENT OF 0.42A.

Use $\quad W = VIt$
$V = 240V, I = 0.42A, t = 1 \text{ min} = 60s.$

So
$$W = 240 \times 0.42 \times 60 = 6048 J$$

ANSWER: ENERGY CHANGED = 6048J.

24.10 THE KILOWATT HOUR AND THE JOULE

1 kilowatt hour = 1 kilowatt for 1 hour
= 1000 watts for 1 hour
= 1000 joules per second for 3600 seconds
= 3,600,000 joules

So $\quad 1kWh = 3.6 \times 10^6 J.$

QUESTIONS

CORE
1. State the voltage of the mains supply.
2. Calculate the current taken by a mains electric kettle when its power is 2.4kW and state which fuse rating should be used.
3. A bulb is labelled 24W, 12V. When used on a 12V supply, calculate the current it will take and its resistance.
4. Calculate the cost of heating a tank of water with a 2kW immersion heater for 90 minutes if electricity cost 5p per kWh.
5. How are the lamps in a lighting circuit connected?
6. Explain why fuses and switches are connected in the live wire?
7. Name a device which is usually doubly insulated.
8. You are connecting a 3 core cable to a three-pin electrical plug. What colour wire should you connect the live terminal?
   A brown   B blue   C black   D green and yellow.   *(L.E.A.G.)*

9. Fig. 6 shows a diagram of a fused three pin plug. The plug is connected to an electric fire.

FIG. 6

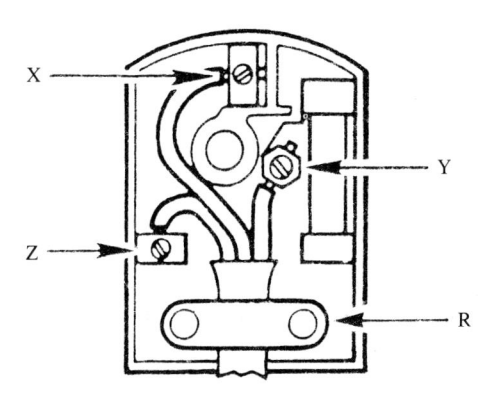

(a) What is the colour of the insulation of the wire connected to
   (i) pin X
   (ii) pin Y
(b) Why is pin X longer than the other two pins?
(c) What is the purpose of R?
(d) Wire X is connected to the frame of the fire. Why does this protect the user from electric shock? *(N.E.A.)*

SUPPLEMENTARY

10. A current of I is passed through an electric fire element of resistance R. The power output of the fire is
    A IR   B I^2R C IR^2 D I^2/R. *(S.E.G.)*
11. A 2kW electric fire is used for 10 hours each week and a 100W lamp is used for 10 hours each day. Find the total energy consumed per month, assuming 1 month = 4 weeks.
12. Convert 3kWh to J.
13. (a) (i) Why is a fuse fitted in a modern 3-pin plug?
        (ii) What causes a fuse to blow?
        (iii) One of the pins is connected to the earth. For a metal electric kettle with a three core cable:
            1. Which part of the kettle should the earth lead be connected to?
            2. What would happen if the casing accidentally becomes live?
    (b) An electric fire is rated 250V 2kW. The fire is operating normally
        (i) How much electrical energy is converted into heat in 1 second?

(ii) On a consumer's bill electrical energy is charged at 6p per unit. What unit of energy is used by the electricity boards?
(iii) What is the cost of having the fire switched on for 5 hours?
(c) An aircraft flies just below a negatively charged thundercloud. Movement of free electrons causes electrostatic charges to be induced on the aircraft.
(i) Draw on the diagram the position and signs of the induced charges on the aircraft

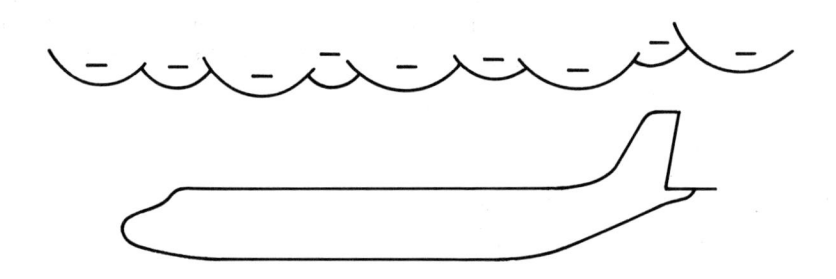

(ii) What rules of force between charges have you used to draw the induced charges?
(iii) What will happen to the induced charges when the aircraft flies away from the cloud? (L.E.A.G.)

Chapter 25
ELECTROMAGNETIC INDUCTION

At the end of this chapter you will know:
CORE: how a changing magnetic field induces an e.m.f. in a circuit and how the effect is used; what the induced e.m.f. depends upon; how an a.c. generator works and the output it gives; what a transformer is and how it is used and the advantages of high voltage a.c. transmission in the national grid.
SUPPLEMENTARY: the rule for the direction of the induced e.m.f.; the principle of operation of the transformer; the power equation for a 100% efficient transformer and how energy losses in a cable may be calculated.

CORE

25.1 INDUCED ELECTROMOTIVE FORCE
Suppose we have the circuit shown in Fig. 25.1.

FIG. 25.1

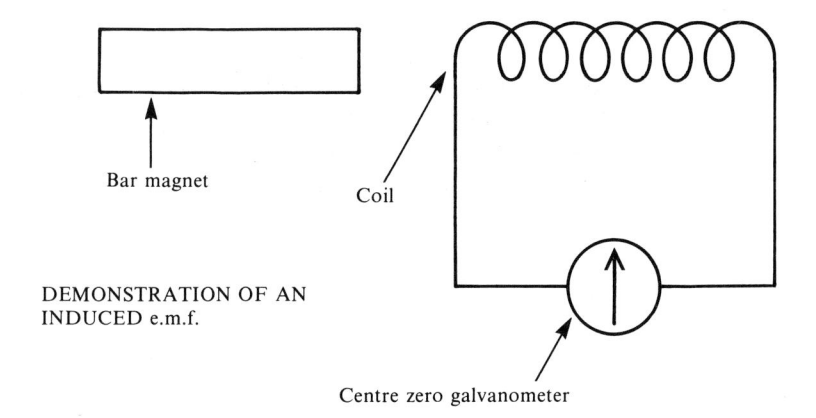

Bar magnet

Coil

DEMONSTRATION OF AN INDUCED e.m.f.

Centre zero galvanometer

A coil is connected to a centre zero galvanometer. A galvanometer detects small currents or p.d.s, often in the range of milliamps or millivolts. Because the zero of the scale is in the centre then currents or voltages in both directions may be measured.

When the magnet is plunged into the coil, the galvanometer deflects, indicating that an e.m.f. has been induced in the circuit. When the magnet is pulled out of the coil the galvanometer deflects again but this time the other way showing that the current is moving in the opposite direction or, in other words, the induced e.m.f. is in the opposite sense. There is no deflection when the magnet is at rest.

We conclude that whenever a magnet moves with respect to a coil, an e.m.f. is induced in the coil and if the circuit is complete, a current will flow. This effect of an induced e.m.f. is used in many devices including bicycle dynamos and tape and video recorder playback heads. It is also the basis of the generation of the mains voltage and this will be considered later in the chapter.

25.2 FACTORS INFLUENCING THE SIZE OF THE INDUCED ELECTROMOTIVE FORCE

Using the circuit shown in Fig. 25.1, we can find that the induced e.m.f. increases if the following quantities increase:
1) the speed of motion of the magnet
2) the number of turns on the coil
3) the strength of the magnet.

When we multiply the strength of the magnet by the number of turns on the coil, we obtain a quantity known as the magnetic flux. We can summarize all three points by saying that the induced e.m.f. increases as the rate of change of flux increases.

In order to explain electromagnetic induction in a conductor, Faraday, who discovered the effect, said that an e.m.f. is induced in a conductor whenever the conductor cuts magnetic field lines or lines of flux. That is, it must move across them, not along them.

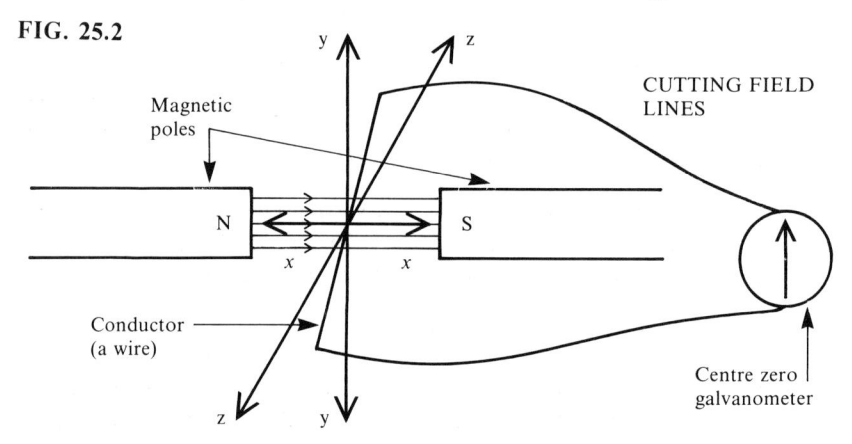

FIG. 25.2

So, in Fig. 25.2, an e.m.f. will be induced when the conductor moves vertically, along y, and cuts the horizontal field lines. If it moves in the x or z directions, it only moves along the field lines and so there will be no induced e.m.f.

25.3 THE ALTERNATING CURRENT GENERATOR

The simplest type of a.c. generator is shown in Fig. 25.3.

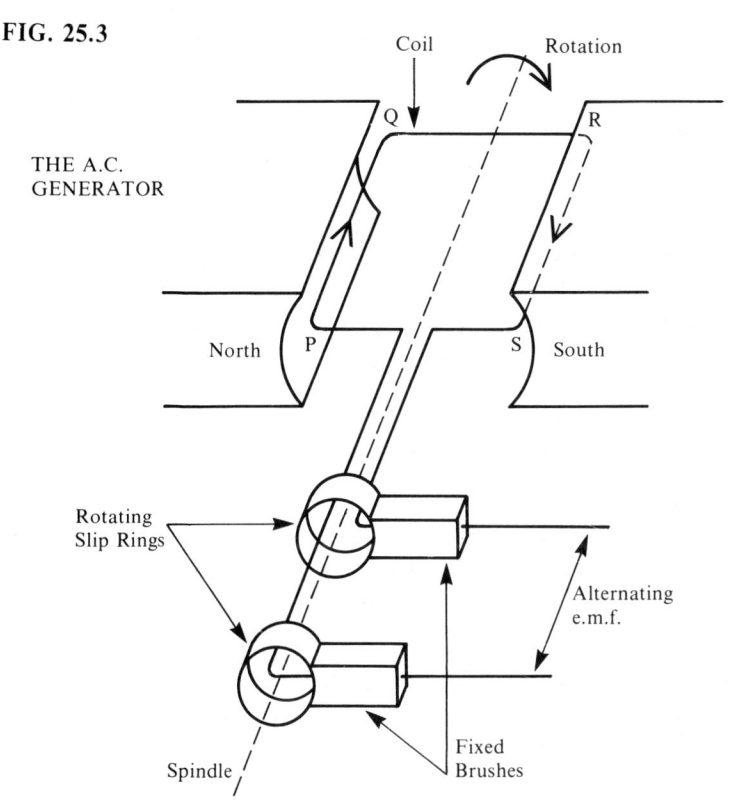

FIG. 25.3

THE A.C. GENERATOR

It consists of a rectangular coil which rotates on a spindle between the curved pole pieces of a U shaped magnet. The ends of the coil are joined to two slip rings which rotate with the coil and press against two carbon brushes through which the current flows.

As the coil rotates, it cuts lines of flux and an e.m.f. is induced. In this device it is the coil which moves while the magnet remains at rest. However it is only the relative motion that is important.

The relationship between the directions of motion of the conductor, the magnetic field and the induced current is given by Fleming's right hand rule which says that if the thumb and first two fingers of the right hand are held at right angles to each other then if the thumb points in the direction of motion of the wire and the first finger points in the field direction then the second finger will point in the direction of the conventional current.

This is shown in Fig. 25.4(a) and Fig. 25.4(b).

FIG. 25.4(a)   **FIG. 25.4(b)**

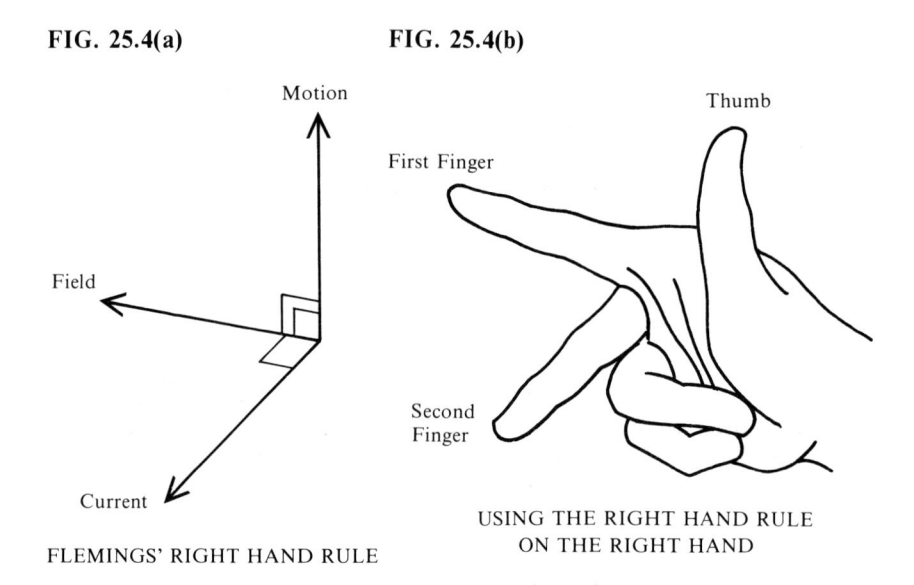

Motion

First Finger

Field

Thumb

Second Finger

Current

FLEMINGS' RIGHT HAND RULE

USING THE RIGHT HAND RULE ON THE RIGHT HAND

We can use this rule to find out how the e.m.f. behaves when it is generated in an a.c. generator.

If the coil is horizontal as shown, sides PQ and RS are moving vertically and are achieving the greatest rate of flux cutting. Using the right hand rule we can see that current moves from P to Q and R to S. As the coil rotates it cuts less flux until when it is vertical, it is cutting no lines of flux at all and the induced e.m.f. is zero. As PQ begins to move downwards and RS begins to move upwards, their direction of motion has been reversed and so the current direction is reversed with current moving from Q to P and S to R. The e.m.f. reaches a maximum when the coil is horizontal again and decreases to zero when the coil is vertical. Its direction is then reversed and reaches a maximum when it is horizontal again, after completing one revolution.

The change in the induced e.m.f. with time is shown in Fig. 25.5.

The alternating e.m.f. generated would cause a.c. to flow in a circuit connected to the generator. The periodic time, T, is the time taken for one complete cycle to be generated and is also the time taken for the coil to make one rotation. The number of coil rotations per second is the frequency of the e.m.f.

FIG. 25.5

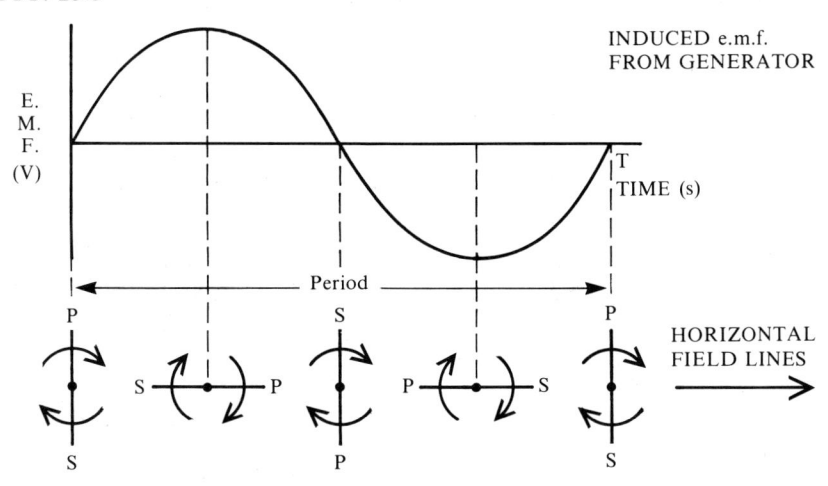

INDUCED e.m.f. FROM GENERATOR

E.M.F. (V)

Period

TIME (s)

P S P

HORIZONTAL FIELD LINES

S —(·)— P   P —(·)— S

S   P   S

25.4 THE TRANSFORMER

A transformer is a device used to change an alternating p.d. or voltage to either a bigger or smaller voltage.

A transformer is shown in Fig. 25.6.

FIG. 25.6

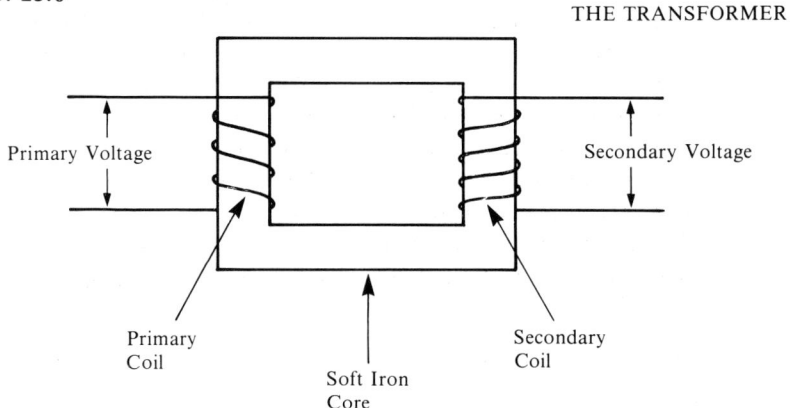

THE TRANSFORMER

Primary Voltage

Secondary Voltage

Primary Coil

Secondary Coil

Soft Iron Core

It consists of a soft iron core onto which two coils are wound. The voltage is applied to the primary and the reduced or amplified voltage is obtained from the secondary.

We find that

$$\frac{\text{secondary voltage}}{\text{primary voltage}} = \frac{\text{number of turns on secondary coil}}{\text{number of turns on primary coil}}$$

or

$$\frac{V_{OUT}}{V_{IN}} = \frac{N_{SECONDARY}}{N_{PRIMARY}}$$

when

V_{OUT} = secondary voltage output
V_{IN} = primary voltage input
$N_{SECONDARY}$ = number of turns on secondary coil
$N_{PRIMARY}$ = number of turns on primary coil.

If there are more turns on the secondary than the primary, the voltage is amplified and the transformer is known as a step-up. If, on the other hand, there are less turns on the secondary than the primary, the voltage is reduced and the transformer is known as a step down.

The circuit symbol for a transformer is shown in Fig. 25.7.

FIG. 25.7

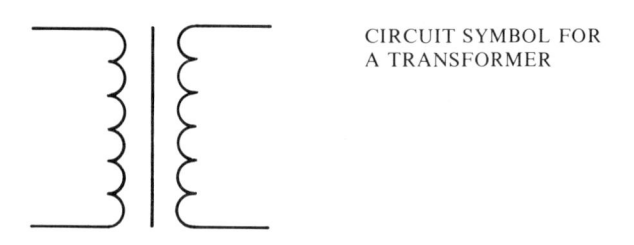

CIRCUIT SYMBOL FOR A TRANSFORMER

Step up or step down transformers can be indicated by changing the ratio of the turns shown on the primary and secondary coils.

PROBLEM
A TRANSFORMER STEPS DOWN THE MAINS VOLTAGE OF 240V TO 12V. IF THERE ARE 2000 TURNS ON THE PRIMARY, HOW MANY TURNS ARE THERE ON THE SECONDARY?

Use

$$\frac{V_{OUT}}{V_{IN}} = \frac{N_{SECONDARY}}{N_{PRIMARY}}$$

So

$$\frac{12}{240} = \frac{N_{SECONDARY}}{2000}$$

$$N_{SECONDARY} = 2000 \times \frac{12}{240} = 100$$

ANSWER: NUMBER OF TURNS ON THE SECONDARY = 100.

In practice, there are small energy losses in a transformer for three reasons:
1. The windings of the copper primary and secondary coils have resistance and heat is produced when the current flows through them.
2. The soft iron core is in the changing magnetic field of the primary. The induced e.m.f. causes currents, known as eddy currents, to flow in it causing heating. These are reduced by using a laminated core. This has sheets separated by insulation to increase the resistance.
3. All the lines of flux generated by the primary may not cut the secondary if the transformer is badly designed.

Large transformers are generally oil cooled to prevent overheating.

25.5 THE NATIONAL GRID

(i) The national grid is a nationwide system of cables, supported on pylons, which connect power stations around the country to consumers.

In the largest modern power station, electricity is generated at 25kV and is immediately stepped up in a transformer to 400kV to be sent over long distances on the Supergrid. Photograph 25 shows part of the Chickerell/Mannington 400kV Supergrid transmission line in Dorset.

Later this is stepped down by a substation to pass along the 132kV Grid. A transformer substation used to step down from Supergrid to Grid is shown in Photograph 26. This shows the Bishops Wood substation near Stourport-on-Severn, Worcestershire.

320 *Electromagnetic Induction*

PHOTOGRAPH 25

PHOTOGRAPH 26

Later still, this is stepped down by local substations to 33kV for use in heavy industry, 11kV for light industry and 240V for domestic use.

The national grid enables electricity to be "shunted" around the country to cope with excessive local demand or the breakdown of local power stations.

(ii) The national grid transmits electrical power across the country. Now

$$\text{electrical power} = \text{volts} \times \text{amps}.$$

The electrical power is transmitted at extremely high voltages, as we have seen and extremely low currents. The less the current flowing in a wire, the less energy wasted as heat. This is the reason for the high voltage used.

The reason for using a.c. instead of d.c. is that it can be transformed up and down.

SUPPLEMENTARY

25.6 THE DIRECTION OF THE INDUCED ELECTROMOTIVE FORCE

It may seem that when we obtain an induced e.m.f. that we are getting something for nothing! In fact, of course, we are not.

Lenz's Law states that the direction of the induced e.m.f. is always such as to oppose the charge producing it.

In Fig. 25.1, consider what happens when the magnet is plunged into the coil. Suppose the south pole of the magnet is nearest the coil as shown in Fig. 25.8.

FIG. 25.8

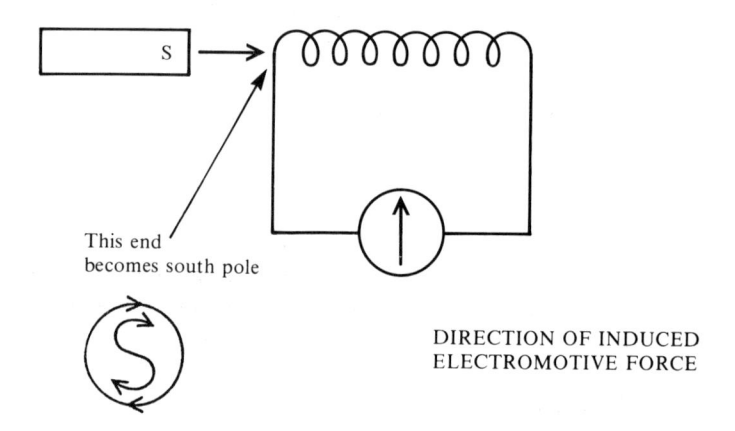

The direction of the induced e.m.f. causes the current to flow in such a direction as to make the near end of the coil a south pole — in other words, the current flows clockwise around the coil, as shown. Work must then be done in pushing the two like poles together. When the magnet is removed from the coil, the current direction reverses causing the end of the coil to become a north pole. Work must now be done to separate the two unlike poles.

We can see that we must do work in order to generate the e.m.f.

25.7 THE PRINCIPLE OF OPERATION OF THE TRANSFORMER

In the transformer, the changing current in the primary produces a changing magnetic flux. This changing flux travels through the soft iron core on which the primary and secondary are wound and cuts the secondary. The secondary coil is therefore cut by a changing magnetic flux and an e.m.f. is induced in it. The flux cutting the secondary coil is changed by changing the number of turns on the secondary.

We can see why it is important that as much of the flux generated by the primary coil cuts the secondary coil.

25.8 THE POWER EQUATION FOR A TRANSFORMER

If a transformer is 100% efficient — that is there are no power (or energy losses) then

$$\text{power in primary} = \text{power in secondary}$$

but $\quad \text{power} = \text{volts} \times \text{amps}$
Now $\quad \text{power in primary} = V_{IN} \times I_{IN}$
and $\quad \text{power in secondary} = V_{OUT} \times I_{OUT}$
where $\quad I_{IN} = \text{primary current}$
$\quad I_{OUT} = \text{secondary current}$

So
$$V_{IN} \times I_{IN} = V_{OUT} \times I_{OUT}$$

or
$$\frac{V_{OUT}}{V_{IN}} = \frac{I_{IN}}{I_{OUT}}$$

Using an earlier equation we have

$$\frac{N_{SECONDARY}}{N_{PRIMARY}} = \frac{V_{OUT}}{V_{IN}} = \frac{I_{IN}}{I_{OUT}}$$

We can see from this that in a step up transformer, the current is stepped down and in a step down transformer, the current is stepped up. This explains why low currents are transmitted along the national grid as a result of the high voltages used.

PROBLEM

A TRANSFORMER STEPS DOWN THE MAINS VOLTAGE FROM 240V TO 12V. IF THE SECONDARY CURRENT IS 2A AND THE TRANSFORMER IS 100% EFFICIENT, CALCULATE THE PRIMARY CURRENT.

Use
$$\frac{V_{OUT}}{V_{IN}} = \frac{I_{IN}}{I_{OUT}}$$

$$\frac{12}{240} = \frac{I_{IN}}{2}$$

$$I_{IN} = \frac{24}{240} = 0.1A.$$

ANSWER: PRIMARY CURRENT = 0.1A.

25.9 CALCULATION OF ENERGY LOSSES IN A CABLE

When electricity flows through a cable, electrical energy is changed into heat.

Now $P = I^2R$
where I = current in A
       R = resistance in Ω
and P = heat power obtained, in Watts.

In a time t seconds, the heat energy generated is given by W where

$$W = I^2Rt.$$

In the national grid this is kept to a minimum for a given length of cable because the current transmitted is small.

W can be regarded as an energy loss since it represents a loss of electrical energy to the system. Obviously the energy is gained by the atmosphere, as heat.

PROBLEM
A CURRENT OF 2A PASSES THROUGH A WIRE OF RESISTANCE 4Ω FOR 3 MIN. CALCULATE THE ENERGY LOSS.

Use $W = I^2Rt$
       $I = 2A, R = 4\Omega, t = 3$ min $= 180$s.
So
       $W = 2^2 \times 4 \times 180 = 2880$J.

ANSWER: ENERGY LOSS = 2.88kJ.

QUESTIONS

CORE
1. State the three factors on which the size of an induced e.m.f. depends.
2. A coil of wire is connected to a centre zero galvanometer. State what would happen if:
   (a) a magnet were plunged into the coil
   (b) the magnet were held at rest inside the coil
   (c) the magnet were removed from the coil but faster than it was plunged in.
3. Draw a diagram of an a.c. generator.
4. State two ways in which the output of an a.c. generator of constant frequency can be increased.
5. A stepdown transformer changes 240V a.c. to 48V a.c. There are 2000 turns on the primary coil. The number of turns on the secondary coil is
   A 40   B 400   C 5000   D 10 000   *(S.E.G.)*

6. The diagram represents a simple transformer with 20 turns on the primary coil and 80 turns on the secondary.

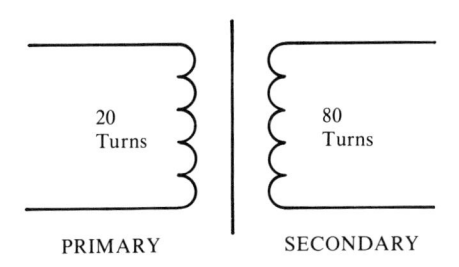

If 4V a.c. is supplied to the primary coil what voltage would you expect across the secondary coil?
A 4V   B 16V   C 100V   D 240V   (L.E.A.G.)

7. Power losses in the National Grid system are reduced by using
A thin cables   B high cables   C underground cables   D high voltages   (S.E.G.)

8. The voltage across the power lines supplying alternating current to an isolated house is 12 000V.
The device D changes the voltage of the supply to 240V

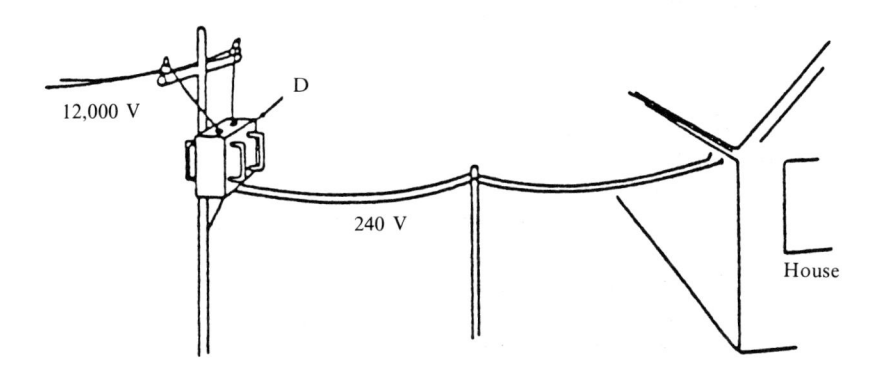

(a) What do we call the device D?
(b) Why is the supply not transmitted all the way at 240V?
(c) Why cannot the 12,000V supply be used, unchanged, in the house? Give two reasons.
(d) Why is alternating current used?   (S.E.G.)

SUPPLEMENTARY
9. State Lenz's Law.
10. Which important principle is the above law an example of?
11. A step down transformer is used to run a 24V lamp from the mains. There are 500 turns on the primary through which the current is 0.5A. Calculate the number of turns on the secondary and the secondary current stating any assumptions made.
12. The current flowing in a wire is halved. What is the effect on the energy loss?

Chapter 26
THE MAGNETIC EFFECT OF AN ELECTRIC CURRENT

At the end of this chapter you will know:
CORE: that magnetic fields are produced by electric currents; the field lines due to currents in straight wires and solenoids and the applications of the magnetic effect of an electric current in electromagnets, bells, relays and reed switches.
SUPPLEMENTARY: the variation of magnetic fields due to currents in straight wires and solenoids with distance and the size of the current.

CORE

26.1 MAGNETIC FIELDS ARE PRODUCED BY ELECTRIC CURRENTS

We saw in Chapter 20, Section 1 that magnetism arises as a result of the motion of charged particles called electrons, in a substance.

Now when an electric current flows through a conductor, it is itself a flow of electrons and as a result whenever a current flows through a conductor, a magnetic field results.

26.2 MAGNETIC FIELD PATTERNS DUE TO CURRENT IN A LONG STRAIGHT WIRE AND A SOLENOID

(i) The magnetic field pattern due to current in a long straight wire is shown in Fig. 26.1.

FIG. 26.1

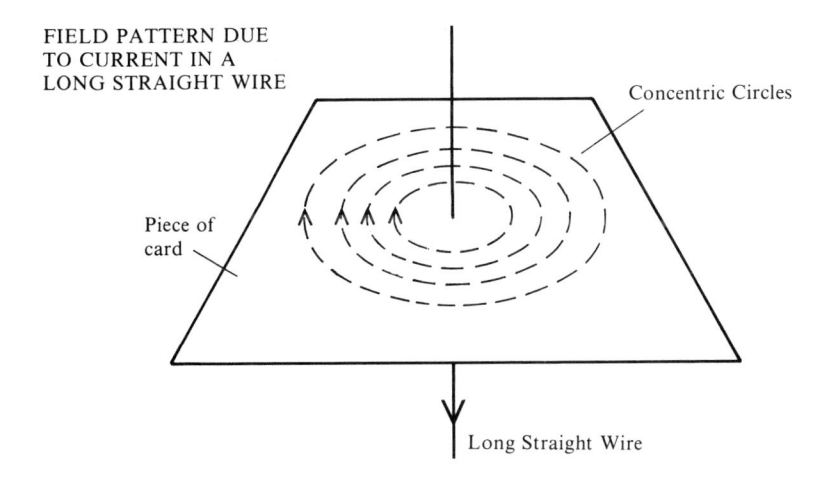

FIELD PATTERN DUE TO CURRENT IN A LONG STRAIGHT WIRE

Concentric Circles

Piece of card

Long Straight Wire

328 The Magnetic Effect of an Electric Current

The lines of field or flux lines are concentric circles centred upon the wire. If the conventional current flows downwards, the direction of the field is clockwise, as shown. If the current direction is reversed, then the directions of the field is also reversed.

The direction of the field is given by the right hand grip rule, which says: If the fingers of the right hand are curled up and the thumb is pointed in the direction of the current then the curled fingers point in the direction of the field. This is shown in Fig. 26.2.

FIG. 26.2

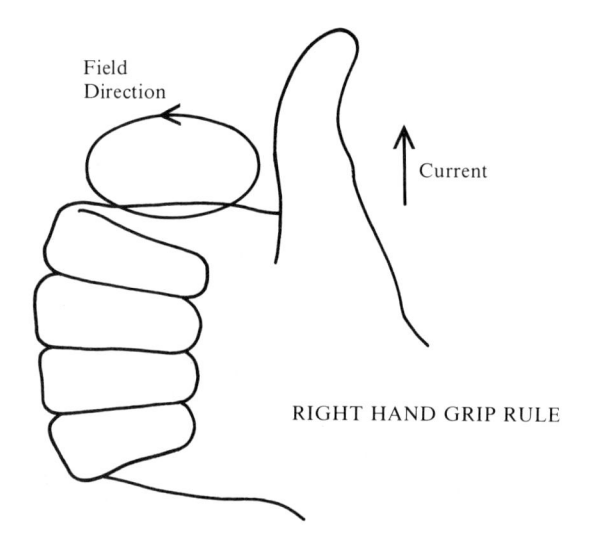

Field Direction

Current

RIGHT HAND GRIP RULE

(ii) The magnetic field pattern due to current in a solenoid is shown in Fig. 26.3.

FIG. 26.3

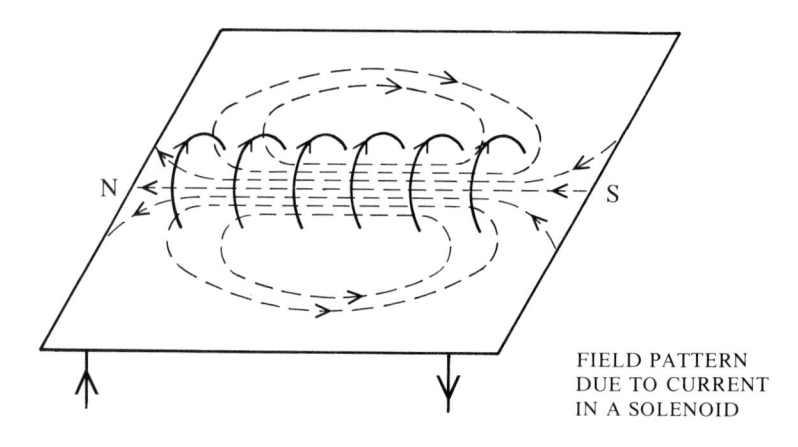

FIELD PATTERN DUE TO CURRENT IN A SOLENOID

The pattern is identical to that of a bar magnet. Each end of coil will become a north and a south pole as shown in Fig. 25.8.

26.3 APPLICATIONS OF THE MAGNETIC EFFECT OF AN ELECTRIC CURRENT

(i) We have seen that certain magnetic materials are soft magnetic materials and lose their magnetism.

These materials are used in electromagnets. An electromagnet consists of a soft iron core around which is wound a coil. When current flows through the coil, the magnetic field which is produced magnetises the soft iron. When the current is switched off, the magnetic field produced by the coil vanishes and the soft iron core loses its magnetism.

A typical electromagnet is shown in Fig. 26.4.

FIG. 26.4

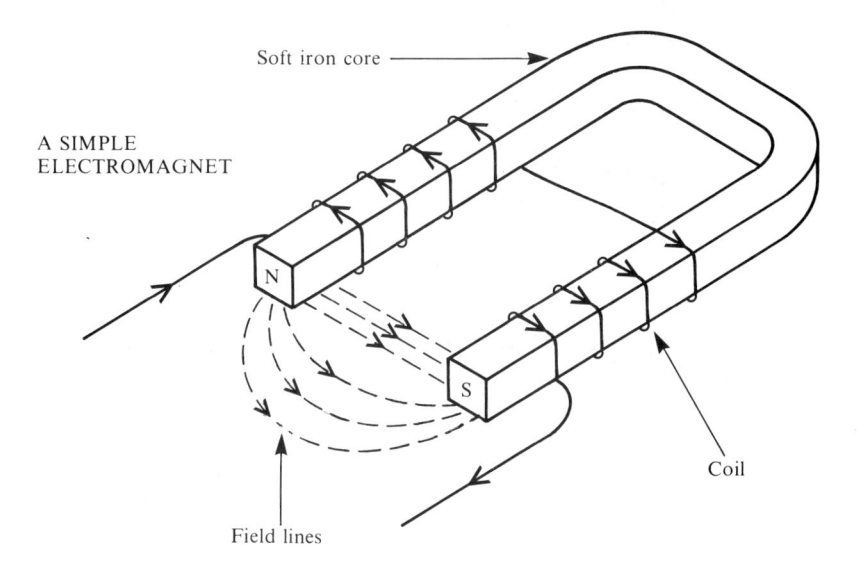

A SIMPLE ELECTROMAGNET

Electromagnets are used to lift scrap iron and in many electrical appliances such as tape and video recorders. In order to lift scrap iron, a soft iron plate with a lifting hook is placed across the poles of the electromagnet.

(ii) An electromagnet is used in the electric bell, shown in Fig. 26.5.

330 *The Magnetic Effect of an Electric Current*

FIG. 26.5

THE BELL

Switch

Springy metal strip

Soft iron bar

X

Contact

Electromagnetic

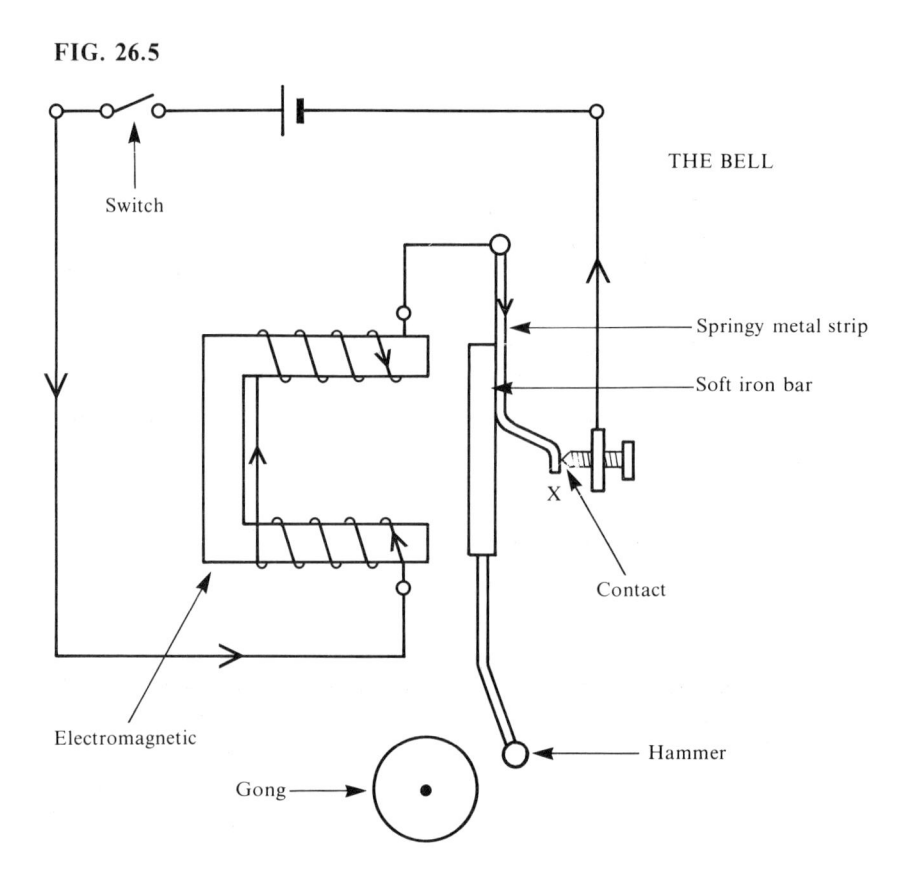

Gong

Hammer

When the switch is closed, the electromagnet is energised. It attracts the soft iron bar causing the hammer to hit the gong. When this happens the circuit is broken at X. The electromagnet loses the magnetism and the springy metal strip pulls the bar back to the contact so that the bell is ready to be rung again.

(iii) A relay is a magnetic switch. It is used when we want one circuit to control another particularly when the current is large in the circuit which we wish to control. Nowadays, it is often used when we interface a computer with a device — that is, we use the electrical output of a computer to control a circuit.

Fig. 26.6 shows a relay.

FIG. 26.6

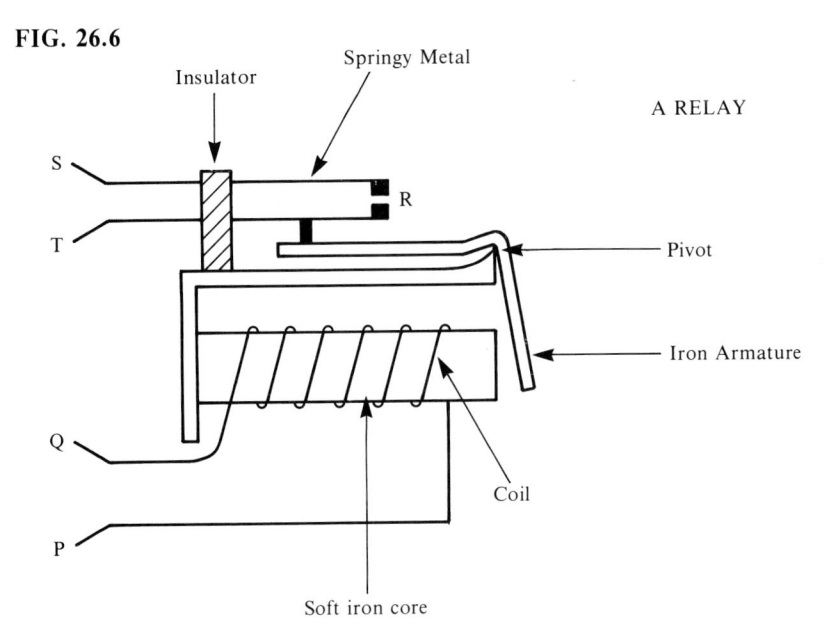

Insulator
Springy Metal
A RELAY
S
T
R
Pivot
Iron Armature
Q
Coil
P
Soft iron core

When current flows in the circuit connected to QP, the soft iron core is energised. It attracts the iron armature, which rotates on its pivot closing the contact at R. The relay is then energised or "on" and allows a current to flow in the circuit connected to ST.

The circuit symbols for a relay are shown in Fig. 26.7(a) and Fig. 26.7(b).

FIG. 26.7(a)   **FIG. 26.7(b)**

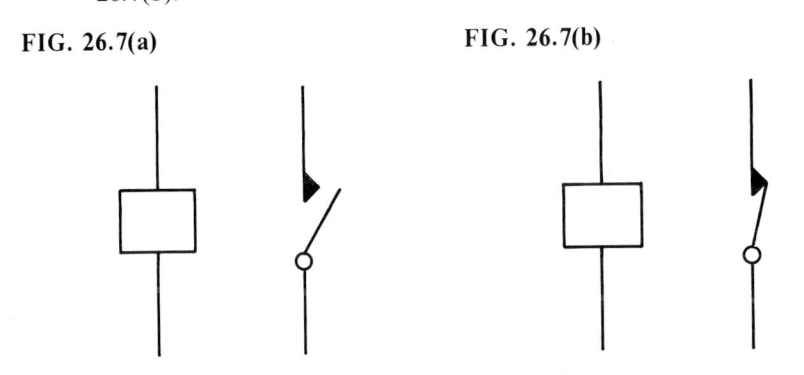

RELAY OPEN OR DE-ENERGISED   RELAY CLOSED OR ENERGISED

(iv) Another type of magnetic switch called a reed switch is shown in Fig. 26.8.

FIG. 26.8   REED SWITCH

```
Magnetic Contact ─────┐  ┌───── Non-magnetic Contact
                      │  │
Glass Tube ───────────┤  ├───── Magnetic Reed
```

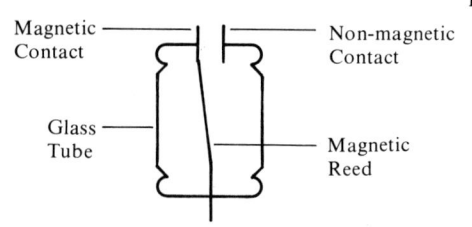

A coil surrounds the switch and when a current flows through it, the reed and magnetic contact become oppositely magnetised and attract each other, causing the switch to close. When the current is switched off, the reed springs back to the non magnetic, non conducting contact and the switch is then open. This type of switch is used when very rapid switching is required. It can also be used in burglar alarms.

(v). Electromagnets are often used together with permanent magnets in devices such as microphones and telephones.

SUPPLEMENTARY

26.4 VARIATION OF MAGNETIC FIELDS WITH DISTANCE AND CURRENT

The field due to a current in a long straight wire decreases as we move further away from the wire.

The field inside a solenoid is constant everywhere inside the solenoid. If we go outside the solenoid, the field decreases rapidly.

Both the field due to current in a long straight wire and in a solenoid are increased if the current is increased.

26.5 THE MAGNETIC FIELD DUE TO AN ELECTROMAGNET

The strength of the magnetic field due to an electromagnet can be increased in three ways:
1) By increasing the current in the coil
2) By increasing the number of turns in the coil
3) By bringing the poles closer together.

QUESTIONS

CORE
1. An electric current flows down a vertical wire. The wire passes through a hole in a board.

The Magnetic Effect of an Electric Current 333

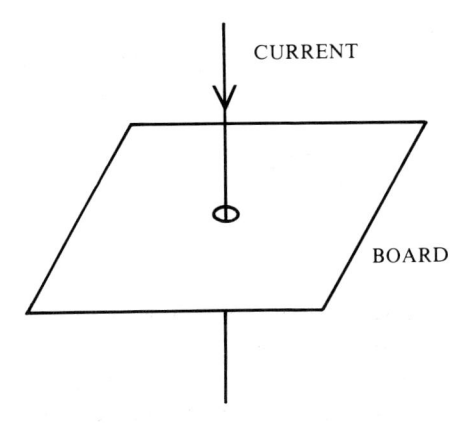

CURRENT

BOARD

Which of these diagrams shows the magnetic field you would find on the board?

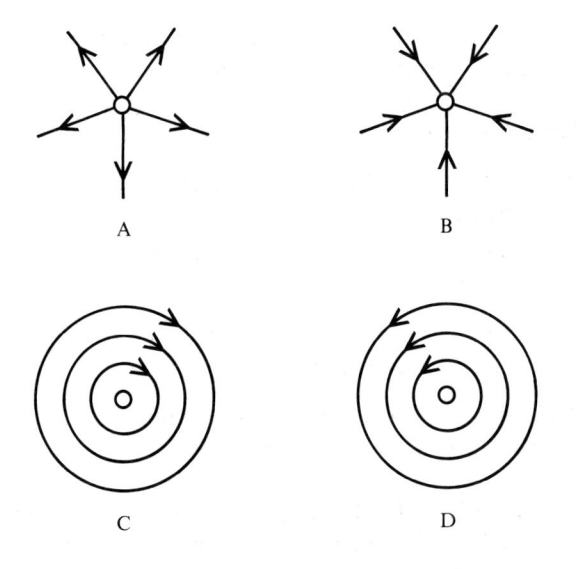

A

B

C

D

(L.E.A.G.)

2. Draw a diagram of the magnetic field pattern due to a solenoid. Label the current direction and the north and south poles.
3. In the diagram the two rectangles represent two light cylindrical iron cores about 1cm apart. The two electrical circuits are identical except that the right hand circuit contains a switch.

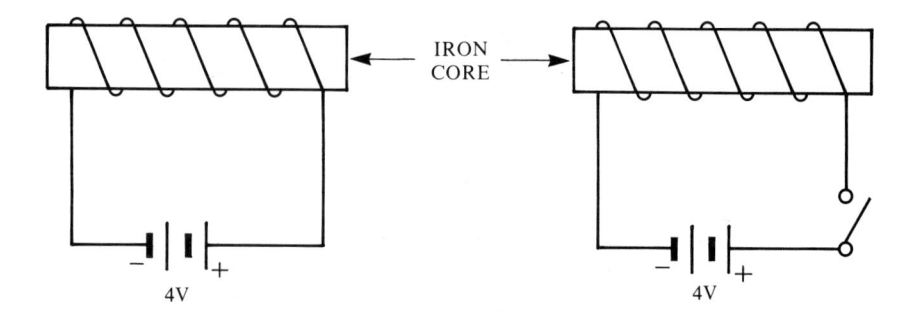

After the switch is closed the two iron cores:
A   attract each other all the time
B   repel each other all the time
C   have no force of attraction or repulsion between them
D   attract each other for just a brief moment.   (L.E.A.G.)

4. What sort of magnetic materials must be used in electromagnets?

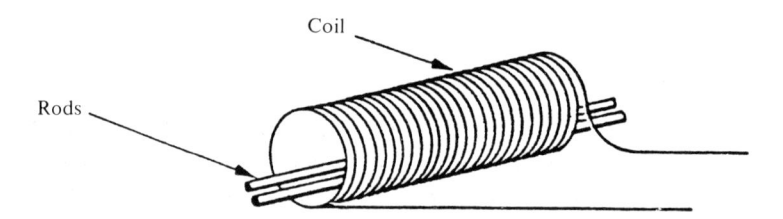

5.

Two metal rods are placed in a long coil as shown. When a direct current flows through the coil, the rods move apart. When the current is switched off, the rods return to their original position.
(a) Why did the rods move apart?
(b) From what metal are the rods likely to be made? Give a reason for your answer.
(c) If alternating current from a mains transformer is passed through the coil, what effect, if any, will this have on the rods? Explain your answer.   (M.E.G.)

SUPPLEMENTARY

6. State how the field due to the current in a long straight wire can be increased at a given distance from the wire.

7. For a given shape of electromagnet, explain how the strength of the magnetic field can be increased.

Chapter 27
FORCE ON A CURRENT CARRYING CONDUCTOR

At the end of this chapter you will know:
CORE: that there is a force on a current carrying conductor in a magnetic field; that this force depends on the size and direction of the current and the field; that there is a turning effect on a current carrying coil in a magnetic field which depends on the strength of the field, the current in the coil and the number of turns in the coil; that d.c. motors and moving coil meters depend on this fact and how loudspeakers work.
SUPPLEMENTARY: the rule relating the direction of the force, current and magnetic field; that a force acts on beams of charged particles in a magnetic field; the field pattern between parallel currents and the forces generated; why a split-ring commutator is used in a d.c. motor and the effect of a soft iron cylinder between the poles of a magnet in a d.c. motor and a moving coil meter.

CORE

27.1 A CURRENT CARRYING CONDUCTOR IN A MAGNETIC FIELD
Suppose a current-carrying wire lies in a magnetic field created by the north and south poles of two bar magnets, as shown in Fig. 27.1.

FIG. 27.1

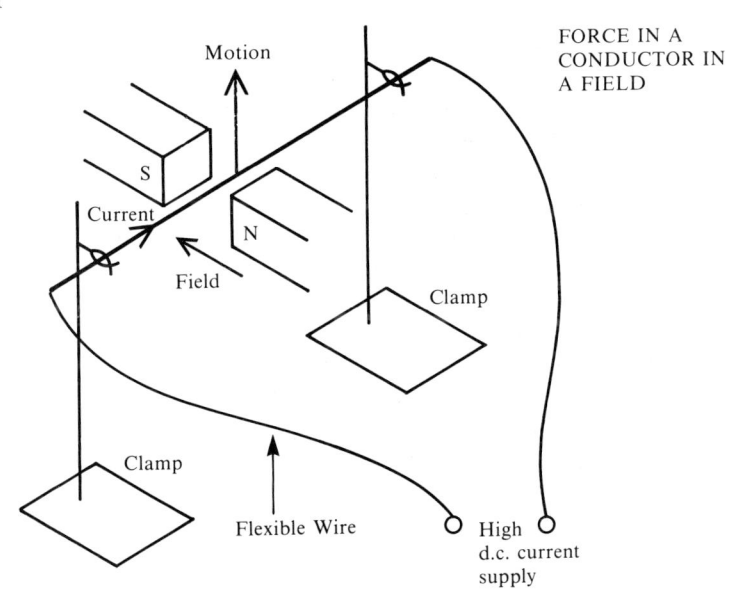

FORCE IN A CONDUCTOR IN A FIELD

336 Force on a Current Carrying Conductor

When the current is flowing, the wire moves upwards as shown, showing that a force is acting on it. If the current is switched off, we find that the wire moves downwards to its usual position.

We find that the wire moves more rapidly, showing that a greater force is acting on it if the current is increased or if the strength of the magnetic field is increased.

The wire moves downwards showing that the force direction has been reversed if the direction of the current or the direction of the magnetic field is reversed.

27.2 THE TURNING EFFECT ON A CURRENT CARRYING COIL IN A MAGNETIC FIELD

Suppose a current carrying coil PQRS is situated in a magnetic field between the curved pole pieces of a U shaped magnet, as shown in Fig. 27.2.

FIG. 27.2

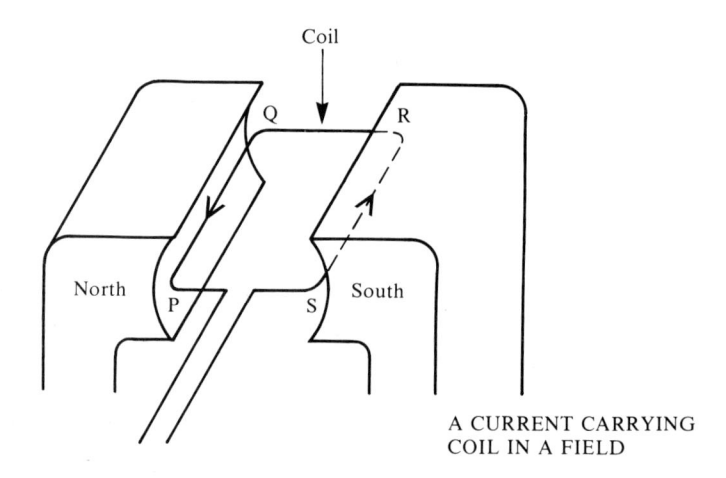

A CURRENT CARRYING COIL IN A FIELD

The side of the coil PQ will experience an upwards force and the side RS will experience a downwards but equal, force. These two forces exert a turning effect on the coil.

The turning effect increases if the following quantities are increased:
1) The strength of the magnetic field
2) The current in the coil
3) The number of turns on the coil.

D.C. motors and moving coil meters depend upon this effect for their operation. In a d.c. motor the coil is allowed to rotate on a spindle. The spindle is then able to transmit the motion outside the motor. In a moving coil meter, the coil is suspended on springs which oppose the rotation. The coil rotates until it is stopped by these springs and in doing so, it moves a pointer over a scale. See Fig. 27.9.

27.3 LOUDSPEAKERS

A moving coil loudspeaker is shown in Fig. 27.3.

FIG. 27.3

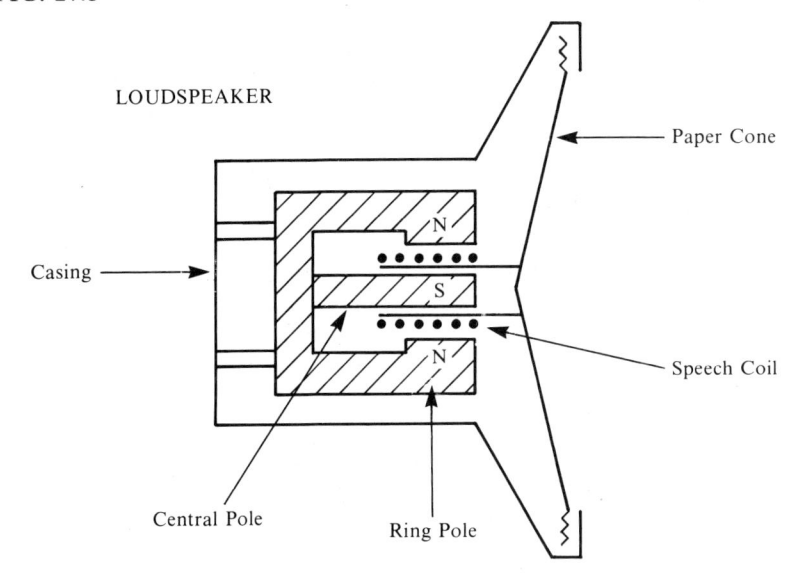

LOUDSPEAKER

Paper Cone

Casing

N
S
N

Speech Coil

Central Pole

Ring Pole

Changing currents from a radio, television or music centre pass through the speech coil which is at right angles to the magnetic field produced by a permanent magnet. Varying forces then act on the coil, causing it to move in and out. A paper cone attached to the coil is made to move in and out and when it does this it generates sound waves.

Adjusting the volume control allows more or less current through the speech coil and causes the paper cone to vibrate with a bigger or smaller amplitude, causing the sound to be more or less loud.

SUPPLEMENTARY

27.4 FLEMING'S LEFT HAND RULE

The relationship between the direction of motion, the current and the magnetic field when a current carrying conductor is in a magnetic field is given by Fleming's left hand rule which says that if the thumb and first two fingers of the left hand are held at right angles to each other, then if the thumb points in the direction of the force or motion, the first finger will be pointing in the direction of the field and the second finger will be pointing in the direction of the current.

This is shown in Fig. 27.4(a) and Fig. 27.4(b).

FIG. 27.4(a) **FIG. 27.4(b)**

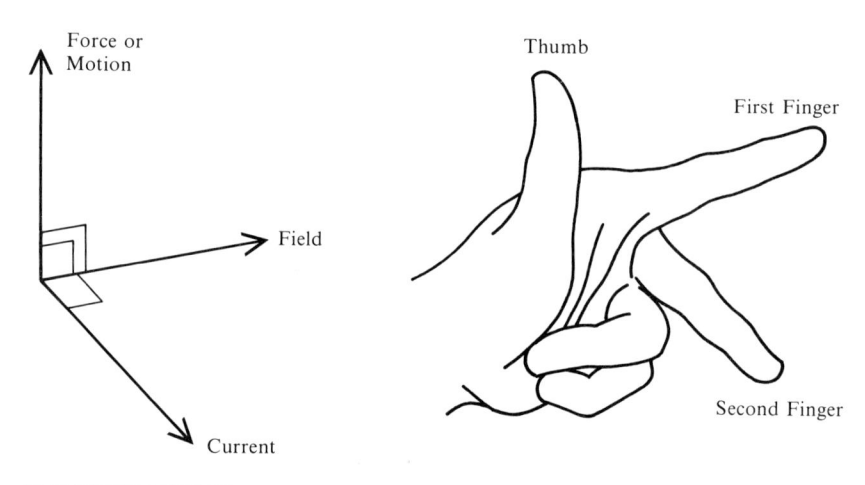

FLEMING'S LEFT HAND RULE   USING THE LEFT HAND RULE

27.5 FORCE ON CHARGED PARTICLES IN MAGNETIC FIELDS

An electric current is a flow of charged particles, with a conventional electric current being a flow of positively charged particles. So, if some positively charged particles move through a magnetic field, a force will act on them at right angles to their direction of travel. The direction of this force will be given by the left hand rule.

Because the charged particles are not confined to a wire, the force can cause them to change direction immediately. As a result of a force which is acting on the particles at right angles to their direction of motion, the charged particles are made to move in circular paths.

If we use negatively charged particles, the direction of the force will be reversed and so will be the sense of the circle moved in. These situations are shown in Fig. 27.5(a) and Fig. 27.5(b).

FIG. 27.5(a)

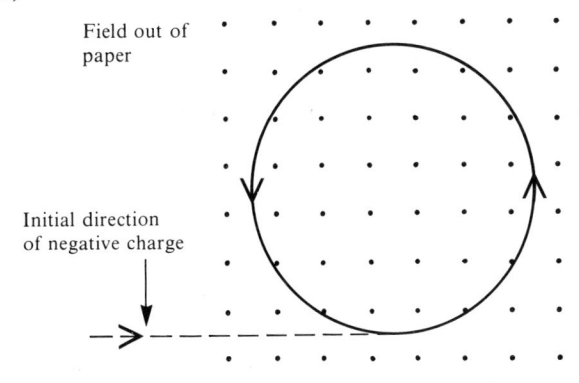

Field out of paper

Initial direction of negative charge

NEGATIVE CHARGE CURVED UPWARDS

FIG. 27.5(b)

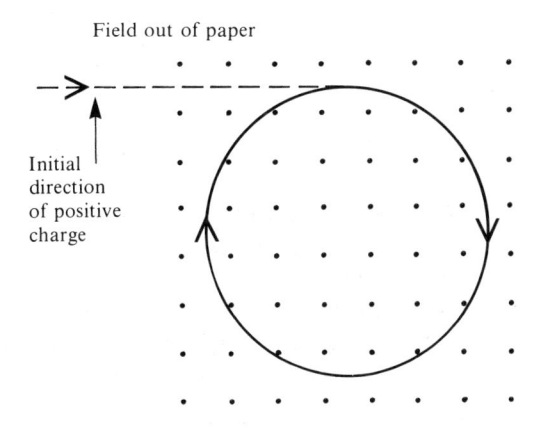

Field out of paper

Initial direction of positive charge

POSITIVE CHARGE CURVED DOWNWARDS

27.6 FIELDS AND FORCES BETWEEN PARALLEL CURRENTS

The reason why a force acts on a conductor in a magnetic field can be understood from Fig. 27.6(a), Fig. 27.6(b) and Fig. 27.6(c).

FIG. 27.6(a)

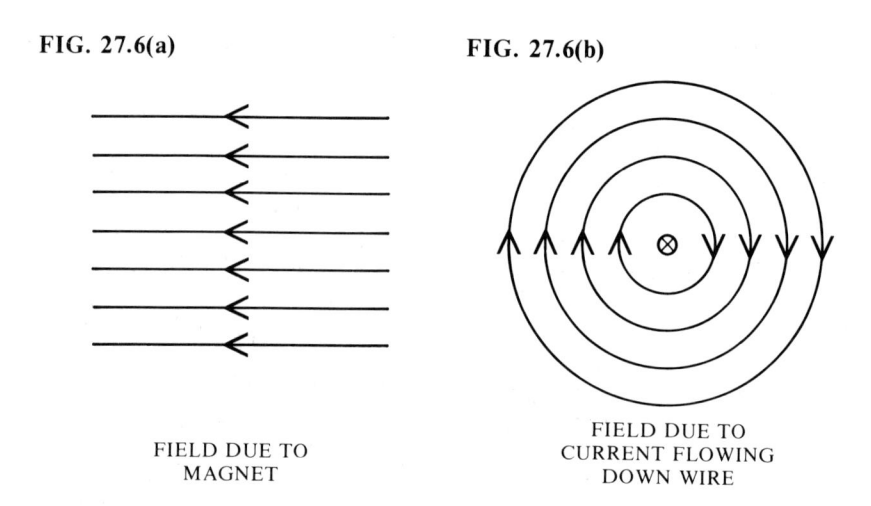

FIELD DUE TO
MAGNET

FIG. 27.6(b)

FIELD DUE TO
CURRENT FLOWING
DOWN WIRE

FIG. 27.6(c)

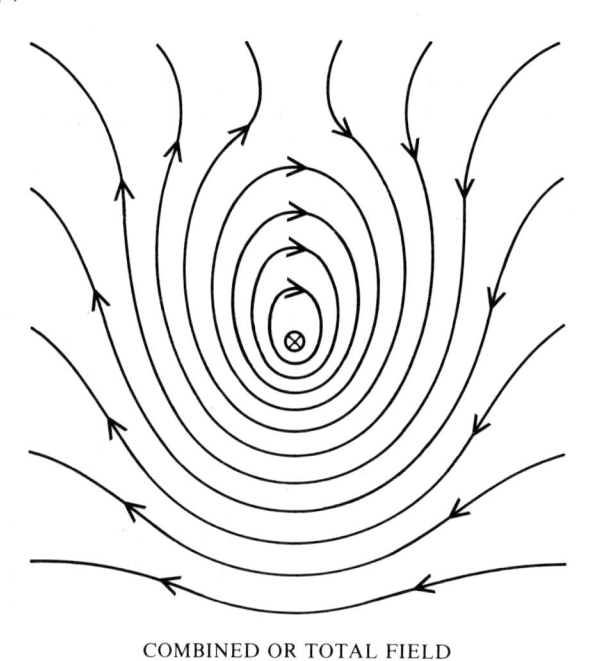

COMBINED OR TOTAL FIELD

Fig. 27.6(a) shows the field lines due to the magnet poles in Fig. 27.1. Fig. 27.6(b) shows the field lines due to the current in the wire. The resultant field obtained by combining both fields is shown in Fig. 27.6(c). These re-inforce at the bottom and cancel at the top and as a result there is a strong magnetic field which pushes the wire upwards.

Force on a Current Carrying Conductor 341

The field pattern between parallel current is shown in Fig. 27.7.

FIG. 27.7

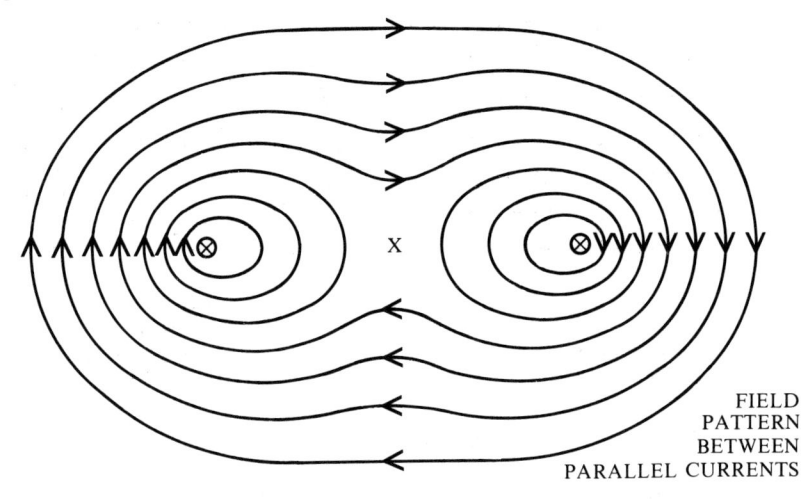

FIELD PATTERN BETWEEN PARALLEL CURRENTS

Between the wires the magnetic fields act in opposite directions. They are exactly equal and opposite mid-way between the wires at a point marked X, the neutral point. Beyond the wires there is a strong field and as a result the wires are attracted to each other. The forces are directed from one wire to the other.

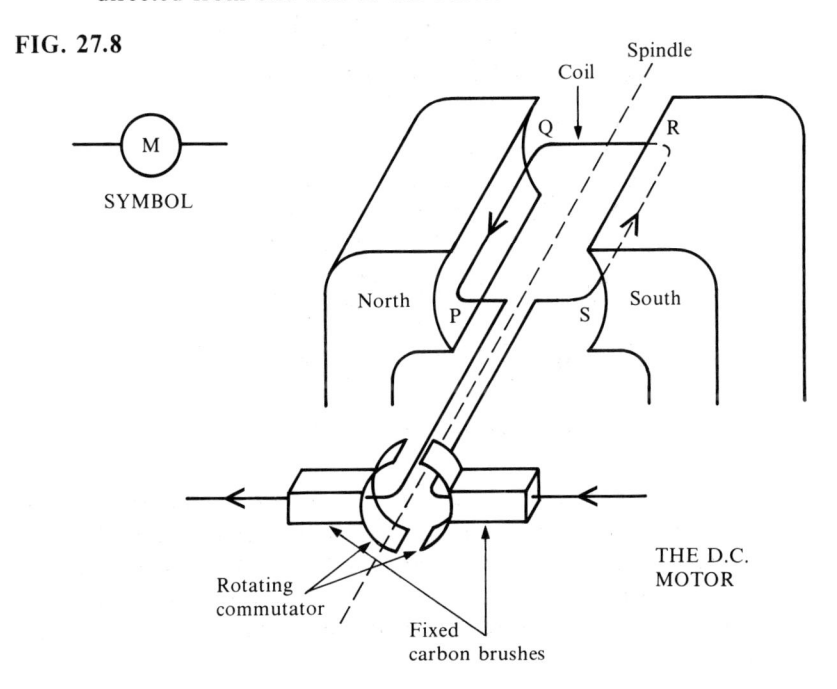

FIG. 27.8

SYMBOL

THE D.C. MOTOR

342 Force on a Current Carrying Conductor

27.7 THE SPLIT-RING COMMUTATOR

When a current carrying coil on a spindle rotates in a magnetic field, we have a d.c. motor. The current is taken in and out of the coil, through a split-ring of copper known as a commutator. Each end of the coil is attached to one half of the commutator. Carbon brushes make electrical contact with the commutator. This is shown in Fig. 27.8.

In the position shown we can see from the left hand rule that side PQ will experience an upward force and side RS a downward force. When the coil is vertical the brushes are in line with the air gaps in the commutator and no current flows through the coil. The coil continues to rotate though, because of its kinetic energy. Contact is again established between the brushes and the commutator but the current direction through the coil has been reversed with current flowing from P to Q and R to S. But PQ is now moving downwards and RS is moving upwards. As a result the force acting on PQ is now downwards and that acting on RS is now upwards. The coil therefore continues rotating clockwise with the current direction being reversed every half turn.

FIG. 27.9

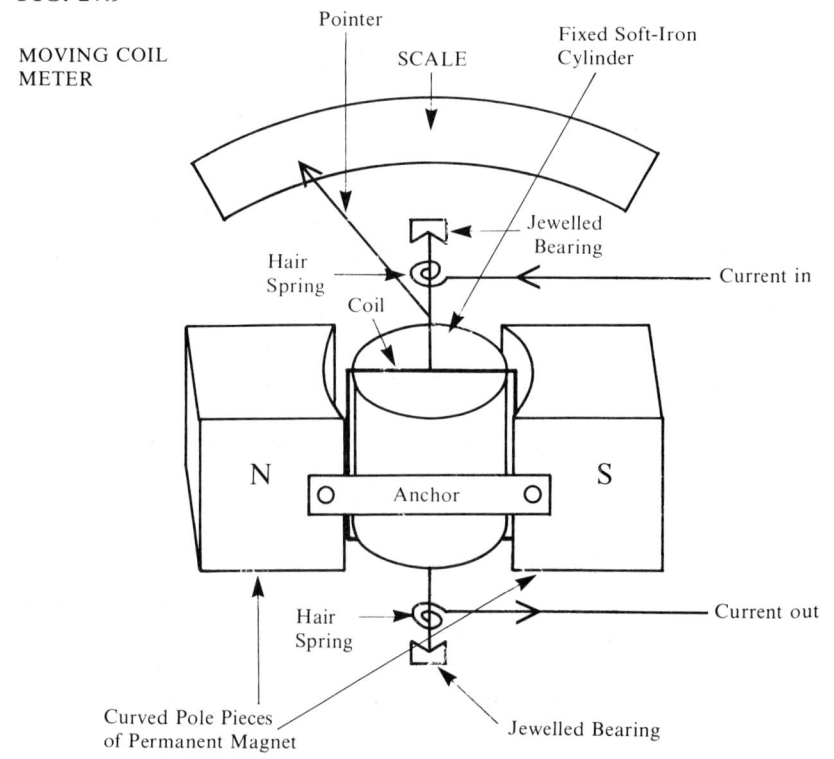

MOVING COIL METER

27.8 THE EFFECT OF A SOFT IRON CYLINDER BETWEEN THE POLES OF A MAGNET IN A D.C. MOTOR AND A MOVING COIL METER

(i) In a practical motor, the coil consists of many turns and is wound on a soft iron cylinder which rotates with the coil. This has the effect of increasing the magnetic field and it makes the motor more powerful. The coil and cylinder together are called the armature.

(ii) A soft iron cylinder is also used in a moving coil meter. Again it has the effect of increasing the magnetic field and causes the meter to deflect more for a given current. A moving coil meter is shown in Fig. 27.9.

QUESTIONS

CORE

1. A horizontal wire carries a current as shown between magnetic poles N and S.

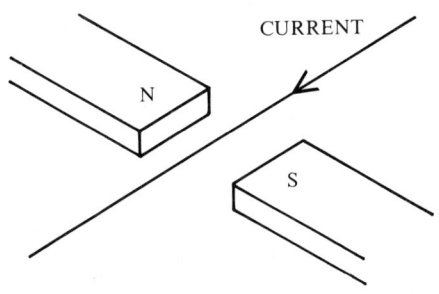

    The direction of the force on the wire due to the magnet is
    A from N to S.   B from S to N.   C in the direction of the current.   D vertically upwards.   *(S.E.G.)*
2. State two ways in which the force in question 1 can be increased.
3. In question 1 what will be the direction of the force on the wire if the magnets are changed over and the current direction is reversed?
4. State three ways in which the turning effect acting on a current carrying coil in a field can be increased.
5. Draw a diagram of a loudspeaker.

SUPPLEMENTARY

6. In question 1, the current in the wire is replaced by a stream of electrons moving in the same direction. What will be the direction of the force exerted by the field on the electrons?
7. Two long parallel wires carry currents in the opposite direction. What will happen to the wires?

Chapter 28
THERMIONIC EMISSION, THE CATHODE RAY OSCILLOSCOPE AND RECTIFICATION

At the end of this chapter you will know:
CORE: what is meant by thermionic emission and how the emitted electrons can be deflected by electric and magnetic fields; the structure of a cathode ray oscilloscope and how it can be used to measure d.c. and a.c. voltages; how it can display waveforms; how a capacitor can be used to smooth a half-wave rectified voltage; what is meant by a smoothed full-wave rectified voltage and the structure of a simple power supply.
SUPPLEMENTARY: how a time base is used on a cathode ray oscilloscope to measure time intervals, periods and frequencies; how a four diode bridge can be used as a full wave rectifier and why a smoothed full wave rectified voltage is not perfectly smooth.

CORE

28.1 THERMIONIC EMISSION

We now know that an electric current consists of moving electrons.

Electrons can be given off in a process known as thermionic emission. The apparatus used to demonstrate the process is shown in Photograph 27.

PHOTOGRAPH 27

Acknowledgement: Philip Harris Ltd.

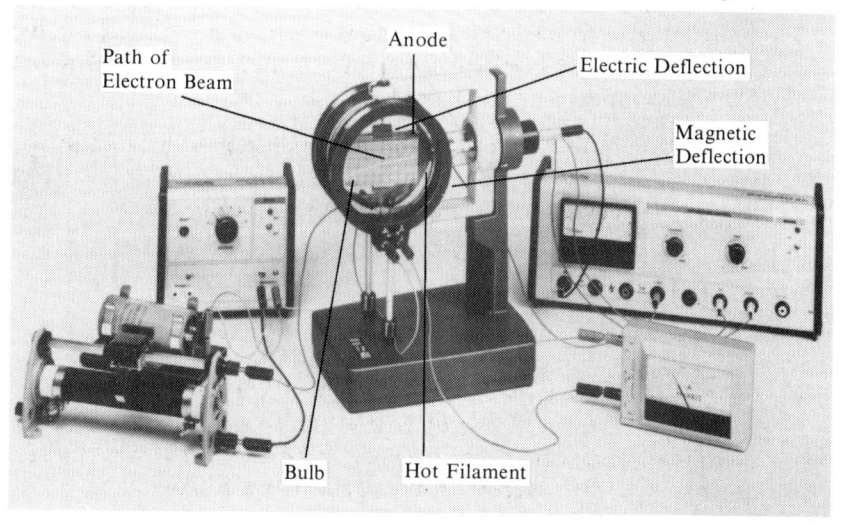

Labels: Path of Electron Beam; Anode; Electric Deflection; Magnetic Deflection; Bulb; Hot Filament

Thermionic Emission, The Cathode Ray Oscilloscope and Rectification

A small coil of wire known as a filament is sealed inside an evacuated glass bulb.

The filament is heated by the current from a 6V a.c. or d.c. supply.

A very large d.c. voltage of at least 500V is applied across the bulb, with the filament connected to the negative of the supply and the positive of the supply connected to another metal contact inside the bulb known as the anode.

When the filament is heated and the high voltage is switched on, electrons are given off from the filament, in a process known as thermionic emission, in which we can consider that the electrons are being "boiled away."

The path of the electron beam can be seen by placing a fluorescent glass screen inside the glass bulb, as shown. Where the electrons strike this screen, it glows green.

The electrons are not given off if the filament is not heated or if the high voltage supply is reversed to make the anode negative. We can check this by observing that when either of these conditions apply, the glass screen does not glow. The reason why the electrons are not given off in these circumstances is that the electrons do not have enough energy to escape from the filament and move away from it.

The filament is behaving as what we call a cathode. When this effect was first seen, the electrons were called cathode rays, because they leave the cathode.

We can deflect the electrons given off in thermionic emission. The deflection can be caused by applying an electric field across two metal plates inside the bulb or by applying a magnetic field generated by two current carrying coils mounted outside the bulb.

By observing the direction of the deflection caused by electric and magnetic fields we can conclude that the particles emitted are in fact negatively charged. We can also calculate the value of

$$\frac{\text{charge of particles}}{\text{mass of particles}}$$

and this value proves that the particles are, in fact, electrons.

28.2 THE CATHODE RAY OSCILLOSCOPE (C.R.O.)

(i) The C.R.O. is a useful device which uses the principle of thermionic emission. It can be used to measure d.c. and a.c. voltages and to display waveforms. A C.R.O. is shown in Fig. 28.1.

346 Thermionic Emission, The Cathode Ray Oscilloscope and Rectification

FIG. 28.1

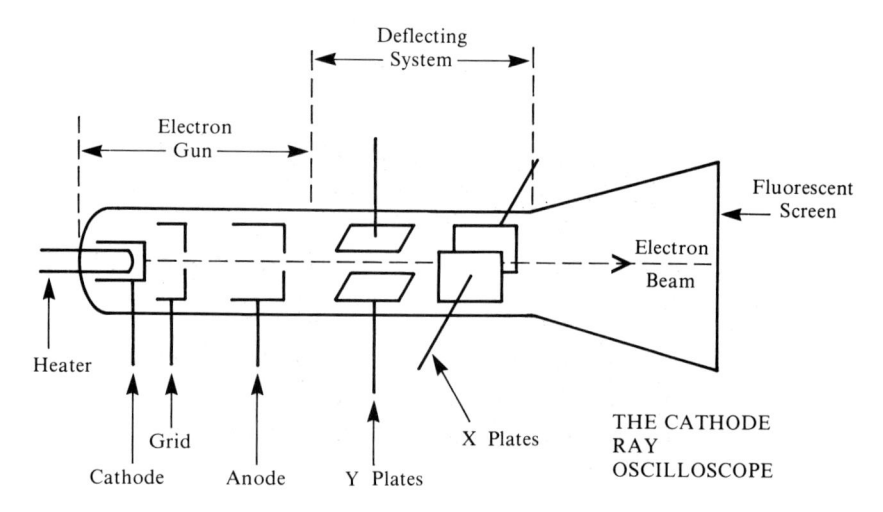

Diagram labels: Deflecting System; Electron Gun; Fluorescent Screen; Electron Beam; Heater; Cathode; Grid; Anode; Y Plates; X Plates

THE CATHODE RAY OSCILLOSCOPE

The inside of the C.R.O. is made up of the following parts:

1) The Electron Gun — this consists of a heater, a cathode, a grid and an anode. Electrons are liberated from the heated cathode by thermionic emission. The grid is at a negative voltage with respect to the cathode and it controls the number of electrons passing through it — this allows it to act as a brightness control. The anode is at a high positive voltage with respect to the cathode. It accelerates the electrons along the evacuated glass tube and focuses them into a narrow beam.

2) The Deflection System — this consists of two sets of parallel metal plates. One set, the Y plates, is horizontal and is used to deflect the electron beam vertically. The other set, the X plates, is vertical and is used to deflect the electron beam horizontally. In order to cause these deflections, voltages are applied across the plates.

3) The Fluorescent Screen — this is the end of the tube which the electron beam strikes. When the electrons hit it, it fluoresces and gives out light. The beam causes a bright spot to appear in the middle of the screen. Application of a voltage across the X or Y plates causes it to move. The brightness of the spot is controlled by the grid.

The outside appearance of a C.R.O. is shown in Photograph 28.

As we have said, the spot is normally in the middle of the screen. To make it move up or down we turn the Y shift control. To make it move left or right we turn the X shift control.

PHOTOGRAPH 28

Acknowledgement: Philip Harris Ltd.

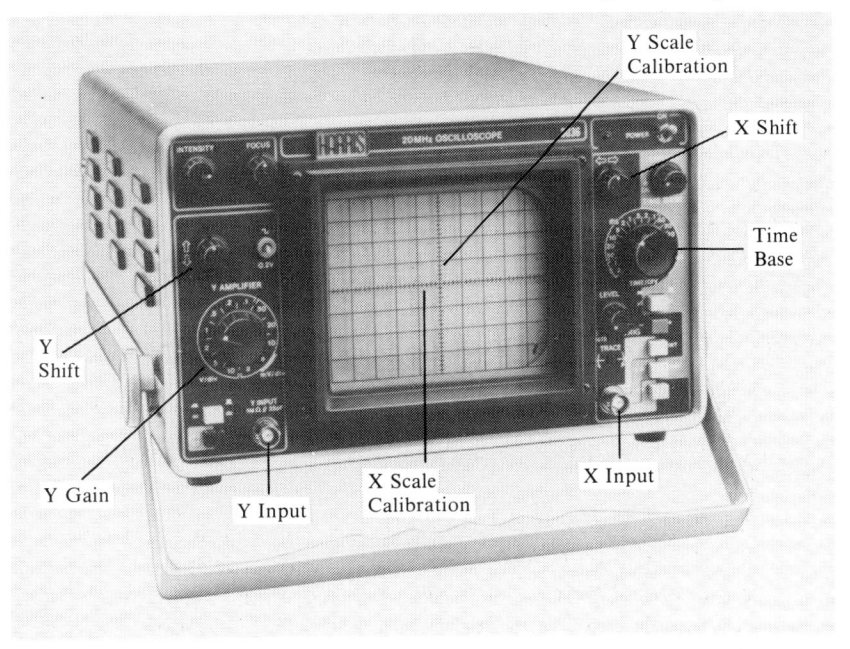

A voltage is applied across the Y plates at the Y input and across the X plates at the X input.

(ii) In order to measure a d.c. voltage, we connect it across the Y input. The spot will move up the screen. We measure this movement on the scale calibration. We then multiply this distance by the Y gain value. The Y gain tells us how the movement is related to the voltage. In the photograph, the Y gain is set at 1V per division telling us that 1cm on the Y scale corresponds to a voltage of 1V. To measure small voltages we increase the Y gain and to measure large voltages we decrease the Y gain.

We can make the spot move down the screen by reversing the voltage that is changing round the terminals connected to the input.

As an example, consider the screen shown in Fig. 28.2(a). The spot has moved 3cm up the screen. Suppose the Y gain is 0.2V per cm. This means that the voltage is
$$3 \times 0.2 = 0.6\text{V}.$$

If the voltage is reversed, the spot will move the same distance downwards, as shown in Fig. 28.2(b).

FIG. 28.2(a)

D.C. VOLTAGE

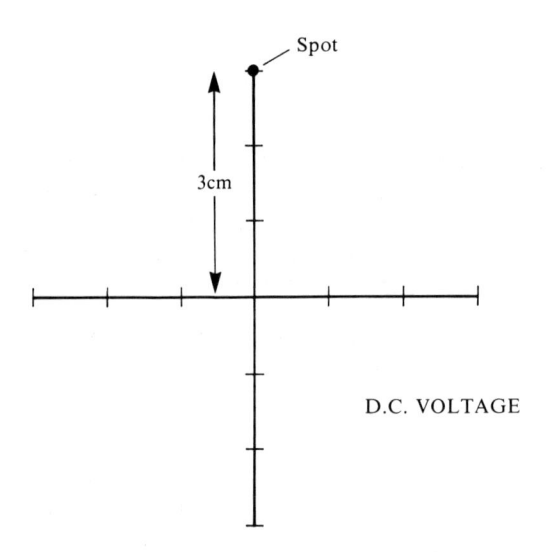

Spot

3cm

FIG. 28.2(b)

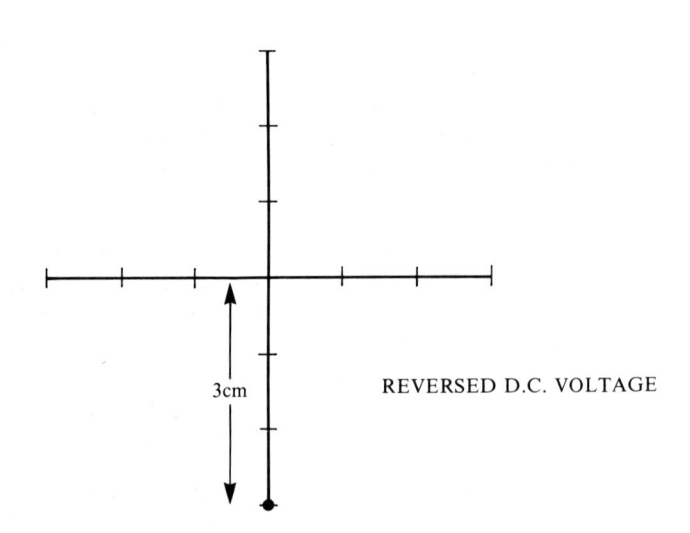

REVERSED D.C. VOLTAGE

3cm

(iii) In order to measure an a.c. voltage, we again connect it across the Y input. Now the spot will move repeatedly up and down the screen. If the frequency of the voltage is 50Hz then the spot will make 50 complete up and down movements every second. It will then appear as a straight line.

The size of the voltage is represented by the amplitude of this straight line, in other words half its length.

Thermionic Emission, The Cathode Ray Oscilloscope and Rectification

Suppose the line is 3.4cm in length. The amplitude is half of this, 1.7cm. If the Y gain is 10V per cm then this corresponds to 17V. This is called the peak voltage of the supply.

When we usually talk about a.c., we quote what is known as the R.M.S. voltage which is a better way to measure a.c. because of the fact that it is repeatedly changing direction. We can show

$$\text{R.M.S. voltage} = 0.7 \times \text{peak voltage}.$$

Here then, the R.M.S. voltage = $0.7 \times 17 = 12V$.

When we discuss the mains supply we are using the R.M.S. value. The peak voltage is in fact given by

$$\frac{240}{0.7} = 339V.$$

(iii) If we draw the change in an a.c. voltage with time, we know that we obtain a wave, as shown in Fig. 25.5. We can demonstrate this on the oscilloscope. The voltage is connected across the Y input and we switch on the time-base. This applies a voltage across the X plates and makes the spot move across the screen at a steady speed from left to right. It then flies back extremely rapidly to the left hand side and repeats its motion. The a.c. voltage makes the spot go up and down and the time-base makes it move from left to right. The combined effect is to cause a transverse wave of the a.c. voltage to appear on the screen.

The time-base is calibrated usually in ms/cm and is the time taken for the spot to travel 1cm across the screen. When the time taken for the spot to travel completely across the screen is exactly equal to the period of the voltage (that is the time for it to make one complete oscillation), then one complete wavelength will be fitted onto the screen. If the time-base setting or frequency is altered then more or less wavelengths will be seen on the screen.

We can use the C.R.O. like this to analyse the waveform given out by tuning forks and musical instruments, when the sound waves enter a microphone and generate a.c. voltages. If the microphone is connected to the Y input and the time-base is switched on, the waveform will be displayed on the screen. A C.R.O. is also part of a television and is used by doctors to observe a patient's heartbeat pattern.

(iv) The circuit symbol for a C.R.O. is shown in Fig. 28.3.

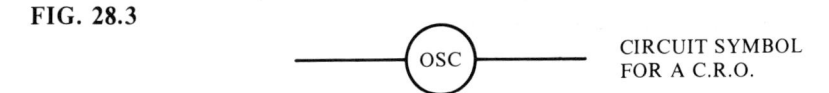

FIG. 28.3

CIRCUIT SYMBOL FOR A C.R.O.

28.3 USING A CAPACITOR TO SMOOTH A HALF-WAVE RECTIFIED VOLTAGE

A capacitor is a device which stores electrical charge and therefore energy. As well as being able to store charge, capacitors allow a.c. to pass through them but not d.c. They are used extensively in modern electrical apparatus wherever tuning is needed — in radios and televisions.

A modern capacitor consists of two long strips of metal foil separated by thin sheets of plastic. These are then rolled into a cylinder, just like a swiss roll.

Capacitance is used to measure the effectiveness of a capacitor. Its units are farads, symbol F. The circuit symbol for a capacitor is shown in Fig. 28.4.

FIG. 28.4

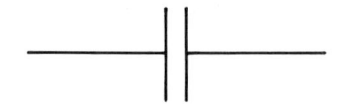

CIRCUIT SYMBOL FOR A CAPACITOR

A diode can be used to convert an a.c. voltage to a d.c. voltage. We then obtain a half wave rectified supply as shown in Fig. 23.11.

FIG. 23.11

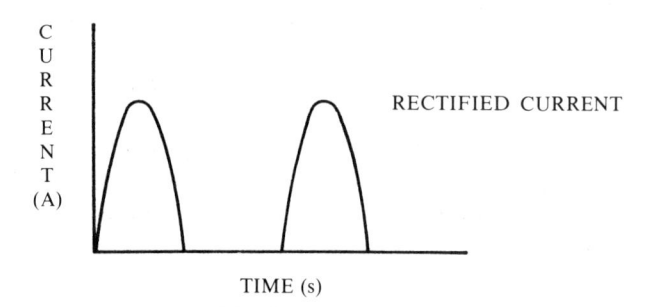

CURRENT (A) vs TIME (s) — RECTIFIED CURRENT

We can see that we have a voltage for only half the time. We can improve upon this by using the circuit shown in Fig. 28.5.

Thermionic Emission, The Cathode Ray Oscilloscope and Rectification 351

FIG. 28.5

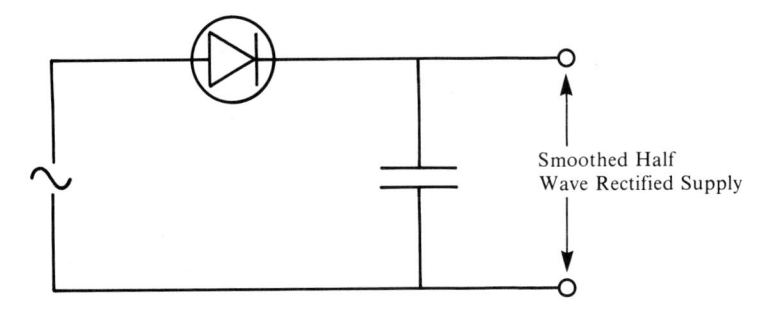

HALF WAVE SMOOTHED RECTIFIED CIRCUIT

The capacitor smooths the rectified voltage by storing charge when the diode is forward biased and releasing the charge when the diode is reverse biased. The smoothed half wave rectified output is as shown in Fig. 28.6.

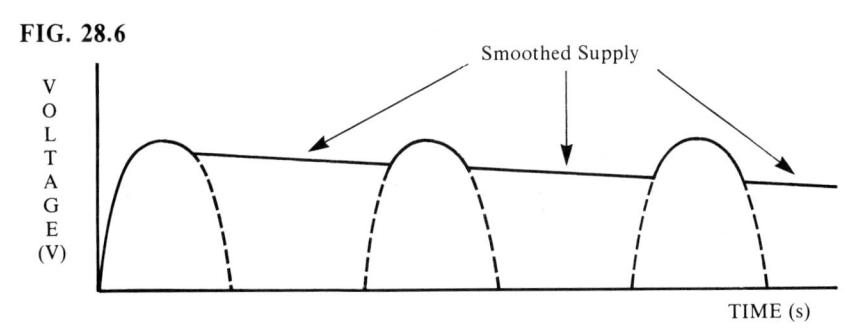

FIG. 28.6

HALF WAVE SMOOTHED OUTPUT

28.4 SMOOTHED FULL WAVE RECTIFICATION

A capacitor can be used with a special arrangement of diodes, known as a diode bridge, to obtain a full wave rectified output, as shown in Fig. 28.7.

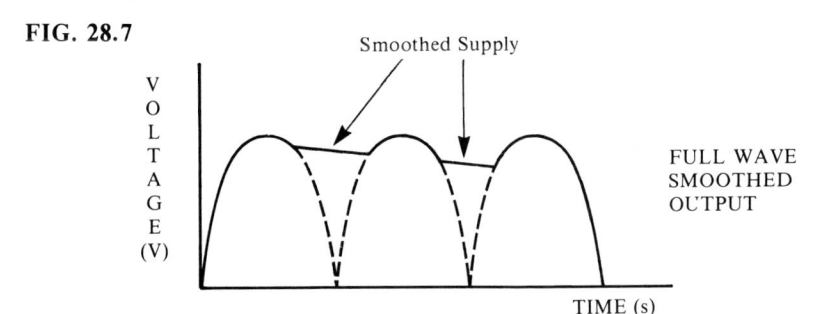

FIG. 28.7

FULL WAVE SMOOTHED OUTPUT

28.5 A SIMPLE POWER SUPPLY

A simple power supply is used to obtain a low voltage full wave rectified d.c. supply from the mains. Its symbol is shown in Fig. 28.8.

FIG. 28.8

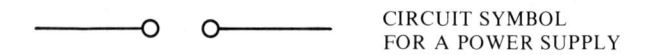

CIRCUIT SYMBOL FOR A POWER SUPPLY

Inside the power supply there is a transformer to step down the voltage, a diode bridge to obtain a full wave rectified output and a smoothing capacitor to give a smoothed supply.

For safety, the core of the transformer is earthed and a switch and fuse are included in the live side of the primary coil. The arrangement is shown in Fig. 28.9.

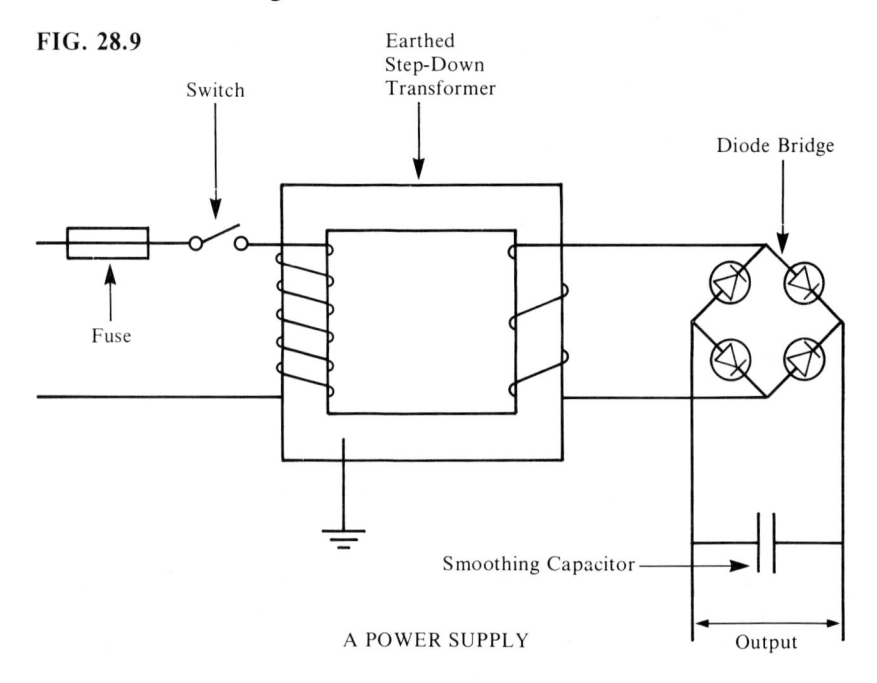

FIG. 28.9

A POWER SUPPLY

A power supply such as this may also be used to re-charge a car battery.

SUPPLEMENTARY

28.6 USE OF THE TIME-BASE ON THE C.R.O.

The time-base on a C.R.O. can be used to measure time intervals, periods and frequencies.

The time taken for the beam to travel across the screen from left to right is given by

time-base setting × screen width.

When an a.c. voltage is applied, the period of the supply — that is the time for one complete cycle — is then given by

time-base setting × the length of one wave

If T = period, t = time-base setting and d = length of one wave
then T = dt

The frequency of the supply voltage is the number of complete cycles per second. If the frequency is f then

$$f = \frac{1}{T} = \frac{1}{dt}$$

PROBLEM
A C.R.O. IS USED TO MEASURE THE FREQUENCY OF AN a.c. VOLTAGE. THE TIME-BASE SETTING IS 10ms/cm. IF THREE COMPLETE WAVES OCCUPY 6cm, CALCULATE THE FREQUENCY OF THE VOLTAGE.

3 waves occupy 6cm
so 1 wave occupies 2cm
so d = 2cm, t = 10ms/cm = 10^{-2} s/cm.
Using $f = \frac{1}{td}$
we have $f = \frac{1}{10^{-2} \times 2} = 50Hz.$

ANSWER: FREQUENCY OF VOLTAGE = 50Hz.

28.7 FULL WAVE RECTIFICATION USING A DIODE BRIDGE
A diode bridge is shown in Fig. 28.10.

During that half of the cycle when C is positive with respect to A, diodes 3 and 1 will be forward biased and 2 and 4 will be reversed biased. Current will pass from C to D and through the output then back from B to A. In the other half cycle when A is positive with respect to C, diodes 2 and 4 will be forward biased and 3 and 1 will be reverse biased. Current will now flow from A to D and through the output then back from B to C.

In order to smooth the output a capacitor is connected in parallel with the output as shown. This charges up while the voltage output is building up to its peak value. After that it begins to discharge slowly, enabling the voltage to be maintained. This continues until the output is climbing up to peak value again at which point the capacitor begins

FIG. 28.10

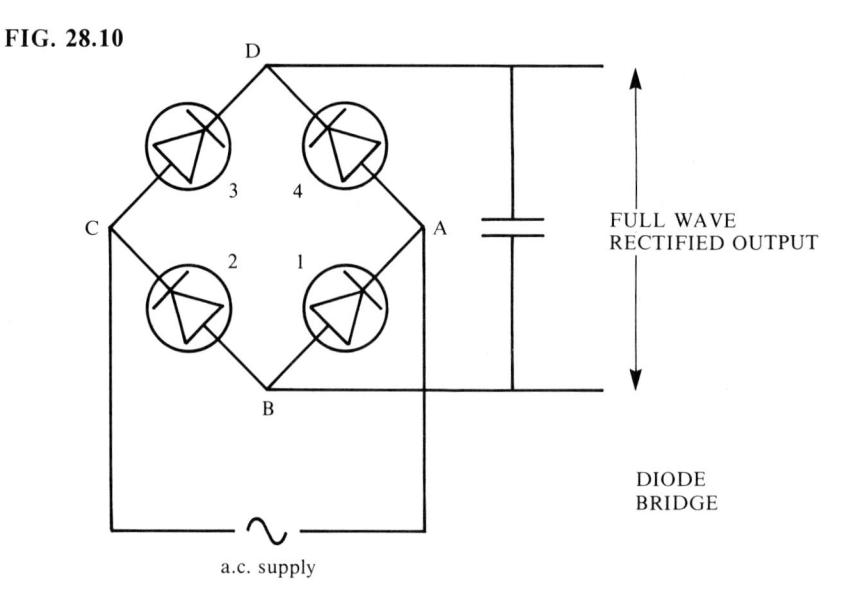

Full wave rectified output — Diode bridge circuit with a.c. supply

to charge up again. The result is the smoothed supply which we have already seen in Fig. 28.7. The amount by which the smoothed supply drops down from the peak value, known as the ripple, can be controlled by suitable choice of a capacitor with a given capacitance.

QUESTIONS

CORE
1. What is thermionic emission?
2. State what an electron gun contains.
3. When a d.c. voltage is applied to a C.R.O. the spot moves up the screen 5cm. If the Y gain is 2V/cm, what is the value of the voltage?
4. State the relationship between R.M.S. and peak voltage.
5. The trace on an oscilloscope is shown in diagram (a). A student then alters one of the oscilloscope controls and obtains the trace in diagram (b).

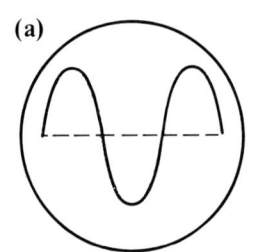

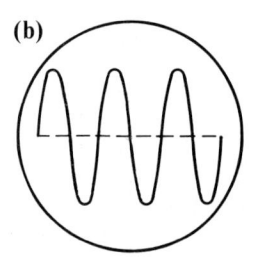

(a) (b)

Which one of the controls did the student alter?
A The Y gain   B The Y shift   C The X shift   D The time-base frequency.
(S.E.G.)

6. State the contents of a simple power supply.
7. Draw a diagram of a half wave smoothed supply.
8. Draw a diagram of a full wave smoothed supply.

SUPPLEMENTARY

9. A C.R.O. is used to measure the frequency of an a.c. voltage. One wavelength is 4cm. If the time base setting is 250 μs/cm, calculate the frequency of the voltage.

10. Fig. 8 shows the screen, Y gain and time base controls from a typical oscilloscope displaying a waveform.

FIG. 8

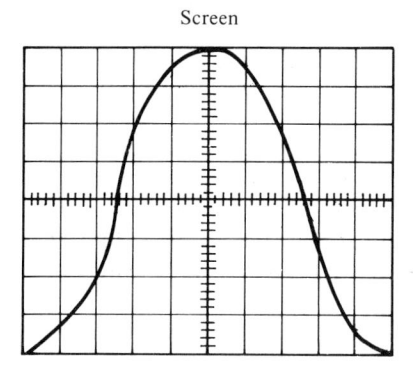

Screen

The graticule has a 1 cm grid.

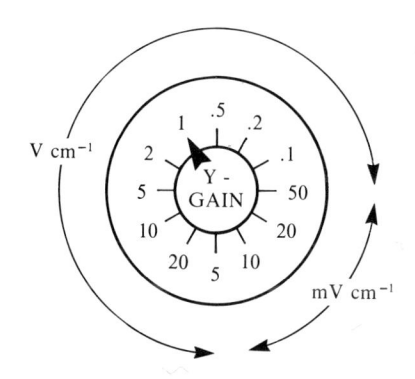

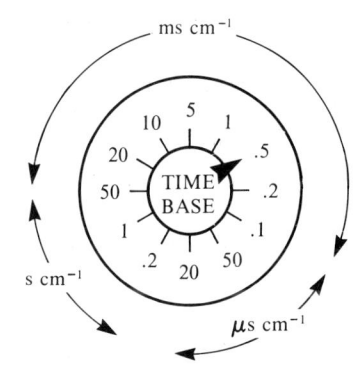

(a) What is the setting of the Y gain control?
(b) What is the peak voltage of the waveform?
(c) What is the time base setting?
(d) What is the period of the trace?
(e) What is the frequency of the waveform?

(f) If the time base setting is altered to 1ms/cm and the Y gain to 2V/cm, draw the resultant trace on the graticule shown below.

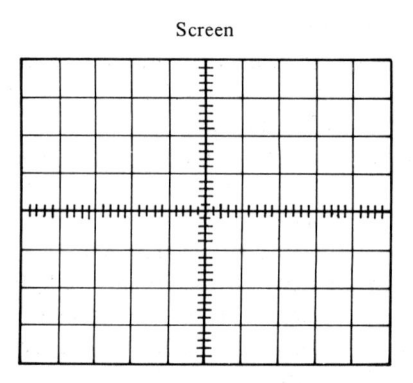

Screen

(N.E.A.)

Chapter 29
ELECTRONIC DEVICES

At the end of this chapter you will know:

CORE: what is meant by potential and how it may be varied using a potential divider; how the resistance of thermistors and light dependant resistors changes; what a light emitting diode is; what a transistor is and its uses in light-operated and temperature-operated switching circuits; how transistors are used in bistable multivibrator circuits; what is meant by a two state system, logic gates and truth tables.

SUPPLEMENTARY: the variation of resistance with temperature of a thermistor, represented graphically; how a light dependant resistor is used in a light meter; why a series resistor is used with a light emitting diode and how a transistor and capacitor are used in time-operated switching circuits.

CORE

29.1 POTENTIAL

We have seen that a cell provides a potential difference. Suppose such a cell has an e.m.f. of 2V. If the negative terminal is earthed, we say that the potential of the positive terminal is +2V. If instead we earth the positive terminal, we say that the potential of the negative terminal is –2V. This is shown in Fig. 29.1(a) and Fig. 29.1(b).

FIG. 29.1(a)   **FIG. 29.1(b)**

NEGATIVE EARTHED   POSITIVE EARTHED

In electronics we often use the symbol 0V instead of the earth symbol.

We often use a potential divider to vary the potential. In Fig. 29.2 we have

The output potential, V_{OUT}, is given by

$$V_{OUT} = V_{IN} \left(\frac{R_2}{R_1 + R_2} \right)$$

This can either by positive or negative depending upon V_{IN}. The equation assumes that there is no output current.

FIG. 29.2

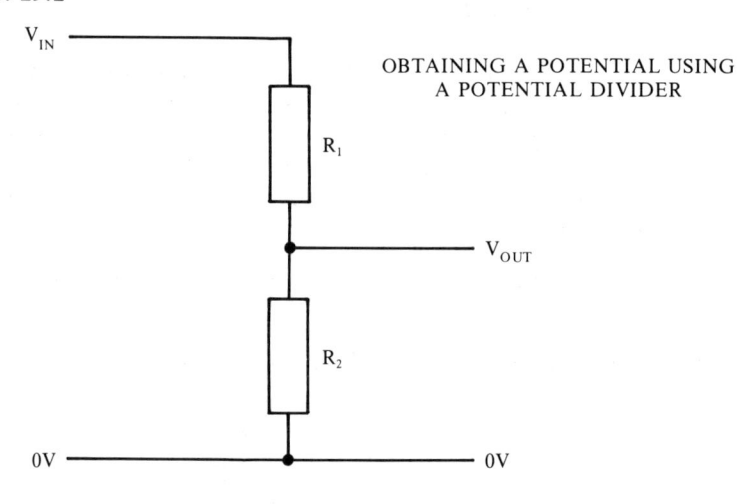

OBTAINING A POTENTIAL USING A POTENTIAL DIVIDER

29.2 THE RESISTANCE OF THERMISTORS AND LIGHT DEPENDANT RESISTORS

(i) A semiconducting device known as a thermistor contains semi-conducting metallic oxides. Its resistance falls greatly as its temperature rises and so it can be used as a sensitive thermometer. The circuit symbol for a thermistor is shown in Fig. 29.3.

FIG. 29.3

CIRCUIT SYMBOL FOR A THERMISTOR

(ii) A semiconducting device known as a light dependant resistor (L.D.R.) is made from a thin layer of cadmium sulphide. When light falls on this layer, its resistance decreases. The greater the light intensity, the greater the fall in resistance — it falls typically from a few megohms in the dark to a few kilohms in daylight. L.D.R.s are used in automatic lighting systems and photographic exposure meters. The circuit symbol for an L.D.R. is shown in Fig. 29.4.

FIG. 29.4

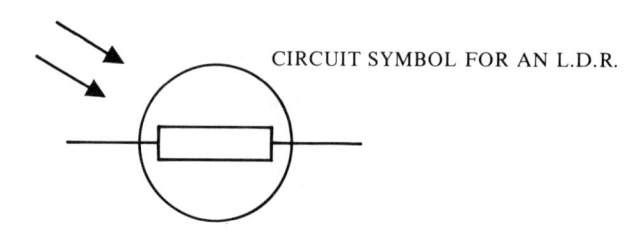

CIRCUIT SYMBOL FOR AN L.D.R.

Electronic Devices 359

29.3 THE LIGHT EMITTING DIODE

A light emitting diode (L.E.D.) is a junction diode which is made from the semiconductor gallium arsenide phosphide. When it is forward biased it conducts and emits light — usually red or green. L.E.D.s are used in many digital displays as seen on some balances, ammeters and voltmeters. They are also used on some calculators, cash registers, clocks, televisions and videos. They are arranged as seven segment displays, as discussed in Chapter 1.

An L.E.D. is an example of a transducer changing electrical to light energy.

The circuit symbol for an L.E.D. is shown in Fig. 29.5.

FIG. 29.5

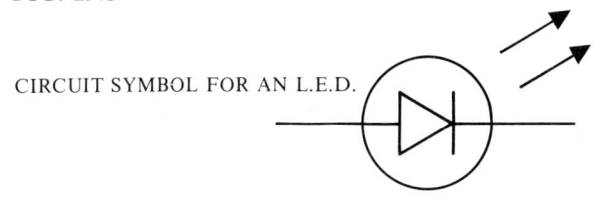

CIRCUIT SYMBOL FOR AN L.E.D.

29.4 THE TRANSISTOR

(i) A transistor is a small three terminal semiconducting device. The most common type is an npn transistor. It consists of a thin layer of p type semiconductor sandwiched between two thicker n type layers.

In practice, it is really two diodes arranged back to back.

Electrical contacts are made to each layer as shown in Fig. 29.6 and the layers are known as the emitter, collector and base.

FIG. 29.6

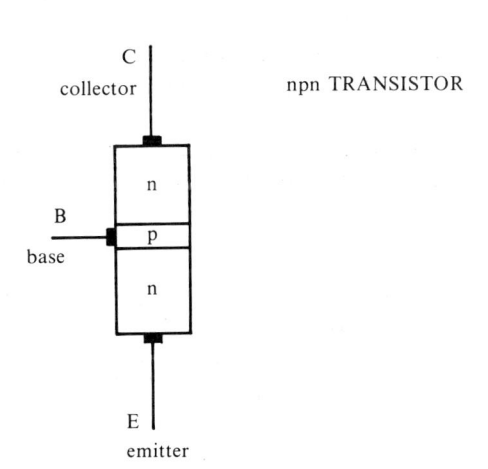

360 Electronic Devices

Suppose we arrange the circuit shown in Fig. 29.7, in which the collector is at +6V with respect to the emitter and the positive potential of the base is varied, using a potential divider.

FIG. 29.7

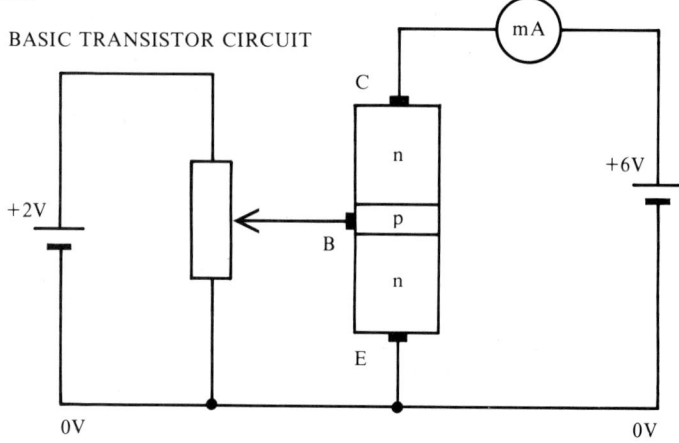

BASIC TRANSISTOR CIRCUIT

When the potential of the base is zero, no current is registered on the milliammeter. As the potential is increased, no current flows until the potential reaches about 0.6V. A current then begins to flow.

The positive potential of the base causes electrons to flow from the emitter to the base, across the pn junction between them. These electrons then continue on to the collector because they are attracted by its positive potential.

FIG. 29.8(a)

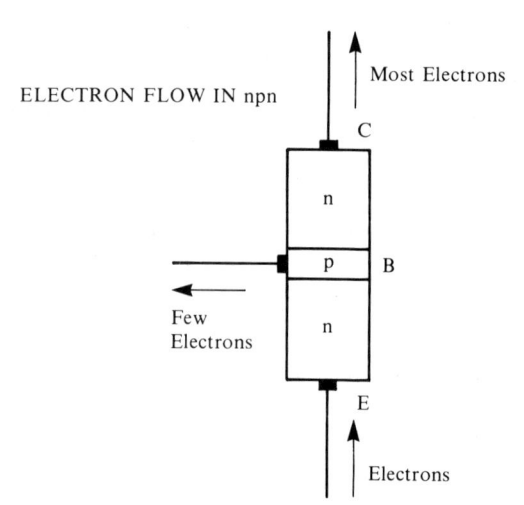

ELECTRON FLOW IN npn

FIG. 29.8(b)   **FIG. 29.8(c)**

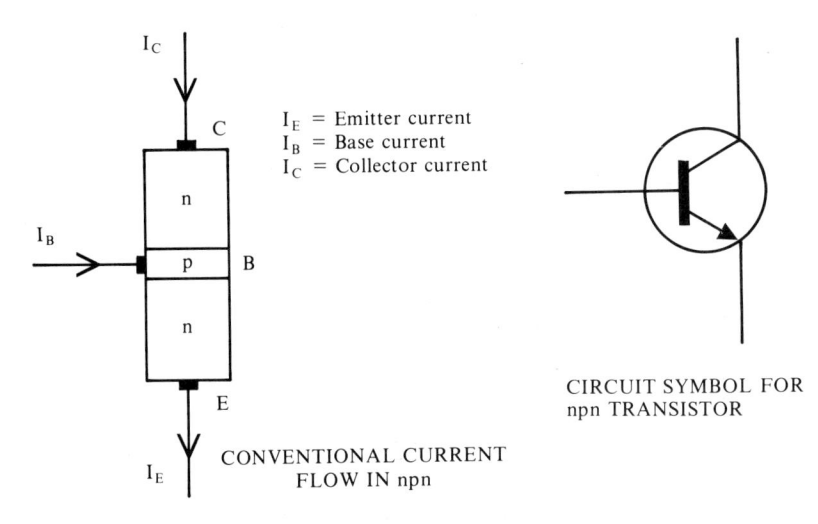

I_E = Emitter current
I_B = Base current
I_C = Collector current

CONVENTIONAL CURRENT FLOW IN npn

CIRCUIT SYMBOL FOR npn TRANSISTOR

No electron makes the journey the opposite way from the collector to the base because the collector-base junction is reverse biased.

Also because the base layer is so thin and contains less doping no holes move across the forward biased emitter-base junction.

(ii) In fact, not all the electrons leave the emitter and reach the collector. Some combine with holes in the base, as shown in Fig. 29.8(a). In order to keep the charge of the base neutral current flows along the connection into the base. So, electrons leave the emitter, a few combine with holes in the base, causing electrons to flow out of the base and most of the electrons arrive at the collector. In terms of conventional current, the current enters through the collector lead, a little enters through the base lead and all leaves through the emitter lead, as shown in Fig. 29.8(b). As a result, the circuit symbol for an npn transistor is shown in Fig. 29.8(c). The arrow points in the direction of the conventional current.

When the transistor is conducting and the base potential is at least 0.6V, the device has a low resistance. Alternatively, when no base current flows and the device is not conducting, it has a very high resistance.

(iii) There are two main uses of a transistor, firstly as an amplifier and secondly as a switch.
1) Typically, the collector current I_C, is about 100 to 1000 times that of the base current, I_B.

362 Electronic Devices

$$\text{Current gain} = \frac{I_C}{I_B}$$

The current gain may be used to obtain a voltage gain by connecting a resistor in series with the collector. The large collector current generates a large p.d. across the resistor.

2) We use the transistor as a switch. If $I_B = 0$ then $I_C = 0$. When the base voltage exceeds +0.6V, the transistor switches on, I_B flows and so does I_C. I_C then continues to increase as I_B does.

A basic demonstration of switching is used in Fig. 29.9.

FIG. 29.9

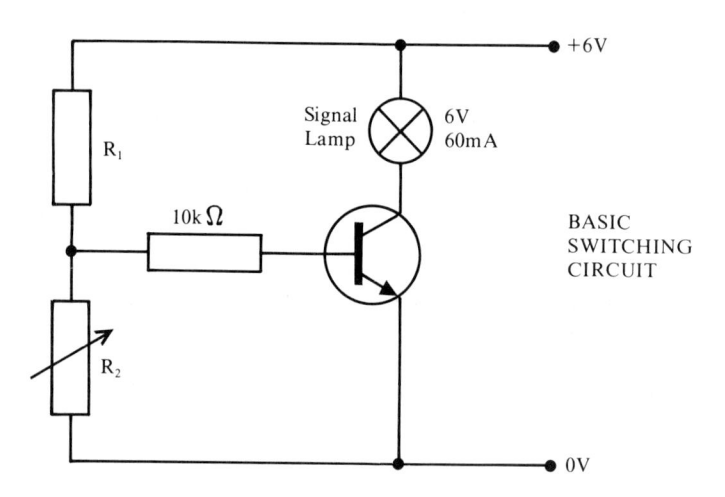

BASIC SWITCHING CIRCUIT

R_1 and R_2 form a potential divider. R_2 is adjusted until the p.d. across it is greater than 0.6V. The transistor then switches on and the collector current causes the signal lamp to light up. The base resistor of $10k\Omega$ is used in case R_2 is made too big. Then the base potential would be large and cause large base and collector currents which would cause the transistor to overheat.

29.5 LIGHT-OPERATED AND TEMPERATURE-OPERATED SWITCHING CIRCUITS

(i) A light-operated switching circuit is demonstrated in Fig. 29.10.

An L.D.R. and a variable resistor make up a potential divider. If no light falls on the L.D.R. its resistance will be high and there will be a large voltage across it. If this is greater than 0.6V the transistor, and hence the signal lamp, will switch on. The actual point at which this takes place depends upon the value of R_1. The bigger R_1, the greater

FIG. 29.10

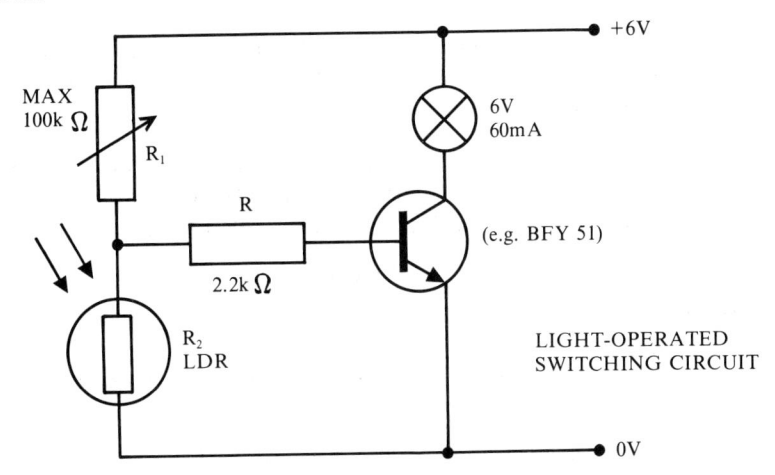

![Light-operated switching circuit: +6V rail to lamp (6V 60mA) and to top of R₁ (MAX 100kΩ variable); R₁ connects down to junction with R (2.2kΩ) going to base of npn transistor (e.g. BFY 51); LDR R₂ from junction to 0V; transistor collector to lamp, emitter to 0V.]

LIGHT-OPERATED SWITCHING CIRCUIT

the voltage across it and the harder it will be to switch on the transistor. This type of circuit can be used to automatically switch on lights when it gets dark.

If the L.D.R. and variable resistor are interchanged, the lamp goes off in the dark.

(ii) A temperature-operated switching circuit is demonstrated in Fig. 29.11.

FIG. 29.11

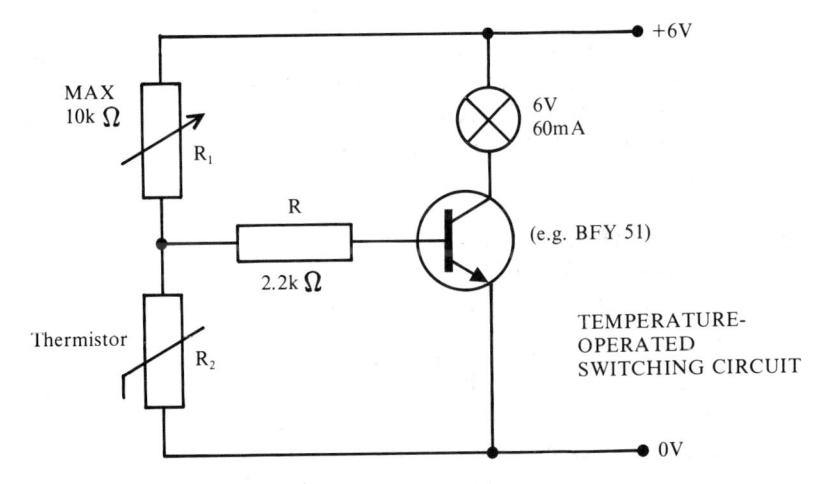

![Temperature-operated switching circuit: +6V rail to lamp (6V 60mA) and to top of R₁ (MAX 10kΩ variable); R₁ down to junction with R (2.2kΩ) to base of transistor (e.g. BFY 51); thermistor R₂ from junction to 0V; transistor collector to lamp, emitter to 0V.]

TEMPERATURE-OPERATED SWITCHING CIRCUIT

The L.D.R. in the potential divider is now replaced with a thermistor. As the temperature drops, the resistance of the thermistor increases and so does the voltage drop across it. If this exceeds 0.6V the transistor, and hence the lamp, will switch on. The actual point at which this takes place depends upon the values of R_1 and R_2. The bigger R_1, the greater the voltage across it and the bigger R_2 will have to be in order to cause switching — in other words, the lower the temperature will have to be. This type of circuit can be used as a frost alarm.

If the thermistor and variable resistor are interchanged, the lamp goes on at high temperatures. This could be used as a fire detector.

(iii) In both the light-operated and the temperature-operated switching circuits which we have considered, the collector current was sufficient to light a signal lamp. It is not sufficient though to activate a mains device such as a domestic light or heater. We then have to use a relay. The collector current is used to activate the relay, enabling a larger current to be switched by a smaller current. The position of the relay in the collector circuit is shown in Fig. 29.12.

FIG. 29.12

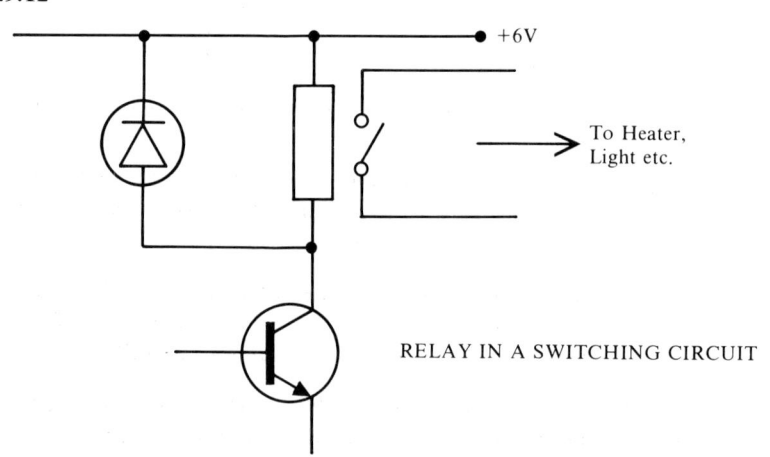

RELAY IN A SWITCHING CIRCUIT

When the transistor is switched on, the collector current goes through the relay and causes its contacts to close. When the collector current falls to zero at switch off, a large e.m.f. will be induced in such a direction as to maintain the current through the relay. This large e.m.f. could damge the transistor. This is prevented by the diode. This is forward biased by the e.m.f. and the current produced can flow easily through it. However, to the 6V supply, the diode is reverse biased and so it does not short circuit the relay when the transistor is on.

(iv) To summarize then, a transistor is off when no collector current flows and is on when collector current flows. For it to be on, a minimum base-emitter voltage of 0.6V is needed. Relays are used when computers are interfaced or used to drive external circuits.

29.6 BISTABLE MULTIVIBRATORS

Multivibrators are switching circuits containing two transistors arranged so that when one is on the other is off.

FIG. 29.13   BISTABLE MULTIVIBRATOR

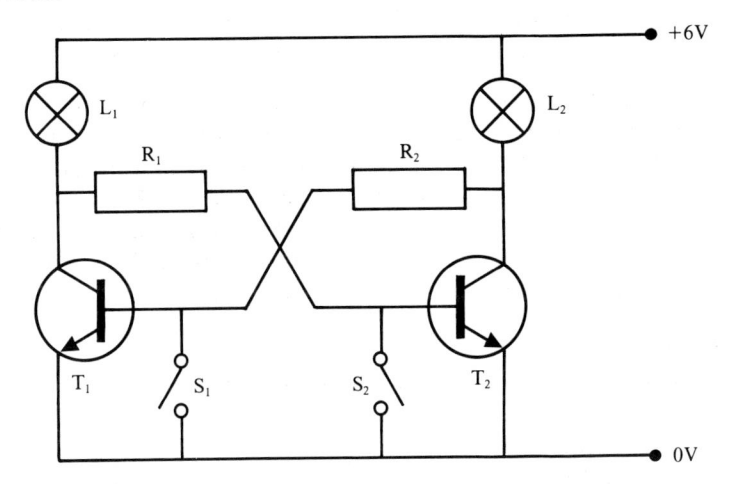

Suppose L_1 comes on when the circuit is first connected. T_1 must then be on and T_2 off. The circuit stays like this — in other words, it remembers its state. We say it is behaving as a latch.

Now suppose S_1 is quickly closed and opened again. The base of T_1 is temporarily connected to 0V, causing it to switch off. T_2 comes on because its base is connected via R_1 and L_1 to +6V.

When one transistor is on the other is off because the base voltage of one — the on one — is connected to the collector of the other — the off on. The one which is off cannot then have a sufficient voltage across it to switch it on.

The circuit stays as it is until S_2 is quickly closed and opened.

Because the circuit has two stable states, we say it is bistable.

29.7 TWO STATE SYSTEMS

We have just considered transistors which can be either on or off. This is an example of a two state system.

29.8 LOGIC GATES

Logic gates are two state switching circuits used in computers and other digital electronic systems. They are off when they give no output voltage and are on when they give an output voltage, typically 5V.

We represent off by 0 and on by 1 and refer to these as logic levels 0 and 1.

The NOT gate, or inverter, has one input and one output. Its circuit symbol is shown in Fig. 29.14.

FIG. 29.14

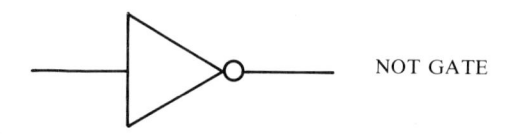

NOT GATE

If the input is at logic level 0 the output is at logic level 1 and vice versa.

The AND gate has two inputs and one output. Its circuit symbol is shown in Fig. 29.15.

FIG. 29.15

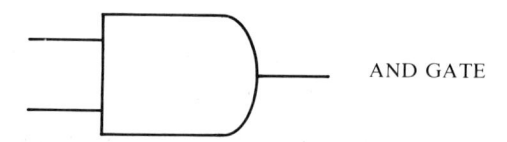

AND GATE

There is only an output at logic level 1 if both the inputs are at logic level 1.

The OR gate also has two inputs and one output — its circuit symbol is shown in Fig. 29.16.

FIG. 29.16

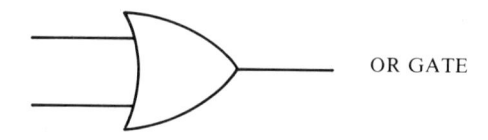

OR GATE

There is an output at logic level 1 if either of the inputs, or both inputs, are at logic level 1.

The NAND gate is an AND gate and a NOT gate. Its circuit symbol is shown in Fig. 29.17.

FIG. 29.17

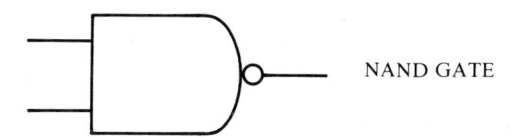

NAND GATE

There is always an output at logic level 1 except when both inputs are at logic level 1.

Finally, the NOR gate is an OR gate and a NOT gate. Its circuit symbol is shown in Fig. 29.18.

FIG. 29.18

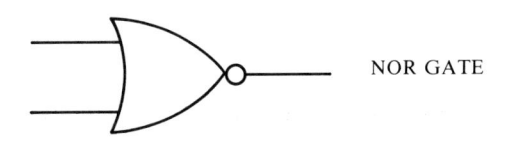

NOR GATE

There is never an output at logic level 1 unless both inputs are at logic level 0.

29.9 TRUTH TABLES

The behaviour of logic gates can be shown using truth tables. These show the outputs for all possible inputs.

Suppose the inputs are A and B and the output is P. The truth table for a NOT gate is

NOT

A	P
0	1
1	0

For an AND gate

AND

A	B	P
0	0	0
0	1	0
1	0	0
1	1	1

For an OR gate

OR

A	B	P
0	0	0
1	0	1
0	1	1
1	1	1

And for a NAND and NOR gate.

NAND

A	B	P
0	0	1
0	1	1
1	0	1
1	1	0

NOR

A	B	P
0	0	1
0	1	0
1	0	0
1	1	0

We may, if we wish label the input and output on the circuit symbols.

SUPPLEMENTARY

29.10 VARIATION IN RESISTANCE WITH TEMPERATURE FOR A THERMISTOR

The variation in resistance against temperature for a typical thermistor is shown in Fig. 29.19.

FIG. 29.19

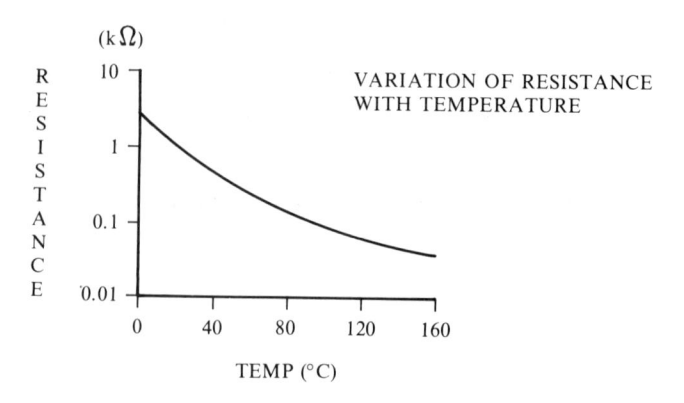

Notice that the fall in resistance is more rapid at lower temperatures.

29.11 USE OF A LIGHT DEPENDANT RESISTOR IN A LIGHT METER

The L.D.R. is the basis of the CdS light meter used by photographers. When light falls on the meter, the resistance of the L.D.R. decreases allowing a bigger current to flow in the circuit of which it forms a part. The current is indicated on a scale which is calibrated in shutter speeds and aperture numbers.

29.12 USE OF A SERIES RESISTOR WITH A LIGHT EMITTING DIODE

The current through a L.E.D. must be limited to about 10mA to prevent damage. In order to limit the current we use a series resistor

FIG. 29.20

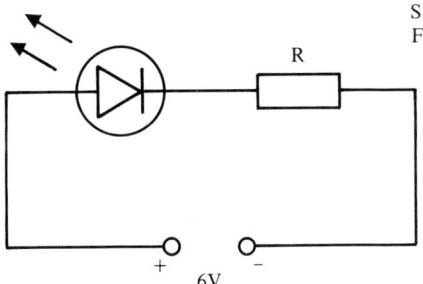

SERIES RESISTANCE FOR AN L.E.D.

In Fig. 29.20, if the p.d. across the L.E.D. is 2V and the current through it is 10mA then the resistance of the resistor R is given by

$$R = \frac{6 - 2}{0.01} = 400 \, \Omega$$

29.13 TIME-OPERATED SWITCHING CIRCUITS

A capacitor may be used with a transistor in a time-operated switching circuit, as shown in Fig. 29.21. Note that in practice a relay would be connected in the collector circuit.

When the switch S is closed, the capacitor C starts to charge through R. After a certain time, the p.d. across the capacitor exceeds 0.6V meaning that the base is at a greater potential than 0.6V, causing the transistor to switch on. The time taken for this to occur depends upon the values of R and C. This circuit can be used in any timing circuit.

370 Electronic Devices

FIG. 29.21

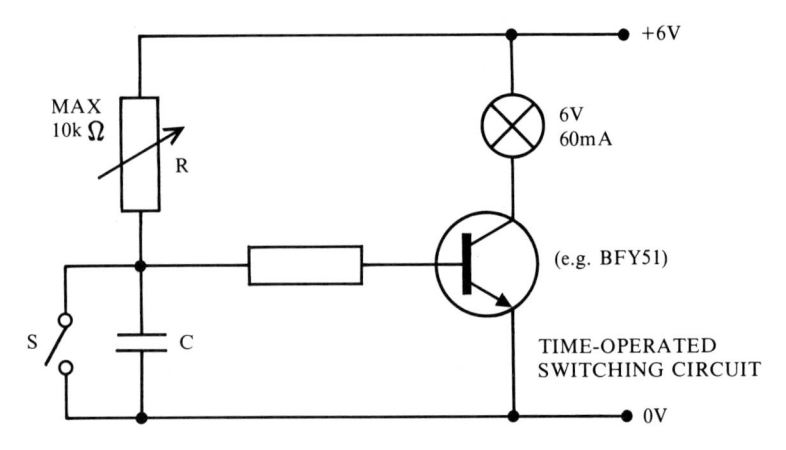

TIME-OPERATED SWITCHING CIRCUIT

QUESTIONS

CORE
1. Draw the circuit symbol for a thermistor.
2. Draw the circuit symbol for an L.E.D.
3. Draw the circuit symbol for an L.D.R.
4. State two types of use for a transistor.
5. Explain why a relay is used when a transistor is used in a switching circuit.
6. The circuit diagram below shows how a transistor may be used to make a switch which makes a light come on when it gets dark.

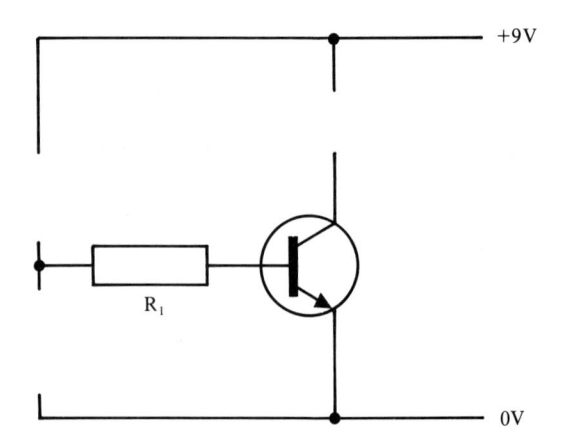

(i) Complete the circuit by adding in the correct places and labelling

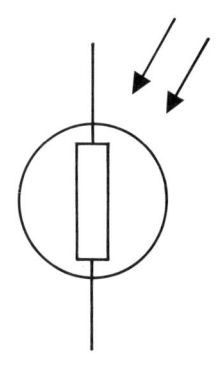

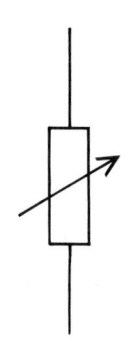

A a light sensitive resistor,   B a variable resistor,

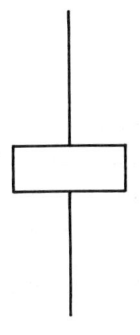

C an electromagnetic relay.

(ii) What happens to the resistance of the light sensitive resistor when it gets dark?
(iii) Explain what effect this change of resistance has on the collector current.
(iv) Why is a variable resistor preferred to a fixed resistor?
(v) Why is a relay preferred to inserting a lamp directly in the circuit?
(vi) How could the circuit be adapted to switch on a warning lamp when an old person's bedroom becomes too cold?

(L.E.A.G. part question).

7.

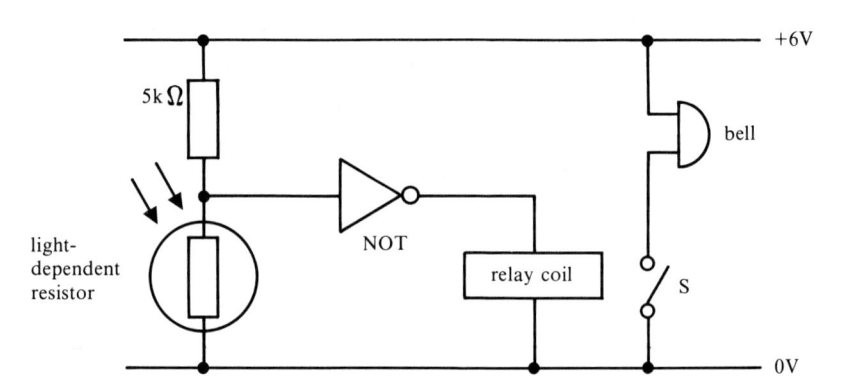

In this circuit the relay coil is energised and can close switch S if the output of the NOT gate is high.
(a) When a bright light is shone on the light-dependent resistor the input voltage to the NOT gate falls.
  (i) Why does this happen?
  (ii) What happens to the rest of the circuit as a result of this?
(b) Suggest a practical use for the circuit shown above. *(M.E.G.)*

8. In a factory, a particular piece of machinery has an alarm system to warn the operator of a fault. The system has a blue lamp (alight when the machine is operating normally), a red warning lamp and a buzzer. There is a fault detection system and an "operator acknowledge" button. If a fault is detected the blue lamp goes out and the red lamp comes on and the buzzer sounds. When the operator acknowledges the fault by pressing the button, the buzzer stops but the red light stays on. Complete the output columns of the truth table below to show what states are wanted.

INPUT		OUTPUT		
FAULT	OPERATOR ACKNOWLEDGE	RED	BUZZER	BLUE
0	0			
0	1			
1	0			
1	1			

(N.E.A. part question)

SUPPLEMENTARY

9. The output of a logic circuit can be displayed using an L.E.D. and an associated series resistor, as in the circuit shown below.

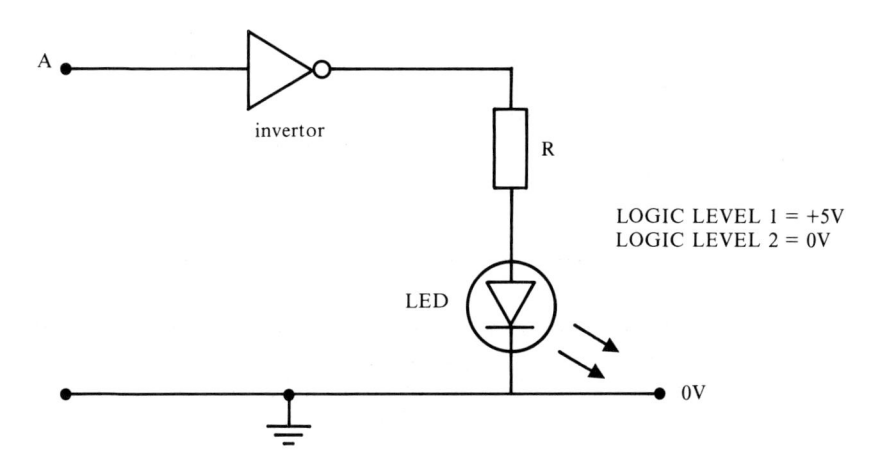

LOGIC LEVEL 1 = +5V
LOGIC LEVEL 2 = 0V

(i) When the L.E.D. is lit, what is the logic state at A?
(ii) The L.E.D. has a potential difference drop of 2V across it and a current of 10mA flowing through it when it is lit. What is the potential difference across resistor R when the L.E.D. is lit?
(iii) Calculate the resistance of R.
(iv) Why is the resistor R needed? *(N.E.A. part question)*

Chapter 30
THE ATOM

At the end of this chapter you will know:
CORE: that an atom consists of a small massive nucleus, surrounded by orbiting electrons; that the nucleus consists of protons and neutrons; what is meant by the term nucleon; how the masses of an electron, a proton and a neutron compare with each other; the charge on the electron, proton and neutron and what nuclides and isotopes are.
SUPPLEMENTARY: how an ion may be formed and the details of the Geiger-Marsden experiment.

CORE

30.1 THE PARTICLES IN THE ATOM

Every substance is made up of atoms. Each atom has a small massive core called the nucleus. This nucleus is surrounded by moving charged particles. The so-called nuclear structure of the atom results from what is known as the Geiger-Marsden scattering experiment in which nuclei were bounced off other atoms.

Today, in order to understand as fully as possible the structure of the nucleus and how nuclei react with each other, we use a tandem Van de Graaff accelerator. Photograph 29 (cover photograph) shows the world's largest such accelerator. It is operated by the Science and Engineering Research Council and is located at Daresbury in Cheshire.

The nucleus contains two types of particles — neutrons and protons. The moving charged particles surrounding the nucleus are electrons. The paths in which they move are called orbits.

An atom which only has a few electrons will have them in orbits close to the nucleus but atoms having more electrons will also have them in orbits which are further away from the nucleus.

The structure of an atom is shown in Fig. 30.1.

Because both protons and neutrons are found in the nucleus, they are called nucleons.

All neutral atoms have the same number of protons and electrons.

The Atom

FIG. 30.1

THE DIAMETER OF AN AVERAGE ATOM IS ABOUT 10,000 TIMES THE DIAMETER OF ITS NUCLEUS

- First Orbit
- Second Orbit
- Third Orbit
- Nucleus
- Atomic Diameter
- Nuclear Diameter

Electrons are represented by dots.

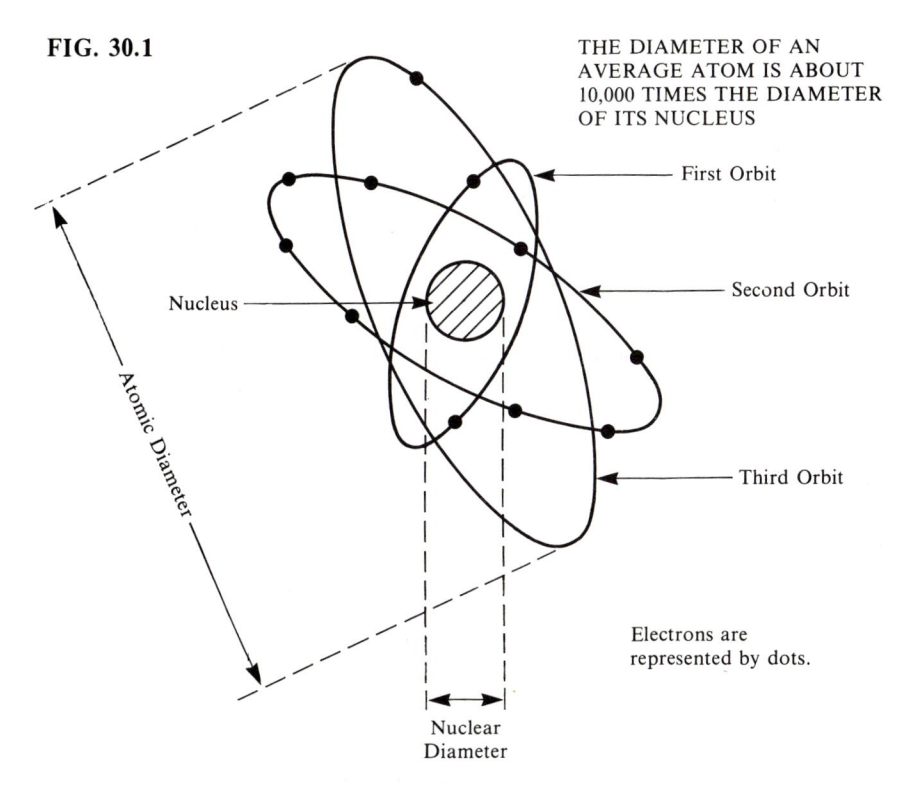

THE STRUCTURE OF AN ATOM

30.2 ELECTRONS, PROTONS AND NEUTRONS

Protons and neutrons have the same mass. Electrons have a much smaller mass — about $\frac{1}{1840}$ of the mass of the proton or neutron.

Electrons carry a negative charge. Protons carry an equal positive charge. Neutrons are not charged.

If we take the mass of the proton and neutron as 1 then the mass of the electron will be $\frac{1}{1840}$ and we can represent mass and charge in a table as shown below:

PARTICLE	MASS	CHARGE
Electron	$\frac{1}{1840}$	-1
Proton	1	$+1$
Neutron	1	0

30.3 PROTON AND NUCLEON NUMBER

The proton number of a nucleus is the number of protons it contains. It is also called the atomic number.

We represent it by the symbol Z.

Since a neutral atom always contains the same number of electrons and protons, then the proton number is also equal to the number of electrons orbiting the nucleus.

So Z = number of protons in nucleus = number of electrons orbiting the nucleus.

The nucleon number of a nucleus is the total number of protons and neutrons in the nucleus — that is, the number of nucleons in the nucleus. It is also called the mass number.

So A = number of protons + number of neutrons
and Z = number of protons
and so A = Z + number of neutrons
Number of neutrons = A - Z.

We can represent an atom of a particular substance X — called a nuclide — by

$$^{A}_{Z}X$$

where X is the chemical symbol for the nuclide, A is its nucleon number and Z is its proton number.

Atoms which do not contain equal numbers of protons and electrons are called ions.

PROBLEM

THE CHEMICAL SYMBOL FOR CHLORINE IS Cl. IF AN ATOM CONTAINS 17 ELECTRONS AND 18 NEUTRONS, WRITE DOWN A NUCLIDE REPRESENTATION FOR THE ATOM.

If the atom contains 17 electrons, then the nucleus contains 17 protons.
So Z = 17
Also A = Z + number of neutrons
So A = 17 + 18 = 35.
The nuclide representation is $^{35}_{17}Cl$

ANSWER: NUCLIDE REPRESENTATION IS $^{35}_{17}Cl$

30.4 ISOTOPES

We have just seen that in a nuclide of chlorine there are 18 neutrons. But in another nuclide there are 20 neutrons. Both nuclides have the same chemical properties. They are called isotopes. Isotopes are nuclides with the same Z but different A.

There are a great number of naturally occurring isotopes — above 280. Certain man-made isotopes can also be made in the laboratory.

Isotopes are very useful because certain natural and all man-made ones are radioactive. Because they are radioactive they can be used in medicine and industry. This will be discussed in detail in Chapter 31.

SUPPLEMENTARY

30.5 THE FORMATION OF IONS

An ion contains unequal numbers of protons and electrons. If an atom gains an electron, it then has more negative charges than positive charges and is called a negative ion. If an atom loses an electron, it then has more positive charges than negative charges and is called a positive ion.

30.6 THE GEIGER MARSDEN EXPERIMENT

The scattering experiments performed by Geiger and Marsden provided evidence for the nuclear atom.

They scattered helium nuclei from a thin gold foil using the apparatus shown in Fig. 30.2.

FIG. 30.2

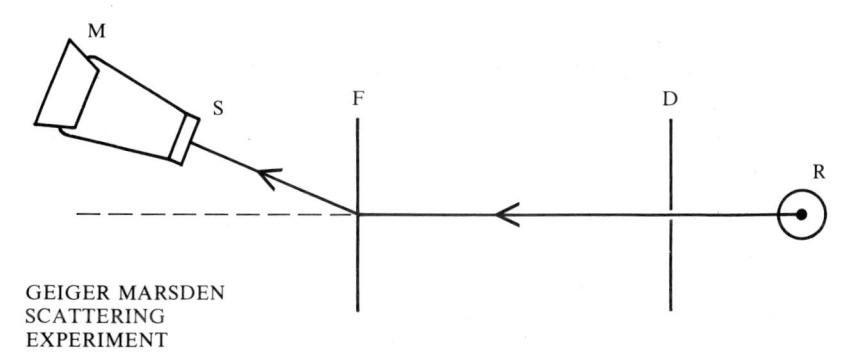

GEIGER MARSDEN
SCATTERING
EXPERIMENT

Helium nuclei from R passed through a slit D. Then they were scattered by a thin gold foil, F. They were scattered from their original direction and when they struck a zinc sulphide screen S, attached to a microscope M, they caused bright emissions of light. The conclusion reached from this scattering experiment was that the positive charge in the gold atoms was concentrated at the centre, in the nucleus.

QUESTIONS

CORE
1. Name the two types of nucleons.
2. An atom contains 17 electrons. How many protons are there in the nucleus?
3. An atom contains 27 nucleons and 13 electrons. How many neutrons are there in the nucleus?
4. State the charge on the neutron, proton and electron.
5. How do isotopes of a nuclide differ?
6. Which of the following is an uncharged particle found in the nucleus of an atom?
   A A proton   B A neutron   C An ion   D An electron?
   (S.E.G.)
7. A nucleus contains 12 protons and 15 neutrons.
   Which of the following gives the atomic number and the mass number?

	Atomic Number	Mass Number
A	12	15
B	12	27
C	15	3
D	15	27
E	27	12

   (M.E.G.)
8. What are nuclides whose proton numbers are the same but whose nucleon numbers are different, called?
9. In an atom, which of the following statements is true?
   A The mass of a proton is smaller than the mass of an electron
   B The mass of an atom is greater than the mass of its nucleus
   C The electron has no mass
   D The mass of a neutron is smaller than the mass of an electron.

SUPPLEMENTARY
10. How is a positive ion formed?
11. What can be concluded from the Geiger Marsden experiment?

Chapter 31
RADIOACTIVITY

At the end of this chapter you will know:

CORE: the three types of radioactive emission from the nucleus; their random nature, ionising properties and penetrating powers; how they are deflected in a magnetic field; how they may be detected by a Geiger Müller tube and a cloud chamber; what is meant by background radiation; how equations can be written to represent the emission of radioactive particles; what is meant by half life and how it may be represented graphically; that safety precautions are needed; the uses of radioactivity; how fission can occur with unstable nuclei; the difference between controlled and uncontrolled fission and the advantages and disadvantages of nuclear reactions.

SUPPLEMENTARY: what happens when a nucleus of U235 or Pu239 absorbs a neutron; what is meant by slow neutrons, a moderator, a chain reaction and control rods; how heat is removed from a reactor core; how waste products need to be safely stored and disposed of and the difference between fission and fusion.

CORE

31.1 THE THREE TYPES OF RADIOACTIVITY

Certain isotopes are called radioactive because they change or decay by emitting radioactivity. This radioactivity is given off at random by the nucleus of the isotope.

There are three types of radioactive emission: alpha, symbol α; beta, symbol β and gamma, symbol γ.

Alpha radiation consists of particles which are helium nuclei and are made up of two protons and two neutrons. They are positively charged. When they travel through a substance they ionise it strongly. They travel about 12cm in air but are easily stopped by paper — typically they are stopped by a piece 0.1mm thick.

Beta radiation consists of particles which are electrons and which must be negatively charged. They ionise a substance less than alpha radiation when they pass through it. They are not stopped by air or paper but need a few millimetres of aluminium or about $\frac{1}{2}$mm of lead to stop them.

Gamma radiation consists of high energy electromagnetic waves. It is only weakly ionising and needs a few centimetres of lead to stop it.

Because they are charged, alpha and beta radiation are deflected by a magnetic field but gamma radiation is not. This is shown in Fig. 31.1.

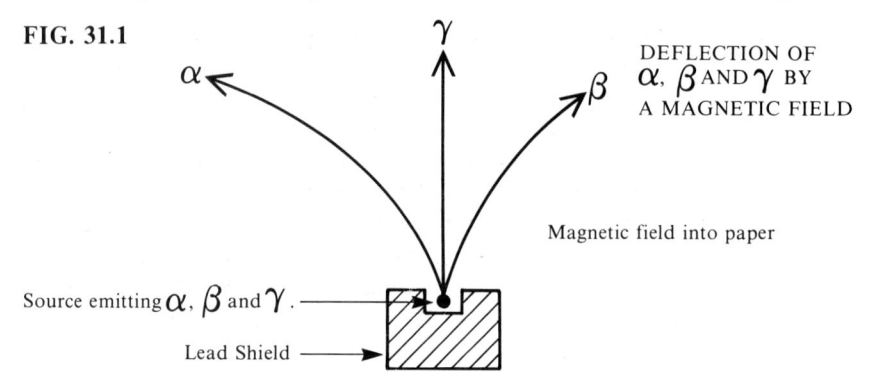

FIG. 31.1 DEFLECTION OF α, β AND γ BY A MAGNETIC FIELD

The directions of deflection can be found by using Fleming's Left Hand Rule.

31.2 THE DETECTION OF RADIOACTIVITY

We use the fact that radioactivity causes ionization to detect it. Two types of detector are available:

(i) The Geiger-Müller Tube.
A Geiger-Müller tube is shown in Fig. 31.2.

FIG. 31.2 GEIGER-MÜLLER TUBE

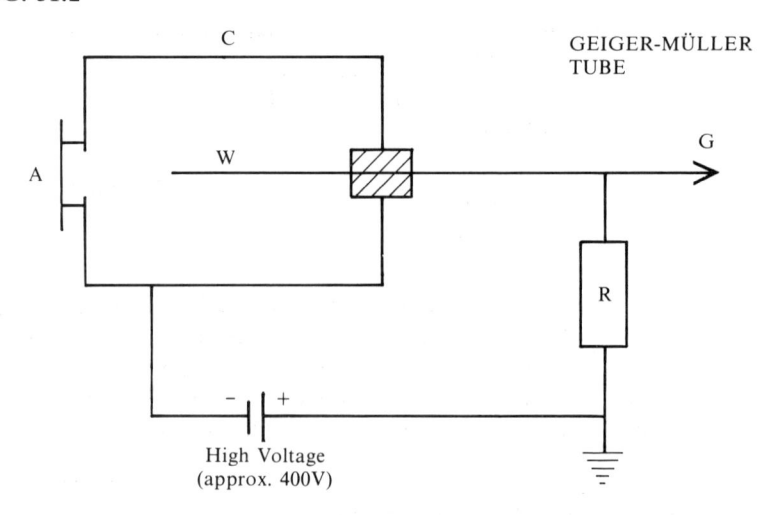

It consists of a cylinder C and a fine wire W mounted parallel to the axis of the cylinder. The wire is insulated from the cylinder. The cylinder contains low pressure air or argon. A large p.d. of around 400V is applied across C and W with the positive connected to W.

Ionizing radiation enters the tube through the window A which is normally covered with a thin sheet of mica, glass or aluminium. It ionizes the gas along its path. These ions are accelerated by the voltage and produce more ions by colliding with neutral atoms and molecules so that the ionization current builds up very rapidly. A very high resistance, R, is connected between the wire and the ground to prevent a constant current flowing and instead give a rapid discharge of a very large current lasting for a very short time. This discharge registers as a "kick" in a device connected at G. The device may be a scaler, which gives a total count, or a ratemeter which gives a count per second or count per minute.

(ii) The Cloud Chamber.

Cloud chambers are used when we wish to follow the path of α, β or γ radiation. Fig. 31.3 shows the typical construction.

FIG. 31.3

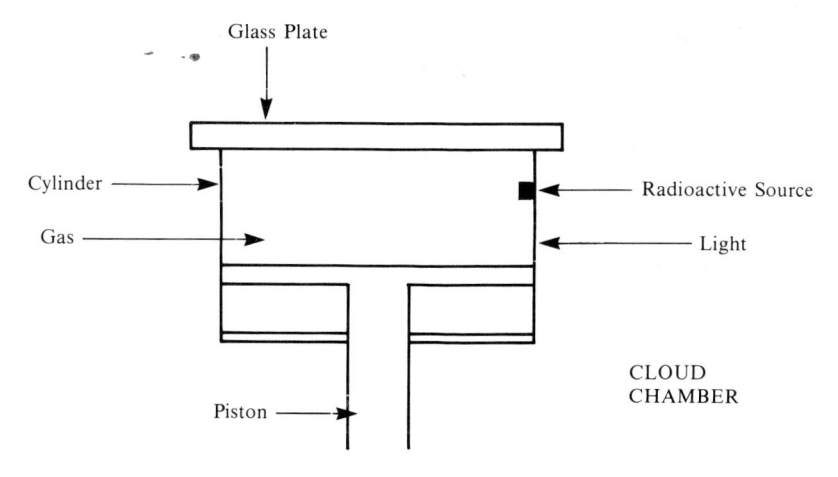

It consists of a cylinder and a piston. The cylinder contains a gas saturated with water vapour. When the piston is quickly pulled downwards, the gas expands and cools. If there are any ions present, the water vapour will condense on them forming small droplets. These can be easily photographed through the glass plate.

If a source of radiation is placed inside the cylinder, the radiation will ionize the gas as it passes through it.

Typical tracks produced by α, β and γ radiation are shown in Fig. 31.4.

FIG. 31.4

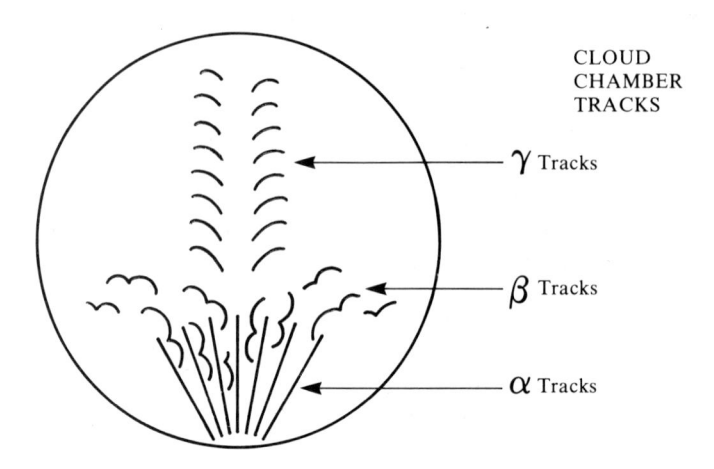

CLOUD CHAMBER TRACKS

γ Tracks

β Tracks

α Tracks

31.3 BACKGROUND RADIATION

Even if no source were near a Geiger-Müller tube or inside a cloud chamber, there would still be signs of radioactivity being present.

All around us, naturally occurring radioactivity or background radiation is present. This radiation comes from space in the form of cosmic radiation, consisting of beta particles. On the earth itself radiation comes from uranium and granite since both are radioactive. Steel in buildings is also radioactive.

Background radiation gives a count rate on a Geiger-Müller tube of around 25 to 30 counts per minute (c.p.m.). In places such as Aberdeen, the granite city, it is higher. It is also higher near places such as nuclear physics establishments and nuclear reactors since these add their own count to the normal background count.

Whenever a Geiger-Müller tube is being used to measure a count or count rate, the background count should always be subtracted from the obtained reading.

31.4 EQUATIONS OF RADIOACTIVE DECAY

When a nuclide decays by emitting gamma radiation, it does not decay into a new nuclide.

But whenever a nuclide decays by emitting alpha or beta radiation it does decay into a new nuclide. We can predict what the new nuclide will be by using a decay equation.

In these equations we represent an alpha particle by $^{4}_{2}\alpha$ and a beta particle by $^{0}_{-1}\beta$.

In decay equations, the total proton number and the total nucleon number add up to the same on each side of the equation.

For alpha decay, suppose a nuclide X decays to Y.
Then

$$^{A}_{Z}X \longrightarrow {}^{A-4}_{Z-2}Y + {}^{4}_{2}\alpha$$

So, by subtracting 4 from the original nucleon number and 2 from the original proton number, we can arrive at the nucleon number and the proton number for the new nucleus, Y.

For beta decay we have

$$^{A}_{Z}X \longrightarrow {}^{A}_{Z+1}Y + {}^{0}_{-1}\beta$$

So, by adding 1 to the original proton number, we can arrive at the proton number for the new nucleus Y.

PROBLEM
WHAT IS THE PROTON NUMBER OF THE NUCLIDE FORMED WHEN A NUCLEUS OF $^{237}_{92}U$ DECAYS BY BETA EMISSION?

Here original proton number = 92
So, new proton number = 1 + 92 = 93.

ANSWER: NEW PROTON NUMBER = 93.

31.5 HALF LIFE

(i) If we start with a particular mass of a radioactive isotope, we find that after a certain amount of time, half of it will have decayed.

The time taken for the mass of a radioactive isotope to halve is called its half life. After each half life the mass of the isotope is halved.

So after 1 half life, ½ the mass remains
   after 2 half lives, ¼ the mass remains
   after 3 half lives, ⅛ the mass remains   and so on.

The half life of a particular isotope is always the same but there is a great difference between one isotope and another.

The shortest half life is $\dfrac{3}{10,000,000}$ s for polonium $^{212}_{84}Po$ and the longest is 2,400y for plutonium $^{239}_{94}Pu$.

If we plot radioactive mass remaining against time, measured in half lives, we obtain the graph shown in Fig. 31.5.

FIG. 31.5

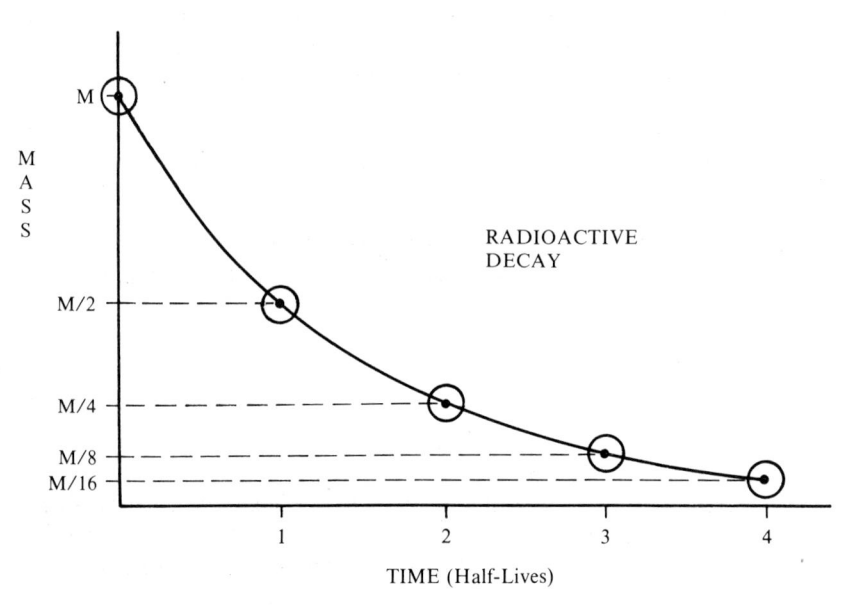

```
MASS
  M ●
        \
         \
          \         RADIOACTIVE
           \        DECAY
  M/2 -----●
              \
               \
  M/4 ----------●
                   \
  M/8 --------------●
  M/16 ---------------●
        1    2    3    4
         TIME (Half-Lives)
```

(ii) A Geiger-Müller tube can measure counts or count rates. We can also define half life as the time taken for the count rate to halve. A graph of count rate against time will have the same shape as the graph shown in Fig. 31.5. In order to measure a half life from one of these graphs we note the time when a particular mass or count rate occurs. We then note the new time when the mass or count rate has halved. The time difference between these two readings is then equal to the half life of the isotope. Its symbol is $T_{\frac{1}{2}}$

31.6 SAFETY PRECAUTIONS

All radioactivity is dangerous to our health. Obviously, radioactive isotopes should never be handled and should be securely stored behind lead walls. We always have to consider the type of radioactive emission given out by an isotope and also the half life of the isotope. Those with long half lives are obviously going to remain radioactive for long periods of time. Those with short half lives will more quickly decay to low activity.

When we talk about exposure to radioactivity we are concerned with two types. In chronic exposure we are concerned with continued, long term exposure. In acute exposure we are concerned with sudden, short exposures.

The direct risks to our bodies from acute exposure are leukaemia, temporary male sterility, burns, radiation sickness and ultimately, death. Chronic exposure can lead to cateracts of the eyes (caused by β particles) and cancer of the bones and lungs.

The genetic risks from both acute and chronic exposure are changes in the ratio of male to female birth rates, changes in the blood and mental impairment.

In cases of chronic exposure the two factors which concern us are the higher probability of cancer and the general risk of damaged genes being passed on.

31.7 USES OF RADIOACTIVITY

(i) Tracers.
Radioactive isotopes are used as tracers when they are used to follow the path of a substance through a pipe. Faults in pipes may be located by introducing an isotope into the pipe and then passing a Geiger-Müller tube over the pipe. The count rate will rise when the tube is near a leak. This technique is used by gas engineers to detect gas leaks.

The thyroid gland takes in iodine. If a person is given radioactive iodine then the extent to which this is taken in can be found by monitoring the thyroid with a Geiger-Müller tube. $^{123}_{53}I$ is used. It has a half life of 13.3h and decays by gamma emission.

(ii) Treatment of Cancer.
Gamma radiation from cobalt $^{60}_{27}Co$, is used. It has a half life of 5.26y.

Cervical cancer is treated by placing a beta emitter such as Cs against the tumour. This isotope has a half life of 30y.

(iii) Welding faults and thickness testing.
Gamma radiation from $^{60}_{27}Co$ is used here. The radiation will easily pass through any cracks giving an increased count rate with a Geiger-Müller tube. If the source is placed above a paper or metal sheet with the Geiger-Müller tube fixed on the other side of the sheet, any variations in thickness of the sheet as it moves by will lead to variations in the count rate.

(iv) Sterilisation.
Gamma radiation from cobalt $^{60}_{27}Co$, can be used to sterilise bodies. This technique is used in operating theatres to sterilise surgical instruments and in the food industry to sterilise food.

31.8 NUCLEAR FISSION

A heavy unstable nucleus such as uranium $^{235}_{92}U$, can be made to split into two nuclei of nearly equal mass. The process is called nuclear fission and it occurs when the heavy nucleus is bombarded with neutrons. During the process, large amounts of energy are released. Three neutrons are also released and the new nuclei are radioactive and decay by emitting radiation.

If the release of energy in fission is controlled then the process can be used in a nuclear reactor. Here two of the released neutrons are absorbed by another material, leaving one neutron free to cause more fission.

If, however, the release of energy is not controlled then the result is an atomic, or more correctly a nuclear, bomb. All the released neutrons go on to cause fission and the enormous amount of energy released becomes explosive.

It is vital that in a nuclear reactor, the supply of neutrons is rigidly controlled. The waste products must be frequently and safely removed to ensure the efficiency of the reactor. The coolant which is used to remove the energy released in the form of heat must be kept in an enclosed system so that it cannot come into contact with radioactive material and the reactor itself must be shielded in lead and concrete to prevent escape of radioactivity.

The advantages of a reactor are: in normal use it is cheap to run, it is efficient, clean and only a small fuel mass is needed compared to the situation where the equivalent amount of energy is obtained from coal. The disadvantages are: the high initial construction cost, the problem of disposing of the waste bi-products, the health risk from the bi-products and the neutrons in the reactor and the risk from terrorists who could obviously use the fissionable materials to make a nuclear bomb.

SUPPLEMENTARY

31.9 RANGE AND IONIZING POWER

Radioactivity which has a high ionizing power has a short range because its kinetic energy is used up in the ionization process. Check for yourself that this applies to all three types of radioactivity.

31.10 THE ABSORPTION OF NEUTRONS BY $^{235}_{92}U$ AND $^{239}_{94}Pu$

In reactor physics we usually just write U235 and Pu239.

Radioactivity 387

When a nucleus of U235 absorbs a neutron, it splits into two nuclei, three neutrons and releases a large amount of energy. A neutron is represented by $_0^1 n$.

We can then represent the fission process by

$$_0^1 n + {}_{92}^{235} U \longrightarrow {}_{56}^{141} Ba + {}_{39}^{92} Kr + 3\,_0^1 n + W$$

The energy W is provided by the difference in mass between the initial products and the final products.

In fact, W is given by
$$W = mc^2$$
where $\quad$ m = loss of mass
$\quad\quad\quad$ c = speed of light in vacuum.

In breeder reactors $_{92}^{238}$ U is bombarded with neutrons to give $_{93}^{239}$ Np. This decays to $_{94}^{239}$ Pu which can be made to undergo fission. Again the energy is provided by a loss of mass.

31.11 MODERATORS AND CONTROL RODS

Both U235 and Pu239 are fissionable when they absorb slow moving, or thermal, neutrons.

The neutrons which are released in the fission process are moving very rapidly and are not suitable to produce further fission. We slow them down and make them suitable to cause further fission by the use of a moderator. Graphite or water are used as moderators.

When the neutrons released in fission are used to cause further fission we say that we have a chain reaction. The reaction in a nuclear reactor is a controlled chain reaction.

The power level at which a reactor operates depends upon the number of neutrons in the reactor. The power level of the reactor can be controlled by controlling the number of neutrons in it. In order to do this, we introduce a neutron absorbing material in the form of a steel rod containing cadmium or boron. These are known as control rods and their position in the reactor can be easily adjusted.

31.12 COOLANTS USED IN NUCLEAR REACTORS

The energy released in nuclear fission appears in the form of heat. It is removed from the reactor by a coolant which must be kept isolated from the reactor itself to prevent contamination by radioactive material. In the advanced gas cooled reactor, the coolant is a gas such as carbon dioxide. In the pressurised water reactor the coolant is water under high pressure. The high pressure prevents the water from boiling and high pressure steam building up.

31.13 WASTE PRODUCTS FROM NUCLEAR REACTORS

We have seen that radioactive bi-products are formed in a nuclear reactor. These are a safety hazard and must be carefully disposed of and stored. We must bear in mind the type of radiation emitted and the half lives of these bi-products.

31.14 NUCLEAR FUSION

Nuclear fusion is the reverse of fission. It is the process where nuclei combine to form a new nucleus of smaller mass than the sum of the masses of the individual nuclei. The loss of mass appears as energy. An important advantage of fusion is that no radioactive isotopes are formed in the process.

Nuclear fusion occurs in the sun and all stars when hydrogen nuclei fuse together to form helium nuclei and release energy. A nuclear fusion reactor would be an ideal safe source of energy.

In order for fusion reactions to occur, the gases used must be heated to very high temperatures. As these gases are heated they become ionized by releasing electrons. This mixture of moving electrons and nuclei is called a plasma. At very high temperatures the nuclei have sufficient energy to overcome their electrostatic repulsion.

At plasma temperatures around 10^8 °C fusion reactions occur between deuterium ^2_1H, nuclei and tritium ^3_1H, nuclei.

The equation for the fusion process is

$$^3_1H + {}^2_1H \longrightarrow {}^4_2He + {}^1_0n + W$$

Water contains deuterium and so there are good supplies of it. Tritium does not occur naturally and has to be made from lithium which is plentiful in the earth's crust.

The fusion produces a helium nucleus, a neutron and energy. 80% of the energy released is given to the neutron making it travel at very high speed and it is this energy that could be used for power generation.

At present, research programmes around the world are aimed at providing the scientific feasibility of using fusion for generating electricity. Within the next few years it is hoped that experiments on the world's largest fusion experiment, the JET will provide fusion reactions. The JET or Joint European Torus is at Culham in Oxfordshire. It is an experiment, not a reactor and is completely European.

During the operation of the JET experiment, a small quantity of gas is introduced into the doughnut shaped vacuum vessel — the Torus.

The Torus is shown in Photograph 30.

PHOTOGRAPH 30

The gas is then heated to form a plasma by passing a large current of up to 5 million amps. through it. This large current is also used to provide magnetic fields to prevent the hot plasma from hitting the walls of the vacuum vessel.

The complete machine is shown in Photograph 31.

It is 15m in diameter, 12m high and weighs around 4.61×10^7N. The experimental programme is expected to continue until 1992.

PHOTOGRAPH 31

QUESTIONS

CORE

1. Name the three types of radioactivity.
2. Which type of radioactive emission is not affected by a magnetic field?
3. Which one of the following is emitted by radioactive nuclei?
   A Gamma radiation   B Infra Red radiation   C Microwaves
   D Radiowaves   E Ultra Violet radiation.   *(M.E.G.)*
4. Complete the blank spaces in the table below:

NAME OF RADIATION	ALPHA RAYS	BETA RAYS	GAMMA RAYS
ELECTRIC CHARGE	POSITIVE		
NATURE OF RADIATION			E.M. WAVES

5. Draw a labelled diagram of a cloud chamber.
6. The half life of radioactive carbon is 5600 years. After how long will the mass be one eighth of its value now:
   A 700 years   B 1867 years   C 19200 years   D 22400 years   E 44800 years.
7. A radioactive isotope is placed near a detector. The graph shows how the count rate changed with time.

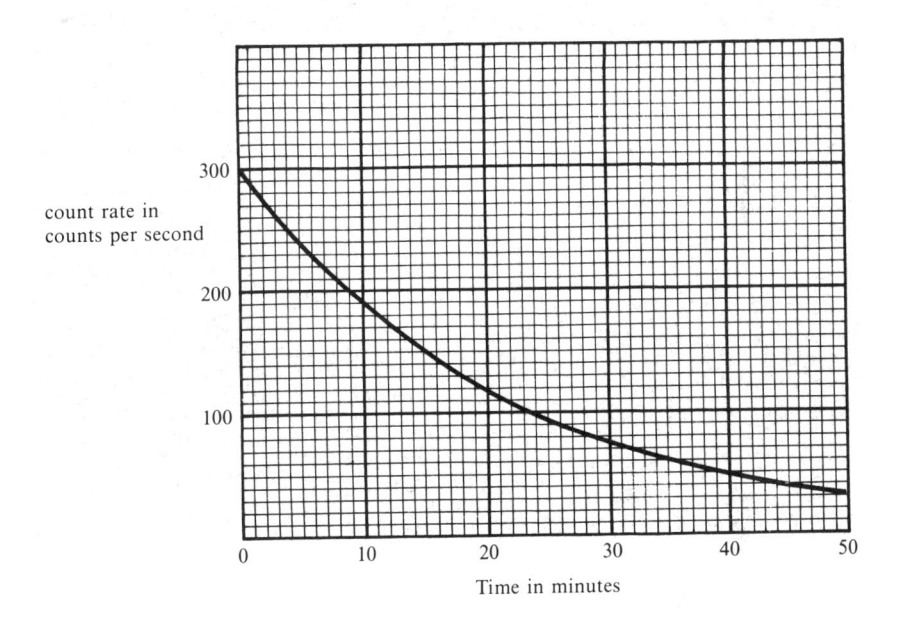

The half-life of the isotope is
A 10 minutes   B 15 minutes   C 25 minutes   D 50 minutes.
(S.E.G.)

8. Figure 5 represents the testing of the thickness of aluminium foil at a factory.

FIG. 5

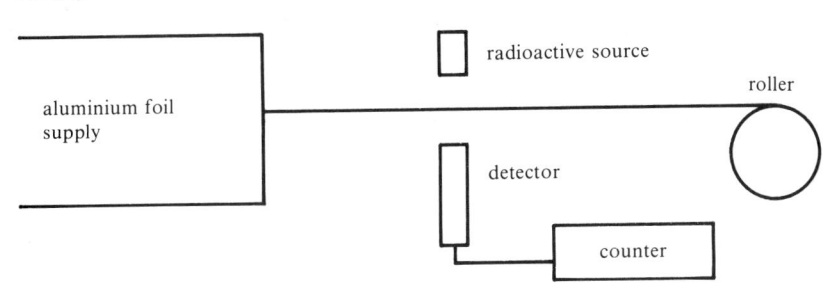

The radioactive source gives out beta particles. It is placed above the sheet of foil and the detector below the sheet.
(a) From which part of the atoms of the sources have the beta particles come?
(b) Why are alpha particles unsuitable for this test?
(c) The readings on the counter for a time of eight seconds are given in the table below.

Time in seconds	0	1	2	3	4	5	6	7	8
Total count	0	40	80	120	165	210	255	295	335
Count in one second	—	40	40	40	45	45			

(i) Complete the table.
(ii) Examine the completed table. Now describe what is happening to the thickness of the foil, giving reasons for your answer. *(N.E.A.)*

9. (a) In a nuclear reactor atoms of uranium 235 split into two nearly equal parts when they capture a neutron. An atom of uranium 235 has 92 electrons and 143 neutrons.
(i) How many protons are there in one atom of uranium 235?
(ii) What is its proton number?
(iii) What is the nucleon number of the uranium 235 atom?
(b) What is meant by the half-life of a radioactive element?
(c) It is proposed to build a Nuclear Power Station at Lower Snodbury, Bumpshire. The Electricity Generating Board support the idea but the local residents oppose it. Suggest three advantages and three disadvantages of the scheme.
(d) Radioactive isotopes have many practical uses. Describe one such use, giving details of how the isotope is used, the type of radiation it emits and an approximate value of its half-life. *(L.E.A.G.)*

SUPPLEMENTARY

10. Write down an equation showing how $^{235}_{92}U$ decays in a reactor.
11. The equation below represents part of the reaction in a nuclear reactor
$$^{235}_{92}U + ^{1}_{0}n \longrightarrow ^{236}_{92}U$$
(a) Explain the significance of the numbers 235 and 92.
(b) $^{236}_{92}U$ atoms are unstable and disintegrate spontaneously into fragments approximately equal in size, together with 2 or 3 fast moving electrons and a large amount of energy. What is

this process called and what is the source of the energy?
(c) $^{235}_{92}U$ is much more likely to absorb slow moving (thermal) neutrons than fast moving neutrons. Describe how neutrons may be slowed down in the reactor core.
(d) Explain what is meant by a chain reaction.
(e) How is the rate of energy production in the reactor core controlled?
(f) The energy is produced in the form of heat in the reactor core. How is the heat removed from the core and how is it converted into electricity?
(g) When the fuel rods are withdrawn from the reactor core they are *radioactive*, containing *isotopes* with long *half-lives*. Explain the terms in italics.
(h) Outline three precautions which must be taken to ensure safe operation of the reactor. *(N.E.A.)*

ANSWERS

CHAPTER ONE
1. a) m   b) m^2 c) m^3
2. 250 cm.
3. 25,000 cm^2
4. 0.25 m^3
5. a) 8 g/cm^3 b) 8000 kg/m^3
6. 189 kg
7. 9 mm
8. 4 ml
9. Vernier calipers, vernier calipers, micrometer screw gauge.
10. The resistance of a body at rest to motion or a moving body to stopping.
11. 3 g/cm^3
12. 4078 kg/m^3

CHAPTER TWO
1. 8 m/s
2. 64 km/h
3. Because the roads cross the cars must be travelling in different directions therefore their velocities must be different.
4. 900 m
5. 50 m/s
6. The first three pieces will be equal in length. The next two will be equal in length to each other but longer than the first three.
7. (a) 200 m   (b) 11 s   (c) 80 m   (d) 15 s   (e) 8 m/s   (f) staying the same   (g) 0 m/s.
8. It accelerates rapidly initially then less rapidly until it reaches a constant speed.
9. 5 m/s^2, 312.5 m
10. It will accelerate rapidly initially, then less rapidly until it reaches a constant velocity known as its terminal velocity.
11. 9.8 m/s^2
12. (a) (i) uniform acceleration, (ii) constant velocity, (iii) uniform deceleration.
    (b) (i) 2.5 m/s^2, (ii) 20 m, (iii) 3.57 m/s.

CHAPTER THREE
1. A scalar quantity has size.
2. A vector quantity has size and direction.
3. Speed
4. Acceleration

Answers 395

5. (a) (i) A scalar quantity only has size but a vector quantity has size and direction.
   (ii) displacement and velocity.
   (iii) distance and speed.
   (b) To add two scalar quantities we add their numbers but to add two vector quantities we have to use a diagram.
6. 2 km
7. 2 km to 8 km
8. 2 cm, 15° south of east.

CHAPTER FOUR

1. It may deform it or twist it.
2. The rod may be stretched, compressed or bent.
3. Shear
4. 10N
5. 25N
6. It can cause motion, an increase in speed or a change of direction.
7. 6000N
8. (a) 980N, (b) 160N
9. (i) push on tyre from road, (ii) 400N, (iii) 1400 kg, (iv) speed increases because of resultant force in forward direction.
10. Its calibration is based on the fact that the elastic limit has not been reached.
11. Towards the centre.
12. At the intersection of the vertical lines drawn through A, B and C.

CHAPTER FIVE

2. 2F
3. 0.5 m
4. 5N
5. D
6. (b) 240N   (c) 220N vertically downwards   (d) increase 20N force; use longer lever.
7. S/He moves it in order to keep his/her centre of gravity directly above the rope.
8. The movement due to the weight causes the ball to rotate clockwise and so roll down the dish.
9. The left side will move down and the right side will move up.
10. 1.2N.

CHAPTER SIX

1. She exerts a greater pressure because although her weight is less, the area of her heel is very very much less.
2. 10 Pa
3. D
4. Its incompressibility.
5. (a)(i) 12.5N, (ii) 20cm², (iii) 0.625N/cm², (iv) 0.3125N/cm²
   (b)(i) 160cm³, (ii) 7.18g/cm³.
6. Low atmospheric pressure is much less than the person's blood pressure.
7. C
8. The barometer would need to be very long.
9. 780mm Hg
10. A line on a weather chart joining points of equal pressure.

CHAPTER SEVEN

1. 20 J
2. 1500 W
3. Energy of motion.
4. Energy of position or condition.
5. Energy can never be made or destroyed but can change into a different form.
6. B
7. C
8. (a) friction in the pulley   (b)(i) 4m, (ii) 800J, (iii) potential, (iv) 840J (v) muscles/food.
9. (a) reservoir, turbine, alternator, p.e. of water to k.e. of water, k.e. of water to electrical energy.
   (b) any three: coal, oil, nuclear, solar, wind, tidal.
10. She does work against gravity.
11. 20 m/s
12. 250 J

CHAPTER EIGHT

1. Solid, liquid, gas.
2. Greater molecular separation.
3. Bombardment of visible particles by rapidly randomly moving invisible particles.
4. Due to its large density its rate of diffusion is very very small.
5. D
6. B
7. Temperature, surface area, draught.
8. D
9. a) increases, b) decreases, c) increases.

Answers 397

CHAPTER NINE

1. It increases.
2. It would bend upwards.
3. A thermostat.
4. D
5. A
6. (a) X, because it contains a gas which expands more than liquid.
   (b) Z, because it contains a smaller initial volume of liquid.
7. The tyre will get hot causing it to expand and enabling the volume of the air to expand. The air will also increase its temperature. We must therefore use the general gas equation.
8. $70 \, m^3$

CHAPTER TEN

1. It is a measure of the kinetic energy of the molecules of a substance.
2. Their temperatures.
3. The lower fixed point — the temperature of pure melting ice and the upper fixed point — the temperature of steam from water boiling at normal atmospheric pressure.
4. C
5. 223 K
6. $-100°C$
7. D
8. Cuts from the glass and mercury poisoning.
9. Large range of variation, linear variation, large variation.
10. $20°C$

CHAPTER ELEVEN

1. J/°C or J/K
2. Low thermal capacity of wick.
3. D
4. $8.8 \times 10^4 \, J$

CHAPTER TWELVE

1. Solid
2. Liquid
3. D
4. Above 100°C
5. The horizontal portion will be below the horizontal axis.
6. Impurities and high atmospheric pressure.
7. 0.16 kg
8. 25.1 kJ

CHAPTER THIRTEEN

1. C
2. D
3. C
4. (a)(i) Conduction, convection and radiation.
   (ii)(A) radiation, (B) convection, (C) convection.
   (b)(i) It is surrounded by a poor conductor.
   (ii) 3p.
5. To eliminate convection currents.
6. Mercury.

CHAPTER FOURTEEN

3. Energy
4. 0.2 m/s
5. 0.5 m
6. 1 m/s
7. 40°
8. Refraction
9. (a) Wavefront same width as slit (b) Wavefronts diffracted.
10. (b)(i) transverse, (ii) longitudinal, (iii) transverse, (iv) transverse.
11. B
12. 1.5
13. D

CHAPTER FIFTEEN

1. Incident ray, normal and reflected ray in same plane.
   Angle of incidence = Angle of reflection
2. Real images are formed by rays which actually meet but virtual images are located where rays appear to meet.
3. Right way up or erect, same size as object, same distance behind mirror as object in front, laterally inverted and virtual.
4. 7 m
5. Large field of view.
6. ƎƆNAJUᗺMA
7. D
8. (a) In line with 0 but same distance behind mirror.
   (b)(i) Infra-red, (ii) concave, (iii) polished metal so that it is smooth.
9. Diffuse reflection occurs.
10. C

Answers 399

CHAPTER SIXTEEN

1. It is refracted.
2. D
3. C
4. D
5. (a)(i) Refraction, (ii) totally internally, (iii) critical angle, (iv) S>R
   (b)(ii) Periscope.
6. 4/3

CHAPTER SEVENTEEN

1. To allow more light through.
2. C
3. D
6. Same size.
7. Real, upside down, reduced, behind lens.
8. One is real, upside down and behind lens; the other is virtual, right way up and in front of lens.

CHAPTER EIGHTEEN

1. They transfer energy, can travel through a vacuum, all travel at the same speed in air.
2. Blue
3. Violet
4. Bright red light has a longer wavelength and bigger amplitude than dim blue light.
5. (a) U.V. and I.R., (b) gamma rays, (c) gamma rays, (d) the same, (e) medicine/sterilization.
6. (a) I.R. at X (b)(i) radio, (ii) gamma rays, (iii) U.V. (iv) radar/radio.
   (b) The clothes will glow brightly because they will fluoresce.
7. No
8. 2m

CHAPTER NINETEEN

1. B and C
2. No, people of that age cannot hear such a high frequency sound.
3. If they emit ultrasonic waves, they can be heard by a dog.
4. Light can travel through a vacuum but sound cannot.
5. (a) C, (b) A
6. To reduce reflections.
7. 198m
8. (a) 70m, (b) it will be reflected from fish at different depths.

9. The temperature is higher in summer and the speed of sound increases with temperature.
10. One sound travels through the air, the other through the fence. The sound through the fence will be heard first.
11. 50Hz.

CHAPTER TWENTY

1. D
2. C
3. B is N, C is N, D is S
4. E
5. (a) N on left, S on right
   (b) in next position, pointer moves by about 45° downwards, then horizontal pointing right, then horizontal pointing left and finally at about 45° downwards.
6. A point where magnetic fields cancel out.
7. A
8. In a moving coil meter. If the field were not radial, the scale would not be linear.
9. The end of each rod would become N poles, each would repel causing the rods to roll away from each other.

CHAPTER TWENTY ONE

1. Electrons leave the cellulose acetate and go onto the cloth.
2. A is uncharged.
3. The region around a charged body where another charged body will experience a force.
4. Electrons can move through conductors but not through insulators.
5. The plastic pen becomes electrostatically charged and attracts the pieces of paper.
6. Coulombs
7. Electrons flow through the connection to earth until the conductor is no longer charged.
8. +10C
9. (a) A   (b) electrons would be repelled to earth leaving the sphere charged   (c) nothing.

CHAPTER TWENTY TWO

1. Amps, with an ammeter.
2. Microammeter.
3. One which continually reverses its direction.
4. A source of electrical energy and a conducting path.

5. Volts
6. Potential difference.
7. The opposition offered by a conductor to the passage of a current.
8. Ohms
9. B
10. B
11. (a) rheostat, (b) changes its brightness, (c) because the resistance in the circuit changes.
    (d) (i) ammeter connected anywhere in circuit, (ii) voltmeter connected with one terminal to each side of lamp.
    (e)

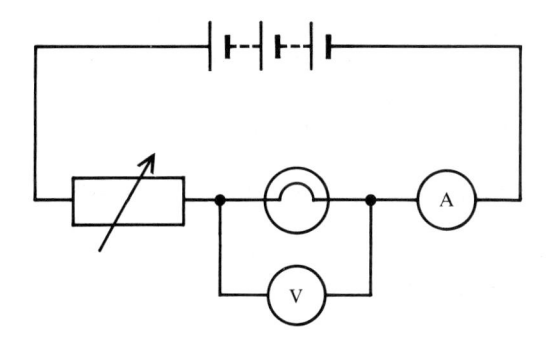

12. 3000C
13. 10V
14. 4Ω
15. 2cm²
16. It increases more rapidly.
17. Yes

CHAPTER TWENTY THREE
1. 4V
2. To decrease the internal resistance.
3. C
4. A
5. 1.5A
6. 3V
7. a) 4A, b) (i) 6Ω, (ii) 2A.
8. D
9. 1.25Ω
10. 6Ω

CHAPTER TWENTY FOUR

1. 240 V
2. 10 A, 13 A
3. 2 A, 6 Ω
4. 15p
5. In parallel
6. So that the device is not live when switched off or the fuse is blown.
7. Vacuum cleaner, hair dryer, food mixer.
8. A
9. (a)(i) green and yellow, (ii) brown   (b) To push aside safety covers   (c) To secure the flex   (d) It takes current to earth.
10. B
11. 108 J
12. 1.08×10^7 J
13. (a)(i) to protect the appliance from an excessive current
    (ii) too much current
    (iii) the outer casing, a large current would flow to earth and blow the fuse
    (b)(i) 2000 J, (ii) 1 kWh, (iii) 60p
    (c)(i) + on top, − on bottom
    (ii) like charges repel, unlike charges attract
    (iii) return to original state.

CHAPTER TWENTY FIVE

1. Speed of magnet, number of turns on coil, strength of magnet.
2. (a) the galvanometer would deflect, (b) nothing, (c) the galvanometer would deflect more.
4. Stronger magnet and more turns on the coil.
5. B
6. B
7. D
8. (a) transformer (step down), (b) the current would be too great, (c) it would be dangerous and difficult to insulate, (d) because it can be transformed.
9. The direction of the induced e.m.f. is such as to oppose the change producing it.
10. Principle of conservation of energy.
11. 50, 5A, 100% efficient.
12. It will be one quarter of its original value.

CHAPTER TWENTY SIX

1. C

3. A
4. Soft
5. (a) they have like poles side by side, (b) soft iron because they lose their magnetism when the current is switched off, (c) they will still repel because they will both change polarity together.
6. Increase the current.
7. By increasing the current in the coil and the number of turns in the coil.

CHAPTER TWENTY SEVEN

1. D
2. By increasing the current and the strength of the magnetic field.
3. Vertically upwards.
4. By using a stronger field, using a larger current and having more turns on the coil.
6. Vertically downwards.
7. They will repel.

CHAPTER TWENTY EIGHT

1. The release of electrons from a hot metal filament.
2. A heater, a cathode, a grid and an anode.
3. 10 V
4. R.M.S. = 0.7 × peak
5. D
6. A step-down transformer, a diode bridge and a capacitor.
9. 1000 Hz
10. (a) 1 Vcm^{-1}, (b) 4 V, (c) 0.5 ms cm^{-1}, (d) 5 ms (e) 200 Hz, (f) two complete wavelengths of half the amplitude.

CHAPTER TWENTY NINE

4. Amplification and switching.
5. To allow a small current to switch a much larger current.
6. (i) Variable resistor in top, LDR in bottom of potential divider, relay in collector lead, (ii) increases, (iii) base potential rises, switches on transistor causing collector current to start, (iv) to change the sensitivity, (v) the collector current is too low for the bulb, (vi) replace LDR by thermistor.
7. (a) (i) resistance of LDR falls, so does the p.d. across it
    (ii) output voltage of NOT gate becomes high, the relay is energised closing the switch and ringing the bell.
    (b) an alarm to detect light.
8. 0, 0, 1; 0, 0, 1; 1, 1, 0; 1, 0, 0.
9. (i) 2, (ii) 3 V, (iii) 300 Ω, (iv) to limit LED current.

CHAPTER THIRTY

1. Protons and neutrons.
2. 17
3. 14
4. Zero, positive and negative.
5. They have different numbers of neutrons.
6. B
7. B
8. Isotopes
9. B
10. By loss of electrons.
11. The nucleus of an atom is small, massive and carries a positive charge.

CHAPTER THIRTY ONE

1. Alpha, beta and gamma.
2. Gamma
3. A
4. First row: negative, zero; Second row: particle, particle.
6. C
7. B
8. (a) the nucleus, (b) they would all be absorbed even by an extremely thin foil, (c)(i) 45, 40, 40, (ii) it becomes thinner then thicker because the count rate increases then decreases.
9. (a) (i) 92, (ii) 92, (iii) 235   (b) time taken for half the radioactive nuclei to decay   (c) Advantages: any three of — cost, efficiency, cleanliness and small fuel mass; Disadvantages: any three of — disposal of waste, high initial construction cost, health risk and terrorist risk   (d) Any suitable use.
10. $^{1}_{0}n + ^{235}_{92}U \longrightarrow ^{141}_{56}Ba + ^{92}_{39}Kr + 3\,^{1}_{0}n + W$
11. (a) 235 is the nucleon number, 92 is the proton number, (b) nuclear fusion where mass is converted into energy, (c) by use of a moderator such as graphite or water, (d) one in which neutrons released in fusion are used to cause further fusion, (e) by control rods, (f) by a coolant, by a generator, (g) emit α, β or γ radiation, nuclides with same Z but different A, time taken for radioactive mass to halve, (h) control rods, adequate coolant, lead shielding.

INDEX

A
A number 375
absorption of sound 234
absolute 123, 138
— scale of temperature 138
— zero of temperature 123
acceleration 22, 23, 27, 37, 40, 71
— centripetal 71
— definition 22
— due to gravity 23, 40
— of free fall 71
— using tickertape timer 37
aircraft cabin pressure 93
air resistance 38
Alnico 247
alpha radiation 379
alternating current 273, 315
— description of 273
— generator 315
altimeter 95
ammeter 272
ampere 271
— micro 271
— milli 271
— the 271
amplitude 172
anechoic chamber 230
AND gate 366
aneroid barometer 94
angle 177, 178, 189, 205
— of incidence 177, 178, 189
— of reflection 177, 189
— of refraction 178, 205
anticyclone 99
aperture 215, 219
— camera 219
— lens 215
apparent depth 205
area 1
atmospheric pressure 92, 93
atoms 116
atomic 118, 375
— diameter 375
— vibration 118
audible frequencies 231
audiotapes 247

B
background radiation 382
balance 11
bar 99
bar magnet 241, 249
barometer 94
— aneroid 94
— mercury 94
bell, electric 330
bending 63
beta radiation 379
bias 285, 286
— forward 285
— reverse 286
bimetallic strip 130
binoculars 208
bistable multivibrator 365
block and tackle 104
boiling 150, 154
— process of 150, 154
— point 150
Brownian Motion 119, 123
Boyle's Law 124
Bourdon gauge 97

C
cable, energy losses in 324
caesium 2
camera 219
car 90, 91
— brakes 91
— hydraulic jack 90
carbon steel 247
cathode ray oscilloscope 233, 237, 345, 352
cell 274, 291
— in parallel 291
— in series 291
— the 274
Celsius scale of temperature 138
centimetre 3
centisecond 12, 16
centre of gravity 61, 72
centripetal 70, 71
— acceleration 71
— force 70
charging by induction 267
circuit 274, 305, 306, 307
— breaker 307
— complete 274
— domestic 305
— house 306
circular waves, reflection of 183
cloud chamber 381

clutter 226
coding device 210
commutator, split ring 342
compressions 180, 236
— in sound 236
— on springs 180
compressing 64, 65
computer memories 247
concave mirror 192, 193
— focal length 193
— focus 193
— principal focus 193
— the 192
concert halls 234
Concorde 57
condensation 151
conduction 159, 160, 164, 168
— applications of 164
— mechanisms 159
— rate 160
— theory of 168
conductors, electrical 262, 266, 280
construction rays 218
constructive interference 179
control rods 387
convection 161, 162, 166
— applications of 166
— currents 162
— mechanisms 161
conventional current 275
converging lens 215
— focal length 215
— focus 215
— principal focus 215
— the 215
conversion of energy 105
convex mirror 193
— focal length 193
— focus 193
— principal focus 193
— the 193
cooling curves 152
costings, electrical 303
coulomb 265
critical angle 207
crushing can experiment 93
crystal lattice 116
cubic 2, 4
— centimetre 4
— metre 2
— millimetre 4
cystoscopes 211

D

deformation 52
density 5, 12, 16
depressions 99
destroying magnets 243, 245
destructive interference 179
deuterium 388
deviation 205, 207
diffraction 179, 185
— explanation of 185
— in waves 179
diffuse reflection 199
diffusion 121
direct current 273, 341
— motor 341
— nature of 273
dispersion 211
displacement 20, 27, 35, 206
— definition 20
— of light 206
— time graphs 27, 35
display, seven segment 8
distance time graphs 27, 35
dog whistle 232
domestic 165, 305
— circuit 305
— hot water system 165
door 78
double 165, 244, 307
— glazing 165
— insulation 307
— stroke method 244
drinking straw 95
driving mirror 195

E

earth 251, 307
— magnetic field due to 251
— wire 307
echoes 234
elastic 65, 66, 107
— limit 66
— materials 65
— potential energy 107
electric 69, 107, 197, 265, 271
— current 271
— field 69
— fires 197
— lines of force 265
— potential energy 107
electrical 303, 304, 310
— energy 310
— power 303, 304

electricity 303, 308
— dangers of 308
— uses of 303
electromagnet 329, 332
— construction of 329
— magnetic field due to 332
electromagnetic spectrum 223, 228
electromagnetic waves 223, 224, 228
— nature of 223
— speed in air 228
— uses of 224
electromotive force 275, 300
electron 375
electrostatic charging 258, 263
— process of 258
— in everyday life 263
emergent ray 206
energy 105, 106, 107, 109, 111, 112, 122
  137, 283, 310, 323
— conversion 105
— definition 105
— elastic potential 107
— electric potential 107
— electrical 310
— electromagnetic 107
— equation 112
— food 109
— fossil fuel 106
— gravitational potential 107
— heat 122
— internal 137
— kinetic 107
— losses 111, 323
— lost by a cell 283
— magnetic potential 107
— nuclear 106
— potential 107
— principle of conservation of 105
— thermal 122
— vegetable fuel 106
— wave 107
— wind 106
equations of motion 39
equilibrium 52, 80, 81
— metastable 81
— stable 80
— state 52
— unstable 81
evaporation 122, 123, 154
— forces affecting 123
— process of 122, 154
exhaustible energy reserves 112
expansion 129
— of gases 129
— of liquids 129
— of solids 129
extraction fans 165

F
ferromagnetic substance 241
field 68, 69, 70, 74, 195, 248, 339
— between parallel currents 339
— force 68
— gravitational 68
— electric 69, 262
— magnetic 70, 248
— strength 74
— view 195
filament lamp 278, 280
fission, nuclear 386
fixed point 140
— lower 140
— upper 140
flask, vacuum or thermos 166, 167
Fleming's rule 316, 337
— left hand 337
— right hand 316
fluorescence 224
flux, magnetic 248
focal length 193, 215, 216
— of concave mirror 193
— of convex mirror 193
— of thin converging lens 215, 216
focus 193, 215
— of concave mirror 193
— of convex mirror 193
— of thin converging lens 215
food 109
force 51, 52, 65, 66, 68, 70, 77, 261, 335,
  338, 339
— between charges 261
— between parallel currents 339
— centripetal 70
— definition 51
— extension graph 66
— field 68
— moment of 77
— on conductor in a magnetic field 335
— on charged particle in a magnetic
  field 338
— resultant 52
— tensile 65
formation of image in plane mirror 19
forward bias 285
fossil fuel 106

408 Index

free 40, 52
  — bodies 52
  — fall acceleration 40
frequency 173
freezing point 151
friction 54
fulcrum 77
fuse 290
fusion, nuclear 388

G

Galileo 38
galvanometer, moving coil 313
gamma 224, 228, 379
  — radiation 379
  — waves 224, 228
gases 91, 118, 119, 129, 133, 134
  — expansion of 129
  — general law of 134
  — pressure of 91
  — properties of 118, 119
  — variation in volume and temperature 133
gates 366, 367
  — AND 366
  — logic 366
  — NAND 367
  — NOR 367
  — NOT 366
Geiger Marsden experiment 377
Geiger-Müller tube 380
general gas law 134
gliders 165
gradient 33, 35, 36
  — of displacement time graph 35
  — of distance time graph 33
  — of velocity time graph 36
gravitational 23, 40, 68, 107
  — acceleration 23, 40
  — field 68
  — potential energy 107
greenhouse 166

H

half life 385
hard magnetic materials 246
headlamps 197
heat 122, 146, 151, 167
  — energy 122, 151
  — engine 167
  — latent 151
  — specific capacity 146
hertz 173

Hooke's law 66, 67
hour 12
house circuit 306
hovercraft 56
hydraulic car jack 90
hypothermia 141

I

ions, formation of 377
incidence, angle of 177, 178, 189
induced 245, 313, 314, 322
  — electromotive force 313, 314, 322
  — magnetism 245
inertia 16, 71
infra red 224, 228
insulation, electric 262, 266, 280
insulation, roof and wall 165
interference 179
  — constructive 179
  — destructive 179
  — in waves 179
internal 137, 206, 207, 295
  — energy 137
  — reflection 206, 207
  — resistance 295
image 192, 210
  — real 192
  — subsidiary 210
  — virtual 192
isobars 99
isotopes 376

J

JET experiment 388
jack, hydraulic car 90
joule 102
junction diode 280, 286, 296, 352, 354
  — as a rectifier 296
  — bridge 352, 354
  — the 280, 286

K

keepers 253
Kelvin scale of temperature 138
kilo 3
kilogram 2
kilometre 3
kilowatt hour 310
kinetic 107, 118
  — energy 107
  — theory 118
krypton 1

L

latent heat 151
lateral inversion 191
lattice, crystal 116
law 24, 56, 73, 125, 177, 188, 190, 197, 261
— of charged bodies 261
— of magnetic poles 242
— of motion 56, 73
— of pressure 125
— of reflection 177, 188, 190, 197
length 1
lens 215
— aperture 215
— thin converging 215
light 177, 188, 203, 224, 358, 359
— brightness 224
— colour 224
— dependent resistor (LDR) 358, 369
— deviation 224
— emitting diode (LED) 359, 369
— ray 188
— reflection 177
— refraction 203
lightening 264
like poles, magnetic field due to 250
liquids 88, 98, 118, 119, 129
— atomic arrangement in 118, 119
— expansion of 129
— pressure in 88, 98
limit of proportionality 70
litre 5
logic gates 366
losses of energy 111, 323
loudness 233
loudspeakers 337
lower fixed point 140
lubrication 56
luminous object 188

M

machine 102
magnifying glass 221
Magnadure 247
magnets, making of 243, 244
magnetic 70, 107, 241, 242, 246, 248, 249, 250, 251, 253, 254, 327, 329, 332
— effect of electric current 329
— fields 70, 248, 249, 250, 251, 254, 327, 328, 332
— flux 248
— materials 246
— poles 241, 242

— potential energy 107
— screening 253
magnetism, induced 245
mains supply 303
mass 2, 10
manometer 96
materials 65
— elastic 65
— plastic 65
matter 116, 122
— effect of thermal energy on 122
— types of 116
measuring cylinder 9
melting 150
mercury 5, 94, 139
— barometer 139
— density of 5
— thermometer 139
metastable equilibrium 81
meter, moving coil 342
metre 1, 2, 3, 4, 8
— cubic 2
— cubic centi 4
— cubic milli 4
— milli 3
— micro 3
— rule 8
— square 1
— the 1
microammeter 272
micrometer screw gauge 14
microphone 233
microsecond 12
microwave 224, 228
milli 3, 5, 12, 272
— ammeter 272
— litre 5
— metre 3
— second 12
mirror 189, 192, 195, 197
— concave 192
— convex 197
— driving 195
— parabolic 197
— plane 189
— security 195
minute 12
mixed networks 298
moderator 387
molecular speed 123
moment 77, 79, 82
— definition of 77
— principle of 79, 82

monochromatic waves 227
motion, non uniform 32
motor, direct current 341
multiple reflection 209
Mumetal 247

N

NAND gate 367
national grid 319
nature of image in a plane mirror 191
neutron 375, 386
— absorption of 386
— the 375
newton 60
Newton's Laws of Motion 56, 73
neutral 64, 252
— filament 64
— point 252
NOR gate 367
normal 177
north pole 241
NOT gate 366
non uniform motion 32
nuclear 106, 375, 386, 387, 388
— diameter 375
— energy 106
— fission 386
— fusion 388
— reactor 387, 388
nucleon 374, 375
— definition of 374
— number 375
nucleus 259, 374

O

Ohm's Law 278, 279, 295
optical 210, 211, 215
— centre 215
— fibre 210, 211
OR gate 366
orbits, electron 374

P

parabolic mirror 197
parachute 38
parallax 8
parallel currents 339, 340
— field between 340
— force between 339
paramagnetic substance 254
pascal 88
photocopiers 264
period 173

periscope 194, 208
Permalloy 247
perspiration 122
pitch 233
plane 181, 182, 189
— mirror 189
— waves 181, 182
plasma 388
plastic materials 65
platinum-iridium 2
plotting compass 248
potential 275, 293
— difference 275
— divider 293
potential, electric 357
potential energy 107
(see also energy)
power 104, 352
— definition 104
— supply 352
pressure 87, 88, 90, 91, 92, 93, 94, 96, 98, 99
— aircraft cabin 93
— atmospheric 92, 94
— definition 87
— gas 91
— gauges 96
— law 125
— liquid 88, 98
— transmission in liquid 90, 99
primary coil 317
principle 79, 82, 105
— of conservation of energy 105
— of moments 79, 82
principal focus 193, 215
— of concave mirror 193
— of convex mirror 193
— of thin converging lens 215
projector 218
proportionality, limit of 70
proton 374, 375
— number 375
— the 374
pulley 103

Q

quality of sound 236

R

radar 224, 228
radiation 162, 166
— absorbers and emitters 162
— applications of 166
— occurrence 162

radiation, background 382
radio 227, 228
radioactive 382, 385
    — decay, equation of 382
    — tracers 385
radioactivity 379, 380, 384, 385, 386
    — detection of 380
    — ionising power 386
    — range 386
    — safety precautions 384
    — types of 379
    — uses of 385
radioastronomy 227
ray 188, 217, 218, 220
    — construction 218
    — diagrams 217, 220
    — light 188
range 8
rarefaction 180, 236
    — nature of 180
    — in sound 236
real 192, 204
    — depth 204
    — image 192
rectification 296, 350, 351, 353
    — half wave 350
    — full wave 351, 353
    — meaning of 296
Reed switch 332
reflection 177, 181, 182, 183, 188, 189, 197, 206, 207, 209, 234
    — angle of 177, 189
    — circular waves 183
    — diffuse 199
    — internal 206, 207
    — law of 177, 188, 189, 197
    — multiple 209
    — plane waves 181, 182
    — regular 199
    — sound 234
    — total internal 207
refraction 178, 183, 203, 205
    — angle of 178, 205
    — change in speed 183
    — light 203
refractive index 184, 212
refrigerator 153
relative expansion 132
relay 331, 364
resistance 276, 280, 284, 295, 338
    — explanation of variation 284
    — factors affecting 280, 284
    — idea of 276
    — internal 295
    — of LDR 338
    — of thermistor 338
resistors 277, 292, 293, 297
    — in parallel 293, 297
    — in series 292
    — material of 277
resultant force 52
reverse bias 286
rheostat 277
right hand rule 328
ringing bell 232
ripple tank 175
rubber sucker 92

S

scalars 44
    — definition 44
    — addition of 44
scales, reading of 7
scales of temperature 123, 138
    — absolute or Kelvin 123
    — Celsius or Centigrade 138
screening, magnetic 253
secondary coil 317
semiconductors 280
seven segment display 8
shearing 63
shutter 219
S.I. system 2
single stroke 244
smoothing 350
soft magnetic materials 246
solidification 151
solids 116, 119
solenoid 244, 245, 328
    — field pattern due to 328
    — nature of 244, 245
sonar 232, 235
sound 230, 234, 236, 237
    — absorption 234
    — frequency 237
    — properties 230
    — quality 236
    — reflection 234
    — speed in air 234, 236
south pole 241
spark discharge 263
specific 146, 147, 154, 156
    — heat capacity 146, 147
    — latent heat 154, 156
speed 19, 28, 123, 172, 174, 234, 236
    definition 19

— molecular 123
— sound 234, 236
— time graph 28
— wave 172, 174
spouting can 89
square metre 1
stable equilibrium 80
storage of heat 148
stretching 64, 65
stroboscope 177
subsidiary image 210
supporting columns 65
switching circuit 362, 363, 369
    — light operated 362
    — temperature operated 363
    — time operated 369
syringe 90

T

telescopes 195, 218, 220
temperature 137, 138, 148
    — definition 137
    — measurement 138
    — mixed bodies 148
tensile force 65
terminal velocity 38
thermal 22, 122, 129, 130, 145
    — capacity 145
    — energy 22, 122
    — expansion 129, 130
thermionic emission 344
thermistor 141, 358, 368
    — the 141, 358
    — variation in resistance 368
thermocouple 141, 143
thermometers 14, 138, 139, 142
    — clinical 14
    — liquid in glass 139, 142
    — properties of 138
thermometric properties 142
thermos flask 166, 167
thermostat 131
tickertape timer 23, 37
time 2, 11, 16
timebase 349, 352
toppling 80
torches 197
total internal reflection 207
tracers, radioactive 385
transducer 105
transformer 317, 322, 323
    — power equation 323
    — principle 322

— the 317
transistor 360, 361, 362
    — as amplifier 361
    — as switch 362
    — npn 360
transmission of pressure in liquid 90, 99
transverse wave 172
tritium 388
truth tables 367
turning effect, current carrying conductor 336
two state system 365

U

ultrasonic 231, 235
ultraviolet 224, 228
unlike poles, magnetic field due to 250
unstable equilibrium 81
U shaped magnet, field due to 254
upper fixed point 140

V

vacuum flask 166, 167
Van de Graaff Generator 264
vector 44, 47, 48
    — addition 44
    — definition 44
    — polygon 48
    — resolution 47
vegetable fuel 106
velocity 20, 30
    — definition 20
    — time graph 30
vernier calipers 12
vibration, atomic 118
videotape 247
virtual image 192
visible wave 224, 228
volt 283
voltmeter 276
volume 9
    — definition 9
    — displacement 9
    — measurement 9

W

wall insulation 165
water, expansion of 132
watt 104, 304
wave 172, 175, 180
    — circular 175
    — longitudinal 180
    — plane 175

— transverse 172
(see also electromagnetic waves)
weather 99
weight 60
wind energy 106
wiring plugs 307
work 102, 112
    — definition 102
    — done 112

X
X rays 117, 224, 228

Y

Z
Z number 375